HUMANISTIC ECONOMICS
THE NEW CHALLENGE

HUMANISTIC ECONOMICS
THE NEW CHALLENGE

MARK A. LUTZ
University of Maine, Orono
Department of Economics

KENNETH LUX, Ph.D.
Clinical Psychologist
Auburn, Maine

Foreword by AMITAI ETZIONI
George Washington and Harvard Universities

THE BOOTSTRAP PRESS

New York, New York

To our children and their generation.

The Bootstrap Press is an imprint of the Intermediate Technology Development Group of
North America, Inc., 777 United Nations
Plaza, New York, New York 10017 (212/972-
9877)

Library of Congress Cataloging-in-Publication Data:

Lutz, Mark A.
    Humanistic economics.

    Bibliography: p.
    Includes index.
    1. Economics. 2. Economics–Moral and ethical aspects.
3. Economics–Psychological aspects.
I. Lux, Kenneth. II. Title.
HB72.L88   1988   330.1   88-7324
ISBN 0-942850-10-6
ISBN 0-942850-06-8 (pbk.)

Printed in the United States of America

CONTENTS

critique of economics

FOREWORD

Neoclassical economics, and the paradigm that underlies it, have been criticized to perfection. No part has been left unscathed. The paradigm has been shown to be extremely unrealistic in its assumptions, especially its notions of a rational, self-centered individual, and of the existence of a self-regulating market. It has also been shown to be tied to a particular ideology, that of laissez-faire conservatism. And it has been found to be highly deductive and rather aempirical; a kind of mathematical form of scholasticism. Professor Mark Lutz, together with psychologist Kenneth Lux, extend and enforce these core criticisms in several powerful segments of their book.

Despite such powerful and repeated challenges, neoclassical economics, and more generally the neoclassical paradigm, continue to reign in the social sciences and in intellectual circles that both draw on the social sciences and feed into them. There may be several reasons for the resiliency of the neoclassical paradigm, but first among them is the fact that one cannot beat a theory with nothing. A constructive challenge must be mounted, a viable alternative advanced. This is what Professor Lutz and Dr. Lux have set out to accomplish.

The Lutz/Lux paradigm of humanistic economics builds on Maslow's and other humanistic psychologies and on the concept of human needs. This yields a much richer, more encompassing, nobler, and more humane perspective than the rational pursuit of pleasure or self-interest. Indeed, the authors make excellent use of the concept of the divided self—or as they call it, the dual-self—recognizing that we all have both a nobler and a more debased element.

The significance of using human needs as a starting point cannot be overstated. Lutz and Lux have much to say on the subject in the body of the volume that need not be repeated here. Human needs are universal. All people in all periods in all countries have the same basic human needs. Cultures may define the ways these needs are served, even the intensity with which this or that need is pursued. However, Spartans and Athenians, Americans and Chinese, Blacks and Whites, and all others have a basic need for affection, self-esteem, and so on. The recognition of this universal condition provides an independent basis for evaluating varying societal structures–those more and those less responsive to basic human needs. In this manner we can counter moral relativism.

The authors also turn economics imperialism, or what they call the "marketization of society," on its head. Economics imperialism is a tendency of economists to explain non-economic behavior in their own terms. Crime, love, and even salvation are explained as utility-maximizing behavior. Lutz and Lux show instead that much economic behavior can be explained in psychological terms. And, they argue against allowing marketing considerations to eat evermore into the societal fabric, considerations that undermine both society and the market that ultimately depends on society. Instead, the authors would rein in the market and thus save both society and the economy.

Another major intellectual need is addressed in the book. Rather than treating economic relations as segregated, as if the market was in one place–and society, polity, and culture in some other–the authors return to the tradition of the original political economics. They treat the economy as part and parcel of the society, the way it is more effectively treated.

Last, but not least, Lutz and Lux demonstrate that one can deal with the subjects at hand with a clarity and style that would allow the educated public to participate in the dialogue, rather than to hide ideological assumptions behind technical vocabulary and mathematical equations. Every reader need not agree with all that the authors write, or the specific conclusions reached, in order to applaud the direction they move us and the way they are proceeding.

Amitai Etzioni

Cambridge, Massachusetts   George Washington and
December 1987   Harvard Universities

PREFACE

Almost a decade has passed since our earlier *Challenge of Humanistic Economics* was published. Although we have reasons to be rather gratified about its general reception both inside and outside academia, it soon became clear that a new and better articulation of a more human economics was needed. Increasingly, ideas of mere revision started to yield to a compelling desire to restructure the book at its very foundation. Only in this manner could the basic vision and argument be given greater coherence, validity, and hopefully also permanence.

For this reason, our present title is a double-meaning variation of the former title, and it is our way of handling the fact that the present book is both a new version of the old and is yet a new book. The present material is almost completely new, with only a little more than 5 percent of its contents taken directly from the earlier work. This is not to say that the present book is just an improvement over our previous *Challenge,* but rather it seeks to further develop some of the theoretical concepts and ideas of that book. For example, we now explicate a new "dual-self" theory of human personality, which is largely implicit in Maslow's hierarchy of the basic human needs concept. We first started to become aware of this in 1982 and proceeded to articulate this new perspective in a paper titled "New Directions in Humanistic Economics."[*]

The present book not only reexamines economic rationality from the new dual-self perspective, but also puts much greater emphasis on the importance, and we think breakthrough, of the development both in

---

[*] Presented at the Allied Social Science Association Meetings in New York, December 27, 1982. This paper was later published in the *Forum of Social Economics* (1984), pp. 1-33.

theory and practice of industrial worker cooperatives. We also discuss topics such as economic imperialism and the perils of unregulated free trade, neither of which was mentioned in the first book, in part because there was less need at that time.

There is also a lot of important and valuable material in the first book that did not find its way into the present one, so that the initial *Challenge,* although now out of print, can be seen as a useful and supplementary addition to what is contained here. This is particularly the case with the history of humanistic economics, our Galbraithian discussion of competition, the treatment of work, freedom, poverty, the European welfare state, and the steady state economy.

With two books now written and both presenting humanistic economics, one would think that all of the important issues and topics have been covered. But that is not the case. Perhaps the fact that the two authors of this book are both white and male is reflected in relatively little discussion in the book pertaining to the particular issues of race and gender. We have also had to refrain from discussing such all-important humanistic topics as the local economy, community self-reliance, environmental economics, land reform in less developed countries, and last but certainly not least, an economic analysis of the arms race and the warfare economy. It is hoped that other books will remedy many of these and other omissions.

In whatever we did accomplish in including here, we owe a great deal to others. Just as with the earlier *Challenge,* we were privileged to rely on three major pillars of support without which this book could not have been written. They are, first, the extremely generous financial support of Robert H. Lutz, combining so effectively the two roles of loving father and accomplished banker. Second, an Economics Department at the University of Maine which not only has tolerated this ongoing, somewhat subversive enterprise, but in many ways also ended up supporting and encouraging it. Thirdly, Gail Fernald, who, once again, took sole charge of not only all the secretarial tasks, but also managed meticulously and cheerfully all the organizational work from beginning to end, as well as attending to proofreading and index-making. There is no way in which we can express adequately our deep indebtedness and gratitude to everybody here.

We are also most grateful to a number of economists and social thinkers for their inspiration, particularly Amartya Sen, Nicholas Georgescu-Roegen, David George, Amitai Etzioni, David Ellerman, and Amritananda Das. Without them there would have been little to write about.

The present book has also greatly benefited from an early and extensive set of critical but highly constructive comments by Kenneth Boulding made on the occasion of our initial 1982 paper. We further benefited from the comments of referees, above all, Herman Daly, Roy Rotheim, Lloyd Little, George Rohrlich, and once again, Kenneth Boulding. Finally, certain aspects of the material contained in this book were greatly improved after repeated discussions with such loyal intellectual friends as Jim Wible and Jon Wisman, and also Abdul Huq and Melvin Burke of the University of Maine. Similarly, we learned to appreciate the valuable input by so many graduate students, including Debbie Thompson, Lisa McGowan, Stephanie Seguino, and Susan Hunt, as well as from the manifold input of large numbers of undergraduate students who participated in one way or another in the classrooms of ECON 320: Humanistic Economics.

A special thanks goes to The Bootstrap Press run by Cynthia and Ward Morehouse and assisted so ably by Peggy Hurley. You three taught us not only that "small is beautiful" but also that publishing a book can still be a real joy.

Last—but, of course, anything but least—there is Carol Arone Lutz, teacher of real human values, loving companion, and patient wife, as well as artist in charge of the cover design. Thank you so very much.

Mark A. Lutz
Kenneth Lux

ACKNOWLEDGEMENTS

Quotation on page 241 is from *The Share Economy* by Martin Weitzman, Harvard University Press. Reprinted by permission.

Quotations on pages 190 and 192 are from *The Economics of Justice* by Richard Posner, Harvard University Press. Reprinted by permission.

Quotation on page 21 is from William R. Allen, *Midnight Economist: Broadcast Essays III*. Reprinted by permission.

Quotations on pages 23 and 49 are from *Basic Economic Concepts: Microeconomics*, 2nd edition, by Werner Sichel and Peter Eckstein. Copyright © 1977 by Houghton Mifflin Company. Used by permission.

Figure on page 48 is from *Basic Economic Concepts: Microeconomics*, 2nd edition, by Werner Sichel and Peter Eckstein. Copyright © 1977 by Houghton Mifflin Company. Used by permission.

Quotation on page 22 is from *Economics* by Campbell McConnell. Copyright © 1981 by McGraw-Hill. Reprinted by permission.

Quotation on page 90 is from *Price Theory and Applications*, 3rd edition, by Jack Hirshliefer. Copyright © 1984 by Prentice Hall.

Quotation on page 303 is by A. J. Liehm in Ken Coates, ed., *Essays in Socialist Humanism*, Spokesman, Nottingham, 1972.

Chapter 1

THE EMERGENCE OF HUMANISTIC ECONOMICS

We need an economics we can live with. This is meant in two related ways. One is that we need an economics that literally can keep us all alive, can physically maintain and sustain us. The second is that we also need an economics that is ennobling, that we can be proud to identify with and proclaim. This is the matter of vision. We need an economics with an uplifting and constructive vision, an economics allowing us to live fully.

We are afraid that at least the issue of vision, and all too often the maintenance of material adequacy for all, are lacking in conventional and mainstream economic theory. This theory is an inheritance largely from eighteenth and nineteenth century British philosophy, with its hedonistic, mechanical, and narrow image of the person. Increasingly, people in our society, and in the economics profession as well, have become dissatisfied with the mainstream economic vision. They have become dissatisfied with the fact that it will not even admit that it is a vision, but instead presents itself as only what is natural, what is inevitable, and, simply, what is "economics."

The problem has often been, however, that in our dissatisfaction with the vision of mainstream or "neoclassical" economics we have not known where else to turn. Socialism was the most prominent and obvious alternative, and for a long time the issue was, in the main, one of either accepting neoclassical economics or turning to Marxism. But this has been an unhappy choice. Any promise that socialism, in at least its

Marxist variety, has held out as the ennobling alternative vision has been largely dashed by results, if not by failures in its theory. So for the most part those numbers of people who cannot adhere to either of these economic visions have been stuck. It has historically been the case, and this may be a necessary way in which the mind works, that until a successful new vision of something has been articulated, people will not be able to leave the old vision.

A significant glimpse of a new vision was offered to us in 1973 with the publication of E. F. Schumacher's *Small is Beautiful: Economics as if People Mattered*. In the magnificent irony of Schumacher's subtitle he pointed out the central problem of contemporary economics—it had lost the person.

What was further striking was that in the related field of psychology a group of psychologists, most notable among them Abraham Maslow, was making a similar criticism in their field. This criticism came to be described in a new conception of psychology called "Humanistic Psychology." It was put forth as a "third force" in psychology to counteract the two reigning dominant schools in psychology—Behaviorism and Freudianism.

Here was quite a parallel. Schumacher was presenting at least the seeds of a new economic vision in contrast to the existing alternatives of mainstream, neoclassical, and neo-Marxian economics, and he was doing it in the name of the person. And Maslow, Carl Rogers, Rollo May, and others were doing it in psychology by offering an alternative that they called humanistic to the existing two dominant forces in that field.

It did not take much to realize that Maslow's new vision of the person was well-suited for the theoretical underpinning that Schumacher in an essentially independent way was bringing to bear on his perception of and prescription for a new economic vision of the future.

We have used the words *new* vision, and we are a little sorry to have to do this because to do so too easily plays into the "cult of the new" which is such a manipulative feature of our contemporary economic and social environment. Something is seen to be good only if it is new—and the word new is trumpeted about as if it is the exact equivalent to the good and the desirable. But we know this is not the case. Indeed, it turns out that this so-called new vision upon close examination is seen to be only a fresh statement of something that is classic and has been presented throughout the history of thought as well as the history of economics.[1]

What this means is that humanistic economics not only steps outside of the dichotomy of capitalism-socialism but also outside of liberalism-conservatism. In terms of a fresh statement it is certainly liberal, but in terms of what it is saying it is only a *re*statement, and in that it is conservative; it conserves perennial truths by attempting to restate them in modern form. To begin to see this we need to take a look at the history of the concept of humanism.

The Concept of Humanism

"How many angels can dance on the head of a pin?" This question has often been used as a parody of the kind of questions and the manner of thought that came to dominate the philosophy of the Middle Ages. This way of thinking, which was known as Scholasticism, was tightly bound by the dictates and dogma of the Church and its semi-official adoption of Aristotelian philosophy. The humanist critic Erasmus described this climate as one of "the God Latin, the crabbed learning, the barren subtlety, and the needlessly elaborate theology of the schoolmen."[2]

Perhaps the earliest dissenter of the scholastic tradition was the early fourteenth century Italian poet Petrarch. In his sonnets and other writings he ignored the courtly and ecclesiastic conventions and expressed real emotion and feeling. Following Petrarch, other more philosophically oriented thinkers arose at the end of the fourteenth and the beginning of the fifteenth century to bring fresh life into the Catholic world view. Looking for new sources of inspiration they turned to Plato and other Greek and neoplatonic sources, as well as writings in Hebrew and Arabic. One of the most important of these new thinkers was the Italian Pico della Mirandola, who in 1486 offered for debate and discussion to the Church theologians a list of several hundred questions. The Pope found these questions heretical and did not allow the debate. Instead, Pico published only the introduction he had written to these questions, and this became the famous *Oration on the Dignity of Man*. In it he has God say to Man:

> We have made you a creature neither of heaven nor of earth, neither mortal nor immortal, in order that you may, as the free and prouder shape of your own being, fashion yourself in the form you prefer. It will be in your power to descend to the lower brutish forms of life; [and] you will be able, through your own decision, to rise again to the superior orders whose life is divine.[3]

The dignity of Man, according to Pico, rests in Man's freedom and his capacity and need to direct and shape his own life. Man is unfinished. He has the freedom either to raise himself above the angels or reduce himself below the beasts. This double nature of the person, its "dual-self," is the essence of what has come to be known as classical humanism. We have within us both the higher and the lower, the noble and the base, and our freedom lies in our capacity to choose between the two.

After Pico we have the Dutchman Erasmus, whom we have already mentioned, and then Giordano Bruno and Galileo. The latter two brought to the new thought an interest and appreciation of the natural world, and believed that knowledge of God or Truth resides not only in books but in nature as well.

Some of this same spirit of opposition to unjustified authority was present in the German priest Martin Luther who in 1517 brought his own famous set of "95 Theses" to the attention of the Church. The Church's negative reaction to him and his eventual excommunication led to a split in Christianity and eventually to the Protestant Reformation. Erasmus, who was a contemporary and friend of Luther, eventually found that his sense of independence could not be tolerated by Luther's own authoritarianism, and he opted to remain within the Catholic church rather than join Luther in his new church. But he still continued as a humanist reformer.

It is important to note in this depiction of classical humanism that these individuals were not in opposition to a belief in the existence of the divine. As a matter of fact, they felt that the overbearing weight of authority was itself in contradiction to the spirit of the divine. Rather, in their conflict with the authorities they were asserting the reality of a higher power or higher truth that existed above the bureaucracy and conventionality of the authorities.

However, in the eighteenth century various thinkers, mostly in France (e.g., O'Holbach, Lamettrie, Voltaire, Diderot), adopted atheism and took the position that only a complete break with any sort of religion would free Man from the oppressions of the churchly, as well as royal, authority. This philosophy became aggressively materialistic and laid the basis for the widespread acceptance of philosophical materialism—the belief that there is no spirit, all is matter—in the nineteenth century. This culminated in the work of Darwin, Marx, and Freud, who together defined the nature of what has been called the modern mind.

We should add to this the note that in the early twentieth century the American psychologist John B. Watson decided that the concept of mind itself was unnecessary; after all, it could not be seen or touched, and therefore psychology need only be the study of behavior. This was the founding of Behaviorism. In our times the leading behaviorist is B. F. Skinner. In 1979 a group called the Humanist Society gave him the award of "The Humanist of the Year." We mention this so we can appreciate the irony that when Abraham Maslow and Carl Rogers challenged Skinner's behaviorism in the 1960s, they did so in the name of humanism.

We thus see that humanism has come to mean almost anything and in fact can be seen, as the eleventh edition of the *Encyclopaedia Britannica* puts it, as "the parent of all modern developments whether intellectual, scientific, or social." A humanism so broad has very little meaning. To be useful for us a critical distinction must be made between humanism's spiritual and its materialistic varieties. This distinction harkens back to the classical humanism of Pico and Erasmus, and from this perspective the title of humanistic must be withheld from any school of thought that denies the reality of higher motives, a higher human nature, a higher Self. In short, the person as person is not just an animal, whether "social" or "tool-using," but something higher than that.

Utilitarianism and the Development of Psychology

All of the social sciences, including psychology and economics, developed out of eighteenth and nineteenth century concepts formed in the natural sciences such as physics and biology.

An important basis of this approach was the philosophical position known as *utilitarianism*, first formulated by the Englishman Jeremy Bentham (1748-1832). Utilitarianism is the idea that people do the things they do because these actions are useful to them (have utility) in the sense of bringing them happiness or pleasure. Here, in a famous phrase, is how Bentham expressed it:

> Nature has placed mankind under the governance of two sovereign masters, pain and pleasure. It is for them alone to point out what we ought to do, as well as to determine what we should do. . . . They govern us in all we do, in all we say, in all we think: every effort we make to throw off our subjection, will serve but to demonstrate and confirm it. In words a man may pretend to abjure their empire, but in reality he will remain subject to it all the while.[4]

According to Bentham, pleasures did not differ between themselves in type or kind, but only in their amount, that is, in their strength or intensity. Therefore, the difference between the pleasure of eating a piece of chocolate and the satisfaction, say, of a job well done was not that they were different kinds of "pleasures," but that they differed in their strength. The importance of this doctrine for the study of the person is that it allowed the newly budding social scientists largely to sidestep the classic human issues of ethics and justice, or values, by treating these problems as if they were only a matter of quantity. The need to discriminate between the good and the pleasurable, between what is true and the personally expedient, was increasingly seen as only the difference between two amounts of pleasure. For the utilitarian, taking a cue from what he or she thought were the lessons of science, what is good is what is pleasurable, and what is bad is what is painful. Therefore, all the philosophical questions of good and bad, right and wrong, could be reduced to the matter of pleasure and pain. In this respect there is little, if any, difference between people and animals–and a basis was laid for the eventual study in psychology of animal behavior as a parallel to human behavior.

A second feature of utilitarianism which appealed to the early social scientists was the comparison made between the operations of the mind or brain and those of a calculator. According to Bentham, the person was a "felicity computer" who calculated the amount of pleasure and pain in each posssible action and took the direction that promised the maximum pleasure or least pain.

This penchant of Bentham and his late eighteenth century colleagues for seeing what was good in terms of intensity of pleasure naturally leads to a focus on the body and bodily sensations. Therefore, it is but a relatively small and obvious step from Bentham to Freud, despite the intervening century, with Freud's theory that sex and sexuality are essentially the origin and mainspring of all human actions–for, indeed, in terms of bodily sensations sex is no doubt the strongest direct body pleasure. It is solidly in the tradition of Bentham and utilitarianism that Freud formulated his central concept of "the Pleasure Principle."*

This physicalistic as well as quantitative emphasis is also the conceptual framework that lay behind the other major theoretical direction in early psychology, Behaviorism. This begins with the Russian physiologist Ivan Pavlov who showed that dogs in his laboratory would

---

*Later in his life, Freud came to see this as limited and wrote the essay "Beyond the Pleasure Principle," but in terms of his influence on society and culture, this reexamination of the whole issue was rather late in the game and except for specialized Freudians is hardly the association that people have with the meaning of Freud in modern life.

come to salivate at the sound of a bell if that bell sound had previously been paired with meat put into the dogs' mouths. This learned association or "conditioned reflex" was seen to be the simple unit, the behavioral atom, as it were, upon which the whole edifice of human personality and culture was built.

Later on in America, the psychologist B. F. Skinner refined and broadened these behavioristic concepts in his formulation of what was called "Reinforcement Theory." Skinner, initially working with rats and pigeons, showed that if these animals were kept in a hungry state they would learn to perform certain operations, such as pressing a lever when that operation led them to receive food. This is the basic principle of what we commonly know as animal training. For Skinner, as for Pavlov, these principles were the actual foundations upon which all other complex and sophisticated human behavior was built, including, no doubt, these writers' very formulation of these theories. The food in the case of the hungry rat, just as, say, the paycheck for the employee, is the "reinforcement" or reward that stamps in or maintains certain desirable behaviors, or behaviors that are in accord with the reinforcement contingencies or "schedules" in the world around us.

The connection between all these concepts, such as utility, the pleasure principle, and reinforcement theory, is very direct and clear, and we can certainly get a sense of their relationship to at least a conventional view of what economics is about. Indeed, it is the case that certain "behavioral" economists have directly used the Skinnerian reinforcement model in their study of economic behavior.[5]

The Rise of Humanistic Psychology

As we have said previously, there is fundamentally nothing new in the humanistic point of view, as indeed there is nothing new about the "utilitarian" perspective that it attempts to criticize and refute. We can trace these issues at least as far back as Plato, who in a most apt quote has Socrates saying to Callias in *The Apology:*

> If your two sons were only colts or bullocks, we could have hired a trainer for them to make them beautiful and good and all that they should be; and our trainer would have been, I take it, a horseman or a farmer. But now that they are human beings, have you any trainer in your mind for them? Is there anyone who understands what a man and a citizen ought to be?[6]

The concept that the person is to fulfill his or her own higher nature–what they ought to be–has existed since antiquity, indeed, from
biblical times. And it has always been in contention with the alternative
view that human nature is constructed entirely out of forces acting upon
it, including instinctual drives, pleasure and pain, and generally the sensations of the body, as we would expect of an animal. The modern twist
on this ancient argument, which humanistic psychologists had to confront, was that the utilitarian or pleasure principle point of view had become the "scientific" point of view. The humanists protested that not
only was this conception a very limited and outdated view of science
but it also had serious logical flaws. This was pointed out by Carl Rogers
in the famous debates he had with behaviorist B. F. Skinner in the early
1960s. Rogers summarized Skinner's position as follows:[7]

> From what I understand Dr. Skinner to say, it is his understanding that
> though he might have thought he chose to come to this meeting, might
> have thought he had a purpose in giving this speech, such thoughts
> are really illusory. He actually made certain marks on paper, and
> emitted certain sounds here, simply because his genetic makeup and
> his past environment had conditioned his behavior in such a way that
> it was rewarding to make those sounds, and that he as a person doesn't
> enter into this . . . .
>
> Skinner: "I do accept your characterization of my own presence
> here."

According to the humanistic psychologists, all forms of
utilitarianism–whether the pleasure principle or reinforcement theory–
become self-contradictory when applied to man as a *total* (one and only)
explanation of his nature. For the behaviorist the very writing of his
reinforcement theory must be seen as itself a product of mere reinforcement and not a freewill expression of what is supposed to be the truth.
In other words, by claiming reinforcement principles as the totality of
human behavior the theory itself rules out the concepts of truth or falsity as meaningful (since all results from reinforcement), while at the
same time trying to claim that it is the truth. This is a direct contradiction and the theory self-destructs.

Therefore, the humanistic psychologist saw that if utilitarian type
pleasure principles were applicable to human behavior, they could not
be the total, but should only describe a part of human behavior. What
the behaviorists had done was to raise a part of human behavior to the
status of the whole. There must be another part of human nature, and
this is the part that is not passively pushed around by forces outside of
itself, and is not a captive subject to Bentham's "sovereign" masters of
bodily pain and pleasure. Furthermore, the human being not only reacts

to past events but also acts with real choice in regard to its goals in the future. Man is a being with goals and intentions or, in other words, a being capable of inspiration and vision.

The Hierarchy of Needs and Self-Actualization

These insights and outlooks of the humanistic psychologists were most constructively and effectively expressed in Abraham Maslow's concept of the hierarchy of needs. This refers to the development and increasing maturation of the self, that inner sense of who one is and what one feels and thinks. In a healthy person this growth takes place throughout life, and is continually moving towards higher levels of self-realization or *self-actualization*, to use Abraham Maslow's term for this process.

The growth of the human being towards self-actualization represents the attainment of full human potential. Maslow has listed the growth necessities in their order of priority for the human being as (1) the needs of physiology (food, clothing, shelter); (2) the need for safety and security; (3) the need for belongingness (meaningful social relationships); (4) the need for esteem and self-esteem (a sense of self-worth); and finally, (5) the need for self-actualization.

While each person naturally grows and evolves in a unique way, all the first four need gratifiers are necessary if this personal evolution is to be realized. It might be said that the observed diversity in human beings lies in how they go about meeting their basic needs, but not in whether they have or do not have these needs. The humanistic psychologists have seen them as characteristic of the human species.

The Hierarchical Nature of Human Needs

Psychologists have long recognized that when the fundamental, basic needs, such as the physiological, are not satisfied they will exert a pressure on the person that will tend to override all other possible concerns and needs. Thus, even though self-esteem, for example, is one of the basic human needs, it remains well in the background if the need for security is unsatisfied.

The converse of this is equally important. Once a basic need is satisfied, then the next basic need emerges to the forefront of attention and interest. Therefore, by satisfying one area or category of need, the person is able to become involved with the needs that exist at a higher level of development. In other words, human needs manifest themselves in a series of stages and, according to Maslow's classic original conception, you have to get through one stage before you can go on to the next. These stages can be seen as priorities, so that a more crucial priority must be heeded before another priority can claim attention. This can be seen to define the process of growth. It has been summarized by Maslow in the following phrase: "Man does not live by bread alone—*if* he has enough bread."

Thus the various basic human needs can be arranged in a hierarchical order in terms of their necessity for growth and development. The more pressing needs have to be satisfied before the higher ones. A depiction of this hierarchy, based on Maslow's work, is shown in Figure 1.1. Let us review these needs.

Figure 1.1

MASLOW'S HIERARCHY OF NEEDS (VALUES)

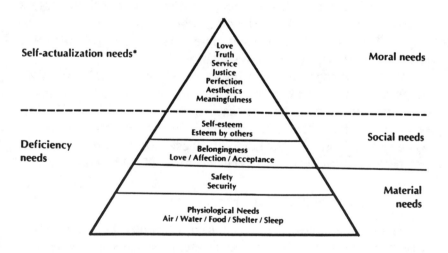

*Self-actualization needs are of equal importance (not hierarchical).

The most basic needs are physiological. We have to survive, and for this we need a minimum of food, water, shelter, and clothing, etc. If not sufficiently satisfied, according to Maslow, these needs will dominate the organism, "pressing all its capacities into their service and organizing these capacities so that they may be most efficient in their service." Relative gratification, on the other hand, submerges them, making room for the next higher set of needs to dominate one's personality. Concern with hunger and other material necessities will now turn into concern with safety and security.

Safety and security needs provide a transition from the physiological area of need to the social area. On a physiological level security means that one can expect to meet one's physiological needs into the foreseeable future. This then blends into the more socially oriented need that one is safe from threat or loss due to the actions of others. All in all, safety and security relate to the feeling of having basic survival needs met and of being protected. Together with the physiological needs they may be seen as part of the *material* needs.

The third cluster of needs revolves around the social area, and is what can be called the need for belongingness. This means being part of a family, community, and society at large, and forming close and meaningful interpersonal relationships.

Maslow spoke about a fourth area of need that also has a strong social focus. This is the need for esteem, which is the need to feel respected, to feel worth something, to have basic dignity as a person. Here we move more clearly into the area of work, and the need to feel that one is productive, and that there is value in what one is doing. We will often refer to the needs of belongingness and esteem as the basic *social* need.

Maslow's studies led him to use the term *deficiency needs* to describe these first four categories of need. He used the term because deprivation in these areas produces illness, very much like the idea of a deficiency disease, such as the absence of certain vitamins. A distinguishing characteristic of a deficiency need is that it is *psychologically* inactive, or latent, in a healthy person. Of course, everyone always needs food, shelter, etc., but the point is that these do not occupy as much consciousness when they are routinely satisfied. Nevertheless, these lower needs can become temporarily dominant as a result of deprivation.

The most basic deficiency needs, such as that for food and water, are cyclical or episodal; they are quieted upon being satisfied, but after a period of time they again press for satisfaction. This is why the safety and security need is closely tied to an adequate fulfillment of the physiological needs. They cannot be satisfied once and for all, but need the assurance of being able to be satisfied in the future. In the same way, once each of the subsequent human needs are met, they tend to decrease in importance for the organism and the way is made for the next need to emerge. This is illustrated in Figure 1.2, which also shows the course of development of the whole hierarchy of needs.

Figure 1.2

THE DEVELOPMENT OF NEEDS (VALUES)

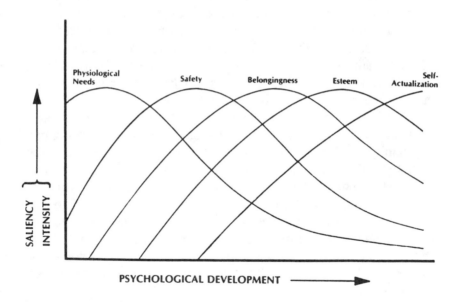

Self-Actualization.   When all the deficiency or lower needs are met the person does not stop growing. On the contrary, at this point the person has the possibility of entering into the most fulfilling phase of human development, which Maslow termed *self-actualization*. These are needs for creative development, and are the paramount needs in the life of a mature and healthy adult.

A major characteristic of growth needs, in contrast to the deficiency needs, is that their gratification leads to an *increase* rather than a decrease in their strength. This is illustrated by the constantly rising curve for self-actualization in Figure 1.2. For example, when a person is able to produce something creative, say, through painting, this generates even further interest in artistic expression. Similarly, the desire for truth is never satisfied but builds upon itself to produce a further and deeper search. These needs tend to be continued and ever-present, in an upward and future-oriented development. They carry a person to the heights of what it means to be fully human. This striving for the good and the beautiful can also be seen as a *moral* need.

It will be noted in Figure 1.1 that there is not a hard and fast line between the deficiency needs and self-actualization, with the social needs being borderline between the two. Note also in the diagram that the lower needs are object-oriented and materialistic, and the higher needs become more socially oriented and more abstracted from objects. This distinction parallels the classic distinction between the material and the spiritual.

What are the qualities of the highly self-actualized person? Research discussed in the work of Maslow and Rogers indicates that they tend to be creative and spontaneous rather than impulsive and self-centered. They are non-power-seeking; they tend to recognize the worth and value of others; their attitudes are highly democratic rather than authoritarian; they prefer decentralized organization structures; and they prefer cooperative rather than competitive relationships with others.[8]

The above is a sampling of qualities that are indicative of the self-actualized person. It is not exhaustive and really cannot be, but it does serve to give the flavor of what a person is like who seems to have reached some of the higher levels of human development. In a word, this is a picture of the fully mature human being.

The Common Sense of a Hierarchy.   What happens as soon as you begin talking about needs is that a hierarchy very naturally emerges. And a hierarchy means an ordering according to relative importance. So talking about needs naturally leads to a scale of relative values. Such a scale of values or needs does not necessarily depend upon using the specific categories that Maslow has settled upon, or even using categories that are at the same level of generality as Maslow's. Talking about needs leads to an ordering of those needs according to relative importance, and that is the critical point.

The existence of a hierarchy of human needs has always been recognized and observed by thinkers at least as far back as Plato. In *The Republic* he writes, "Now the first and chief of our needs is the provision of food for existence and life . . . . The second is housing and the third is raiment and that sort of thing." As the economist Walter Haines notes, the phrase "food, clothing, and shelter" goes back a long way.[9]

We find this same recognition in Adam Smith: "After food, clothing and lodging are the two great wants of mankind."[10]

The late nineteenth century economist Karl Menger, one of the fathers of mainstream utility theory in economics, proposed this specific list: water, food, clothing, shelter, coach (transportation), tobacco.[11] The list is given in the order of importance that Menger himself proposed for these needs—water being the most important and tobacco the least. You may find yourself agreeing or disagreeing with the exact ordering of needs as Menger proposes them, but you can easily accept that such an ordering is basically on the right track.

Another economist who was also central to the nineteenth century development of utility theory, William Jevons, was perhaps the first to use specifically the term hierarchy: "My present purpose is accomplished in pointing out this hierarchy of feeling and assigning a proper place to the pleasures and pain with which Economy deals."[12] Jevons, however, was to decide that economic needs occupied a place *within* the hierarchy, a hierarchy which includes a moral dimension, a sphere not belonging to the scope of economics.

Jevon's decision was to prove to be a most unfortunate move, as seen from the standpoint of a humanistic economics. It soon led to the rejection of the idea of a hierarchy of needs and along with it the elimination of the concept of needs itself. The reasoning behind this rejection of needs will be explained and examined in the next chapter. But the upshot was that economics, following Jevons and others of his time, did away with the concept of needs and instead substituted the concept of "wants," or more specifically what is called *demand*. That is, there is no recognition of objective human needs in economics. This is all determined subjectively by each individual, and backed up by his or her purchasing power. Economics as it is practiced today makes no distinction on the level of its basic theory between needs and non-needs, or necessities and non-necessities. All is seen as wants or demand, and this is expressed through that individual's purchase. For economics it is strictly a case of one man's meat is another man's poison. And thus the common sense of a hierarchy is no longer common as far as economists are concerned. And needs make no sense.

Does Human Development Depend on Money?   Some people reading Maslow's theory interpret it to mean that money is either necessary for or allows personal growth, and that only the wealthy and economically successful can be self-actualized. That is, the wealthy have the resources to meet their lower needs, and thus to allow the higher needs to emerge.

This interpretation is false and contradicts the spirit of what Maslow was trying to do. By looking at the hierarchy we can see that money is much more pertinent to the material needs than the social and self-actualization needs. This shows us that money is relevant and even necessary for growth, but up to a point, and that point is right about the level of the security needs. And as can be seen from our depiction of Maslow's hierarchy, the need for security marks the gateway between the material needs and the social and self-actualization needs. We will eventually see that the provision of basic security becomes a primary objective of a humanistic economics.

From the perspective of the hierarchy of needs, the single-minded and exclusive pursuit of money past the point of security not only fails to facilitate growth but impedes it. This fact is well recognized in the ethical and moral teachings of almost all of our social, cultural, and religious traditions. A clear-cut example is the legend of King Midas in Greek mythology. His wish was that everything he would touch would turn to gold, and this was granted. Then when he went to pick up a piece of bread to eat it, it turned to gold, and when he went to hug his beloved son, his son turned to gold. And King Midas realized that his all-consuming passion for gold had curtailed his happiness as well as his very life.

The hierarchy shows us that in order to grow, an individual must eventually turn his or her energy to other interests besides the pursuit of material wealth, and these are described as social needs and self-actualization. Although people may use money to try to buy social and self-esteem, this is a classically false way to go about it since these needs cannot be bought. Likewise, and even more so, for the top of the hierarchy—Love, Truth, Fairness, Perfection, Service. This is not to say that wealth prevents or blocks the attainment of the higher states of human development. Wealth may well come as a byproduct of the pursuit of excellence. Someone who does excellent work in their chosen vocation may become financially well-off as a result, but it is the pursuit of money, instead of the pursuit of excellence and fulfillment, that is the problem for human development.

Maslow Updated: The Dual-Self

In his later work, particularly beginning in 1968, Maslow recognized a problem with his step-wise, all or none hierarchy of needs "in which the basic needs are gratified, one by one, before the next higher one emerges into consciousness." He admitted this view was "static," and instead recognized that self-actualization is not some far-off distant goal at the end of a long series of steps, but is present as a possibility all the time, even when the lower needs are still operating. He furthermore recognized that his tendency to see self-actualization as something only achieved later in life at the end of the fulfillment of the hierarchy of needs was partially an artifact of his mostly studying self-actualization in older people.[13]

As a result of this reconsideration, Maslow leaned towards classifying human needs into two types, with a more fluid boundary between the two. These types were the *deficiency* or basic needs and the *growth* or self-actualization needs. Deficiency needs include all needs in the hierarchy except self-actualization, the latter making up the growth needs. Maslow wrote:

> If we define growth as the various processes which bring the person towards ultimate self-actualization, then this conforms better with the observed fact that it is going on *all* the time in the life history . . . . Growth is seen then not only as progressive gratification of basic needs to the point where they "disappear," but also in the form of specific growth motivations over and above these basic needs.[14]

Maslow related these two types of needs to the basic duality of the human being, "the predicament, of being simultaneously merely creaturely and godlike, strong and weak, limited and unlimited, merely animal and animal-transcending . . . yearning for perfection and yet afraid of it, being a worm and also a hero." In short, "the human being is simultaneously that which he is and that which he yearns to be."[15] Here we have a perfect echo of what Pico said 500 years ago.

Maslow developed his ideas primarily on the basis of psychological and clinical insights and his own experiences as a therapist. Most of the empirical and experimental work has followed since. An extensive review of the relevant research comes to the interesting conclusion that "a dual-level hierarchy of needs may provide a valuable alternative to Maslow's need hierarchy" and interprets the evidence so far as consistent with deficiency (or maintenance) and growth needs constituting such a dual-level hierarchy.[16]

We can see then that Maslow's original conception of a hierarchy of needs is really an extension of the idea that the human being has two poles or endpoints in his or her motivational makeup. Maslow's spectrum or panorama of human needs is like a bridge that spans from a material pole (deficiency needs) on one end of human nature to a spiritual pole (growth needs) on the other end. The movement through the hierarchy of needs can be seen as the increasing dominance of growth needs over deficiency needs in the individual's decision making.

A problem with the original hierarchy conception is that it could easily obscure the fact that both poles are always present, and that a choice always exists for the person between expressing lower needs or higher ones in a given situation where the two are mutually exclusive.

A person does not progress automatically, but only does so by making the right choices. As we shall soon see, it is a sense of security and trust that facilitates the choice of the higher.

The presence of inner conflict is one of the inevitable conditions of human existence. Its recognition goes back to Greek antiquity and is also a prominent part of the Judeo-Christian tradition. For Plato there were two categories of human motives, the passions and reason, and the human being had to use the latter to subdue and override the former. In the New Testament the Apostle Paul says, "That which I would do, I do not, and that which I would not do, I do."[17] Any student trying to discipline himself to study knows what this is all about. In the same vein is a classic line out of Geothe's *Faust*: "Two souls, alas, do dwell within his breast; the one is ever parting from the other." The psychologist William James recognized this fundamental fact of human existence in his concept of "the divided self."[18] We are not just one harmonized integrated self, but face conflict between parts of our selves, or different values, or a dual-self.

Each side of the dual-self, or the two selves (which corresponds to the two types of needs, deficiency and growth), can be characterized in a number of ways through different pairs of terms. Table 1.1 lists some of these pairs to help the reader gain a sense of the difference between the two parts of the self. It should also be kept in mind that these two parts of the self exist relative to each other so that each of these characteristics listed are not absolute but only have that particular quality in contrast with the other pole of the self.

Table 1.1

SOME BASIC CHARACTERISTICS OF THE DUAL-SELF

Higher self	-	Lower self
Growth needs	-	Deficiency needs
Self-actualization	-	Ego-aggrandizement
Truth seeking	-	Self-interest seeking
Reasonable	-	Rational*
Principled behavior	-	Instrumental behavior
Altruism and love	-	Selfishness
Objective	-	Subjective
Transpersonal	-	Personal (individual)

*Economic rationality

In conclusion, then, we understand humanistic psychology as a dual-self psychology allowing us to see how it connects with the tradition of classical humanism, rather than with materialistic humanism and its one-level or flattened conception of Man. As we shall see, the dual-self conception is what economics needs in order to break out of its overly narrow and distorted image of what people are and how they operate.

Humanistic Economics

An economics which is based on this narrow image–an image which is called "Economic Man"–reduces the whole Man (or person) to only self-interest motives. Humanistic economics seeks to restore the person in economics to its fullness and wholeness by recognizing another class of motives, and then to derive an economics that is in accord with this wholeness.

The beauty of the classical humanistic conception is that this whole image of the person can very simply be attained by recognizing two kinds, or a duality of motives, in human beings–a recognition that matches common sense and has been acknowledged by students of human nature throughout the ages. It is only reductionist, mechanistic science (derived from physics, which is already changing its characteristics) that cannot accomodate the dual-self image, and thus has to see the human being as a creature whose only aim is to maximize its single individual advantage.

Mainstream economics is not necessarily wrong in itself. It is certainly the case that people often do seek their own personal advantage. As the next chapters will show, the problem is that economics took this to be the whole picture, or at least the whole picture as far as the science of economics need be concerned. People end up as merely self-interested seekers pursuing in all their actions their own individual advantage or gain. But, if there is another side to human nature that operates alongside the self-interest side, then to reduce the human being to only the former side is to distort reality. Policies and recommendations that come out of such a science will naturally tend to embody those distortions and pass them on to the general population. Then we have an interesting "reflecting mirrors effect" where society reflects back to economists the very same self-interest images that economists have passed on to society.

Humanistic economics aims for a more complete image of the person. In addition to the self-interest side it posits a mutual interest side or, put in other terms, in addition to advantage seeking it posits the existence of truth or fairness seeking. The relationship between these two basic kinds of motivations and the often necessary trade-offs or compromise between them sheds new light on the whole range of economic phenomena.

The building that is Man not only has a basement but also an upper floor. The real economic questions from the humanistic standpoint of humanism are: Where will Man choose to spend his time, in the basement or on the upper floor? And what factors influence those choices? At least if there is an upper floor there is a chance for sunlight and fresh air to come pouring in through the open windows.

References

1. Mark A. Lutz and Kenneth Lux, *The Challenge of Humanistic Economics*. Menlo Park, California: Benjamin/Cummings, 1979, pp. 25-55.
2. William H. Coates, Hayden V. White, and J. Salwyn Shapiro, *The Emergence of Liberal Humanism*. New York: McGraw-Hill, 1966, p. 40.
3. Quoted in "What Is Humanism," editorial essay in *Manas*, XXXII, no. 5 (January 1980), p. 2.
4. Jeremy Bentham, *An Introduction to the Principles of Morals and Legislation*. London: T. Payne & Sons, 1789, chapter 1, part 1.
5. John Kagel, et al., "Experimental Studies of Consumer Demand Behavior Using Laboratory Animals," *Economic Inquiry*, 13 (1975), pp. 22-38.
6. Quoted in Jane Loevinger, *Ego Development*. San Francisco: Jossey-Bass, 1976, p. 6.
7. Transcribed from tape of "Education and the Control of Human Behavior," University of Minnesota, Duluth, June 11-12, 1962.
8. Abraham H. Maslow, *Motivation and Personality*. New York: Harper & Row, 1954, chapter 11, pp. 149-180.
9. Walter Haines, "The Hierarchy of Needs in Classical Theory," paper presented at the Eastern Economic Association Meetings, New York, March 1985.
10. Adam Smith, *The Wealth of Nations* [1776]. New York: The Modern Library, Random House, 1937, p. 161, book 1, chapter 10, part II.
11. Karl Menger, *Principles of Economics* [1871]. Glencoe, Illinois: The Free Press, 1950, chapter 3.
12. William Jevons, *The Theory of Political Economy* [1871]. New York: Augustus M. Kelley, 1965, pp. 26-27.

13. Abraham H. Maslow, *Toward a Psychology of Being*. New York: Van Nostrand Reinhold, 1968, p. 26.
14. *ibid.*
15. *ibid.*, p. 176 and p. 160.
16. M. Wahba and L. Birdwell, "Maslow Reconsidered: A Review of Research on the Need Hierarchy Theory," *Organizational Behavior and Human Performance* (1976), pp. 212-240.
17. Romans, 7:14-20.
18. William James, *The Varieties of Religious Experience* [1902]. New York: Mentor Books, New American Library, 1958, lecture VIII.

Chapter 2

THE PLACE OF HUMAN NEEDS IN ECONOMICS

It is probably amazing for the newcomer to the study of economics to learn that mainstream theory does not acknowledge that there are such things as needs. Are not economics books full of references to the difference between necessities and luxuries, he or she wonders? Well, there sometimes are references to necessities and luxuries in economics books–but they are mentioned almost as a practical afterthought and do not appear as part of the fundamental concepts of the profession.

Reducing Needs to Wants

Some economists do us the service of making this explicitly clear. One of these is the "midnight economist" Bill Allen:

> . . . in economics, "need" is a non-word. Economics can say much which is useful about desires, preferences, and demands. But "need" presumably is a moral, psychological, or physical imperative which brooks no compromise or adjustment–or analysis. If we "need" something, we must have it: there is literally no alternative of either substitution or abstinence.

> But the assertion of absolute economic "need"–in contrast to desire, preference, and demand–is nonsense. What do we do if I "need" a certain amount of something and you also "need" a particular minimum amount and both of our "needs" cannot be satisfied? It actually is the condition of the world that we have conflicting claims which

must somehow be resolved, for not everyone–if indeed, anyone–can be fully satisfied all the time. It does no good for each of us stubbornly to stamp a foot, spit downwind, and proclaim inalienable "needs" which in the aggregate cannot be satisfied. Scarcity, by its nature, gives rise to competition, to conflict, to the necessity of rationing in some manner the things we desire.[1]

Instead of needs the economist talks about desires, preferences, or demand, as Allen makes clear, or–in a word–wants. For the economist there is no distinction between needs and wants because everything is a question of wants.

When an economist talks about wants, he or she is talking about something that is infinite–because wants are infinite. There is no end to our wants, and economists are the first to point this out. For example, McConnell in his textbook tells us:

As a group, these material wants are for practical purposes *insatiable*, or *unlimited*. This means that material wants for goods and services are incapable of being completely satisfied. A simple experiment will help to verify this point: Suppose we are asked to list those goods and services we want but do not now possess. If we take time to ponder our own failed material wants, chances are our list will be impressive. And over a period of time, our wants multiply so that, as we fill some of the wants on the list, at the same time we add new ones. Material wants, like rabbits, have a high reproduction rate. . . . Not too many years ago, the desire for color televisions, air conditioners, video recorders, digital watches, and tubeless tires was non-existent. Furthermore, we often cannot stop with simple satisfaction: the acquisition of a Pinto or Chevette has been known to whet the appetite for a Porsche or Jaguar. In summary, we may say that at any given time, the individuals and institutions which constitute society have innumerable unfulfilled material wants.[2]

One of the most salient facts about the concept of a need, as opposed to that of a want, is that it has a natural capacity. When that capacity is fulfilled–such as in hunger and the need to fill a stomach–then the need is satiated and the person can go on to something else. This is one of the prime ideas behind Maslow's concept of the hierarchy of needs.

This observation–that consumption leads to satiation or fulfillment–is so basic to the living organism that economics could not very well continue to exist and not recognize this. So how does economics reconcile the idea of insatiable and unlimited wants and the natural satiability of a need? It does so in the concept of *diminishing marginal utility*. Here is how a text explains it:

Diminishing marginal utility is an expression of the "variety is the spice of life" philosophy of most individuals–that people prefer to have one or a few of a lot of different goods and services rather than a great many of only a few goods and services. For example, diminishing marginal utility suggests that an individual will derive more satisfaction from eating a first apple than a second apple, which in turn provides more satisfaction than a third apple, and so on–where all the apples are eaten at one sitting . . . . Exceptions to diminishing marginal utility are only infrequently observed.[3]

We notice in the above statement that for the economist it is not a fulfilled capacity that leads an individual to go from one item of consumption to another, but only because "variety is the spice of life" (or, in other words, wants).

Very striking in this example is the demonstration that economics applies its wants doctrine to all consumption, even that of a food item like an apple. In this example the person is not seen to stop eating the apple because a hunger need has been fulfilled, but rather because the apple has somehow become less interesting, lost its "spice"–increasingly so with each bite–so that eventually he loses interest in apples and goes on to something else.

This example is not a stray one or accidental, but really does set forth the mainstream economics view of the nature of the person–being a collection of infinite wants. Paul Heyne in his successful and well-written textbook, *The Economic Way of Thinking*, uses the example of water to demonstrate the economist's conviction that "needs turn out to be mere wants when we inspect them closely."[4] We will focus rather closely on Heyne's explanation because it both gives us a good account of the economist's reason for rejecting needs in favor of a want or demand concept, and at the same time inadvertently reveals the fallacious thinking underlying such a position.

"Do we need water," Heyne asks? "No. The best way to turn a drought into a calamity," Heyne observes, "is to pretend that water is a necessity." Expressing the point of view of standard economics, his point is that if we take a supposed need, such as water, and we increase its price, then people will use less of it, just like anything else. Therefore, the economist reasons, it is not a need. Critically, Heyne says, "Well-intentioned people and some not so well-intentioned talk constantly of basic needs . . . ." The economist does not like such talk. Heyne tells us that "The 'law of demand' is preferable to the concept of need, because demand relates the amounts that are purchased to the *sacrifices* that must be made to obtain these amounts."[5]

Needs and the Paying of Interest

The unreality or falsity of this position is also revealed in the same textbook, although unintentionally, to be sure. This occurs in a later section when Heyne is attempting to explain why people will pay interest to borrow money. He gives an example of Robinson Crusoe, a familiar figure in economists' arguments. His Robinson Crusoe "can keep himself alive," says Heyne, from day to day only by digging for clams. The most he can dig with his bare hands, without a shovel, is five clams a day, and these five clams "will barely enable him to keep body and soul together." In Heyne's example he posits that Robinson would be able to dig ten clams a day if he had a shovel, and thus move to a higher income level. But a shovel costs thirty-five clams. "Since Robinson would starve," says Heyne, if he took a week off to earn the shovel, he cannot attain this higher income level. Therefore, he points out, Robinson will gladly borrow thirty-five clams and pay back even more, say forty, for the opportunity to dig ten clams a day. With the shovel he will have five clams a day above his bodily needs, and thus in eight days he will be able to pay back the forty clams (cost of the shovel plus five clams interest), and then he will own the shovel and merrily go on digging ten clams a day for the indefinite future. So Robinson has to work an extra day to pay for the interest on his loan.

Interesting. If there are no needs, only wants, as author Heyne told us earlier in this chapter, why cannot Robinson simply take time off from his clam consumption and save for a shovel? How foolish and irrational it is for him to have to spend an extra five clams (interest) for the privilege of borrowing. If he did not bother consuming (which according to Heyne he does not have to because there are no needs, only wants) he could save his five clams a day and in only seven days of work buy the shovel rather than working eight to pay off the shovel plus the interest. In this example Heyne is being much more in touch with reality, and has already told us that Robinson has to "keep body and soul together" and not "starve." It is true that Robinson "wants" the shovel, but the reason he will borrow at interest is that he *needs* to eat.

With this example, we can now look back at the argument Heyne gave earlier against needs and see its problem. Let us say the price of water goes up, and a certain person stops drinking it and he dies. The economist's conclusion would be: He just did not want it enough, was not willing to "sacrifice" enough, to pay the price. One has to wonder if it just does not seem to occur to the economist that the person could not afford the higher price. The "sacrifices" that the economist refers to in his concept of demand is purchasing power. By this standard a rich man will make more "sacrifices" for water than a poor man. To the economist it seems to be the case that somehow a poor person just does not seem to want water as much as a rich person.

Rather than showing us that there is no such thing as need, what the law of demand shows us is that for any good–even water–some people are consuming more than they need to, and when the price goes up they are able to cut down on usage, which is to say, they can economize. But to say that there is no such thing as a minimum for basic goods is absurd. Heyne points out some existing water "substitutes" that can be used if the price goes up–dirty automobiles, brown lawns, plumbers to fix leaky faucets, deodorants, plus a host of small inconveniences.[6] Unfortunately, none of these can be drunk when thirsty.

Heyne intends his Robinson Crusoe example to show that "capital [the shovel] is productive," that Robinson's shovel will increase his wealth. In the example he gives us a picture of someone eking out a marginal existence–with no resting space–but then interprets the borrowing as the same thing as an investor attempting to expand his wealth. It indeed is the case that from the standpoint of want-based economics there is no difference between these two kinds of instances, because there is no such thing as a difference between wants and needs. Of course, in economics textbooks writers will talk about necessities and luxuries, or the difference between necessary spending and discretionary spending, but not at all see that this common sense distinction–which they can hardly avoid and still in any way be talking about the real world–is denied in their basic image of the person.

Is Everyone Better Off? Needs and Market Exchange

It is a basic axiom in conventional economics that in economic transactions in the market (exchange), all parties become better off. After all, if a person would not become better off in a transaction, economists argue, why would he or she enter into it? Furthermore, following from this logic is the belief that the more free exchange the better, and the higher the level of economic activity the better.

This logic is based on the assumption that there are only wants and no recurrent needs. Once we recognize that there are needs, the whole picture changes fundamentally and we can see that the economic axiom about exchange has a critical flaw.

If someone is pressed by a need, and let us take hunger as the prototype of need, the longer they go without fulfilling that need the worse it becomes. That, in fact, can be seen as one of the defining characteristics of a need which distinguishes it from a want. A need tends to grow in intensity with the passage of time, and if not fulfilled leads to serious deterioration of the health of the individual, if not his or her death.

Wants, on the other hand, can be seen as wishes or whims. Something that would be nice to have, perhaps spicy, something that will "tickle the palate." However, if not obtained, a want can be easily forgotten or another one may take its place. Therefore, while it is the characteristic of needs that if not met their intensity *increases* with time, wants tend to have the opposite characteristic. If not met, their intensity *decreases* with time. (Of course, there is a grey area between the categories of needs and wants where one shades into the other. And this is because needs are not just biological. Needs are also socially defined and developed as well, such as technologically developed products, like a car. One may need a car to get to work, or other reasons.)

What the above analysis lets us see is that someone who enters into a market transaction in order to meet a need does not really do so in order to become better off, but in order to *prevent being worse off*. As should be recognized from the discussion, this difference is not just semantics. The issue here is the different relationship between the passage of time and a need versus a want. Waiting makes needs worse, while it tends to make wants better. These are opposite effects. Sticking with the prototype need of hunger, we can see that as a person waits with that need he or she will be under increasing pressure to make a transaction in order to meet it. And the need of hunger occurs cyclically. By constantly exchanging to meet a hunger need we can hardly characterize that person as becoming better off each time. What they in fact are doing is merely maintaining their existence.

The meeting of a person's needs in the market is a parallel concept to that of *replacement costs* in the matter of the business enterprise. The distinction is made in the analysis of the firm between replacement costs and new investment, with the former going to maintain the existing enterprise, while new investment has the purpose of expanding or enhancing it. This is also the difference between an expense and a capitalization. This distinction is almost exactly equivalent to one between exchange in the marketplace to meet vital needs versus exchange to meet wants. The former prevents the economic entity from becoming worse off, while it is only the latter exchange that enables the entity to become better off. Conventional economic theory has no way to recognize this very obvious and real distinction in its mono-dimensional theory of utility, which excludes a distinction between needs and wants.

The introduction of this new concept opens the doors to the recognition of the possibility of power and coercion in what is otherwise called "free exchange." All we need to see is that one partner is compelled by need, the other motivated by want; the latter can wait while the former, pressed by needs, cannot. As a result, the terms of trade will mirror the distribution of power. This type of problem remains invisible within the theoretical apparatus of mainstream economics. Only after we have removed the blinders of one-dimensionality can it be apprehended within a theoretical framework. What we now are able to appreciate in economic theory is that there is an inherent imbalance in market transactions where some traders are trading for necessities and others for luxuries in the same market, which is very often the case. When people with significantly different income levels are in the marketplace together, the poor person is at a disadvantage in relation to the wealthy person.

Because of this imbalance we can see that the logic of the market will, other things being equal, work to "over-price" necessities and "under-price" luxuries. This tendency is brought about by uneven pressures operating in the shopping for consumer goods and, more importantly, in the selection of employment. The needy will not be able to enjoy the same opportunities that competition affords to the more well-to-do. Waiting for good opportunities and careful educational and career preparation often entails costs so high that only the rich can afford to pursue advancement through them. The poor are too busy working in order to survive. That is, the rich can afford the cost of waiting, while the poor cannot. The market thus has a built-in tendency to under-supply the needs of a population, while at the same time over-supply its desires. What we see here is that from a humanistic perspective, on a fundamental theoretical level the market by itself will fail to allocate properly.

As stated above, this issue is most significant in the case of what is called the labor market, or the market where employers hire workers. There is a distinctly inherent imbalance between the position of the two parties to this exchange, so that there is never a symmetrical relationship between those who "supply" the labor and those who "demand" it (the employer). Particularly, there is an asymmetry in the consequences of unemployment for workers and employers. The English economist and social theorist Lord William Beveridge phrased it this way: "a person who has difficulty in buying the labor that he wants suffers inconvenience or reduction of profits. A person who cannot sell his labor is in effect told that he is of no use."[7] Of course, the "no use" phrase should not hide from us the fact that a person who cannot sell his labor literally faces death (unless maintained by a social welfare system, of which Beveridge himself was one of the leading proponents).

We can now recognize that the concept of "market failure" as used in conventional economics is misleading. It implies that the market is an inherently perfect allocator, and when left to operate by itself it will lead to optimum economic conditions. From the above analysis this would appear to be false. Contrary to what conventional economics posits, so-called market failure is inherent in the nature of the market itself. Conventional economics has missed this because its conceptual apparatus has not been able to distinguish between necessities and luxuries.

The Mainstream Hierarchy

At this point, it may be instructive to note that not all mainstream economists would deny that there is some kind of hierarchy of needs—it is just too obvious for all of them to do so. But the economist would construct a different kind of hierarchy than the humanist does. It is a hierarchy reflecting their view that there is only one uniform self-interest, and no notion of a dual-self. Let us look at what kind of hierarchy would come out of such a view.

An early description of it is given by the eighteenth century French philosopher Jean Jacques Rousseau as he describes "man in society" as opposed to his man in nature:

> ... With man in society, things are very different: first the necessary must be taken care of, then the superfluous: then come the delights, then the accumulation of immense riches, then of subjects, then of slaves; never is there a moment of respite. What is most remarkable is that the less the needs are natural and pressing the more the passions increase and, what is worse, the power to satisfy them.[8]

What Rousseau reveals to us here is what we might call the "mainstream economist's hierarchy" which we can contrast with the humanistic hierarchy. First, necessities are acknowledged and the person seeks to fulfill them. But then, when this is met, instead of the increasing appearance of the higher motives as Maslow would predict or describe, we find the coming to the fore of the "passions," "superfluous," the "delights," desire for riches, for power, and so forth. Here is a more understandable framework than we usually get in the more dogmatic anti-needs presentation of economics. It says, let us acknowlege that there are needs, and that a person must take care of them before everything else. But after this is done, then what emerges are the wants, and these truly are infinite. So all we do, the economist might go on to say, is short-circuit or simplify this process a bit, and for theoretical elegance just assume that all is wants.

The eminent humanistic economic scholar and theorist, Nicholas Georgescu-Roegen, explains why such a view is probably what lay behind the economists' development of the idea of utility (or diminishing marginal utility):

> The modern utility theory reduces all wants to one general abstract want called "utility." In line with this reduction, one need not say "these people need more shoes"; instead, "these people need more utility" should suffice. . . . All this may again be due to a particular feature of the economies in which the builders of the modern theory of utility lived. Those were not economies in which a low income kept basic wants in front of everybody's eyes; they were economies where *most people* were able to satisfy even many personal wants. Modern utility theory is a theory of a consumer who has a relatively ample income and whose economic choice is guided only by the quantities of commodities.[9]

Thus the economics of utility comes out of a world view, or an image of society in which all needs have been met. Only in that context does it make sense and carry any realism. The shocking thing about an economics that relies on this picture is that it begins at a place where the fundamental economic problems are already assumed to have been solved.

However, back in the real world, even in those affluent societies in which these neoclassical theorists lived, there were vast numbers of people who had great difficulty in meeting basic needs, and there were great disparities in wealth and in market power. So in these societies, anxiety and insecurity also existed as one of the basic realities of economic life, as is well recognized in any account of the stresses and strains of life in the industrial economies and the corrosive competitive spirit that this can breed. As Bill Allen told us at the beginning of this chapter, "It actually is the condition of the world that we have conflicting claims which must somehow be resolved, for not everyone—if indeed, anyone—can be fully satisfied all the time." Allen says, "if indeed, anyone," and in so doing he is being true to his principles. Infinite wants can find no satisfaction no matter what a person's level of wealth. Scarcity is a permanent and inevitable condition. Allen goes on, "scarcity by its nature, gives rise to competition, to conflict, to the necessity of rationing in some manner the things we desire."[10] But, if it should turn out to be the case that things we desire are not the same things as the things we need, then at a basic theoretical level a profoundly different picture of economics can emerge.

What happens to economics when we recognize that there are needs in contrast to wants, and that the human being may be a creature of other motives in addition to self-interest? Do we see new economic possibilities? Does permanent and inevitable dissatisfaction then appear to be a myth, and a dark one, arising out of false economic thinking? Can we see that scarcity is not inevitable?

Commensurability: The Essence of Wants and Utility

Within the statement quoted above by Georgescu-Roegen is another and revealing critical insight into a wants-based economics. By reducing all human needs and desires to the same thing—wants, economics makes no distinction between activities as different as, say, reading a book, eating a hamburger, going for a walk, or getting drunk. They all provide the same thing, the fulfillment of a want; and whether this is called satisfaction, pleasure, or utility, it is all seen as the same thing. For economic theory these activities are not different, but each only provides amounts of "utility."

Thus, in a wants- or utility-based economics there are no distinctions in quality or kind between different activities. Each activity, regardless of what it is, provides utility, and the only question is how much—and that is indicated by how much the person is willing to pay for it (or "sacrifice" as some economists would say). A person does not eat an apple to meet a hunger need, but only to get utility—"variety is the spice of life." He or she may get that spice or utility from playing pinball as well.

The problem here is that if you are hungry, playing pinball just will not do, and this principle carries through throughout the whole hierarchy of needs. Even on the most basic physiological level we find this to be the case; if you are thirsty you need water and if you are hungry you need food. They cannot substitute for each other. As we look at the more social needs and compare them to the physiological, this is even more profoundly true. A social need cannot be satisfied by food, and vice versa (although we may, in fact, try to do so, and then we have what psychologists refer to as "consumption disorders," such as obesity). All these needs fall into different categories or types. Therefore, they cannot really be measured together, so that the different *kinds* of satisfaction that one gets from, say, a good meal and a good discussion with a friend cannot meaningfully be added up to an overall total called total utility or total satisfaction. But this is precisely what conventional economics tries to do. All consumption (indeed, all economic activity) is seen as commonly additive or measurable or, to use the somewhat more technical term, commensurable (from the Latin word *mensure*, which means to measure). In other words, economics attempts the trick of adding together apples and oranges. To do this we would need to add them together in the category of fruit. In the concept of "utility," economics has invented a category into which all things fit. But this category is fallacious and anything but self-evident. Expressing needs as wants allows the economist to do things that are impossible when needs are seen as needs. Some implications of the explicit recognition of needs on economic theory will be demonstrated in a slightly more technical appendix at the end of this book (Appendix I).

One advantage or appeal of this commensurability step can easily be guessed. It allows economics to apply mathematics and mathematical concepts across the board to human activity. While this may be a convenience from the standpoint of mathematics, it makes little sense if it violates the fundamental nature of human life. We know that the modern world has the penchant for turning everything and everyone into a number, and that the concept of quality gets crushed out in the process. The philosopher René Guenon referred to this tendency of our times as "the reign of quantity," and here we can see how the utilitarian core of modern economics contributes to this process, or perhaps is the main driving force of this process.[11]

Humanistic economics seeks to construct an economics that can help reverse the reign of quantity. It knows that the different needs cannot be added together–they are incommensurable. If you need good clean drinking water, all the newsprint turned out at the pulp mill up the river will not do. We need clean drinking water first, and then newsprint, and each one is not a substitute for the other, as conventional economics would have us believe. The humanistic insight into needs can be succinctly stated as follows: Wants are commensurable and needs are not.

The doctrine of wants and utility came about in economics through the particular way in which the ideas of economics developed, as indicated by Nicholas Georgescu-Roegen. It is a product of the history of economic activity, the key role played by England in that history, and the special attention that was given there to the concept of self-interest. We will look at this history in the next chapter.

References

1. William R. Allen, *Midnight Economist: Broadcast Essays III*. Los Angeles: International Institute for Economic Research, 1982, p. 23.
2. Campbell McConnell, *Economics*. 8th edition. New York: McGraw-Hill, 1981, p. 23.

3. Werner Sichel and Peter Eckstein, *Basic Economic Concepts*. Chicago: Rand McNally, 1974, pp. 128-129.

4.   Paul Heyne, *The Economic Way of Thinking*. 4th edition. Chicago: Science Research Associates, 1983, p. 16.

5. *ibid.*, p. 32 (emphasis added).

6. *ibid.*, p. 23.

7. William H. Beveridge, *Full Employment in a Free Society*. New York: W.W. Norton, 1945.

8. Quoted in Hirschman, *The Passions and the Interests*. Princeton: University of Princeton Press, 1977.

9. Nicholas Georgescu-Roegen, "Utility and Values in Economic Thought" in Philip P. Wiener, ed., *Dictionary of the History of Ideas*. Vol. 4. New York: Charles Scribner & Sons, 1973, p. 458.

10. William R. Allen, *Midnight Economist: Radio Essays II*. Los Angeles: International Institute for Economic Research, 1980, p. 10.

11. René Guenon, *The Reign of Quantity and the Signs of the Times*. Baltimore: Penguin Books, 1972.

Chapter 3

SELF-INTEREST AND ECONOMIC
MAN: A HISTORY

The modern commercial economy had its beginnings with the breakup of feudalism and the old order of the Middle Ages.

Perhaps the seed point of what was to be the progression towards the modern world was the First Crusade in 1095 in which Europeans travelled eastwards to rescue the Holy Lands from Islam. These roving bands of religiously motivated soldiers eventually became international journeying "merchants" and engaged in trade of the exotic spices, silk, and ivory of the East for the basic goods of the West. This trade was profitable, and the opportunity through commerce to acquire wealth burst rather suddenly upon the stage of human history. Frederick Braudel, the eminent historian, locates the critical event of this development in the huge profits to be made in overseas trade, occurring in dramatic fashion for the first time in the sixteenth century.[1]

From Mandeville to Adam Smith

In England this new economic climate led to what has been called *the enclosure movement*. Large areas of land, once considered common and which anyone could use for farming and for raising and grazing animals, were enclosed by powerful lords and nobles to be privately used for commercial purposes, particularly the raising of sheep, whose wool was now finding a lucrative market. The peasantry was displaced from this increasingly valuable land, and in time after much disruption and uprooting, became the mobile labor force for the also newly developing factory system.

With wealth and its acquisition becoming the new order of the day, the whole tone and temper of society underwent profound changes whose net value is still today the subject of much debate.[2]

Bernard de Mandeville (1670-1733) and *The Fable of the Bees*

A key early figure in this debate was the Dutch physician Bernard de Mandeville, who first lived in the Renaissance city of Leiden, also an important commercial center in Holland, and then moved to London. In 1705 he published a small booklet in verse in London, first called *The Grumbling Hive*, and in a later edition he gave it the title by which it became best known, *The Fable of the Bees*. It is a satiric social commentary that catches the paradox of the times and created a sensation. While lauded by Ben Johnson, Swift, and Voltaire, it was condemned by all with ties to the tradition of classical morality, including John Wesley, William Law, and a certain Francis Hutchenson.

In the analogy of *The Fable of the Bees* Mandeville states that the various vices—pride, indulgence, avarice, and so forth—are actually the cause of social and economic development:

> Vast numbers thronged the fruitful hive;
> Yet those vast numbers made 'em thrive;
> Millions endeavoring to supply
> Each others lust and vanity
>
> ...Thus every part was full of vice,
> Yet the whole mass a paradise[3]

It was observed to be the case that the very basis of national greatness lay in such doings. However, in the story of the poem the moralists in the beehive complain about all this sinfulness, and finally Jove, moved by indignation, turns "all the knaves honest" and brings the supposed benefits of virtue upon them. But these "benefits" turn out to be dubious since the presence of virtue removes the motivation, the means, by which all their luxuries and comforts came to be. As a consequence, the whole economy of the hive runs down, and the hive's honey stock wealth diminishes. In his conclusion to the poem Mandeville calls on the moralists to stop complaining:

> Then leave complaints; fools only strive
> to make a Great [into] an honest hive.

> To enjoy the world's conveniences,
> Be famed in war, yet live in Ease,
> without great vices, is a vain
> Utopia seated in the Brain.

To attempt to have a society of wealth and yet be without great vices is a contradiction, says Mandeville. One of Mandeville's critics, Francis Hutchenson, occupied a chair of Moral Philosophy at the University of Glasgow in Scotland. Hutchenson's student, and in turn the occupant of that same chair of Moral Philosophy in 1752, was none other than Adam Smith, the venerable father of economics.

Adam Smith (1723-1790): The Father of Economic Science

Smith's first book, which originally brought him to public recognition, was *The Theory of Moral Sentiments* published in 1759. In the opening lines Smith states the nature of his inquiry: "Howsoever selfish Man may be supposed, there are evidently some principles in his nature which interest him in the fortune of others, and render their happiness necessary to him, though he derives nothing from it, except the pleasure of seeing it." In general, Smith's theory of the basis of moral sentiments is a person's ability to take the position of a third party, an impartial observer, and in this way form a sympathetic idea of the moral, as opposed to the selfish, merits of the situation. If man in society should lose this ability, states Smith, then "the agreeable bands of love and affection . . . are broken asunder" and the cohesion and integration of its members are "dissipated and scattered abroad":

> All the members of human society stand in need of each other's assistance, and are likewise exposed to mutual injuries. Where the necessary assistance is reciprocally afforded from love, from gratitude, from friendship, and esteem, the society flourishes and is happy. All the different members of it are bound together by the agreeable bands of love and affection, and are, as it were, drawn to one common centre of mutual good offices.

> Society, however, cannot subsist among those who are at all times ready to hurt and injure one another. The moment that injury begins, the moment that mutual resentment and animosity takes place, all the bands of it are broken asunder, and the different members of which it consisted, are, as it were, dissipated and scattered abroad by the violence and opposition of their discordant affections.[4]

Near the end of the book, under the category of "Licentious Systems," Smith deals with Mandeville. All traditional systems of morality rest, as Smith says, on the belief that there is a real and essential distinction between vice and virtue and "to encourage," he adds approvingly, "the best and most laudable habits of the human mind." A licentious system, such as that of Dr. Mandeville, on the other hand, says that such a distinction is false, "a mere cheat and imposition upon mankind," so that one need not attempt restraint and control of the so-called lower passions because they are not really lower after all. In that way it gives "license." Furthermore, as Larouchefoucauld delineated in his epigrams and Mandeville satirized in his fable, the so-called virtues are really disguised or masqueraded forms of what we ordinarily call vices, such as pride and vanity. In other words, so many of the seemingly virtuous are really hypocrites.

Smith regards Mandeville's ideas as "holy pernicious," and "in almost every respect erroneous." Yet he says *almost*, and in this lies what will be a fateful gap. In disdainfully dispensing with Mandeville, Smith does acknowledge the following: "But how destructive soever this system may appear, it could never have imposed upon so great a number of persons nor have occasioned so general an alarm among those who are the friends of better principles had it not in some respect bordered on the truth." But this truth for Smith, at least in his first book, is just a bit of "sophistry" by which Mandeville "establishes his favorite conclusion that private vices are public benefits." So Smith is unperturbed: "Such is the system of Dr. Mandeville, which once made so much noise in the world."

Seventeen years later, in 1776, Smith comes out with *The Wealth of Nations* and the book goes down in history as the origin of the economic theory of self-interest. In one of its most famous passages, which is often quoted as the keynote of the book, Smith says the following:

> It is not from the benevolence of the butcher, the brewer, or the baker, that we expect our dinner, but from their regard to their own self-interest. We address ourselves not to their humanity but to their self-love, and never talk to them of our own necessities, but of their advantages. Nobody but a beggar chooses to depend chiefly upon the benevolence of his fellow citizens.[5]

In his introduction to the Modern Library Edition to Smith's book, the editor and well-known economist Edward Cannan notes that "we can scarcely fail to suspect that it was Mandeville who first made him [Smith] realize that it is not from the benevolence of the butcher . . . that we expect our dinner."[6] Whatever the influence, Smith, who began as a moral philosopher upholding the traditional values—and even the concept of virtue itself—ends up espousing the new doctrine of self-interest in what was to be its most influential presentation.

The Influence of Isaac Newton and Naturalism.   There are probably many ways that we can account for this apparent change in Adam Smith's thinking—at least the change in emphasis in his later work that became the foundation of the new field of Political Economy. But perhaps the most significant and far-reaching source of this shift was the climate of intellectual thought in Britain that resulted from the epochal triumph of Sir Isaac Newton's celestial mechanics. Newton's work was *The Mathematical Principles of Natural Philosophy*, published in 1687. And the effect of this milestone work changed Western thought ever since and nowhere so profoundly as in Smith's Britain. The Scottish universities of which Smith was a most prominent member were highly active in spreading the ideas of Newton. In one of Smith's essays he describes Newton's system as "the greatest discovery ever made by man."[7]

The keynote of Newton's system was the law of universal gravitation. It stated that a universally present "force," which Newton called gravitation, caused a phenomenon to follow mechanical and mathematically regular laws. This arrangement applied to the smallest particles as well as the movements of the planets and stars. From the time of Newton's publication henceforth (at least until the work of twentieth century physicists) scientists conceived of nature as a giant mechanical contrivance, very much like a universal clock.

Even before Smith's *Wealth of Nations*, mechanistic thinking was very much in the air. On the continent, the mechanistic ideas of Helveticus were stirring great controversy. Around 1760 he wrote, "As the physical world is ruled by the laws of movement, so is the moral universe ruled by the laws of interest."

Although he was not necessarily making a specific comparison with Newton's system, Adam Smith in the joint concept of self-interest and "the invisible hand" advanced the principle that could be to economics what gravitation was in physics. The economic agent seeks only his own gain, Smith says in *The Wealth of Nations*, but he is in this "led by an invisible hand to promote an end which is no part of his intention." The invisible hand here is a close parallel to the action-at-a-distance, which was the way that the force of gravity was conceived of as acting on physical bodies.

The passage from moral science to natural science, at first so subtle but ultimately so deep and vast, can be glimpsed in the differences between Smith's *Moral Sentiments* book and his *Wealth of Nations*. In the former book Smith actually uses the invisible hand concept for the first time, before it is most famously used again in *The Wealth of Nations*. Here is how it appears in *Moral Sentiments:*

The produce of the soil maintains at all times nearly that number of inhabitants which it is capable of maintaining. The rich only select from the heap what is more precious and agreeable. They consume little more than the poor; and in spite of their natural selfishness and rapacity, though they mean only their own conveniency, though the sole end which they propose from the labours of all the thousands whom they employ be the gratification of their own vain and insatiable desires, they divide with the poor the produce of all their improvements. They are led by an *invisible hand* to make nearly the same distribution of the necessaries of life which would have been made had the earth been divided into equal portions among all its inhabitants; and thus, without intending it, without knowing it, advance the interest of the society, and afford means to the multiplication of the species. When Providence divided the earth among a few lordly masters, it neither forgot nor abandoned those who seemed to have been left out in the partition.[8]

Here the invisible hand is equated with "Providence" (Smith's capitalization), which was how the moral tradition conceived of the workings of a just God. The effect of the invisible hand is "to make nearly the same distribution of the necessaries of life which would have been made had the earth been divided into equal proportions among all its inhabitants." That is how we ought to know it is operating, when there has been a more equal division of the necessities of life, regardless of the "vain and insatiable desires" of the rich.

When Smith introduces the invisible hand concept in *The Wealth of Nations*, it no longer refers to a guiding force moderating the social effects of the vain and insatiable desires of the rich, but now more of a justification for every economic agent only following their self-interest. Smith's complete statement in *The Wealth of Nations* is as follows:

[The economic agent] intends only his own gain, and he is in this, as in many other cases, led by an invisible hand to promote an end which was no part of his intention. Nor is it always the worst for the society that it was no part of it. By pursuing his own interest he frequently promotes that of the society more effectually than when he really intends to promote it.[9]

Smith no longer talks here of Providence overseeing and moderating selfish and insatiable desires, and the invisible hand comes close to being equated with self-interest. Later, Hermann Gossen was to complete the equation.

This is really quite a remarkable statement, and these ideas in their own way had as wide an influence on subsequent thought as did Newton's. Smith is saying that good intentions may be less beneficial for society than self-interested intentions. This is the prime foundation thought of mainstream economics. With such a statement Smith hooks up with Mandeville and departs from the moral tradition of all previous social thought which he himself upheld in his first book.

Even though self-interest is ordinarily thought of as a highly personal motivation, in Smith's usage it becomes an impersonal natural force, very much like gravity. Just as gravity harmoniously orders the great multitudinous and sprawling heavenly phenomenon, self-interest is the basic and universal flywheel of social behavior. The invisible hand is a marvelous verbal coinage that may well describe how Newton's gravity acts to move about the planets in their orderly course, and now is applied to society.

Nassau Senior, a later English follower of Smith, in 1836 saw the attempt to maximize wealth as an element in economic theory "like gravity in physics," and as the "ultimate fact beyond which the reader cannot go, and of which almost every other proposition is merely an illustration."[10]

From a Science of Wealth to a Science of Human Behavior

In the early formulations of the principle of self-interest by Smith and his followers, we still find the focus on economics as the science of material wealth. That was the purpose of the inquiries of Smith and others–to investigate the causes and the reasons that made for or allowed accumulation of wealth. The reason for such a study was their interest in seeing the betterment of society at large, and particularly for Smith, the adequate provision of material needs for the less well-off. This time period was still thought of as the age of accumulation and the essential question concerning these early economists was how to expand production.

Taking off from Smith's work, David Ricardo (1772-1823), another of the great "classical economists," emphasized the key role of the businessman or merchant, and lamented that in the long run he saw only what he believed was the "unproductive" landlord benefiting from his ability to collect rents. For Ricardo self-interest and business motivation were perfectly compatible. In one of his letters to Thomas Malthus he writes, "It is self-interest which regulates all the speculations of trade; and where that can be clearly and satisfactorily ascertained, we should not know where to stop if we admitted any other rule of option."[11] The entire economics of Ricardo presupposed self-interested individual motive and actions, but being more interested in explicating the development of an economic system (particularly as affected by the income distribution), he left the question of individual behavioral laws largely implicit.

John Stuart Mill (1806-1873): The Ambivalent Father of Economic Man

The emphasis on wealth production and capitalist development of the early classical economists underwent a shift in the writings of John Stuart Mill, the last of the great classical economists. Mill's textbook *The Principles of Political Economy*, first published in 1848, held sway in the field through numerous editions until it was finally replaced as the premier text in the field by Alfred Marshall's *Principles of Economics* in the 1890s.

John Stuart was raised by his famous philosopher father, James Mill, in the dry, demanding, and rigorous atmosphere of an almost religious belief in Utilitarianism. The elder Mill was a personal friend and disciple of Jeremy Bentham, the father of the pleasure-pain calculus doctrine discussed in the first chapter.

At the tender age of three John Stuart had to learn ancient Greek, next came Latin, algebra, Aristotle's logic, and at the age of thirteen, economics. To cap it all off, at fifteen he started to imbibe Bentham's philosophy. So far so good. The education seemed to work out perfectly: John Stuart joined the circle of England's most respected intellectuals. He seemed happy, but then, at the age of twenty, he was unexpectedly struck by a "mental crisis." Suddenly his life seemed empty and hopelessly meaningless.

The detailed description of this intense and prolonged depression is movingly described in a special chapter of his *Autobiography*, written shortly before he died in 1873. We mention it here since it relates intimately to the issue of self-interest and the calculated economic way of thinking as a philosophy of life. Looking back, Mill was led to adopt a new theory of life when he came to realize that the stress on analytical thinking had a tendency to destroy a person's ability to have feelings, and that Bentham's pleasure- and pain-based view of human nature reducing everything to self-interest was not the whole picture. In destroying one's ability to have feelings it ironically destroyed the prime goal of Bentham's doctrine: to be happy. Only by forgetting one's own happiness could one really gain genuine happiness. Here is how he put his new insight:

Mill maintains are 2 selves; the affectionate, bonded self and self-seeker after wealth & pleasure. ——— —

I have never, indeed, wavered in the conviction that happiness is the test of all rules of conduct, and the end of life. But I now thought that this end was only to be attained by *not* making it the direct end. Those only are happy . . . who have their minds fixed on some object other than their own happiness; on the happiness of others, on the improvement of mankind, even on some act or pursuit, followed not as a means but as itself an ideal end. Aiming thus at something else, they find happiness by the way. The enjoyments of life (such was now my theory) are sufficient to make it a pleasant thing, when they are taken *en passant*, without being made a principal object.[12]

The young Mill turned to the poetry of Wordsworth, whose work "seemed to draw from a source of inward joy, of sympathetic and imaginate pleasure, which could be shared by all human beings . . . and which would be made richer by every improvement in the physical or social condition of mankind." Soon the cloud of depression drew off, and as Mill writes, "though [he] had several relapses, some of which lasted many months . . . [he] gradually, but completely, emerged from his habitual depression and was never again subject to it."[13]

After the events described above, Mill began the slow process, which was to continue all his life, of turning away from the stifling concepts of the abstract and mechanical utilitarianism of his father, towards a more human and person-centered approach to social thought and economics. In this process he also broke with the strict quantitative utilitarianism of his father and Jeremy Bentham. He criticized the poverty of this view of human nature:

Man is conceived by Bentham as a being susceptible of pleasures and pains, and governed in all his conduct partly by the different modifications of self-interest and the passions commonly classed as selfish, partly by sympathies or occasionally antipathies towards other beings. And here Bentham's conception of human nature stops. . . .

Man is never recognised by him as being capable of pursuing spiritual perfection as an end; of desiring, for its own sake, the conformity of his own character to his standard of excellence, without hope of good or fear of evil from other source than his own inward consciousness. . . .

Nor is it only the moral part of man's nature, in the strict sense of the term–the desire of perfection or the feeling of an approving or of an accusing conscience–that he overlooks; he but faintly recognises, as a fact in human nature, the pursuit of any other ideal end for its own sake. The sense of *honour* and personal dignity–that feeling of personal exaltation and degradation which acts independently of other people's opinion, or even in defiance of it; the love of *beauty*, the pas-

sion of the artist; the love of *order*, of congruity, of consistency in all
things and conformity to their end; the love of *power* not in the limited
form of power over other human beings, but abstract power, the
power of making our volitions effectual; the love of *action,* the thirst
for movement and activity, a principle scarcely of less influence in
human life than its opposite, the love of ease. None of these powerful constituents of human nature are thought worthy of a place among
the "Springs of Action"; and though there is possibly no one of them
of the existence of which an acknowledgment might not be found in
some corner of Bentham's writings, no conclusions are ever founded
on the acknowledgment. Man, that most complex being, is a very
simple one in his eyes.[14]

And later on in his life he was to champion the emancipation of
women, the concerns and aspirations of the poor, and the development
of labor unions and farm cooperatives, and offered with the assistance
of Harriet Taylor, his wife, a landmark essay in Western social thought,
On Liberty (1859).

At the same time, however, some of his earlier classical conceptions of economics stubbornly refused to be outgrown and remained
with him, and economics in general, ever since. During his mental crisis,
he wrote several essays on how to recast economics into a science
"depending on laws of human nature," particularly those which did *not*
relate to the feelings of affection, love, conscience, and duty. Economics
for him was no longer to focus on national wealth, but on the nature of
the individual seeking wealth. The correct way to proceed was to
"reason from assumed premises that might be totally without foundation in fact, and which are not pretended to be universally in accordance with it." Born was a hypothetical image of a man that "makes entire
abstraction of every other human passion or motive, except . . . aversion to labor, and desire of present enjoyment of costly indulgences."[15]

But Mill also clearly recognized that the conclusions of such an
abstract science are *only* true in the abstract, only to the extent that
people really do want to maximize their wealth. If there are other motives that "excite the human will to action," as for instance, "social affection," and which are also operative, the truth derived in the abstract
is no longer really true. As he put it: "Effects are commonly determined
by a concurrence of causes. If we have overlooked any one cause, we
may reason justly from all the others, and only be further wrong. Our
premise will be true, and our reasoning correct, and yet the result of no
value in the particular case."[16]

This methodological thought of Mill is significant since it establishes firmly that Mill, the father of the analytical abstraction of the
economic actor (later to be named "homo oeconomicus"), also was well

[handwritten annotation: unfortunately only Mill's self-seeking person remained, to become the centerpiece of economics.]

aware that there are other aspects to human nature, some of which he had become acquainted with only during his immersion in poetry when facing a philosophical crisis. That other domain (pursuit of truth, love of beauty, sense of personal dignity, etc.) was not relevant for economics, he thought, but it did indeed exist and may interfere with the applicability of economics. In other words, self-interested Economic Man had a more noble brother, both of them sharing fully in making up human reality. For Mill, however, economics was only one part of human reality, which was that tendency in human nature to maximize wealth.

Ironically, then, with John Stuart Mill the powerful idea gains further currency that economics is about self-interested wealth accumulation only. It ought not to concern itself with the other higher activities of Man. This theme would then be voiced again four decades later by Jevons and others, establishing itself as the primary one in England and some parts of the continent.

Karl Marx (1818-1883)

A spur to the refinement of the prevailing classical economic thought was provided by an alternative economic perspective to that fashioned by Mill. In the same year that Mill published his textbook, 1848, another economics document was put forth: *The Communist Manifesto*.

The economic sources of Marx and Engels were impeccable–the works of Adam Smith himself. And, surprisingly, Marx is generally seen to be an economist in Smith's classical tradition. What Marx did was take a concept of Smith's and develop it as the centerpiece of his own economics. The concept is referred to as the Labor Theory of Value. Smith had written that the labor put into producing a good is its only source of value.

> In the early and rude state of society which precedes both the accumulation of stock and the appropriation of land, the proportion between the quantities of labour necessary for acquiring different objects, seems to be the only circumstance which can afford any rule for exchanging them for one another. . . . In this state of things, the whole produce of labour belongs to the labourer; and the quantity of labour commonly employed in acquiring or producing any commodity is the only circumstance which can regulate the quantity of labour which it ought commonly to purchase, command, or exchange for.[17]

Marx was then to theorize that since labor was the only source of value, the profit of the capitalists or the return to capital, as opposed to the return to labor, was sheer exploitation of the laborer.

In regard to the theme of self-interest Karl Marx made equal use of that assumption as did his classical predecessors. His economics as articulated in *Das Kapital* (1860) and elsewhere is essentially the economics of the development of capitalism, emerging from medieval feudalism and ending in violent revolution that ushered in a new age of state ownership of the means of production (meaning essentially factories). The driving engine of such self-destructive economic dynamics was the urge of the capitalist to accumulate for the sake of accumulation and domination of markets. As one contemporary Marxist observes: "He is driven by exactly the same urge to get rich as the miser, only he satisfies it not in the illusory form of building a hoard of gold and silver, but in capital formation which is actual production."[18] Like the miser, he is "essentially greedy." Again, as with Adam Smith, it is pure self-interest that fuels the economy and the expansion of market values. Unlike Smith, however, such a natural urge is seen not to promote the welfare of all, but a society that is torn by conflict, social antagonism, recurring crisis, mounting unemployment, and what Marx called the "immiseration" of society at large. In short, in the Marxian cosmology of a world without Providence, self-interest had lost much of its goodness. Far from being some sort of mystery glue binding society in social harmony, self-interest now looked like an explosive, if not a self-destructive force. Such was the disturbing insight classical economists gained almost a century after Adam Smith. A deadly blow, and perhaps not surprisingly the end of the classical tradition.

Hermann Heinrich Gossen (1810-1858): Pioneer of the Neoclassical Revolution

Karl Marx died in 1883 waiting in vain for the long expected revolution in England and the subsequent rebirth of society. Instead, a very different kind of revolution was in the making; a revolution not of the expropriated proletariat but in the way economists perceived their very subject.

The new spirit which was to sway economists onto a new track first manifested itself in Germany in the year of 1854 with the publication of a highly unusual book by an obscure and long ignored Prussian civil servant, Hermann Heinrich Gossen. The book, published at the author's own expense, carried the title of *The Laws of Human Relations*. In the preface, the author, seemingly more inspired than modest, claims: "I

[handwritten at top: God gave us pleasure and we are ungodly not to pursue it]

believe I have accomplished for the explanation of the relations among humans what a Copernicus was able to accomplish for the explanation of the relation of heavenly bodies."[19] Not surprisingly, the book was a little too much ahead of its time to become a best seller, especially in Germany. Most of the copies never sold and were delivered back to the author at his own request. It was only decades later that some of the best known economists started to hunt for the handful of copies kept in public libraries in Germany, Switzerland, and at the British Museum in London. At that time, the so-called neoclassical revolution had already begun sweeping full force through England, Austria, and Switzerland. We mention Gossen's work here because he was the first to be moved to articulate in no unclear fashion a new and more powerful perspective concerning self-interest. It marks the birth of a new economy of pleasure-seeking, atomistic individuals interacting with one another in market exchange.

Maximization of individual pleasure, "viewed by all men without exception as life's ultimate purpose," was seen by Gossen as instilled and willed by none other than God. By following self-interest we follow God's will. Any moralist-type self-control would inhibit God's plan. As Gossen put it: "It would frustrate totally or in part the purpose of the Creator were we to attempt to neutralize this force in total or in part, as is the intention of some moral codes promulgated by men." And he asks with moral indignation: "How can a creature be so arrogant as to want to frustrate totally or partly the purpose of his Creator?"[20]

Nevertheless, too many are inclined to fail to observe "the relevations of the Creator," and to hanker after some sort of human or social morality. Now, with a limited or less than perfect God this would indeed be a problem, but, Gossen assures us, we need not fear such misguided attempts: "He (the Creator) must have anticipated this erring too, and for this reason He gave this force (the quest for maximum "Lebensgenuss" or life pleasure) such an extraordinary strength that all human resistance to it can only weaken but not paralyze it. And no matter how much man may try to suppress this force in one of its manifestations, it will always reappear with increased strength in an unexpected and unforeseen new manifestation."[21]

So most humanitarian-type legislation to help the poor will indirectly backfire and make the poor even worse off. It is the task of economics to demonstrate the social reformers and moralists wrong. The latter believed to have discovered in egoism an evil force, and "they held that egoism would destroy human society were it allowed to work unchecked." Economics was now seen as the science of pleasure, realizing that the Creation is indeed perfect, that the world as it is needs no improvement, and that human beings need not be (mis)guided by moralistic prohibitions. Instead, Gossen observes, "we have learned to recognize the (true) force whose strength we have occasion to admire daily and in innumerable instances, namely, the *egoism* of the human race."[22] Discovering the laws and interplay of self-interested pleasure-maximizing beings is discovering the content of the only *true religion* of the Creator. The dogmas of such religion are the laws of nature. The moral principle of such religion is to organize actions in harmony with the natural laws of pleasure and egotistical human nature. The rituals of such religion are the exercises man has to perform in order to understand the laws of nature and to develop the facility to act accordingly. Finally, the priests of this religion are those individuals who succeed in discovering new more refined laws of pleasure and in achieving for it wider recognition; in other words, the true priests of this new religion of self-interest and laissez-faire are to be found within the ranks of the economists. For divine revelations we have to turn to the sacred texts such as Gossen's pioneering book. Not inappropriately, it concludes by calling on the reader to contemplate in what "beautiful a fashion did the Creator know how to remove the obstacle that egoism seems to oppose to the welfare of society and to bring about through this egoism exactly the opposite: *He made egoism the sole and irresistable force by which humanity may program in the arts and science for both its material and intellectual welfare.*"[23]

Whether Hermann Gossen was a reincarnation of Bernard de Mandeville or not we do not know, but he certainly was a most ardent and radical disciple of Adam Smith's invisible hand doctrine. He raised egoism to a divine principle and declared it the root of all that's good, not only in the economic sphere but for the entire social domain as well.

Appropriately, his book ends with a moral exhortation for the reader to steep him or herself in adoration of God, to make oneself worthy of Him, to help speed up the coming of His Paradise, all by casting away unnatural moral restraint and by following the new oracle:

o r g a n i z e   y o u r   a c t i o n s   f o r   y o u r   o w n   b e n e f i t.

With Gossen, the Gospel of self-interest became rearticulated and revived at the very time when Karl Marx was busily engaged in scribbling down his thesis of capitalist doom. What Gossen did in such outspoken prose and frank manner was decades later to emerge as the new a-b-c in approaching economic reality: (a) base economic analysis on so-called laws of individual behavior; (b) trust the natural God-given goodness and power of self-interested behavior; and (c) view as highly suspect the promise of all kinds of well-meant attempts to improve the socioeconomic world through legislation inspired by some humanitarian motive, whether it be minimum wage legislation, social security, or relief for the poor. Realistically, nobody could be expected to outsmart God, i.e., the results of self-interest in the free marketplace.

The Neoclassical Marginalist Revolution

Gossen's new framework of divinely ordained individual self-interest was contained within several hundred pages of terse text, interrupted by numerous graphs and occasional algebra. All of this was essentially ignored until the rising stars of late nineteenth century economics discovered in Gossen a precursor of their own marginal utility revolution that proved to be so successful.

The New Economics of William Stanley Jevons (1835-1882)

One of them, W. S. Jevons, wrote in the preface to his second (1879) edition that "it is quite apparent that Gossen has anticipated me as regards the general principle and the theory of economics," and he even went further to admit graciously, "So far as I can gather his treatment of the fundamental theory is even more general and thorough than I was able to scheme out."[24]

Nevertheless, it is Jevons' own work and not Gossen's that constitutes the vital link in the evolution of mainstream thought in economics. In particular, defenders of capitalism at the time of Marx's attacks on its legitimacy finally found what they wanted: a move away from the labor theory of value held by classical economists since Adam Smith. For it is the case that there are some fundamental problems in the labor theory of value, whether advocated by Smith, Ricardo, or Marx. Two of the most important ones are the question of the productivity of capital, and the issue of market value.

The productivity of capital problem is that tools or machines increase the output of labor. As we saw in the case of our Robinson Crusoe, a worker can dig more dirt per unit time with a shovel than with his hands. If it is the capitalist that provides him with the shovel, cannot it also be said that capital itself is productive and so legitimately should share in a portion, perhaps even the largest portion, of the price received for a good? Thus began the debate in economics: Is capital productive?

Then there was the problem of market value. The prices people are willing to pay for goods are determined in markets. Should not the "value" of a good, after all, be what someone is willing to exchange (or pay) for a good? A given worker and capitalist can turn out a lot of widgets, but what if no one really needs or wants any widgets, can it still be said then that they have any value, at least in an economically meaningful sense of the word? And the problem can also be phrased in the reverse. What if a worker is turning out what appear to be widgets, and yet they seem to be in great demand; should they be seen to have value?

Smith was particularly troubled by this latter problem and phrased his dilemma in what has been called the paradox of value: Why is it that something which has great use, such as water, should cost us so little, while something with very little use, such as diamonds, should be so dear in its exchange value in the market place? Thus Smith recognized two kinds of value, use value and exchange value, and pondered over their relationship.

Jevons' new theory lay in an ingenious explanation of the paradox of value which seemed to resolve the century-old dilemma. The key lay in concepts of marginal and total utility. They are typically presented in standard textbooks by the following graph:

Figure 3.1

THE PARADOX OF VALUE

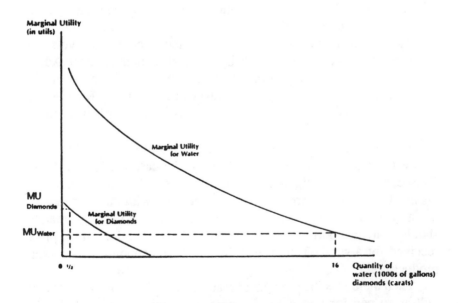

We should think of marginal utility as the present or current utility–how much the consumer is willing to spend for the last unit bought. In the neoclassical framework of Jevons and his followers, the individual units of an item consumed add up overall to its total utility.* The paradox of value is solved because use value is the total utility of a good, whereas exchange value is its marginal utility. Here the graph is explained by the conventional textbook:

> Note that for all the units of water, which most consumers consider to be essential to their survival, marginal utility is significantly higher than it is for diamonds. But the marginal utility for water drops off sharply after some large number of units are consumed, so that the marginal utility for the fifth unit of diamonds is actually considerably larger. . . . Value in exchange is not determined by total satisfaction, but rather by what people are willing to pay for the last unit they buy. While the expected total satisfaction from water can be much higher than from diamonds, the additional satisfaction derived from the last unit of water is expected to be very low relative to diamonds, since the typical consumer buys so many more units of water than he does diamonds.[25]

In this discussion of the problem of adding up their "satisfaction" or utilities from different kinds of goods, we can recognize a fatal flaw in the above explanation. It is revealed in the phrase, "the typical consumer buys so many more units of water than he does of diamonds." Here is the old bugaboo of commensurability. In what way can it be said that the consumer buys more *units* of water than diamonds? What is a comparable unit of water and diamonds? Indeed, what is a unit of water? An ounce? A glassful? A gallon jug? And what is a unit of diamond? A carat? A stone? An ounce? Obviously, a unit of anything can be anything you choose as long as it is relevant to the kind of good it is. Generally, for water it happens to be volume and for diamonds it is carats. Since water and diamonds satisfy two quite different kinds of needs it is ridiculous to talk about their units as comparable and to say that the consumer consumes more water than he does diamonds. There is simply no commensurability between these two goods.

Can't equate diamonds & water

---

* It may be noted that the same insight as presented earlier by Gossen used a different language. The marginal utility of a community was to him an incremental "atom" of a particular "means of enjoyment."

So the distinction between so-called total and marginal utility as an explanation for Smith's use value and exchange value simply "does not hold water," so to speak.

This failure was not easily recognized in the late 1800s, and even today the utility explanation of the paradox of value is presented to students as something that is still legitimate. Perhaps the reason is that the concept of utility seemed to be a quantity, and that would make self-interest directly measurable.

One of the earliest and greatest humanistic economists, John Hobson, saw through the fallacy of marginal comparisons between different qualities, and set forth a realistic alternative theory of how the economic actor allocates. Hobson's critique and reformulation is presented in Appendix II.

The Quest for Measurability. Jevons, like Gossen before him, was a strong advocate of a more mathematically oriented economics: "Most persons," he regretfully observed, "appear to hold that the physical sciences form the proper sphere of mathematical method, and that the moral sciences (economics) demand some other method, I know not what. My theory of economy, however, is purely mathematical in character."[26] What was for Mill still an "arbitrary assumption" was now converted to an axiom "known to us immediately by intuition" from which economic theory as some "mechanics of utility and self-interest" was to be analytically deduced by Jevons.

At the same time, however, we encounter a major difference relative to what Gossen said; it pertains to the treatment of self-interest. Gossen had criticized established political economy for limiting itself to the pleasure (utility) from only *material* goods and instead had proposed that "we set aside this limitation and extend the purpose of this science to its real dimensions—*to help man obtain the greatest sum of pleasure during his life.*"[27] In short, for Gossen economics was more generally "the science of pleasure" with laws pertaining to pleasurable material and non-material things alike.

Jevons, on the other hand, addressed what he felt was the legitimate question of the relation of economics to *moral* science or ethics. He was unenamored of the type of utilitarian perspective advanced by Bentham in which all pleasures are essentially of the same quality differing only in permanence and intensity. Instead, Jevons recognized that the mental and moral feelings are of a more elevated and different kind than the ones arising from "bodily wants and susceptibilities." Economics and its calculus of utility—rather than dealing with the whole gamut of feelings—needs to be limited to these ordinary material wants and wealth, while a higher calculus of moral right and wrong would be required in deciding how to employ that wealth. There is as a result, at least in theory, room for moral action to be left to philosophers and other non-economists which a general Gossen-type "science of pleasure" cannot possibly encompass. Self-interest and calculated utility-maximization in economics, yes, but not for *all* human actions. In this, Jevons confirms for neoclassicism the point of view put forth by his British predecessor, J. S. Mill.

In this perspective Jevons was followed by his younger English contemporary, F. Y. Edgeworth (1845-1926), author of *Mathematical Psychics* (1881). He, too, considered that there might be other motives to account for than mere self-interest, "admitting that there exists in the higher part of human nature a tendency towards and feeling after utilitarian institutions . . . could we seriously suppose that these moral considerations were relevant to war and trade; could eradicate the controlless core of human selfishness, or exorcise an appreciable force in comparison with the impulse of self-interest? . . . The first principle of economics is that every agent is actuated only by self-interest."[28] Here Edgeworth perfectly echoes Jevons and to a lesser extent J. S. Mill. But now, adding the neoclassical enthusiasm for the mathematization of everything economic, Edgeworth went on to say that utility could be measured scientifically just as soon as a "hedonimeter" could be developed.

Economic Man into the Twentieth Century

Meanwhile, the seeds of the neoclassical revolution had also sprouted independently in Switzerland in the work of Leon Walras, who built his purest of pure theoretical constructs on selfish and calculating economic agents.

While having recognized him as a most important conveyer of Economic Man into the twentieth century, we will, in what follows, focus on the developments in the Anglo-Saxon world. It is here where the economics of the twentieth century were essentially formulated and presented to the rest of the world.

Alfred Marshall (1842-1924) and the Pursuit of Excellence

The neoclassical development in economics culminated in the work of Alfred Marshall. As we have already mentioned, his *Principles of Economics* (1890) replaced Mill's as the leading text in the field.

Jevons' and Menger's concept of Economic Man was crude ore that was worked and refined in the hands of the foremost British neoclassical economist Alfred Marshall. Marshall's work still forms the basis of much of contemporary economic thinking.

Marshall came out of a strict Evangelical Protestant background, and he entered college as a theology student with the goal of becoming a minister. He soon concluded that he could better serve humanity through the more worldly field of economics, where he was introduced by his British elders, Jevons and Edgeworth, to the utilitarian tradition.

In utilitarianism Marshall encountered a long-standing economic principle that in a fundamental way is ethically deficient. This was the problem to which Mill was sensitive. To restate the problem: it is the case that the "good" action often involves a restraint of impulse, or a resistance to temptation, and these are efforts that are anything but pleasant. The good often means the *resistance* to pleasure. In the same way growth or maturity means the restraint of previously indulged desires. The hedonism that was first encountered in Gossen's book and which by now had become established doctrine in economics had eliminated this distinction. Good and pleasure were now made one. How well this belief met the demands of an increasingly affluent and consumption-oriented British economy.

Into this milieu came Marshall, the ex-theology student. Inevitably, it became his task to resolve the various ethical conflicts that both economics and industrial British society faced. In the first edition of his *Principles of Economics* he freely uses the hedonic terms *pleasure* and *pain*. But in the later editions he deleted pain and pleasure and changed to the more temperate *satisfaction*, or *benefit* and *cost*.

Marshall, in his usual scholarly spirit, devoted more than one of the initial chapters in his text to a reexamination of the question pertaining to the correct substance and scope of economic science. He found that the proper focus of economics was "a study of men as they live and think in the ordinary business of life." But, he adds immediately, "it concerns itself chiefly with those motives which affect, most powerfully and most steadily, man's conduct in the *business* part of life."[29] And the steadiest motive to such "ordinary business work" is the desire for material rewards.

For Marshall it is on the consumer side, the way income and wealth is spent, where different kinds of motives need to be recognized. He writes, "while wants are the rulers of life among the lower animals, it is to changes in the forms of efforts and activities that we must turn when in search for the keynotes of the history of mankind." But even here, Marshall comes to the conclusion that the higher motives cannot be included within the scope of economics: The "higher study of consumption must come after, and not before, the main body of economic analysis; and though it may have its beginning within the proper domain of economics, it cannot find its conclusion there, but must extend far beyond."[30]

So once again, just like J. S. Mill and Jevons, Marshall recognizes non-economic (or higher) motives, but in the end refuses to incorporate these into the discipline. To him it was a worthwhile topic only for some distant future. Meanwhile, he proceeded to treat the consumer, at least in his graphs and his algebra, much as Jevons and Gossen did before him, as a self-interested utility maximizer who interacts with a basically profit-maximizing businessman. And he did so confessing his faith that "progress chiefly depends on the extent to which the *strongest* and not the *highest* form of human nature can be utilized for the increase of social good."[31] By this Marshall was expressing the long-standing belief in Western social thought, which can be traced to Hobbes and then Machiavelli, that the higher aspects of human nature were largely ineffective in curbing the much more powerful human *passions*. Therefore, in order for social progress to occur, another one of the passions—economic interest—had to be set against the others. Virtue could not override vice; only another vice, although more benign, could be made to overrule the destructive vices.

Under the influence of Alfred Marshall, economics emerged as a much more homogenous discipline. The marginalist revolution seemed successfully completed and with the new *neo*classical economics firmly entrenched. Much of this new consensus may be attributed to Marshall's genius as a wide-ranging synthesizer who managed to weave together the best strands of the various competing schools of thought, particularly Mill's thought with the new marginalist revolutionaries. At the same time, we should add that another element was involved as well. During the first decade of this century, almost all British students preparing for their qualifying university exams ended up being tested on questions drawn up at Cambridge University under Marshall's direction.[32] And the success of Marshallian economics also meant the enthronement of utility maximizing Economic Man, on whom Marshall relied throughout his analytical work—particularly his graphs and his algebra—despite his expressed preference and rhetoric for a more realistic and holistic image of Man.

The Baptism of Economic Man.   It was Marshall who, in his lectures of 1885, first coined the term "Economic Man" and so gave a name to the already forty-year-old intellectual offspring of J. S. Mill. Not long thereafter, Walras and his follower, Pareto, also used the new label.

Let us briefly summarize here the "neoclassic" meaning of the concept: Economic Man-type of behavior was only meant for behavior that was considered "economic." In that domain men were seen to behave selfishly and motivated only with regard to their own welfare. The psychology was derived from Bentham's utilitarianism and since J. S. Mill, great care was taken to ensure that any kind of ethical or moral considerations were not allowed to determine, or even co-determine, his behavior. Economic Man was not only the prime pillar in the economic foundation but also responsible for making economics the science of self-interested behavior.

Although the neoclassical tradition of taking utility and self-interest as the mainspring of economic behavior has continued to dominate the mainstream of economics, there have always been critics and it is the work of these critics and countervoices that constitute a history of the humanistic alternative tradition; a tradition whose origins centered around the names of Simonde de Sismondi, John Ruskin, and John Hobson. Some of their contributions will be discussed later.

In Marshall's Shadow: Philip Henry Wicksteed (1844-1927)

While Marshall increasingly dominated academic economics during the first decade of this century, few were aware of a Unitarian minister who was appointed in 1874 to the Little Portland Street Chapel in London, a position he held until 1897, after which he supported himself and his family by lecturing and writing. Wicksteed, like Marshall, could not withstand the temptation to immerse himself with the more worldly gospel of economics. In 1882 he had purchased a copy of Jevons' book and not long after that he was the first to throw himself full force against Marx's labor theory of value in an article that was published in a socialist journal in 1884. Later, increasingly influenced by a line of thinking that originated in Austria and is now known as the Austrian School of economics, he started to devote his energies to the writing of book-length monographs, the first of which was published in 1888, his *Alphabet of Economic Science*, and another, his magnum opus, *The Common Sense of Political Economy* (1910).

The Common Sense was to introduce readers with little or no background in economics to a point of view centering almost exclusively on the new marginal utility principle. Jevons had gone far, he believed, but not quite far enough. The new reconstruction was still shackled by a general adherence to traditional terminology, categories, and the like. Here is how Wicksteed expressed it so eloquently when introducing his book:

> The new temple, so to speak, has been built up behind the old walls,
> and the old shell has been so piously preserved and respected that the
> very builders have often supposed themselves to be merely repairing
> and strengthening the ancient works and are hardly aware of the ex-
> tent to which they have raised an independent edifice.[33]

The author believed that "the time had come for a frank recognition of these facts," and his *Common Sense* was to be the vehicle to accomplish the task.

The book is quite significant for our purposes in that it was to be
an important influence upon Lionel Robbins' later work that was to
shape twentieth century economics. Secondly, Wicksteed addressed the
issue of the scope of economic science with the hope of universalizing
it. Here he was the first *English* economist to follow a path similar to
the one taken by Gossen and his followers in Austria, particularly
Wieser: The marginal principle was not, as Jevons and Marshall
believed, *only* applicable to industrial or commercial affairs, "but runs
as a universal and vital force through the administration of *all* our
resources."[34] In short, all deliberate or conscious human action is part
and parcel of economics. Wherever there is a question of choice, for
example whether to study or go out with a friend, we are in the process
of managing our time. And our time is indeed limited to twenty-four
hours a day and the span of our life. This was a new way of looking at
life. Economists like Jevons and Marshall identified scarcity and the
application of the material condition with *material* shortage and scarcity. It was only Gossen who, long before anyone else, pioneered in
taking time itself as the bedrock of scarcity. And when he talked about
maximizing pleasure it was always specified that it be "the total pleasure
during one's entire life that should be a maximum."*

The ramifications of this new idea were far-reaching. It allows not
only the consumer but also the human being in general to be analyzed
exactly the same way we look at a businessman–calculated, often cold,
and certainly commercial and impersonal in his dealings. Everything
we do relates to the economic category. Simply because we all have to
live with finite time, we are all administrating that limited resource in

---

* Wicksteed could not have gotten the idea by reading about Gossen in Jevon's
  book. He must have either rediscovered it himself or picked it up from
  reading Gossen or the Austrians. But wherever it originated, Wicksteed was
  the first to introduce it into the English intellectual scene.

order to squeeze out maximum gain, pleasure, or utility. The non-economic category either does not exist or is subordinated to the economic. Gone are the reservations of Mill, Jevons, and Marshall, as well as the traditional focus emphasizing applications in business and commerce. What comes in instead is much more subtle: economics becomes a new *way of thinking*, the way of extremely time-conscious beings always aware of what they are foregoing by doing what they do. If such *is* the consciousness of restless modern man and woman, then economic science in the style of Gossen and Wicksteed becomes the ready-made instrument to speed up such consciousness among freshmen and sophomore students, and to further inculcate them into true practitioners of such a mentality and lifestyle.

In addition to defining and conceptualizing economics as a way of thought that applies to all human behavior, Wicksteed also believed that he was able to show that this way of thought had nothing to do with selfishness. Economic Man may be constantly calculating to achieve his own ends, but these ends need not be selfish. Indeed, they could be philanthropic. All the hard bargaining and constant calculation of gain that the economic actor engages in could be either for charitable purposes or selfish purposes, or any purposes whatsoever, but these purposes had nothing to do with what economics was about. Economics was merely about means, the ways of achieving purposes, and the most efficient use of those means. So one can drive a hard bargain and very coldly indeed maximize one's wealth in business dealings because one is interested in making a large contribution with this wealth to a favorite cause or charity. The purposes or ends of one's economic behavior *may* include any human motive, including the altruistic. This could hardly be called selfish, could it?

Wicksteed referred to this as the principle of "non-tuism." "Tu" is the French affectional word for you, which has traditionally been translated into English as "thou." So, with reference to Martin Buber's dialogical concept, non-tuism could be translated as "non-I-Thou." For Wicksteed, what defines the economic relationship is that each party enters into it with only the intent of serving his or her own purposes and not those of the other with whom one is dealing—a situation typically characteristic of an "arms-length" transaction. The critical point for Wicksteed is that one's purposes in entering into the exchange need not be selfish. The only thing that matters from the standpoint of economics is that genuine altruism or benevolence (to use Adam Smith's original word) *is not applied to the person one is dealing with and exchanging with.* Therefore, the self-interest principle going back to Adam Smith is still maintained, and yet the discipline need not conceive of itself as the science of selfishness.

Whatever the supposed effects of this new interpretation of self-interest, Wicksteed's influence in the academic community and among the new students of the discipline was modest at best. Just as for Gossen, it must have been a bitter pill to swallow for the clever, perhaps even brilliant, Wicksteed. Tragically, perhaps symbolically, he died suddenly in 1927 of an obstruction in the throat.

Lionel Robbins and the Hiding of Economic Man

Meanwhile, there was mounting criticism of the underlying non-human, even inhuman, image of man in economics—a criticism that was bound to make even the orthodox defenders of conventional economics a little uneasy.

One of the most celebrated attacks on self-interest came from the American economist Thorstein Veblen (1857-1929). One can still easily find even in many mainstream texts his famous caricature of nineteenth century economic man:

> The hedonistic calculator of man is that of a lightening calculator of pleasures and pains, who oscillates like a homogenous globule of desire and happiness under the impulse of stimuli that shift him about the area, but leave him intact. He has neither antecedent nor consequence. He is an isolated, definitive human datum in stable equilibrium except for the buffets of the impinging forces that displace him in one direction or another. Self-imposed in elemental space, he spins symmetrically about his own spiritual axis until the parallelogram of forces bears down upon him, whereupon he follows the line of the resultant. When the force of the impact is spent, he comes to rest, a self-contained globule of desire as before.[35]

If there was a way to somehow silence critics such as Veblen once and for all, demonstrating that self-interest, money, and pecuniary incentives were neither dominating nor even necessarily characteristic of the discipline, it would certainly be a most tempting new road to take. Wicksteed's *Common Sense* had fully laid out such an alternative.

It was Robbins' genius to see the significance of Wicksteed's work and develop this in his 1931 publication of a book called *The Nature and Significance of Economic Science.* In the work Mr. Robbins did what neither Gossen or Wicksteed could do: reach the main currents of economic thinking. Robbins saw in Wicksteed a promising avenue for deflecting once and for all the perennial charge of self-interest, and unlike Gossen or Wicksteed, Robbins was a prominent and respected professional economist teaching at the prestigious London School of Economics.

He was then able to announce to a wide and receptive audience that Economic Man was a fiction, and that economics was really not about self-interest after all. Indeed, Robbins claimed that those who still clung to the old image of self-interested Economic Man showed "a failure to understand the significance of the last sixty years of economic science." Robbins further tells us that "Before Wicksteed wrote, it was still possible for intelligent men to give countenance to the belief that the whole structure of economics depends on the assumption of the world of economic men, each accentuated by egocentric or hedonistic motives. For anyone who has read *Common Sense*, the expression of such a view is no longer consistent with intellectual honesty. Wicksteed shattered this misconception once and for all."[36]

Robbins relates Wicksteed's non-tuism principle in the following way:

> So far as we are concerned, our economic subjects can be pure egoists, pure altruists, pure ascetics, pure sensualists or–what is more likely–mixed bundles of all these impulses. The scales of valuation are merely a convenient formal way of exhibiting certain permanent characteristics of man as he actually is. . . .

> All this means is that my relation to the dealer does not enter into my hierarchy of ends. For me (who may be acting for myself or my friends or some civic or charitable authority) they are regarded merely as means.[37]

Perhaps the fallacy of this conception is already apparent to the reader. The clue comes when we recognize that egoistic and non-ethical behavior comes about precisely when other people are treated as means rather than as ends in themselves. The popular terminology for expressing this type of relationship is "using people." What Robbins, harkening back to Wicksteed, is trying to tell us is that one can have ethical and noble ends, such as giving to charity, and yet treat the person with whom one is dealing in the economic sphere without any regard to that person's own welfare or well-being. This, of course, is a contradiction and should readily be seen as moral hypocrisy. It is not that people do not act that way. They can and they do. But this is hardly a defense of the Economic Man principle as morally neutral (which is Robbins' aim).

There is one more fallacy in Wicksteed's principles that Robbins naturally took on, which we should also point out here.

In Robbins' quote above he says, quite rightfully, that the economic actor could have a mixture of various motives, such as egoism and altruism, or sensuality and asceticism. But then Robbins wants to go on to claim that we can still take this actor as maximizing his utility across this very same mixture, so that the standard economic outcomes are still predicted:

> If, e.g., for purposes of demonstrating the circumstances in which a single price will emerge in a limited market, it is assumed that in my dealings in that market I always buy from the cheapest seller, it is not assumed at all that I am necessarily actuated by egotistical motives.[38]

The problem is, and this is the critical point for the dual-self, that these motives are mutually exclusive or incompatible. When you fulfill one you defeat the other. An altruist is an altruist precisely because he is not an egotist; an ascetic becomes an ascetic by renouncing sensualism. Therefore, purposes or motives such as these are incommensurable and cannot be treated as a mixture whose total can be added together and maximized. When Robbins recognized correctly that most people were a mixture of purposes or motives such as these, he did not realize that at the same time he was giving a fatal blow to the cherished concept of utility maximization.

History of Self-Interest in Economic Science: Conclusion

The history of ideas is usually much more complex and intriguing than the history of events and, in fact, often underlies and interacts with that history. The same is true for the idea of self-interest. We have tried to indicate some of the main currents in and around the mainstream of economics–or we should say, the two historically separated branches of the mainstream, one flowing largely on British soil, while the other originated in the German-speaking part of Europe (above all in Austria). Today, they both have merged into what now constitutes the modern mainstream point of view. In many respects this merger is not yet complete, and the philosophical differences that used to separate the two branches of the mainstream are still active. In a nutshell, then, these differences amount to the following: The British current–as articulated by Mill and Jevons and the great Marshall–was willing to recognize the existence of non-self-interested action, higher motives, or Marshall's "activities," but for various reasons it did not consider it the task of economics to reckon with them. Economics *qua* economics had to deal only with self-interest.

The other, more continental strand, particularly emanating from Gossen and the great Austrian economists, left its mark on the British Wicksteed and Robbins. Here a much more radical position reigns: Since time is the ultimate resource, everything we want and do is inherently limited. By nature, we have to manage our time; logic compels choices, and we make these choices in order to enhance our *own* purpose, whatever that may be. Here we are all more or less self-interested all the time, not just in the domain of what traditionally had been regarded as economics—in production, consumption, work, and leisure—but also in our family and love life. In any deliberate action there is only one purpose; there can be no other—we have to make the best use of *our* time. And that purpose is decisive.

Not surprisingly, the intrinsic policy implications of the Austrian- or British-type strands of self-interest lead to different basic positions. So the British tradition ever since J. S. Mill has been able to point out problem areas where *economic* laws left to themselves will produce undesirable outcomes as judged from a "higher," or holistic point of view. In short, what may appear as good economics may not be in the interest of the common good. But as an *economist*, he or she cannot really do too much about that other than leave the matter for the social philosopher, the social psychologist, and the politician. The Austrian-type tradition, on the other hand, claims to be speaking *not* about economic laws but about *human* laws. What such type "economic" or human science recommends is only limited by the limitations of human nature itself. There is no social (non-economic) point of view from which to criticize "economic" outcomes. The policy recommendations of such an all-encompassing human science are seen as firm and conclusive, and it is the economist's task to fight for their implementation, regardless of the observed hesitations of sociologists, psychologists, and politicians.

Which of the two rival views we hear propagated in the economics classroom or elsewhere depends on the nature and origin of the waters with which the preaching economist has been baptised. But remember that in both, the English or Austrian case, we are presented with the gospel of *self-interest* of one kind or another. The two strands of self-interest merging into our contemporary mainstream can be pictured in the following historical map.

In Chapter 5 we will address the modern economist's contention that self-interest is no longer assumed in the contemporary discipline.

Figure 3.2

SELF-INTEREST INTO THE MAINSTREAM:
A GEOGRAPHY

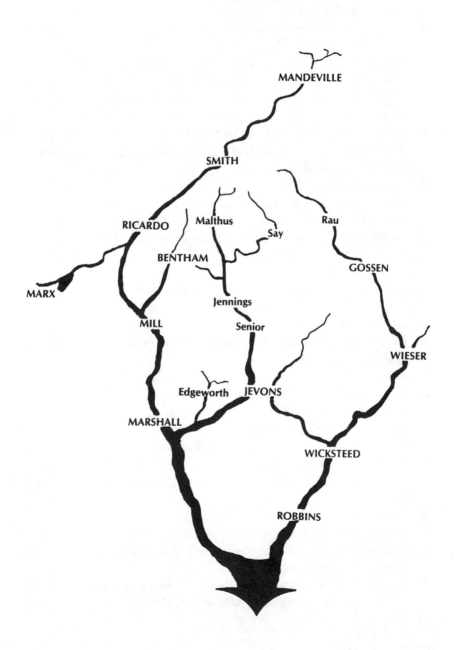

References

1. Frederick Braudel, *The Wheels of Commerce.* Vol. 2. New York: Harper & Row, 1985.
2. E. Ray Canterbery, *The Making of Economics.* Belmont, California: Wadsworth, 1976, pp. 61-70.
3. Bernard de Mandeville, *The Fable of the Bees* [1714]. Vol. 1. London: Oxford University Press, 1966, pp. 18, 24, 36.
4. Adam Smith, *The Theory of Moral Sentiments* [1753]. New York: Augustus M. Kelley, 1966, pp. 124-125.
5 . Adam Smith, *The Wealth of Nations* (1776). Edward Cannan, ed. New York: The Modern Library, Random House, 1937, book 1, chapter 11, part II, p. 14.
6. *ibid.*, p. Liv.
7. Quoted in Canterbery, *op. cit.*, p. 35.
8. Quoted in Jacob Oser, *The Evolution of Economic Thought.* 2nd edition. New York: Harcourt, Brace & World, 1970, p. 16.
9. Adam Smith, *The Wealth of Nations* [1776]. New York: McGraw-Hill, 1973.
10. Quoted in Israel Kirzner, *The Economic Point of View.* Kansas City: Sheed & Ward, 1960, p. 67.
11. Quoted in *ibid.*, p. 53.
12. John Stuart Mill, *Autobiography* [1873]. Indianapolis: Bobbs-Merrill, 1957, p. 92.
13. *ibid.*
14. John Stuart Mill, *Utilitarianism, On Liberty, Essay on Bentham and John Austin* [1838]. M. Warnock, ed. Cleveland: World Publishing, 1962, pp. 88, 99-101.
15. John Stuart Mill, *Essays on Some Unsettled Questions of Political Economy* [1844]. Reprinted in David Hausman, ed., *The Philosophy of Economics*, New York: Cambridge University Press, 1984, p. 57.
16. *ibid.*, p. 66.
17. Smith, *Wealth of Nations, op. cit.* (McGraw-Hill, 1973).
18. Paul Sweezy, *The Theory of Capitalist Development.* New York: Monthly Review Press, 1942.
19. Hermann H. Gossen, *The Laws of Human Relations* [1854]. Cambridge, Massachusetts: MIT Press, 1938, p. cxlvii.
20. *ibid.*, p. 4.
21. *ibid.*, p. 6.
22. *ibid.*, p. 218.

23. *ibid.*, p. 299 (emphasis added).
24. William Stanley Jevons, *The Theory of Political Economy* [1871]. Reprint. New York: Augustus M. Kelley, 1965, p. xxxv.
25. W. Sichel and P. Eckstein, *Basic Economic Concepts.* Chicago: Rand McNally, 1974.
26. Jevons, *op. cit.*, p. 3.
27. Gossen, *op. cit.*, p. 39 (emphasis added).
28. F.Y. Edgeworth, *Mathematical Psychics: An Essay on the Application of Mathematics to the Moral Sciences.* London: C.K. Paul, 1881, p. 16.
29. Alfred Marshall, *Principles of Economics* [1890]. London, Macmillan Press, 1949, p. 12.
30. *ibid.*, pp. 72, 76-77.
31. Dennis Robertson, *Economic Commentaries.* London: Staple Press, 1956, p. 148.
32. A.W. Coats, "Sociological Aspects of British Economic Thought" in *Journal of Political Economy,* 75 (October 1967), pp. 706-729.
33. Philip Wicksteed, *The Common Sense of Political Economy.* London: George Routledge & Sons, 1933, p. 2.
34. *ibid.*, p. 3.
35. Thorstein Veblen, *The Place of Science in Modern Civilization and Other Essays* [1915]. Reprint. New York: Caprice Books, 1969, pp. 73-74.
36. Lionel Robbins in his "Introduction" to Wicksteed, *The Common Sense of Political Economy.* London: George Routledge & Sons, 1933, p. xxi.
37. Lionel Robbins, *The Nature and Significance of Economic Science* [1932]. London: Macmillan, 1984, pp. 95, 97.
38. *ibid.*, p. 96.

Chapter 4

THE PROBLEM OF SELF-INTEREST, AND THE HUMANISTIC RESPONSE

What we today call humanistic economics first came into existence when early social thinkers looked at the world about them and saw that much was in painful contrast to the glowing theoretical expectations generated by the self-interest model of the classical economists.

Here we will focus on two outstanding pioneers of this tradition: the Swiss Count Sismondi and the English social critic John Ruskin. One was concerned with the inability of self-interested market decisions to assure stable, uninterrupted economic growth; the second questioned whether reliance on self-interest delivered the kind of quality society we really would want to have. The chapter will conclude with some basic, more analytical reasons why the pursuit of individual advantage will often fail to generate the common good.

Jean C. L. Simonde de Sismondi (1773-1842) and His Impact on Economic Thinking

The Swiss Count J. C. L. Simonde de Sismondi was an early admirer of Adam Smith's ideas, and he popularized them in a book that was a French presentation of Smith in 1803, *De La Richesse Commerciale* (On Commercial Wealth). Like his teacher, he advocated free trade and came out strongly against monopolies, custom houses, colonial privileges, and government intervention in general. The book was not a brilliant success, but it did generate enough professional reputation to induce the Dutch university of Wilna to offer him the vacant chair of political economy. He decided to refuse that opportunity and devote himself to the study of history. And it was here that he learned to be more cautious in trusting the prevailing method of abstract theoretical deduction from first principles, especially when applied to the complex social reality. Instead, he was led to look at political economy from a more historical and empirical point of view.

In 1819 he published his second book on economics titled *New Principles of Political Economy*. It was an attempt to rewrite the science anew in the light of some of the newly recognized facts—particularly the novel and so far unexplained economic "panics" or crises, which he personally witnessed afflicting the less privileged workers in England and the European mainland.

The timing of his book was helpful for its promotion, since 1819 marked the worst commercial crisis yet. Another one hit in 1826, and from then on there were recurring ups and downs at roughly four-year intervals. Sismondi, visiting England in 1818, 1824, and 1826, observed:

> In this astonishing country [Great Britain], which seems to be submitted to a great experiment for the instruction of the rest of the world, I have seen production increasing whilst enjoyments were diminishing. The mass of the nation here, no less than philosophers, seems to forget that the increase of wealth is not the end in political economy, but its instrument in procuring the happiness of all. I sought for this happiness in *every* class, and I could nowhere find it.[1]

At the same time, he felt that events since 1819 had confirmed his *new* principles:

> Seven years have passed, and the facts appear to have fought victoriously for me. They have proved, much better than I could have done, that the wise men from whom I have separated myself were in pursuit of a false prosperity; that their theories, wherever they were put in practice, served well enough to increase material wealth, but that they diminished the mass of enjoyment laid up for each individual; that they tended to make the rich man more rich, they also made the poor man more poor, more dependent, and more destitute.[2]

All the suffering he encountered in England and so vividly described, he now attributed to a "false economical system" where wealth took precedence over people.

Self-interest under the operation of the invisible hand, rather than producing widespread prosperity and happiness in uplifting the laborers and the poor as had been one of Smith's original intentions, had instead produced a new and miserable social grouping, the industrial workers. They were victims of what Sismondi was one of the first to discover, the business cycle manifesting itself in periodic crises of overproduction and high unemployment.

He explained the problem as a recurring lack of consumption power among the masses of laborers. The newly manufactured goods could not be sold at a profit and so glutted the markets. The chief villain was an unfettered drive to expand output, in part fueled by new technologies, which boosted the profits of the entrepreneurs but which did not trickle down to raise the subsistence wages of a workforce that lacked any bargaining power.

However, the standardbearers of Smith's political economy, especially his contemporary, Jean Baptiste Say, refused to see this as a major problem and took little time in pointing this out. Sismondi was confronted with Say's *Law of Markets*: "Supply creates its own demand," meaning that the process of producing goods automatically provides the purchasing power enabling all those goods to be bought. Every good that was produced cost something and every cost was someone else's income. Thus, according to Say's Law, there could never be such a thing as a general glut (the buildup of goods for sale without the purchasing power to buy them).

Sismondi did not necessarily dispute the logic of this, but to him what was true in abstract theoretical terms was still misleading in the real world, where owners and workers had to adjust painfully to the ever-changing economic realities. It may be true that after a large increase in labor productivity caused, let us say, by a new labor-saving technology, the entrepreneurs did have higher profits and more purchasing power. Most of it, however, would get translated by those entrepreneurs into a new demand for fancy luxury goods, many of them custom-made or imported. Although luxury goods producers will eventually experience a boom allowing workers to find new work there, the adjustment takes time: New machines have to be built, new capital has to be found, and workers will have to be retrained. In the meantime, demand for the expanded output of standard manufactured goods would be insufficient, workers would be laid off herewith further decreasing purchasing power and increasing social misery. Of course, in a textbook world of perfect information and smooth adjustments, things would work out differently, but that was not the real world Sismondi tried to describe and understand. This is illustrated by means of an example he used to argue against McCulloch, the leading disciple of David Ricardo who had just died the previous year. Unfortunately, his arguments were not sufficiently persuasive for the abstract Smithian-trained economists of his time.

Sismondi's example is as follows. Imagine an old-fashioned book fair. Each merchant brings to a city each year fifty copies of each of the five books he has printed, sells them all and goes home with 250 newly acquired books. So far so good; production and demand are the same. But, what if one merchant brings a book nobody wants? Not knowing what the others wanted, he has made a mistake. Now he cannot sell those copies and as a result he lacks the purchasing power to buy fifty books from the other merchants who in turn have to go back with an unsold surplus. The book market is glutted and some printers may be laid off. The beginning of a crisis results just because one producer made an error in forecasting demand. Had he had perfect knowledge of the market, everything would have gone smoothly, but now the disease is likely to spread into other industries, some related to printing presses, others to the ones producing goods that printers' households buy.

In conclusion, Sismondi advanced the new principle of a balance that needs to be maintained between production, income, and consumption. Such balance was constantly upset by the restless drive to expand production, with some incomes lagging behind, particularly those of workers. To maintain this balance Sismondi sought to enlist the help of government whose task he saw as ensuring the material well-being of all. This could be done by public work jobs for the unemployed and by legislation encouraging profit-sharing. He observed: "Let the law constantly favor the division and the accumulation of inheritance; let it compel the master to find a pecuniary and political advantage in binding his workmen more closely to himself, in hiring them for longer periods, in sharing his profits with them, and perhaps private interest, being better directed, will itself repair the evil it has done to society."[3]

The Mainstream Rushes On

Sismondi's attack rendered the laissez-faire doctrine somewhat more controversial in the profession, particularly in France. Antoine Buvet, one of his disciples, was quick to reword the doctrine as "Laissez-faire la misere, laissez passer la mort," meaning: "Let wretchedness do its work, do not interfere with death."

But, by and large, the mainstream thinkers of his time and thereafter paid little attention. The eminent Joseph Schumpeter had at least some kind words for Sismondi, whom he credited for first realizing "that transitional phenomena are the essence of the economic process—and hence not only relevant to its practical problems but also to its fundamental theory. The economic process is chained to certain sequences and enforces others, [and it] is a system of periodicities and lags and, by virtue of this alone, harbors a world of problems that do not exist for Ricardian economics or any other economics of the same type."[4]

Sismondi was disappointed but not surprised. "There are subjects on which each has his opinion settled, and finds it more easy to let his adversary's book fall unnoticed than to answer it."[5] Tormented by the thought of the immense suffering of humanity, he spent the last years of his life in despair. His last words on political economy were, "I cry, take care, you are bruising, you are crushing miserable persons who do not even see from whence comes the evil which they experience, but who remain languishing and mutilated on the road which you have passed over. I cry out and no one hears me: I cry out and the car of the Juggernaut continues to roll on, making new victims."[6]

The influence of Say's *Law of Markets* was strong within the economic profession, and lasted over 100 years later right through the Great Depression of the 1930s. When society turned to the economists to ask what to do about the Depression, the general advice was "do nothing." Gluts were impossible. So the recent and admittedly worsening period of economic stagnation and increasing unemployment and poverty was only a quickly passing phase in which the automatically adjusting system of the market would soon take care of everything. According to economists, workers were obviously demanding too high a wage and as soon as they moderated their wage demands down to the "natural" level of the market they all would be hired back again. Furthermore, this decline in wages was a necessary precondition to a decline in prices and would have consumers rushing back to the stores to snap up goods at bargain prices.

This was the advice and explanation offered by the influential Lionel Robbins in his 1934 book, *The Great Depression.*[7] Yet Robbins' own data in his statistical appendix contradicted his laissez-faire policy recommendations. His index of wages in the U.S. showed them dropping by about 20 percent from 1929 through 1933, while his data showed unemployment going from nearly nil in the boom year of early 1929 to over 13 million in 1933–25 percent of the labor force. Similarly with prices, the cost of living in the U.S. dropped 25 percent during the same period, and yet industrial production still dropped by almost the same amount during those years.

The Great Depression and the Birth of Macroeconomics

The Depression ground on for ten long years with its traumatic misery which has left permanent scars on the generation that experienced it, only to be really ended by the advent of World War II in 1939. The prevention of the absolute collapse of the system before then and some provision of human needs were the result of President Franklin Delano Roosevelt's vigorous actions to intervene in the market system and "prime the pump," despite the advice of most economists. The notable exceptions were the Englishman John Maynard Keynes and Keynes' few American adherents, such as Alvin Hansen and his other Harvard associates. They rejected the logic of laissez-faire and demonstrated theoretically that an economy could settle in an equilibrium at a level of glut, stagnation, and unemployment. But this time, in contrast to when Sismondi was writing over a century previously, the international massiveness of the Depression compelled widespread attention and the eventual adoption in the economic profession of such heretical ideas. Each individual pursuing his or her own self-interest on a micro level (that of the individual, the firm, or even industry) could add up to aggregate or macro conditions that were to the detriment of the whole society. This tended to be the direct opposite of Mandeville's original dictum that private vice makes public virtue.

One would think that the severe lessons of the Depression—which eventually reached the following proportions, to quote Roosevelt, "I see one-third of a nation, ill-housed, ill-clad, ill-nourished"—would have been enough to transform the economic profession forever, but the vital memory of actual experience slips in time, and each generation seems to need to learn the lessons of the past anew.

The possibility that economic traumas, such as the Great Depression, are not yet behind us was signaled by the stock market crash of October 1987, which rivaled the crash of 1929.

Although Keynesian macroeconomics has permanently altered the face of the field of economics, the old ways of thinking have over time made their reappearance. Generally, Keynesian doctrine was effective and supreme, right through the 1960s. Then it seemed to falter and no longer provided remedies for a period of the new "stagflation" that occurred in the 1970s. This was the simultaneous existence of both economic stagnation and inflation, a condition which was not likely to occur according to Keynesian theory. Just exactly what caused the problem is still a matter of unresolved and intense debate. But whatever the reason, it is worth noting that the Keynesian remedial policies can no longer be expected to work in a free-trading global economy with no *central* control over its money supply and fiscal policies. In effect, we are drifting back into an economic world akin to the nineteenth century when Sismondi first cried out. We will discuss this problem in depth when considering the globalization of the economy in Chapter 13.

This brings us to another giant of humanistic economics, the Englishman John Ruskin, who was also uncomfortable with the self-interest assumption of his contemporary economists.

Economics of an Invented World

In the decades after Adam Smith his followers aspired to be considered more as scientists than as mere social philosophers. They sought to logically deduce from a first principle of self-interested motivation meaningful implications and consequences applying to society. Such tendency was particularly apparent in the works of David Ricardo, Jean Baptiste Say, Nassau Senior, James Mill, and in the earlier works of John Stuart Mill. Economists of that time wanted to explain prices or "exchange value," as well as the production and distribution of social wealth, and to do so by means of some generalizable, law-like behavior, as in the physical sciences. Except for a few (such as Senior), most of them readily admitted that since they were reasoning from rather abstract and hypothetical assumptions their conclusions were bound to be similarly hypothetical and "only true in the abstract." Nevertheless, the job of the economist was now seen to work out and to demonstrate what one can expect to happen in a society where all aspire to realize what they understand to be in their own individual interest and interact with each other accordingly. It was in this way that nineteenth century economics as a science was moving into full gear.

Economists have assumed that there is nothing wrong per se with such an approach, especially if it could be confined only to the purposes of a description of reality. All science makes simplifying assumptions. The Nobel prizewinning economist Robert Solow writes, "No one believes these assumptions to be true," but, "the only way to make progress is to invent a simplified world."[8] The problem is that just because an assumption simplifies, it does not mean that it *correctly* simplifies. The wrong simplification when applied in practice has deadly consequences.

Economic theories almost always have implied applications, and they have been applied to society ever since the inception of economics as a discipline, so that the idea that there is no connection between description in economics and prescription is quite misleading. We can see this in the instructive case of the first official university professor with a chair in political economy, the British Nassau Senior.

Aspiring to teach "purely scientific" economics, Senior taught his students that although the conclusions of the science as they relate to the "nature and production of wealth are universally true," these same conclusions "do not authorize [the Political Economist] in adding a single syllable of advice." So far, so good. Apparently Professor Senior moves on safe ground. But wait. Only a few years earlier this very same professor had published *Three Lectures on the Rate of Wages* (1830) where he argued that the way to produce greater social wealth was (1) to remove all restrictions of free commerce and (2) to abolish the Poor Laws. Not only unauthorized, but rather stern advice here. But why criticize the Poor Laws? Because they were "unnatural," and would decrease the incentive to work. In the more natural state—without Poor Laws—the laborer, when his resources were in distress, would respond with "greater exertion and severe economy, and what they cannot supply, he receives with gratitude from the benevolent."[9]

Worse yet, the beneficiaries of Professor Senior's scientific economics not only were his students in the classroom but the members of the British Parliament as well. As somebody who evidently was somewhat informed on the subject, he was two years later appointed to a Poor Law Inquiry Commission. Its report, largely Senior's work, became the basis of the new law passed in 1834. It legislated that any relief be kept lower than the lowest wage paid anywhere and that it be confined to jail-like workhouses where spouses were to be separated to discourage procreation of more paupers. In Senior's own words: "The report, or at least three-fourths of it, was written by me, and all that was not written by me was rewritten by me. The greater part of the Act, founded on it, was also written by me; and in fact I am responsible for the effects good or evil . . . of the whole measure."[10]

So much for Professor Senior's comments on policy advice. But, it is not Senior's history alone which reveals the contradiction and problem. On the very same page where Professor Senior was quoted earlier disqualifying the economist from giving advice, we can see in another sentence the entire contradiction: "The business of a Political Economist," Professor Senior tells us, "is neither to recommend nor to dissuade, but to state general principles which it is fatal to neglect."[11] Fatal for whom, one wonders? Hardly for the inmates of the workhouses, and probably not for the English working class as a whole.

With Science Against Poverty

Senior believed in the so-called wage fund theory which claimed that at any time there was a fixed amount of money available for workers' compensation. Any unnatural interference by government which sought, one way or another, to raise wages would naturally result in fewer workers getting paid and more unemployment and misery for the rest. Similarly, more generous poor relief would merely induce the paupers to produce more offspring, who would later compete for the scarce wage fund and lead to ever-costly relief paid out of ever-rising taxes. Overall, he would argue that humanitarians, lacking an under-standing of the scientific laws of economics, would end up causing much more harm than good to the working class as a whole. The same kind of analysis underlay the opposition to relief for the poor of other well-known classical economists from Smith to J. S. Mill. For example, David Ricardo concluded in his *Principles of Political Economy and Taxation* (1817):

> The clear and direct tendency of the poor laws is in direct opposition to those obvious principles (making for the natural price of labour); it is not as the legislature benevolently intended, to amend the con-dition of the poor, but to deteriorate the condition of both poor and rich; instead of making the poor rich, they are calculated to make the rich poor; and whilst the present laws are in force, it is quite in the natural order of things that the fund for the maintenance of the poor should progressively increase till it has absorbed all the net revenue of the country . . . . [12]

Just like Senior after him, Ricardo, soon to become a member of Parliament and its Poor Law Committee, could effectively see to it that the body politic would be guided by the sound principles of scientific political economy. Others, like his followers McCulloch and Torrens, also made sure that the political opposition to the Poor Laws could make their case in a climate of great intellectual respectability. The "laws" of the market advised against any government interference into the labor market, provided, of course, that the misery of the paupers would not generate a dangerous climate of revolutionary unrest, a fear that prodded Senior to merely toughen the Poor Laws rather than to abolish them altogether.

Meanwhile, and not at all surprisingly, the economists of the period, by their equation of public and private benefit, quickly gained a reputa-tion as high priests of laissez-faire capitalism. And nothing helped create this image more effectively than a couple of popular books penned by women. One of them, *Illustrations in Political Economy*

(1834) by Harriet Martineau, greatly outsold not only the better known scholarly texts but also the more successful novels by Charles Dickens which showed the other side of the story. *Conversations of Political Economy* (1819) by Ricardo's intimate friend, Jane Marcet, went through sixteen editions and was hailed by her more famous contemporary McCulloch as "the best introduction to the science that has yet appeared."*

Here is a short paragraph taken from Jane Marcet's crusading book for laissez-faire:

> The natural causes which tend to develop the wealth and prosperity of nations are more powerful than the faults of [government] administration which operate in contrary direction. But it is nevertheless true that these errors are productive of a great deal of mischief; that they check industry and retard the progress of improvement.[13]

It clearly shows why the people in England could not have had any doubts in associating political economy with laissez-faire capitalism.

The Moral Protest of John Ruskin (1819-1900)

Against this background, we can now move on to the second great pioneer of humanistic economics: John Ruskin. At the time the Poor Laws were revised, and when Senior lectured his students about economic advice, Ruskin was less than twenty years old and about to start a highly successful career in art history and art appreciation. Romantic idealist that he was, he wanted to bring the wonders of art to the ordinary working man. Unfortunately, he soon encountered a serious problem: workers were neither interested in art nor interested in attending the evening lectures especially designed to make them learn to appreciate it. After some years, Ruskin concluded that the real problem was not with the workers, but their degraded economic status having stunted their aesthetic needs and sensibilities.

---

* Similarly to McCulloch's endorsement of Ms. Marcet, it was J. B. Say, another famous contemporary, who heaped praise on Ms. Martineau. It is important to point this out, since modern students are often led to believe that these popular "vulgarizations" distorted the truth and conveyed a public image of political economy that was not shared by the great practitioners themselves.

As a result of this discovery, Ruskin turned his interests to economic affairs and political economy. The end product was a book titled *Unto This Last*, published in 1866, two years after Senior died. It starts out with the following paragraph:

> Among the delusions which at different periods have possessed them-selves of the minds of large masses of the human race, perhaps the most curious–certainly the least creditable–is the modern soi-disant science of political economy, based on the idea that an advantageous code of social action may be determined irrespective of the influence of social affection.

In a nutshell, Ruskin accuses economists of trying to prescribe so-cial policy on the basis of self-interest only. He then continues:

> Of course, as in the instances of alchemy, astrology, witchcraft, and other such popular creeds, political economy has a plausible idea at the root of it. The social affections, says the economist, are acciden-tal and disturbing elements in human nature; but avarice and the desire of progress are constant elements. Let us eliminate the incon-stants, and, considering the human being merely as a covetous machine, examine by what laws of labour, purchase and sale, the greatest accumulative result in wealth is attainable. Those laws once determined, it will be for each individual afterwards to introduce as much of the disturbing affectionate element as he chooses, and to determine for himself the result on the new conditions supposed.[14]

In other words, the would-be economist policy maker starts out with the principles based on abstract self-interest, and then tries to adjust the results here and there to approximate real world behavior of real people.* Ruskin strongly disagreed, saying that "the disturbing ele-ments in the social problem are not of the same nature as the constant ones; they alter the essence of the creature under examination the mo-ment they are added; they operate, not mathematically, but chemically, introducing conditions which render all previous knowledge unavail-able."[15] He then masterfully compares economics to an abstract science

---

* So far Ruskin has been merely attempting to paraphrase his contemporary, J. S. Mill, with the most respected learned opinion on the subject. To Mill, self-interest was not the only motive force; there were, of course, other "disturbing" forces, but those, according to his principle of the "Composition of Forces," could be taken into account later and mechanically added or subtracted from the conclusion deduced from initial principles grounded in self-interest.

of gymnastics which assumed that men had no skeletons: "It might be shown, on the supposition, that it would be advantageous to roll the students up into pellets, flatten them into cakes, or stretch them into cables; and that when the results were effected, the re-insertion of the skeleton would be attended with various inconveniences to their constitution."[16]

Similarly, in considering men as actuated "by no other moral influences than those which affect rats or swine," political economy ends up denying the motive power of the Soul, and "the force of this very peculiar agent, as an unknown quality, enters into all the political economist's equations, without his knowledge, and falsifies every one of their results."[17] Ruskin proceeds to illustrate the point by referring to the employer-employee relationship. There the "greatest average of work" cannot be attained on the basis of antagonistic self-interest, but instead derives from justice, mutual good will, and a co-operative spirit. True, he admits that it is not "so easy to imagine an enthusiastic affection among cotton spinners for the proprietor of the mill"; similarly, it may be asking too much to expect a general attitude of self-sacrifice towards the company. But to him, all this lack of "moral animation" is to a considerable degree to be explained by the prevailing practice of engaging "a workman at a rate of wages variable according to the demand for labour, and with the risk of being at any time thrown out of this situation by chance of trade." "Now," he warns, "under these contingencies, no action of the affections can take place, but only an explosive action of disaffections."[18] The remedy suggests itself in the regulation of wages and employment. Only if workers are assured a just and living wage as well as permanent employment will they see any reason to more fully exert themselves on behalf of their employer.

As much as Ruskin turned again and again to government to protect the poor by interfering into the wage determination process, he, like Sismondi, was more of a social reformer than a socialist. He was even, as the following quote demonstrates, a true believer in genuine private enterprise.

> "Private enterprise" should never be interfered with, but, on the contrary, much encouraged, so long as it is indeed "enterprise" (the exercise of individual ingenuity and audacity in new fields of true labour), and so long as it is indeed "private," paying its own way at its own cost, and in no wise harmfully affecting public comforts or interests. But "private enterprise" which poisons its neighborhood, or speculates for individual gain at common risk, is very sharply to be interfered with.[19]

Whatever Ruskin's ideology, he had few kind words for economists: "As no laws but those of the Devil are practicable in the world, so no impulses but those of the brute [says the modern political economist] are appealable to in the world. Faith, generosity, honesty, zeal, and self-sacrifice are poetical phrases; there is no truth in man which can be used as a moving and productive power."[20] To Ruskin and his numerous sympathizers political economy as preached by its mercenaries was indeed "a lie" and responsible for *all* the evil of his times.

Needless to say, Ruskin's vituperative phrases were largely ignored by his adversaries. Still, he may have been the first to cry out loudly against the dangerous tendency of assuming self-interested Economic Man in social description because of the inherent tendency to imply its use for prescription as well.

Ruskin, thanks to his strongly developed moral sense, could see deeper in these matters than his contemporaries. What he saw made him angry and perhaps even drove him to his sporadic bouts with insanity. On the other hand, his penetrating and outspoken critique also threatened the intellectual and commercial establishment of his day as is evident by the following comment published in the *Manchester Examiner and Times:* "He [Ruskin] is not worth our powder and shot. Yet, if we do not *crush* him, his wild words will touch the springs of action in some hearts, and ere we are aware, a moral floodgate may fly open and drown us all."[21] Of course, he was not crushed and he did touch some hearts, among them John Hobson, Mohandas K. Gandhi, Arnold Toynbee, and Richard Tawney. He also had some effect on the British development of economics. So the great Alfred Marshall, for example, credited Ruskin's "splendid teachings" with having clarified something that the earlier economists were not making sufficiently clear; namely, that "sordid selfishness" and the desire for material wealth are by no means the only human motives.

Where Ruskin had little or no influence was on continental thought, especially the new developments sprouting out of Gossen's and Menger's new vision (time-is-scarce and economics-is-human-action) discussed in the last chapter. Their modern spokesman, Lionel Robbins, has only contempt for "suchlike critics." He observes that, "If Carlyle [Ruskin's mentor] and Ruskin had been willing to make the intellectual effort necessary to assimilate the body of analysis bequeathed by the great men whom they criticized so unjustly, they would have realised its profound significance in general, even if they had been unable to provide any better description than its authors."[22]

Those economists, subsequently able to overpower the British influence, have in a sense been even more harmful than the Ricardos, Mc-Cullochs, and Seniors. By teaching that economics is ultimately about the right ("the economic") way of thinking, they may have had some influence in how we actually now think. In the process one easily forgets that approaching everything in terms of considering opportunity costs has an opportunity cost of its own: the inability to appreciate actions based on commitment to ecological and social values and moral concerns. An example of even empirical support for the fact that there has been a subtle indoctrination of self-interest in the mind of the economist will be found in the next chapter, when we discuss the concept of the "free rider."

Additional Limitations of a Science of Self-Interest

The problems of a science relying on a self-interest-only description of Man do not end with these criticisms. Such an approach drastically narrows the questions that can be asked and the types of problems that can be addressed. So, for instance, ask an economist how to create a more motivated and productive work force. The answer, if at all forthcoming, will be limited to such items as modifications in the way compensation is paid or how supervision is conducted. Ask about how we can get more broadly based cooperation in terms of voluntary compliance with tax laws; his or her answer will revolve around *incentives*. In these answers you will not, for example, find any reference to fairness. It is simply not in the vocabulary of the economist to talk and think in such terms.

We need an economics we can live with, one that is able to weigh the benefits *and costs* of individualistic competition, the costs *and benefits* of social cooperation. We need an economics that benefits not just Economic Man, but real men and women who have the capacity to live a life of values, integrity, and wholeness.

Adam Smith's celebrated proposition that we can expect our daily provisions from the butcher, the baker, and the brewer, thanks to their self-interest, loses force when it is found that large segments of the population are likely to go without their daily bread unless they are able to successfully appeal to public benevolence, namely, public welfare or charity. It was in terms of mass poverty and human degradation that Sismondi and Ruskin questioned the unalloyed wisdom of an economy relying on the springs of self-interest.

Self-Interest and "Market Failure"

Over the decades other shortcomings of Smith's invisible hand doctrine were revealed and articulated by scores of economists. But their primary argument was not that self-interest is bad or limited, but that there can be situations where it cannot be adequately expressed in a free market economy. Economists saw this as a failure of the free market as a social institution, rather than a failure of self-interest in itself. Criticism along those lines usually points to undefined property rights, missing markets, or the like. Similarly, it could be shown that consumers often lacked the necessary information and foresight to act in their true interest. Things sometimes turn out differently than they first appear to the self-interested economic actor, and knowing the end result one would have acted differently. Take the following example.

Let us say an enterprising businessperson buys a franchise into a cut-rate bookstore, perhaps being opened in a shopping mall. He is an honest merchant who is offering the public a good deal. And let us say that his enterprise prospers, so much so that a smaller privately owned bookshop in the nearby central city begins losing customers and eventually has to shut down. From the standpoint of self-interest alone, all of this would appear to be of social benefit. People are given a choice between books at a higher price and books at a lower price and naturally choose the latter, and society's resources are directed towards less expensive books. But what if the older, privately owned bookstore offered some goods and services that were not available at the larger bookstore—a more careful selection of quality and unusual books, personal service from a staff that really loved books, and in general a comfortable atmosphere for reading and browsing? All of this is now gone with the economic success of the new discount bookstore, and when the old store closes the customers are disappointed and feel that they have lost something of value. By diverting some of their book purchases to the new store at discount prices they have inadvertently caused the demise of the old bookshop. Had they known that this would be the result they may very well have opted to buy books at a higher price to keep the old bookstore in business. Or they may not have opted to do so. The point is that they were not given the choice, and the self-interest-driven market alone does not give them the choice.

To repeat, the problem according to economists here rests not necesssarily with self-interest but with the free market as a vehicle to express and realize that self-interest. Similarly, the problems of unwanted pollution and insufficient public goods, such as not having enough safe and beautiful city parks, are blamed on so-called "market failure," not on self-interest. These blemishes and the subsequent necessary policy correctives generally did little to shake the economists' basic faith in the socioeconomic value of self-interest.

As time progressed, the Age of the Economist and the faith in self-interest slowly managed to displace the moral injunctions of the Church, the ethicists, and the philosophers. In the twentieth century, strongly influenced by the new themes of Darwin and Freud, even leading philosophers joined hands with scientists and mathematicians in pushing the self-interest creed. Thus the pronouncement of Bertrand Russell: "If men were actuated by self-interest, which they are not–except in the case of a few saints–the whole human race would cooperate."[23] This identifies the saintly with self-interest and defines self-restraint and cooperation as a mere subset of self-interest.

Enter the Prisoner's Dilemma

All this changed rather drastically in 1950 when Merrill Flood and Melvin Dresher created, and A.W. Tucker (a mathematician) subsequently formalized, the so-called "Prisoner's Dilemma." Under this heading the following parable is told.

Secret police hold two political prisoners who are suspected of belonging to an illegal opposition party. Each prisoner is held and interrogated in an individual cell. The police need a confession for conviction, otherwise they will be held and interrogated for one year and then let go. In the case that both of them confess, their cooperation will be taken into account and they will each get five years. On the other hand, if only one of them confesses, thereby implicating the other, the confessing one will immediately be set free while his tight-lipped partner is put into the slammer for eight years. The prisoners can either confess or not confess, but since they are kept in separate confinement, neither knows what the other will do or does.

The figure below summarizes formally the options that each prisoner faces. The numbers indicate the (negative) payoffs in terms of years of incarceration.

Figure 4.1

PRISONER'S DILEMMA

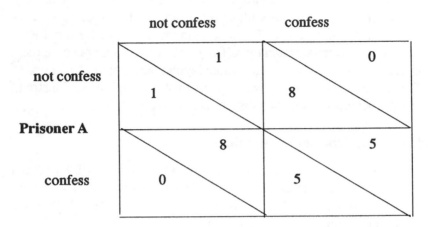

Let us look at the situation of Prisoner A as he contemplates what to do from a self-interested perspective. Not knowing what B will do, he first simply assumes that B will not confess. Under this circumstance Prisoner A would be better off by *confessing* since 0 is less than 1 year in terms of the jail sentence. Second, he reexamines the entire matter, now assuming instead that his partner will indeed confess. The situation for A then looks as follows: If he does not confess he is stuck with 8 long years, but if he would confess it's only 5. So here, too, confessing would be in A's rational self-interest. We may conclude that whether B confesses or not, A is better off confessing. Not knowing what B will do, A has a rational self-interest in confessing. The second prisoner's self-interested reasoning will follow the equivalent analysis and come up with the same conclusion: it's in his self-interest to confess. Both accordingly confess and both are locked up for five years each (lower right-hand box). In theory, at least, there would have been a much better way out of the dilemma. If both had not confessed, they both would be out in one year. What was really working against them was their self-interest. As the logic of the parable suggests: self-interest imprisons.

One could say that their self-interest in this situation had not served them well, or, more paradoxically, that self-interest was not in their real self-interest.

What about a prior agreement made between them, but also based on self-interest? Could they not earlier have agreed never to tattle on each other if they are ever caught? Of course, they could, but imagine now what would happen. Prisoner A now thinks he can count on Prisoner B to keep his promise to remain silent. But how about himself now? If he breaks the agreement he would walk home free, while his more honest friend gets locked up for a long time and is unable to punish his cheating partner. All things considered then, even with such an agreement, self-interest would dictate *confessing*. Of course, a symmetrically identical way of reasoning will also induce Prisoner B to break his agreement. In the absence of an enforceable pact, if both think they can get away with cheating, self-interest will make them both cheat (i.e., confess) and spend the next five years behind bars.

This agreement version of the prisoner's dilemma helps us better understand some terms that will be extensively made use of in the chapters to follow.

If there is an agreement to team up with each other in this matter, each prisoner has to choose to either cooperate and do his proper share, or else gain at the expense of the other–to get something (instant freedom) for nothing (no penalties for his cheating). This selfish desire to gain while letting the other(s) foot the bill goes by the name of being a "free rider." In contrast, the choice *not* to exploit the opportunity, the refusal to free ride, is what *cooperation* is all about. It is intrinsically linked to self-denial, not self-interest. Ironically, in order to realize the self-interested outcome one has to let go of self-interest. In this light we would have to question Bertrand Russell's faith, and may want to turn his saying upside down: Only if men were actuated by moral self-sacrifice, could they serve the interest of the whole human race.

How can the prisoner's dilemma be successfully overcome? What is the best road to liberation? There are two: First, if both are altruistic and are pained by the thought of their friend in prison, they may conclude that both confessing is positively the worst, yielding a total of ten years behind bars. Almost as bad would be the total outcome if one confesses and the other does not: eight years. As a result, each partner altruistically decides not to confess, and they both submit to only one year of incarceration.

Alternatively, each prisoner could decide that it was morally wrong to tattle on the other or to break a prior mutual understanding. The golden rule, for example, admonishes to treat the other as one would want

to be treated oneself. Clearly, that means non-confession or cooperation, no matter what. And such moral commitment also gets rewarded
by the minimal stay in prison, one year.

In terms of self-interest motives we may now ask ourselves, what
has gone wrong? Why does the logic of self-interest suddenly not work?
The answer is that self-interest produces the results that are considered
in one's self-interest if, and only if, the outcome of one's action is entirely confined to one's own action, and nothing else. In contrast, self-
interest does not produce optimal results if the outcome of one's action
depends also on the actions of others. Since so many human actions
take place in a social context, if these actions are based entirely on self-
interest, it appears that much social activity would produce prisoner's
dilemma-type outcomes. There are numerous applications of this
problem in economics; the analysis has been applied to inflation, work
motivation, oligopolistic pricing, public goods, and other topics.

A Tale of Two Ford Plants.   Let us illustrate the limitations of a self-
interested economic thought with a news story that was published in
the *New York Times*.[24] There we read about the productivity differences between otherwise identical plants producing Ford Escorts. One is
in Germany, the other near Liverpool in England. Both plants were
designed and built to produce 1,015 cars a day. At each, according to
the *Times*, "shiny Escorts, Ford's hot new car, roll off bustling production lines dominated by robot welders and vast automated presses
punching out steel as if it were aluminum foil." Yet, in spite of the almost identical technological set-up the British work performance does
not compare well with its German counterpart. It produces only two-
thirds in terms of output with about 25 percent more labor input. As a
result, it takes about forty man-hours to produce an Escort in England,
while it only takes twenty-one man-hours in Germany for the same car.
So, in spite of the fact that the hourly pay in England was $8.25, signifi-
cantly lower than the $13.50 in the German plant, it cost Ford Motor
Company $1,000 *more* to produce an Escort in Britain than to make one
in Germany and ship it to England.

The problem has been attributed to low work morale of British
workers. The plant there, according to the report, "seems to overflow
with workers–some of them reading or eating, others kicking a soccer
ball–while [the German plant] seems almost depopulated and nearly
every worker in evidence is hard at his job."[25]

The story above is not atypical of the industrial relations and the
climate generally prevailing in the two countries. In England the
worker, protected by various union rules, sees himself in an adversarial
position *against* management and airs his grievances in numerous

strikes and walk-outs as well as by putting out only the lowest effort he can get away with. The German worker, on the other hand, is imbued with a much more cooperative spirit. Management and labor tend to work together and accomodate each other wherever possible. In part, this may be explained by the greater job security (deemphasizing the importance of work rules) and a general climate of significantly higher industrial democracy. The workers, through their representatives on the Board, co-determine the fundamental decisions affecting them. The result is lower costs, higher profits, *and* higher wages. Everybody gains.

The prisoner's dilemma approach can now summarize the problem here. Workers can either cooperate with management by giving their best effort or they can follow their self-interest by minimizing their extra effort. Similarly, management can be cooperative and generous towards the employees or, alternatively, pursue their own self-interest by granting as little as absolutely necessary to workers. These alternative strategies can now be summarized in Figure 4.2.

Figure 4.2

INDUSTRIAL RELATIONS:
COOPERATIVE OR ANTAGONISTIC?

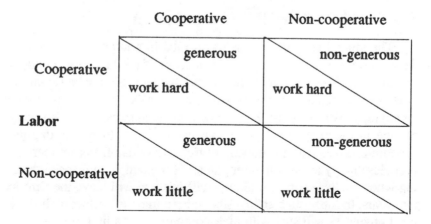

We have, for the sake of simplicity, omitted here any numbers relating to quantitative outcome, but we can see that the mutually cooperative strategy is best for both parties, while the mutually non-cooperative one is worst for both. It seems to be the case that the highly paid and hard-working Germans illustrate the most desirable strategy, while the British partners are locked into the low pay, low productivity cell. Note that since the amount of work effort is difficult to measure and police, a formal enforceable agreement on that variable is impossible. As a result, self-interest and distrust of management compels a non-cooperative strategy for labor. Ideally, they would work little under a generous management, but even if management is hard-nosed and stingy, they would be better off by exerting themselves as little as possible. The same argument applies to management. Their self-interested strategy is to adopt a non-cooperative attitude regardless of what labor may do. Best for them: labor would cooperate by exerting themselves while they themselves do nothing more than they absolutely have to. Instead, if labor were to economize on its efforts, a non-cooperative management strategy would be called for as well.

The mutually cooperative outcome is not within the reach of self-interested parties. But a willingness to abstain from self-interest or utility-maximizing (pay-off) considerations opens the door to economic success. As such, all this is not only a real world case study but very much an illustration of what John Ruskin talked about when criticizing the economist's perspective that relies on self-interest while ignoring the power of the higher human motives.

Trust and Loyalty as Economic Lubricant

The mutual cooperation that is so vital in a large-scale economy depends on trust and loyalty. As the success of the Japanese economy has shown, when employees are assured that they will not be summarily let go in an economic downturn they are less likely to leave for a better paying job in an upturn. To find and train good employees with every change in the economy is very expensive. Trust, then, has definite economic value. With the erosion of trust American firms are increasingly less likely to offer their engineers, for example, advanced training when studies show that almost half of them will leave the firm in two years. In Japan such an investment in training is well worth it since most engineers will stay with their companies for a lifetime. This explains in part why American companies are increasingly finding it more economical to buy complex and sophisticated parts and equipment from the Japanese than to develop their own resources and personnel to produce it.[26]

The problem exists not only for the employer. Mergers and buyouts by outside companies abrogate and undercut the positions of employees loyal to the original firm. For example, Eastern Airlines faced bankruptcy in 1984, and its workers responded to requests to help save the company by accepting reduced wages and benefits. Two years later, however, Eastern's board accepted a takeover from Texas Air Corporation. The chairman of Texas Air then repudiated union contracts, laid off two-thirds of the labor force, and cut wages by half. So that is what the Eastern employees could now look forward to as thanks for their former concessions.[27]

The erosion of trust in an economy leads to the development of ever complicated and extensive legal procedures in which each party tries to protect itself against being sold out or taken advantage of. This multiplies the red tape involved in economic transaction. Contract requirements proliferate, and litigation over their interpretation correspondingly increases. Between 1970 and 1985 the yearly total of private contractual disputes brought before federal courts tripled. Thus the "transaction costs" of doing business increases and the economic system becomes more cumbersome and inflexible. The effect of this has been described by Robert Reich as "economic gridlock."[28] (This is an analogy to the gridlock situation in city traffic. Drivers going through an intersection opportunistically crowd into the same intersection in order to avoid getting cut off by drivers coming into the intersection from the cross-moving direction. The cumulative effect of this behavior is to ensnarl traffic for everyone and lock up the whole system of movement.) Also, these forces feed on each other in a vicious cycle. The more gridlock seems imminent, the more drivers tend to thrust themselves into intersections.

The implications of the prisoner's dilemma do not stop at only narrowly defined "economic" problems, such as the examples and description above, but touch on a broad range of human concerns up to the most vital and critical. A tourist may like to visit a quiet unspoiled place of nature. But each visit may spoil it a bit for everyone else. If the individuals have no way to mutually coordinate their actions, the best self-interest tactic for every individual is to rush in before the others have spoiled it even more. This is the logic that generates in other contexts what is popularly described as the rat race. I need to get there first or else it will be too late for me. Larger meanings should become clear. At its worst, individual self-interest with no other available principle or means of mutual moderation leads to the problems of resource depletion, pollution, and ultimately another deadly race, the arms race.

The Patching Up of Self-Interest Doctrine

The prisoner's dilemma is the dilemma of individuals who are prisoners of only self-interested action and have no way to cooperate for their own mutual well-being. The broad reach of this problem casts a deeply critical light on the economist's long cherished inheritance from Adam Smith, that the pursuit of individual self-interest alone leads to the public good. Economics has generally avoided facing up to this problem in its core theoretical structure in a twofold way–first by redefining or attempting to transform what is meant by self-interest (and we will look at this in the next chapter), and second by spinning off new divisions of the field of economics while leaving the core structure intact.

The most prominent of these new divisions is that between micro- and macroeconomics. As we saw earlier in this chapter, macro-economics came into existence with Keynes' theory explaining how the Great Depression was economically possible. Up until Keynes, what we today call macroeconomics was expressed in Say's *Law of Markets*, which in turn was only an elaboration of Adam Smith's original concepts. Smithian economics did not need a separate micro and macro because Smith's thesis was that self-interest on an individual or firm level led to the general good on a national level–the "micro" and the "macro" were one, and that in fact was part of the theoretical power of what Smith had to say. However, when the tragedy of the Depression showed the failings of Smithian and neoclassical economics, a macroeconomics came into being. At the same time, economists still adhered to Smith's self-interest doctrine as essentially valid, only now its relevance was confined to what came to be called microeconomics.

Another important division in economics that serves a similar purpose is that between economics proper and what is called "welfare economics," the economics of the general or social good of society. Again, the need for a welfare economics arises out of problems that have been recognized in the standard self-interest economics as we have discussed here. We will examine the basic concepts of welfare economics in Chapter 7.

We will now look at the contemporary attempts to redefine the concept of self-interest.

References

1. J.C.L.S. de Sismondi, *New Principles of Political Economy* [1827]. 2nd edition. Preface reprinted in Sismondi, *Political Economy and the Philosophy of Government*. New York: Augustus M. Kelley, 1966, p. 115.
2. *ibid.*
3. de Sismondi, *op. cit.,* reprinted in P.C. Newman, et al., eds., *Source Readings in Economic Thought*. New York: W. W. Norton, 1954, p. 239.
4. Joseph Schumpeter, *History of Economic Analysis*. New York: Oxford University Press, 1954, p. 495.
5. J.C.L.S. de Sismondi, "Extracts from the Private Journal," *Political Economy and the Philosophy of Government*. New York: Augustus M. Kelley, 1966, p. 454.
6 . *ibid.,* p. 455.
7. Lionel Robbins, *The Great Depression*. London: Macmillan, 1934.
8. *New York Times*, December 30, 1984 (book review), p. 7.
9. Quoted in E. K. Hunt, *History of Economic Thought: A Critical Perspective*. Belmont, California: Wadsworth, 1979, p. 124.
10. Quoted in Lionel Robbins, *The Theory of Economic Policy*. London: Macmillan, 1953, p. 95.
11. *ibid.,* p. 127.
12. David Ricardo, *The Works and Correspondence of David Ricardo*. Vol. 1. P. Sraffa, ed. Cambridge, Massachusetts, Cambridge University Press, 1951, pp. 105-106.
13. Jane Marcet quoted in Rajani K. Kanth, *Political Economy and Laissez-Faire*. Totowa, New Jersey: Rowman & Littlefield, 1986, p. 20.
14. John Ruskin, *Unto This Last*. New York: John Wiley & Son, 1866, pp. 17-18.
15. *ibid.,* pp. 18-19.
16. *ibid.,* p. 19.
17. *ibid.,* pp. 21, 23.
18. *ibid.,* p. 28.
19. John Ruskin, "Letters on Political Economy," in *Arrows of the Chase*. Vol. 2. Boston: Colonial Press, 1880, p. 282.
20. John Ruskin quoted in Sherbourne, *John Ruskin or the Ambiguity of Affluence*. Cambridge, Massachusetts, Harvard University Press, 1972.
21. *Manchester Examiner and Times*, October 2, 1860.

22. Lionel Robbins, *The Nature and Significance of Economic Science* [1932]. 3rd edition. London: Macmillan, 1984, p. 27.

23. Quoted in Fred Hirsch, *Social Limits to Growth*. Cambridge, Massachusetts: Harvard University Press, 1976, p. 135.

24. *New York Times*, October 13, 1981, D1, 4.

25. *ibid.*

26. Robert Reich, *Tales of a New America*. New York: Times Books, Random House, 1987.

27. *ibid.*

28. Robert Reich, "Enterprise and Double Cross," *Washington Monthly,* January 1987, pp. 13-19. Adapted from his book, *Tales of a New America. ibid.*

Chapter 5

SELF-INTEREST AND CONTEMPORARY ECONOMICS

Economic theory in its traditional flagship country–England–underwent some facelifting only several years after Robbins' famous book gave it the impetus. The primary reconstruction came from two of Robbins' British colleagues, John Hicks and R. G. D. Allen, who reconsidered and reinterpreted the neoclassical marginal utility theory. To a large extent, they had been moved by the scientifically troublesome insight that utility and with it the law of diminishing marginal utility were both non-observable and, in the the case of utility, also non-measurable. In an age of increasing scientific rigor, economics had been relying too much on excessive metaphysics to build their demand and labor supply curves. And although the end product of the reconstruction ended up being more in outer form than inner substance, it did provide economists with a brand new tool: indifference curve analysis. We discuss this new analytic device as well as its significance from a humanistic perspective in Appendix I at the end of the book. Let us instead focus on another aspect of the Hicks/Allen revolution: its effect on nineteenth century Economic Man and the behavioral assumption of individual self-interest.

At first sight, modern economics appears to deny that it entails any postulate of self-interest, or at least such is the view taught by the textbooks. In one of the dominant microeconomics textbooks by Jack Hirschleifer we read:

It is sometimes charged that economics also postulated that people's preferences are completely selfish. This is an uninformed criticism. It is true that, observing facts as they really are, the economist ordinarily operates on the premise that individuals seek their own advantage, "It is not from the benevolence of the butcher, the brewer, or the baker, that we expect our dinner, but from their regard to their own interest." That this is a main truth about human activity it would be absurd to deny. Nevertheless, charity is an important feature of economic life; people have, in a sense, a taste for benevolence.[1]

Similarly, Edwin Mansfield in his textbook cautions the student that "[the person's] tastes may be judged to be shallow or deep, lofty or mean, selfish or generous: this makes no difference to the theory."[2] In the same vein Browning and Browning devote two whole pages to denouncing the stubbornly perennial criticism that "economics assumes people are greedy and care only about material possessions"; or that "economics disregards the fact that individuals are benevolent and are concerned with the welfare of other people."[3]

The Emergence of Rational Economic Man

Did our old friend Economic Man really get flushed out of the mainstream? The answer lies in a new concept that began to assume a central place in the modern economic image of the person, and that is rationality. If the long-standing emphasis on the self-interest orientation of the person in economics was taken to mean selfishness, then that implication was misleading, thought economists. Thus they refined what they meant by self-interest. This refinement was expressed as rationality: The modern Economic Man was put forth as Rational Economic Man.

Certainly, economics gains here in terms of the connotations of the word. It is definitely more appealing to be concerned with the investigation of a being who is rational, rather than one who is merely self-interested and all the negatives which that may imply. Therefore, almost all contemporary economics texts state the assumption that man is rational. This is taken to simply mean that he or she will seek their more preferred outcomes or consequences rather than their less preferred. As Mansfield states it, "Given the consumer's tastes . . . we assume that he is rational. . . . This is an assumption so general and so reasonable that most people would accept it as a good approximation to reality."[4]

Before going on with our analysis of this new emphasis, it is worthwhile to examine economics' adoption of this specific term, rationality.

The Meaning of Rational Behavior

We have said that the connotations of the word rationality are positive, and this no doubt would make it quite congenial to any student of economics encountering the field for the first time. But a curious and important transformation occurs in the meaning and use of this term. We find out that by referring to the rational economic actor, economics intends this term in a very particular and technical way, and is not using the word as it is most generally and popularly understood. Let us see what the common understanding is and compare it to the economic usage.

Dictionaries define rational behavior as "behavior that conforms to the dictates of reason." In other words, if we say that one is rational we are saying that the person is reasonable. Incidentally, we note in the above quoted statement by Mansfield, that it is "reasonable" to accept that the economic actor is rational. So although Mansfield himself in the quote above uses the idea of *reasonable* to promote the economist's concept of rationality, we will now see that reasonable is not what economists really mean by rational. Confused? Well, perhaps for good reason.

In the common usage of the term rational one would not think of describing the robbing of a bank as a rational or reasonable act. However, we find out that for economics this is quite possible (not because economics supports crime). Robbing a bank can be described in economics as rational, because for the economist the word rational strictly means the logical application of means to attain particular ends, *regardless of what these ends are.* For economics, therefore, a bank robber is behaving rationally if he goes about his work in an efficient and effective manner.

This use of rational to refer to the relationship between means and ends, and not to the choice of ends themselves, reflects a change in the concept of reason that is generally seen to be initiated with David Hume's *Treatise on Human Nature* (1739). Previous to Hume, in any philosophical discourse and still currently in popular usage, the term rational also meant the choice of ends. The late German philosopher Max Horkheimer, founder of the Frankfurt school in philosophy, observes: "'Reason' for a long period meant the activity and assimilating the eternal ideas which were to function as goals for men."[5] But since David Hume considered a person to be nothing more than a bundle of passions or desires, there was no more room for any kind of existence of eternal ideas which could be counted on to rule our goal-seeking behavior. In the Anglo-Saxon academic world, and particularly in the philosophy of social sciences in economics, this new and naturalistic view of the concept of rationality caught on and prevails until this day.

Rational Man in Modern Economics: Indifference Analysis

Now that we know what economics means by rationality we can turn to its application in the concept of Rational Economic Man.

Let us take three goods–pens, candles, and apples. Then let us assume that a particular individual prefers candles to apples, and apples to pens. Therefore, this individual would rank his order of preference as candles, apples, and pens. All that is necessary here in terms of rational choice is that this rank order obeys the *axiom of transitivity* which rules out that someone might prefer A to B and B to C, but then C to A. Another individual might, of course, have a different preference order, so that pens would be her first choice, then candles, then apples.

The economist also applies this same logic to collections or "baskets" of goods. There can be any number of goods in the basket, but let us just take the simplest two goods case, say, books and meal tickets. If someone is offered a basket of five books and five meal tickets versus a basket of four books and four meal tickets, it would be rational for the person to choose the first basket. This follows in a straightforward fashion from the principle that if something is good, then more is better than less. At this point in the discussion we will agree with the economist that the choice of the second basket would be irrational. So far so good.

But now the going gets a little more tricky. Modern economics goes on to say that this choice or ranking of goods or collections of goods can be applied to all possible collections, and this is called the *axiom of comparability. All* baskets of goods are comparable, and either one is preferred to the other or the consumer is indifferent between the two. With the axiom of comparability the economist believes that he or she has settled all of the metaphysical problems with the old concept of utility. Now utility could just mean a rank order of preference.

But there is a rub, and that is in the concept of indifference. As a result of the axioms of comparability and transitivity, economists claim that one of the possibilities is the condition of indifference between baskets. Let us look at this in terms of our books and meal tickets example. The economist would want to say that there are several alternatives that would all be equally preferable. Above, we saw that the basket with five books and five meal tickets was preferred to one with four and four. The economist would want to say that the five and five could be split up in different combinations and the consumer would not mind at all, so that he or she would be indifferent as to whether the basket contained six books and four meal tickets, or seven books and three meal tickets, or six meal tickets and four books, or seven meal tickets and three books. Each of these baskets would be preferred to the four and four. (In this example, for the sake of simplicity we assume a linear curve with a slope of -1. This would, of course, imply that books and meal tickets were perfect substitutes.)

Indifference and Incommensurability.   The importance of this is that in the concept of indifference lies the economist's old friend commensurability. The economist wants to say that units of one good in the basket can be traded for units of another in the basket and the consumer's preference for the basket would remain the same.

Now we can see why it is not only single goods that the economist wants to put in a preference order but baskets of goods as well. By assuming that the economic actor can rank order entire baskets of goods, or collections, the economist can continue to assume that the consumer can assign a total value to a collection, regardless of what items make up the collection. For the economist it is expressly important that it does not matter what is in the collection. In addition to food, books, and other material goods, it can include such noble goods as a happy neighbor, a better world, a meaningful life, or other equally lofty goals. But what matters is that the collection can be dealt with as a total value derived from its individual components, in other words, commensurability.

Thus, again, the rational economic actor is not seen to be a real person with a variety of qualitatively different needs, but the Economic Man abstraction of only having wants, each of which is additive to or substitutable for the other. Thus it is important for us to recognize that the concept of rationality, while sounding very appealing and desirable, does not change the underlying economic conception of commensurability for all goods and services, and thus posits an economic being of wants rather than needs.

Rationality and Self-Interest

Although the Hicks/Allen reconstruction now occupying the very heart of microeconomic textbooks can be seen as amounting to only a change in form or language, it does allow choice to be pictured in more general and comprehensive terms. There is no requirement that preferences ought to be selfish and greedy. So, for example, an altruistically minded person may most prefer a particular consumption bundle that would be heavily oriented towards feeding the hungry and the poor. Or a mother may prefer that the youngest child obtains the most attractive bundle. In the case of the altruist or the mother the ranking of bundles gives heavy emphasis to consumption sets that are not one's own. But even though consumption does not have to be one's own, satisfaction is. Both the altruist and the mother do whatever they are doing because it is taken to maximize their satisfaction. It is their pleasure, so to speak, to be altruistic or full of sympathy.

But let us be clear; if our goal is assumed to be maximum satisfaction of our own preferences, then we are really in a way still self-interested. This was clearly recognized by I. M. D. Little in his attack on this type of approach: "In the past economists have often been attacked on the grounds that their theories applied only to selfish people; such attacks were brushed aside as absurd. But they were not absurd." And he goes on to explain, "the usual way of answering these attacks was to say that an altruistic man might still be maximizing his satisfaction, because altruism is itself a pleasure. But this is to deny that one ever suffers, or expects to suffer, by helping others, which is absurd."[6]

Little's observation, which was made in the context of proposing another reconstruction of consumer choice along the lines of behavioristic psychology, had little effect on the profession. Such further reconstruction was meant to explain choice *not* on the basis of psychology or preferences, but by externally observed behavior alone. In this he sought to refine Samuelson's revealed preference theory proposed in 1939. We ignore here these theories of choice since it is by now generally agreed that they did not achieve what they initially sought to do, as already indicated in the Appendix discussing wants, needs, and indifference.

Meanwhile, the great majority of economists seem quite comfortable in the assertion that in pure theory such a Rational Man is not necessarily selfish. He may on one occasion or another be acting with a certain degree of altruism or even enlightened self-interest, the latter being commonly understood by philosophers as *prudent* behavior. In such a perspective self-interest is simply being motivated by our *own* purposes, preferences, and satisfactions, however constituted. What we do "rationally" is by definition necessarily self-interested. It cannot be otherwise; there is no more contrast class, no *non*-self-interest.

In such a perspective any ethical issue based on the fact that the self-interested person is selfish becomes immaterial, and the word "self-interested" is seen as equivalent to the words "*rational*" or "*purposeful*." At least with purpose and rationality one can envision a contrast class: namely, impulsive, irrational, self-contradictory behavior. Such is the nature of Man according to pure modern economic theory: not really selfish but in fact only rational. Thus Rational Man may appear to be less obnoxious than its nineteenth century counterpart.

Economic Rationality as Psychologically Empty

The formal theory of rational choice and Rational Man outlined above does not say much about his actual character. But there is some such information contained in the axiomatic model, although primarily implicitly.

As first character witness, let us hear the following brief testimony by Hollis and Nell concerning our idealized Rational Man:

> He is neither tall nor short, fat nor thin, married nor single. There is no telling whether he loves his dog, beats his wife or prefers pushpin [an old-fashioned game] to poetry. We do not know what he wants. But we do know that, whatever it is, he will maximize ruthlessly to get it.[7]

Ruthless maximization, constant calculation, and an eagerness to take advantage of every possible opportunity, all are certainly important characteristics of such an "idealized and abstract" individual. The term "ruthless" here should not be taken as a biased value judgment by Hollis and Nell, but is used to mean that this person has only one purpose. No doubt it is not an entirely unreasonable description of the pressured businessman who does well to calculate and recalculate the best ways to advance himself, and it is clear that advancement means profitability. But outside of business, this may be quite an unrealistic description. Let us now see what it entails.

For one, the emphasis on calculation implies a one-dimensional process. The very possibility of calculation means that all relevant information of the variables can be expressed in—or reduced to—a common measure, allowing for variation in quantity only. Instead of truly deciding or *choosing* between alternative ends and actions, he merely calculates and determines with mathematical precision which one yields the highest value. In economics this is considered to be choice. It is an equivalent mental exercise to "choosing" the square root of nine as a bigger number than the square root of four. Truly qualitative considerations cannot be fitted into such a one-dimensional world. Once again, this is part and parcel of the commensurability assumption.

Such passion for dispassionate calculation may make for "modern" or "instrumental" rationality in behavior, but it is not compatible with the temporary suspension of calculation which is and always has been seen as the hallmark of moral or ethical conduct. Moral behavior, or action based on rules or with regard to principles, has to be seen as the very opposite of opportunistic behavior. This is also brought out clearly in the dictionary where the taking advantage of opportunities is described as "dispensing with a fixed and moral program." If "taking advantage" or rationality really dispenses with morality, economic theory appears to leave out something essentially human, some principles of action which a meaningfully humanistic economics cannot afford to ignore. We have to make room for ethics and morality in Economic Man, and we will show how this can be done in the next chapter.

But let us here sketch the problem with an example. Let us assume that rational economic behavior consists in selecting the best available action, the "number-one" selection in one's preference ordering. A kidnapper has to decide what to do with his victim. One action is to let him go and so risk being identified and caught. The other is to kill his victim. Considering all these things, the kidnapper chooses killing as his action. That is his rank order of preference. Economic rationality leaves matters at this level of rationality. It never asks about the would-be murderer having preferences about his preferences. What if he does not like to kill or, to be more exact, to submit to killing out of fear of getting caught? Now, although he does kill—the action which is his number-one selection—he does not like his own rank ordering; he does not feel good about himself. In other words, he has a meta or a higher preference about his preferences. This is where ethics and morality will have to come in.

We can see how this fits together with the dual-self theory. Rationality, whether selfish or not, is about a single-self, the interests and purposes of that self. As long as we do not admit another and higher phase of our self there cannot be a higher purpose, a higher force, and a higher-order preference ordering. By the same logic there cannot be an inner conflict between following two purposes. In contrast, humanistic economics clearly recognizes what economic orthodoxy ends up denying: the possibility of an inner conflict of interest, a conflict between two incommensurable interests, one of the ego-self, the other of the higher (and more ideal) self. And such recognition, as we will see in the next chapter, is far from irrelevant when considering economic behavior, institutions, and policies.

The Real Soul of Rational Economic Man: Selfishness.   Such is the psychological frame of mind of our abstract Rational Man animated by the basic axioms (transitivity and comparability) of modern preference theory. We are dealing with a fellow who is constantly calculating, trying to accomplish whatever he wants in the best possible way. The key words here are "whatever he wants." If we leave the motivating goals as wide open as that, no economic theory as we presently know it is possible. For instance, take the basic law of demand that, other things equal, we want to buy more of a good if the price drops. Let us say Brazilian coffee drops in price because a new Brazilian government breaks a labor union. Will our rational American coffee drinker buy more Brazilian coffee? It depends on what she wants. If she maximizes for her own consumption purposes, yes, she would buy more coffee. But if she strongly sympathizes with all Third World coffee workers, the answer is not so clear. It is not so clear because our coffee drinker suddenly no longer has the compatible interests of liking coffee and also wanting Third World advancement. The Brazilian move against labor threatens the export revenues of all other Third World coffee producers together. As a result, her sympathies for those producers may override her interest of having as much coffee as possible at the lowest possible price. Similarly, if sellers and buyers maintain a personal interest in one another, we cannot predict or explain any outcome in their transactions. This problem, of course, was long recognized in Wicksteed's stipulation that exchange had to be "non-tuistic."

So, we have to know *what* the maximizer maximizes, the content of maximization. Is it a selfish concern for one's *own* feelings and consumption, or are we to assume some altruistic predisposition to exhibit a significant concern for others? Is a businessman operating to acquire a maximum amount of income or profits, or is he trying to maximize the level of employment in the community—or some combination of both?

In order to build the economic principle of supply and demand, we need to assume something beyond mere abstract rationality: formal preference theory has to be given some substantive content. And economists have done just that, herewith transforming the potentially appealing Rational Man underlying preference theory into an unappealing Rational *Economic* Man underlying the *application* of such theory. Here is how he is described in the authoritative and comprehensive new textbook of Samuelson and Nordhaus:

> Economic Man is an idealized conception of a person who is purely rational, and whose only motivating forces are economic. In such a view, consumers are endowed with a given set of tastes that they try best to satisfy, while entrepreneurs are solely trying to maximize profits.[8]

The allusion to profits indicates that the tastes are now solely confined to tastes and preferences for one's own welfare or "consumption bundles" without any concern for other people's consumption and welfare. No more altruism here, just the conventional self-interest of the nineteenth century type. This is further illustrated by how modern economists apply their theory in viewing government action. Samuelson and Nordhaus describe it as follows: "The theory of public choice cuts through [the] thicket of complex motivations by making a simple [indeed, overly simple] assumption: *politicians are assumed to behave so as to maximize their chances for reelection.* They are assumed to be vote maximizers–just as firms are taken to be profit maximizers."[9] Similar statements, perhaps presented with somewhat greater conviction and enthusiasm, can be found in other leading texts, particularly the one by the well-known economist Jack Hirschleifer.[10] Others are even more outspoken. So, for example, UCLA professor William R. Allen whom we have met before, a respected colleague of Mr. Hirschleifer, has no qualms in telling radio listeners: "Rule number one for the social analyst is to take people as they are. They are–among other characteristics–acquisitive and grubby, interested in their own well-being, preferring more rather than less of what they desire. They have been like that since the fiasco in the Garden of Eden. . . ."[11] Allen, in the foreword to the collection of his radio addresses, is correct when he notes that although the words are generally his, "as any fellow professional in economics would recognize, the essential substance comes entirely from the common heritage."[12] This is the heritage described in Chapter 4, the heritage of Gossen's divinely inspired pleasure maximizer and Adam Smith's baker.

Explaining the Resilience of Selfishness.   The question has been asked by open-minded scholars, why is it that modern economics remains so preoccupied with nineteenth century Economic Man in his new garment of contemporary preference or choice theory? Why do economists choose to interpret their theories of constrained maximization with a content that favors selfish motives over other motives?

Edmund Phelps simply claims that while egalitarians and other humanitarians must have a "new breed of human beings" in mind, economists like him deal with the *present standard breed.*[13] Economics in this view simply reflects how people are–acquisitive, grubby, and interested in their own well-being. Any economics insisting on seeing things differently is at best a dreamy forecast of a remotely distant utopia. The fundamental misconception inherent in this credo of the standard breed of economist has already been pointed out, but more will become apparent as we proceed to unfold the humanistic alternative.

Another and more reasoned explanation has been offered by Amartya Sen.[14] He points out that economists ever since Adam Smith have been exploring the 200-year-old question of how Smith's invisible hand theorem could indeed be true. This is no different today where this question is examined in what is called General Equilibrium Analysis. This branch of economic theory, occupying the very core of modern analysis, is technical and need not be dwelt on here. But one central aspect is clear: in order to demonstrate that selfish individuals in "unsympathetic isolation" from their fellow men are indeed capable of unintentionally maximizing social welfare, we have to assume that they are selfish, otherwise the invisible hand trick of pulling an unselfish rabbit out of a selfish hat cannot be performed. And not surprisingly, the necessary behavioral assumption of selfishness naturally spills into the rest of economics as well.

But what is not surprising is also very unfortunate. The highly technical exercises relevant to general equilibrium theory and its normative kin, the economics of social welfare, occupying as they do much effort, time, and space in graduate-level economics instruction, tend to generate dubious generalizations of how we should best organize an economy in order to assure maximum social well-being. They are taken as guides in how to structure or restructure socioeconomic institutions to the benefit of selfishly interacting individuals. And such general equilibrium theory-based advice may very well work to the detriment of people who are trying to be less selfish than the accomodated "standard breed." So, in spite of the protests and assertions of economists presented at the beginning of this chapter, we have regrettably to conclude that for a variety of reasons, modern economic science still embraces self-interest as the heart and soul of Economic Man.

The puzzle remains, however, why would economists of high respect and reputation want to deny what would seem to be the fact of the selfish core of their science? One somewhat cynical explanation–but at the same time fully consistent with the theory advocated in their texts–is that the denial of self-interest may very well maximize the satisfaction of the authors of modern theory texts. In other words, the denial of self-interest may indeed be fully "rational" and in their own self-interest.

Nevertheless, before concluding this chapter we want to address and discuss an issue that sadly confirms our basic claim, while further undermining the authoritative assertion that any complaints about modern economics operating on the underlying predisposition of selfish Economic Man constitutes an essentially "uninformed criticism."

To demonstrate this, and more, we will turn to a paradigm case study of modern economic theory.

The Free Rider Assumption: A Paradigm Illustration

All intermediate and advanced texts discuss what is called the "free rider" problem. This generally comes up in the area of the public good —a good such as roads, or a lighthouse, or a park, where everyone can benefit from using them whether they pay for them or not. Economists predict that individuals will not pay for the benefits if they can allow other people to pick up their costs—in other words, they will naturally become free riders. Thus Browning and Browning state, "When public goods are involved, free rider behavior is rational, but it hinders the ability of private markets to cater efficiently to the demand for a public good."[15] Similarly, a Nobel Prize authority on public choice economics argues: "Regardless of how the individual estimates the behavior of others, he must always rationally choose the free-rider alternative."[16]

The authors here merely echo what others a long time ago have seen as obstacles to effective cooperation. Perhaps the first was David Hume in 1739 who illustrated the problem of two sheep raisers both bordering a swamplike meadow that they would like to see drained and fenced for their mutual benefit. Each will have an incentive to leave the bulk of their joint enterprise to the other. Similarly, our old friend Gossen— one of the most articulate prophets of egoism—observed in his celebrated book "that in any undertaking involving a joint project, even if everyone has the same interest in its completion, each one will try— as far as possible—to evade the effort for which he has obligated himself."[17]

Our point here is not whether the free rider prediction about human behavior is accurate or not, but that economics makes this prediction as a matter of theoretical principle, and not as an empirical statement. It may be empirically accurate, or it may not, or something in between. What we will try to show is that the theoretical principles of humanistic economics, which not only include self-interested behavior, can handle various empirical outcomes of the free rider problem, while mainstream economics cannot. To show this we turn to the following research study, which not only demonstrates the problems that conventional economics has with the data of free ridership, but also makes a telling point about economics' self-interest bias.

The study is ironically entitled, "Economists Free Ride, Does Anyone Else?"[18] A clever series of twelve experiments were conducted in which subjects had the option of investing tokens in either a "group exchange" (public good) or an "individual exchange." They then would get a set monetary return per token for the investment in individual exchange, as well as a separate return based on the overall level of group investment, regardless of how much that individual subject invested his or her tokens in the group exchange. (All participants in the experiments received the same amount of group return, which varied from experiment to experiment.) From a self-interested free rider hypothesis it would be most advantageous for an individual to invest all of his or her tokens in the individual exchange, and hope that everyone else invested in the group exchange.

Along with this experiment, six economists ("acknowledged experts") were sent a description of the experiment and asked to predict the outcome. One declined to answer, arguing that economic theory made no relevant predictions. But five out of the six agreed that theory clearly supported a strong free rider hypothesis, with relatively few tokens being invested by individuals in the group exchange.

The actual results of the study were reported by the authors as follows:

> Over and over again, in replication after replication, regardless of changes in a score of situational variables or subject characteristics, the strong version of the free rider hypothesis is contradicted by the evidence. People voluntarily contributed substantial portions of their resources–usually an average of between 40 and 60 percent–to the provision of the public good. This despite the fact that the conditions of the experiment are expressly designed to maximize the probability of individualized, self-interested behavior. Free riding does exist–subjects did not provide the optimum amount of the public good and tend to reserve a meaningful fraction of their resources. The "weak" free rider hypothesis is supported. Nevertheless, the amount of contribution to the public good is not easily understood in terms of current theory.[19]

This study, although carefully and seriously conducted, is written up and presented with at least a touch of irony, and we are using it here in that light. Therefore, in this spirit it is worthwhile mentioning one of its additional findings.

There was one exception to the above quoted results. This was a part of the study done with a very special and non-representative group of subjects–thirty-two first-semester graduate students in economics. Only in this case were the results different. The economics graduate students contributed only an average of 20 percent of their resources to the group exchange, and thus "they were very much more likely to free ride than any of the other groups of subjects." It is interesting to note that when questioned later, only two of the graduate students could specifically identify the theory on which the study was based. The authors then draw this conclusion in regards to this most special group: "As first year students they had yet to reap the full benefits of the remarkable education assuredly to be theirs."[20]

Modern economists, with their virtually universally accepted free rider hypothesis, clearly support the view that we have not moved very far since nineteenth century days when it earned the reputation of a dismal science. As one scholar put it recently and succinctly:

> From one point of view the orthodox assertion of the eminence of the free-rider seems to resurrect the old image of economics as the dismal science, for it seems to stress the corruptibility of man. Free-rider behavior involves after all what is frequently referred to as cheating strategy. Each individual, betraying the confidence of his community, engages in deceit to avoid paying the price that he himself regards as an appropriate measure of its value.[21]

It is hard to find a better support for Marshall's assertion that in economic theory the stronger motive is what counts, not the higher one, nor even the one that is empirically supported.

Conclusion

What we have tried to show in this chapter is that for over fifty years, students in economics have received the full benefits of a remarkable education. It is an education in viewing man as a self-centered and self-interested utility maximizer. Where it has been acknowledged that human behavior might have another dimension than self-interest it has been decided that this part of the person is irrelevant to economics and therefore is outside of the scope of the science, at least for the "present standard breed of people." As we have already indicated, humanistic economics believes that such an exclusion is theoretically wanting, empirically questionable, and a serious social mistake with unfortunate consequences. The most alarming of these may be that by only assuming a standard breed of people, economists may be helping to legitimize self-interested behavior and so breed more greed. Humanistic economics, both in theory and in practice, aims towards overcoming these mistakes and their consequences.

References

1. Jack Hirschleifer, *Price Theory and Application.* 3rd edition. Englewood Cliffs, New Jersey: Prentice Hall, 1984, p. 10.
2. Edwin Mansfield, *Microeconomics.* New York: W.W. Norton, 1970, p. 21.

3. Edgar Browning and Jacqueline Browning, *Microeconomic Theory and Application*. Boston: Little, Brown, 1983, p. 52.

4. Edwin Mansfield, *Microeconomics*. 5th edition. New York: W.W. Norton, 1985, p. 53.

5. Max Horkheimer, *Critique of Instrumental Reason*. New York: Seabury Press, 1974, p. vii.

6. I. M. D. Little, *A Critique of Welfare Economics*. 2nd edition. London: Oxford University Press, 1957, p. 21

7. Martin Hollis and Edward Nell, *Rational Economic Man*. New York: Cambridge University Press, 1975, p. 54.

8. Paul Samuelson and William Nordhaus, *Economics*. 12th edition. New York: McGraw-Hill, 1983, p. 903.

9. *ibid.*, p. 703 (emphasis added).

10. Hirschleifer, *op. cit.*

11. William R. Allen, *Midnight Economist: Broadcast Essays III*. Los Angeles: International Institute for Economic Research, 1982, p. 23.

12. William R. Allen, *Midnight Economist: Radio Essays II*. Los Angeles: International Institute for Economic Research, 1980, p. 2.

13. Edmund S. Phelps, *Political Economy*. New York: W. W. Norton, 1985, p. 134.

14. Amartya Sen, "Rational Fools: A Critique of the Behavioral Foundation of Economic Theory," *Philosophy and Public Affairs*, 6 (1977), pp. 317-344.

15. Browning and Browning, *op. cit.*, p. 538.

16. James Buchanan, "The Demand and Supply for Public Goods" in J. Margolis and H. Guitten, eds., *Public Economics*. International Economic Association Conference Proceedings, 1969.

17. Hermann H. Gossen, *The Laws of Human Relations* [1854]. Cambridge, Massachusetts: MIT Press, 1983, p. 254.

18. Gerald Marwell and Ruth Ames, "Economists Free Ride, Does Anyone Else?" in *Journal of Public Economics*, 15 (1981) pp. 295-310.

19. *ibid.*, pp. 307-308.

20. *ibid.*, p. 306.

21. E. R. Brubaker, "Free Ride, Free Revelation, or Golden Rule?" in *Journal of Law and Economics*, 18 (1975), p. 153.

Chapter 6

BEYOND RATIONAL MAN: THE REASONABLE PERSON

Until now, we have spent most of our time following the footsteps of Economic Man. We have witnessed his evolution in theory from a self-interested utility maximizer to the present-day rational agent depicted in the last chapter. In the process we could establish that modern "Rational Man" is not only singularly one-dimensional but, when caught off guard—as in the case of the free rider assumption—still selfish.

Rediscovering Ideals

It is now time to demonstrate that Rational Man, contrary to entrenched belief, is far from manifesting a reasonable and widely applicable behavioral pattern. Instead, he is a creature lacking essentially human characteristics. There is something important missing from the economist's standard image of Man, and we can see this by looking again at the marvelous study by Marwell and Ames titled "Economists Free Ride, Does Anyone Else?"[1] There we learned that while graduate students in general did not "free ride," economists were observed to do so. Now, in an attempt to explain the results, the researchers asked all subjects two additional questions, both relating to fairness. When asked what would be the fair amount of their tokens to be "invested" in the (collective) group exchange, just about everybody answered at least one-half of their tokens, and some even said all. The group of graduate economists, on the other hand, typically refused to answer the question or did not understand the question, which led the researchers to observe that "the meaning of 'fairness' in this context was something alien for this group." Moreover, the few young economists who chose to respond felt that little or no contribution to the common project was fair.

And similarly, another question asking if subjects were concerned with fairness when making their experimental investment decision was answered much less favorably by the economics graduate students than anybody else.

Obviously, there is evidence of a serious problem here. Economics students, following their mentors, cannot easily comprehend the meaning of fairness, and–not surprisingly–find it difficult to be motivated in that respect as well. What is it that renders fairness so incomprehensible for them? Why would George Stigler, when accepting the Nobel Prize, say that "any preoccupation with fairness and justice is uncongenial to a science in which these concepts have *no* established meaning?"[2] An answer to these questions has to involve the recognition that there might very well be a fundamental problem relating the Rational Man assumption to the concept of fairness. It seems that the two are incompatible. In other words, to be fair in economic terms seems to mean to be irrational, and vice versa.

What a curious conclusion. Fairness, at least as defined in the free rider context, is for the economist irrational. However, by now we should probably find this not surprising since we have already examined the very particular and perhaps peculiar way in which the economist defines irrational. It has nothing to do with the choice of one's goals or ends–it could be getting fat, robbing banks, or murder, but only in the choice of the most efficient (i.e., rational) means to those ends.

Unfortunately, the term rational still carries with it the meanings and connotations that it has in ordinary language, such as reasonableness, wisdom, dispassion, and, yes, even fairness. Can we rescue rationality from the confines of the distorting box that conventional economics has trapped it in? The happy answer is that we can, and easily and cleanly so.

Rational Economic Man Gets a Reasonable Partner

First of all, let us meet with another "Man," in contrast to the economist's Rational Man, and that is the legal profession's concept of the "Reasonable Man." Economist Werner Hirsch in his 1979 book *Law and Economics* informs us that the law uses a standard of the "Reasonable Man" to make legal judgments. Hirsch says, "He is a person who is not only protective of his own rights, but also has a fair regard for the welfare of others . . . . For example, the law holds that a person whose acts deviate from the standard of the 'reasonable' can be found negligent and held liable." Hirsch continues, "Economics, on the other hand, is built around the concept of the 'rational man' who in the extreme is totally self-serving, seeking to maximize his self interest."[3]

What is interesting here is that the two concepts of the person, the economic Rational Man and the legal profession's Reasonable Man, sound so close to each other verbally or semantically that one would think they mean the same thing. However, as we have just seen, they are really so far apart as to be essentially opposites. The Rational Man pursues his or her self-interest and the Reasonable Man is precisely reasonable because he or she is following other principles than sheer self-interest. If it were considered legally permissible to do whatever one wanted ("taking the law into one's own hands") then the legal concept of the Reasonable Man would have no meaning.

In this contrast between the conventional economic image of the person and the image of the person in law, we find another way of appreciating the power of the humanistic image of the person. Humanistic economics, through the concept of the twofold or dual-self, comprises both the self of Rational Economic Man and the self of Legal Reasonable Man. The fact is that we have already met Reasonable Man in the context of Maslow's psychology when we first introduced the idea of the dual-self. There it was the higher part of our being that was motivated by such values as truth, and no longer by any such personal deficiency as unmet needs or desires. It suggested that there was a "vertical" dimension, a higher and a lower, and not just a horizontal dimension of a single plane of wants and inclinations. In the process we also noted Maslow's belief that the human being is both animal and animal-transcending, existing in some sort of perpetual tension between what he is and what he yearns to be, sandwiched, if you will, between a higher and a lower self-conception. This higher/lower polarity was characterized not only by the dichotomy of growth needs versus deficiency needs, but also by truth seeking in contrast to self-interest seeking, and by contrasting principled behavior with instrumental behavior. Additionally, the higher self was depicted as objective and transpersonal rather than subjective and personal, the latter characterizing the lower self.

Besides the self-interested ego there is also the more ideal self that deep down yearns to be realized and makes itself felt in our moral values and aspirations. To contrast the two, we can either act so as to maintain our personal integrity or we can yield to our momentary desires and temptations. Reflecting on our daily experience will teach us quickly that the "ideal" self need not be high up in the clouds, like some unattainable metaphysical essence completely detached and divorced from our practical daily conduct. Instead, it is intrinsically bound up and involved with our daily decision making. Furthermore, it also accords with the great traditions of classical thought, both East and West, until Hobbes and Hume changed the story in eighteenth century England. Similarly, it was also deeply embedded in German philosophy, and managed to inspire the subsequent movement of European Existentialism with its actual and "authentic" self.

Visiting Kantian Man: A Close Cousin

Let us look, for example, at one of the greatest philosophers of the last two centuries, the German Immanuel Kant. For him, a dual-self perspective served as the alpha and omega of his entire ethical philosophy. He recognized what he called the *Phenomenal Man*, relying on instrumental thought to best satisfy inclinations and desires in order to feel good. He was seen as existing in the world of nature and its laws and being readily accessible to empirical and sensory observation. In other words, our skin-encapsulated ego is Kant's Phenomenal Man. But, at the same time, there is a more central *noumenal self* beyond the world of the senses.* This is a moral self. In contrast to the other, it is self-determined by the principles of reason, not only in the selection of the most appropriate means towards a given end but also in the selection of the end itself. Therefore, our glutton or murderer would hardly be seen as rational from the standpoint of Kant's noumenal self.

According to Kant, it is only the noumenal self that has the power of free will. The phenomenal self is subject to the passions or desires. To Kant, we as mortal beings have one foot in the sensory (or "sensible") kingdom of nature, and the other in the intelligible or comprehensible kingdom of reason. The former determines our actions ac-

---

*Noumenal means undiscovered, new, not knowable in the subject-object split as phenomena, but as a "thing-in-itself." Hegel later realized that in its full maturity this was ultimate self-awareness or self-realization. If we see the three-dimensional phenomenal self as "material," the noumenal may be contrasted as "spiritual."

cording to the principle of pleasure. The latter provides the moral directions of actions; it informs us what we *ought* to do, regardless of incentives and considerations of self-interest. When the person dwells in the realm of the noumenal, he acts "rightly" and in true freedom—not determined by the inclinations of nature.

The foothold in this realm, according to Kant, not only manifests itself in our capacity of free will, but also gives each of us infinite individual worth. Each and every person is an end, endowed with absolute values and priceless dignity. To be an end is to have one's own purposes. The direct implication of this is that it is wrong and unreasonable to use or exploit another person merely as a means to some end of our own. In other words, it may be economically "rational" to use and exploit others, as for instance a free rider would, but it is definitely not reasonable to do so in the sense here of reason. This was the problem with the Wicksteed-Robbins approach discussed in Chapter 3.

It is helpful to mention one more of Kant's distinctions which ties in with what we saw through Maslow. The physical Phenomenal Man is not only incapable of anything beyond self-interest. We can also understand that his will, motives, and tastes are purely *subjective,* colored by his conceptions of happiness, which are his desires. In contrast, the spiritual Noumenal Person has the potential of egoless action and has a will informed by purely *objective* considerations. That is, in being guided by *reason* alone, ends became common ends because reason is not just one's own reason. Of course, as soon as self-interested rationality and incentives intrude, the chosen action is no longer purely selfless or purely objective.

Meanwhile, economists since Hume and Smith have been writing as if free will and a moral self do not really exist. All actions are assumed to be motivated by considerations of individual advantage no matter how broadly the terms individual advantage end up being defined. Everything is seen as subjective; all values, judgments, oughts, or principles are no different than any want, opinion, urge, or taste. This is well illustrated in the economic perspective of altruism. Following Wicksteed and Robbins, economic theory defined altruism as just another taste, "a taste for altruism." Let us look at how such a world of interacting rational men compares with one where the reasonable self is also granted a place.

The Question of Altruism

The term "a taste for altruism" comes out of the economist's belief that if altruism exists, it is only because my bundle of goods that gives me utility may include your utility, or goods that give you utility. Another way of saying this is that your pleasure gives me pleasure, and this is what altruism is. This is seen as a result of the interdependence of utility functions. My utility function and your utility function are seen to have common points. So just as you may have a taste for chocolates, I can have a taste for altruism. This may mean that I would be happy if you had a chocolate to enjoy, or, in general, I feel good when you do.

Note in the above that my feeling good is taken to be no different *in kind* than your feeling good. You enjoy a chocolate, and my feeling good about this is just like your enjoyment of the chocolate, or my own enjoyment of the chocolate. This altruism, then, is nothing other than my ability to vicariously experience pleasure in your pleasure. Now, there is nothing wrong with this in itself, and it does describe something that occurs. A person has a good time and tells somebody an exciting story about that experience, and the other person enjoys that story and can personally participate in the excitement. But, unfortunately, this does not really describe altruism. The term altruism, as coined in the last century by the French sociologist Auguste Comte, meant "the discipline and eradication of self-centered desire, and a life devoted to the good of others."[4]

This phrase, "good of others," shows the problem of the economist's conception of altruism. The good of others refers to another's needs and well-being, and not necessarily their tastes or wants. You may be overweight and should stay away from chocolates, but you just love them and cannot resist—even though they are *no good for you*. The genuine altruist does not say, "this is great that you're eating chocolates, because you really must love them a lot. Go ahead and have some more." That person would be a pusher or enabler in the language of the psychology of addiction, and not an altruist. A real altruist would urge you to stop eating chocolates, because although you may like the taste of chocolates, it is not in your best interest to eat them.

Therefore, we can see that an individual's tastes or pleasures are of a different type than the other person's altruistic concern or caring for that individual. The tastes or "goods" that are contained in the utility function are of a different order or quality than the good of altruism, so that that good cannot be part of the standard utility function. This problem shows us again what is wrong with the reductionist concept of one-dimensional or mono-utility.

Second Order Preferences and the Higher Self

A very clear and penetrating elucidation of this problem, with the implications of the solution, came to light in 1971 when Harry G. Frankfurt published a landmark article that has inspired countless social scientists and philosophers ever since.[5]

Frankfurt makes a distinction between what he calls *first* order desires and *second* order desires. Examples of first order desires, wants, or preferences, are what one finds talked about in all economic textbooks. Sentences such as "I desire to eat chocolate," I want meat," "I feel like watching a little TV right now," and "I would like a cigarette," all express first order wants. All human beings as well as all members of the animal kingdom share desires of this type. Economics operates as if all desires and preferences are of this type only.

But human beings have a particular and distinctive capacity in that they are able to reflect on their desires and evaluate them. So, we might find someone saying, "I wish I didn't watch so much TV," or, "I wish I could give up smoking." What Frankfurt recognized is that these kinds of statements, while also being desires or preferences, are preferences about preferences or second order preferences. All preferences can be seen as evaluations. "I like to smoke," is one evaluation and "I hate to smoke" is another evaluation. But the statement, "I like to smoke, but I wish I could give it up," can be seen as an evaluation of an evaluation, and thus of a different type. Therefore, the statement, "I have some pretty awful desires," is a perfectly sensible and meaningful human statement, but one that has been completely excluded from being understood within the framework of conventional one-dimensional or one-self economics.

What Frankfurt's analysis points to is that, like it or not, conventional economics is the economics of pigeons, dogs, rats; indeed, the very animals studied in behavioristic psychology, but not of humans as humans. Frankfurt uses the term "wantons" to refer to these creatures and humans operating on these low levels. More precisely, a wanton in Frankfurt's terms is someone whose "desires move him to do certain things, without its being true of him either that he wants to be moved by those desires or that he prefers to be moved by other desires."[6] If Frankfurt is right, then conventional economics sadly emerges as nothing but the economics of wantons. Furthermore, to touch again on a point in the previous chapter, this wanton is also rational in the sense that economics uses that term. All the formal requirements defining rational behavior for the economist are fully present. These requirements are called the axioms of rational behavior and include, among other elements, transitivity and comparability. If he wants something he will duly employ his 'reason' (understood in its economic garb) to deliberate the best possible way to obtain it. Frankfurt's wanton is a very Rational Economic Man.

Self-Consciousness as the Basis for the Dual-Self

Man's self-reflective ability, the ability to have second order preferences or evaluations, means that the self can be an object to itself. This is referred to as self-awareness or self-consciousness. An animal is conscious, but it differs from human beings in that it is not self-conscious.

This self-consciousness is the very basis of the dual-self. The two selves should not be seen as two static entities that exist separately and side-by-side, but rather, they are the duality principle inherent in the human capacity for self-reflection. When I say, "I want a hamburger," there is the *I* and the *hamburger,* and they are referred to as subject and object. However, when I say something like, "I wish I could give up hamburgers," we note that there are two I's here, which are contained in the phrase "I_2 wish I_1 could give up hamburgers." I_1, the subject of the first statement, becomes an object for I_2 in the second statement—thus the dual-self. In the second statement the identification shifts from I_1, desiring the hamburger, to I_2, wanting not to desire the hamburger. Besides this shift in self-identification, we can also note that this example is fairly representative of the nature of second order preferences. The first order self, the one that wants the hamburger, is generally more identified with the skin-encapsulated ego than the second order self. This I_1, identifying with the body, craves a hamburger and tasting it would feel good. The second order self (I_2) identifies with concerns beyond one's body, perhaps the principle of not killing animals, or the issue of world hunger (implied by the huge amount of grain that is needed to feed animals in order to produce a hamburger).

The existence of this self-reflective capacity makes not only for a dual-self, but, in William James' term, a divided self. The full surrender of the lower to the higher is rarely easy, but we could say, just as Robbins did about self-interest, that the conflict between higher and lower or between second order and first order preferences is "so much the stuff of our everyday experience that it has only to be stated to be recognized as obvious." The real human condition involves this everyday tension and struggle. If we define the first order self as the economist's usual "maximizer," or maximizing self, then the presence of the second order self allows for the possibility of *restraints* on that maximization, so that we have *restrained* maximization. No such idea is logically possible without the dual-self.

Economists attempt to get around this in their usual way by positing, along with other desires or tastes, a "taste for moral commitment" or a "taste for non-maximization," but we have already discussed the problem with this kind of conception in the phrase "a taste for altruism." As economist Harvey Leibenstein has pointed out, all tastes for non-maximization lead to a direct logical contradiction: A person is seen as maximizing by acting on his inclination not to maximize.[7]

We should also note here that the restraining higher self is different from the classic Freudian super ego, although it may superficially appear to be similar. Unlike the super ego, the higher self is not externally imposed by parental authority or otherwise. It comes out of our innate human capacity to be self-reflective. Of course, guidance by our higher self, or conscience, is anything but infallible. All too often, well-intended actions end up having unintended deplorable consequences. Yet through a critical and open-minded attitude, we can learn to consistently reform–or better, fine-tune–our intuition and moral capacity to reason; and by this very process we learn to critically reevaluate long-held cultural values and personal beliefs. This postulation of restraint on maximization amounts to recognizing "inner obligation" or moral commitment. We are often bound by such considerations or obligations whether it maximizes our "utility" or not; in such cases, it is said that we act by an inner necessity, an inner need for personal integrity, self-respect, self-actualization, or ego transcendence.

To illustrate what a difference this makes let us reexamine the mundane coffee example of the last chapter. As a coffee lover, I buy a lot of coffee beans, usually an assortment from many countries/regions, including some from Brazil. Now Brazilian coffee gets cheaper due to some unilateral unfair move that reduces its cost, say, the breaking of a labor contract. As a utility maximizer, I will obey the law of demand and exhibit a tendency to buy more Brazilian coffee. But as a moral being, I may very well condemn such action and, out of commitment to principles of fair play, boycott Brazilian coffee. As a result, I will, when responding to the lower market price, *reduce* my consumption. It seems that violating the law of demand may indeed be irrational from the one-self economic point of view, but my "irrationality" is certainly not emotional or arbitrary but instead quite reasonable. It is simply a manifestation of an end that eludes standard economics: a commitment to fairness that effectively restrains a gut-orientated maximizing inclination.

The Economist Fights Back: Overarching Utility

The actor is the ego. It can identify with the concerns of the higher self or it cannot. If it does not, we have the ordinary utility-maximizing ego described by the economist which is literally driven by its desires and inclinations and uses its reason to accomplish these goals. But in identifying with the higher self, the ego engages in what can be called restrained maximization or commitment. So, for instance, one of these restraints could be a deeply held commitment to the value of fairness. If so, the agent would show a cooperative spirit and abstain from free riding.

We can think of this as two different egos; one is the unrestrained maximizing ego, the other the self-restrained, committed, or principled ego. Each will have its own way of ranking alternative actions. Let us examine this with our previous example of liking meat versus abstaining from meat. This can be shown by the following two alternative rankings of preferences as shown in Figure 6.1 under (B).

Figure 6.1

THE PROBLEM OF OVERARCHING UTILITY

(A)
OVERARCHING UTILITY

Meta-Ranking I	*Meta-Ranking II*
Maximizing ego	Self-restrained ego
Self-restrained ego	Maximizing ego

(B)
MAXIMIZING AND NON-MAXIMIZING ORDERINGS

Maximizing Ego	*Self-Restrained Ego*
Hamburger	Vegetarian dish
Fish sandwich	Fish sandwich
Vegetarian dish	Hamburger

In each case the different egos do the ranking according to different criteria (which in effect defines the different egos). The criterion for the first is taste alone, while the second has other values as criteria. In our example these may be the killing of animals, world hunger, or the like. (Both of these egos exist within the same individual.)

Some economists have gotten themselves to the point of recognizing such coexistence of different preference orders. There has been much talk recently of two kinds of utility, one being the ordinary kind reflected in self-interested behavior and the other a moral utility reflected in moral behavior. In our above example this could correspond to the "maximizing ego" going for taste alone, or the "self-restrained ego" which is bound by principles.

James Buchanan, for example, distinguishes between two different kinds of motivation: economic self-interest versus community. This is intriguing, yet puzzling because neither Buchanan nor most of the others who have acknowledged the existence of "moral utility" would be identified as humanistic economists.[8] On the contrary, they happen to be, as in the case of Buchanan, economists with a reputation for ardently pushing the all-is-self-interest school of Rational Economic Man.

The solution to this apparent paradox is to be found in the way economists "solve" the problem of motivational alternatives issuing in two preference orders.[9] Buchanan, for example, after having distinguished self-interest from community, tries to show that this new moral-ethical category can be contained within the old utility-maximization model.[10] This is accomplished by a two-stage process where an agent first maximizes an "overarching utility function," one that contains as items both self-interested utility and the so-called moral utility. Depending on the outcome of that initial calculation, the agent then proceeds to operate either with the self-interested ego or the moral ego.

So, using our example above, what the economist proposes is that the two egos would first be ranked themselves, which would be a ranking of the rankings or overarching utility. Economist Amartya Sen has also called this a "meta-ranking."[11] Therefore, the agent would have a choice between the meta-rankings as shown in Figure 6.1 under (A).

Then, depending on this first choice, that of "overarching utility," the agent would then proceed to the second choice as shown under (B). He or she would make a choice between the two alternative rankings of preferences, either according to the maximizing ego with hamburgers first, or according to the restrained ego with the vegetarian dish first.

In this way the economist tries to show that examination of different kinds of utilities can be accommodated within the usual maximization framework. This is done by bringing in the concept of two stages of choice, each of them a separate maximization. Thus no problem is presented to standard utility theory by a principle of community or commitment (or higher self).

However, it does not work. The problem with it is that the two stages of choice are not independent of one another. Once the agent has made the first choice in this two-stage sequence–that of the so-called overarching utility–the second choice is fixed and there really is no second choice. So from a maximization standpoint there cannot be two stages and it all reduces back to the first stage as the example shows. Let us say that the agent has chosen meta-ranking I which places what we have called the maximizing ego first (in Figure 6.1 under [A]). Once this is done, the agent *must* choose the following preference order: hamburger, fish sandwich, vegetarian dish. It would be contradictory and meaningless to choose meta-ranking I and then choose the preference order of the self-restrained ego in Figure 6.1 (B): vegetarian dish, fish sandwich, hamburger.

The economist probably assumes that a two-stage utility choice is possible because he or she imagines that the two-stage choice process is parallel to a means/ends choice distinction. In such a case it certainly is possible to have a legitimate two-stage process.

Let us say that the person wanted to decide to go to Paris or Rome. That is the choice corresponding to the economist's overarching utility, and in this case represents the choice of ends (or goals). Then the agent would decide how he or she wanted to travel, let us say, either by car, train, or plane, and this corresponds to the choice in Figure 6.1 (B), or in this case the choice of means. However, the economist does not have this situation because the distinction between ends and means is already contained in Figure 6.1 (A), with the two egos being the ends and the means. The information in Figure 6.1 (B) is only a repeat of what is contained in Figure 6.1 (A). Another way to put this is to note again that a particular kind of ego is *defined* by its preference order of items.

What the above shows us is that the choice of ends can never be a maximization choice. That kind of choice can only be confined to means. The concept of utility as used in economics always must refer to means and not ends. To try to have it otherwise the economist runs into contradiction as shown above. He would wind up saying that the vegetarian could choose to eat meat and still be a vegetarian.

In broader terms the economist here is courting what is known as Russell's Paradox. A set of items cannot be contained in itself as a member of that set. The economist is trying to say something similar to the assertion that an individual can choose choice, but this is a contradiction. The problem comes up for the economist whenever he or she talks about two kinds of interest or two kinds of utility, such as self-interest versus community interest, or between short-term interest and long-term interest, and still endeavors to keep the analysis within a one-dimensional utility framework.

Once the economist admits that there are different kinds of utility, that is tantamount to obviating the concept of utility. Different kinds of "utility" mean different ends, and the choice between these ends must be made on a basis other than maximization of utility, since utility itself is a single end.* A value cannot be the basis of judging between itself and other values.

The Emergence of Free Will

But what is the basis of choice between ends or values? How do we choose among different preference orders, one sanctioned by the higher self, the other not, if it is not possible to apply the mechanisms of choice theory to solve the problem? The answer to this question may be startling, but it is an answer that restores fundamental human dignity to the image of the person in the social sciences.

All these terms, and many others that could be used—utility, mechanisms, criteria, calculi—have something in common. They are all deterministic concepts. That is, they are ways of explaining how things or events (such as choices) are determined. This is a foundational concept in standard social science, taking its cue from the cause and effect orientation of the physical sciences. In this case the effect is the particular preference ordering and the cause is utility maximization.

---

* In the language of formal rational choice theory, utility maximization can be applied to ordering these meta-preferences if they are not only transitive but also comparable. We can see that the condition, comparability, is violated by the choosing of a choice criterion, which is foreshadowed for us by the logical contradiction. The economist's comparability assumption implies that there is a single choice criterion by which alternatives, including alternative choice criterion, can be evaluated. But that criterion must itself be a member of the set of all choice criteria, so that it would have to be compared to itself and chosen between itself! Again, contradiction reigns, and the conventional solution does not work.

Everything is determined, and to explain something is to describe the principles of its determination. Therefore, utility maximization is seen as determining a preference ordering.

What we see here is that when all these deterministic concepts are stripped away, and stripped away they must be, what is left is simply nothing at all, or–in another word–freedom. And this freedom, which comes to us in the context of the logic of this discussion, is nothing other than the age-old concept of free will. What we find is that lying above all determinations, causes, principles of rational choice, mechanisms, utility calculus, and so forth, is nothing other than freedom itself. The ultimate choice is free choice, which is precisely what it says. If it is free, it has no antecedents, no determining principles, and no maximization. We have no way of "explaining" free choice precisely because it is free.

The Everyday Evidence of a Dual-Self: Conflict of Interest

There is a type of phenomenon that is commonly observed and widespread which presents severe problems for the standard self-interest conception, while at the same time lending great support to the dual-self idea. This phenomenon is referred to as the conflict of interest.

At the outset, to avoid unnecessary confusion (especially by economists) it may be helpful to point out that we are taking the concept of conflict of interest in the way it is generally used in ordinary language. In particular, we do not interpret the term as it is often used in decision theory, to indicate the conflict or incompatibility of the goals of two or more actors. Rather, the concept is meant to refer to an ethical conflict relating incompatible goals *within* a single actor.

What is striking about this problem for economics lies in the very term conflict of interests. This basic social concept shows the inadequacies of a one-self model. If there is just one self-interest, there can be no conflict of interests. For there to be a conflict of interests there must be two different and incompatible self-interests, and thus the two selves from which these different interests are generated.

According to the *Guide to American Law,* conflict of interest is "a term used to describe the situation in which a public official or fiduciary who, contrary to the obligation and absolute duty to act for the benefit of the public or a designated individual, exploits the relationship for personal benefit, typically pecuniary." And it goes on to provide the following illustration:

Certain relationships in which people or the general public place their trust and confidence in someone to act in their best interests, are recognized at law. When an individual has the responsibility to represent another person–whether as administrator, attorney, executor, government official or trustee–a clash between professional obligations and personal interests arises if the individual tries to perform that duty while at the same time trying to achieve personal gain. The appearance of a conflict of interest is present if there is a potential for the personal interests of an individual to clash with fiduciary duties, such as when a client has his or her attorney commence an action against a company in which the attorney is the major stockholder.[12]

It is significant that the paradigm cases of conflict of interest arise in cases of public servants and professionals. In the case of the former the idea of *service* is explicit, while in the latter it remains implicit. However, according to *Webster's Dictionary,* the word "profess" is derived from the middle English "professed," meaning "bound by a vow." In joining a profession we are in a sense openly declaring or "avowing" to be the votaries of a solemn promise, a promise to devote oneself to some act or service. Obviously, the type of service that is involved here is not self-serving but a commitment to identify oneself with something other than one's ego.

Presently, we are concerned with the ramifications of the conflict of interest doctrine for the so stubbornly persistent economic presupposition that all is self-interest and maximization. The concept of conflict of interest doctrine clearly implies an image of the person that is different than that–and twofold. There is first of all an agent with a preference order that he or she is bent on maximizing. He may be foolish or he may be prudent, but in either case he has his interests which are ultimately self-regarding and grounded in desires related to his lower self, his ego. In this logic of economics there can never be a conflict between two self-interests or purposes, the one-dimensional agent has only *one* overall interest and he is sure to choose that preference which will maximize his particular preference function. No conflict here except mutually conflicting means, as reflected in the idea of opportunity cost.

However, the idea of a conflict of interest clearly implies *another* and conflicting interest within the same person. It arises from his acting by identifying with something other than his narrow self: the public interest, the common interest, a client's interest, and so forth. In the case of professional obligation, or where the protection of a fiduciary interest is entrusted to an agent, what is involved is a commitment, an obligation, a loyalty to something explicitly distinct from one's personal interest. And that commitment implies personal integrity and the concomitant trust of others, or the public, in his or her integrity.

Humanistic economics clearly recognizes what economic orthodoxy ends up denying: the possibility of an inner conflict of interest, a conflict between two incommensurable interests, one of the ego-self, the other of the higher self. And such recognition, as we will see, is far from irrelevant when considering economic behavior, institutions, and policies.

The Relevance of the Dual-Self for Economic Theory

Recognizing a dual nature of the person applies directly to such topics as behavior involving public goods, the prisoner's dilemma, the motivation to work, and consumer boycotts. Work motivation and the prisoner's dilemma are of particular relevance to economics, and we have already pointed to it in Chapter 4, "Tale of Two Ford Plants."

Let us focus here on another example: the concept of what goes under the name of *implicit contracts*. There are unwritten contracts that have never been formally negotiated, but are instead based on some unarticulated understanding of how we are to interact with one another. Such an orientation is particularly called for by the *Guide to American Law*'s observation that the potential for conflict of interest is involved where "groups, associates and enterprises usually operate on informal and unwritten codes of conduct," suggesting that implicit contracts have some sort of intimate connection with the idea of professional conduct and obligation.

The idea of implicit contracts is no longer taboo in economics. For the last two decades economists have been exploring them. That economics, the theory of exchange and contracts, should finally have acknowledged and analyzed such implicit contracts has to be seen, at first sight, as an encouraging sign. As we take a closer look at this pioneering work, however, it becomes quickly apparent that we may be witnessing another instance where theories projecting their own narrow image of reality are ultimately helpless when confronted with the real world.

The problem with implicit contracts, viewed from the conventional economics perspective, is that they often cannot be easily enforced. One reason for this is that they are almost by definition vague and unspecific. A party to such a general understanding will often find it in their interest to withhold total compliance, especially when the degree of non-compliance is likely to go undetected and therefore cause no harm to either one's social reputation or in terms of retaliation by the other side. A good illustration of this possibility is the amount of effort an employee is expected to contribute to his employer. Within the context of self-interest, it certainly pays to withhold extra effort. Similarly, sellers of fresh fruit or fish, for example, have an incentive to underperform by cutting corners in representing the actual freshness of their goods. Or, self-interested guests, dining out at a fancy restaurant in a city that they never expect to visit again, would definitely have an incentive to neglect proper tipping of the waitress, assuming, of course, that the tip is not included in the bill.

Now, of course, many workers do not shy away from extra effort: Many, if not most, farmers and fishermen are committed to fully deliver in terms of freshness. Similarly, most one-time guests dining in restaurants can be observed to leave a tip that is generally understood to be appropriate. But, they mainly do so not because of self-interest but because they feel morally obliged. And it is this feeling of moral obligation that greatly facilitates the carrying out of transactions with a minimum of constraint, thereby reducing transaction costs and encouraging exchange. Imagine commerce marked by mutual suspicion and uncertainty. It certainly takes much pleasure out of dining out when the self-interested waitress will fight back by reducing her own effort to the lowest common denominator of effort. Taxi drivers would rarely find the shortest route to a destination. Medical doctors would engage even more in defensive tactics (e.g., ordering unnecessary and expensive tests) just to decrease the likelihood of malpractice suits. Thus we would find bureaucratic countermeasures, such as more elaborate contracts, more fine print, more regulatory interference, which all tend to choke economic activity.

Perhaps we have yet to get to such a stage of total social and moral stalemate, but from the standpoint of humanistic economics it is a sickness of modern society, a society that operates increasingly on the principle of self-interest. Economists may deplore the increased fragility of implicit contracts, especially in view of the high economic costs. But as economists they have little to suggest by way of preventive or ameliorative action. From an all-is-self-interest model, this is simply a "positive fact," i.e., how things are.

Humanistic economics, on the other hand, does see it as a problem and does have something to say about it. If we can encourage more identification with the higher self, we will better economics, leading to a better economy. Humanistic economics addresses itself to that identification, as we shall see.

Another example of the relevance of an economics going beyond self-interest pertains to the macroeconomy. Suppose inflationary pressure is to some extent the result of market power, where strong trade unions aim for socially irresponsible gains and strong corporations fight back by raising their prices to be swallowed by the more unorganized consumer. If such unrestrained power is the problem, how can we induce moral restraint that would benefit the common good? We find an answer to that question in the next section.

Preparing the Way for Higher Self-Identification: Fairness and Security

A worthwhile, relevant economics should be able to recognize voluntary restraint and suggest ways that would encourage it, rather than ignore the problem and in the process misguide policy makers towards inadvertently promoting the decay of the common good. The contribution of a humanistic economics to this very question is addressed through two principles: fairness and security.

The Need for Basic Fairness

When people discuss the tax system, a key word that usually arises in connection with it is that of "fairness." People want a tax system that is fair. It is generally accepted that if a tax system is perceived as fair, there will be a lessened propensity for people to try to defraud the system and avoid paying taxes—their fair share of taxes, as it is often put.

The concept of fairness also shows up with no less frequency in other areas of the economy as well, such as wages and prices. People want a fair wage for a fair day's work, and do not want to see others skimming off the cream. They also want to pay prices that are fair, and not be cheated or "gouged" at the marketplace. Trade unions can be expected to restrain their demands in a society where they are confident that the distribution of national income among the various classes is guided by considerations of fairness. In contrast, as long as the industrial actors fail to see any rationale behind the distribution of income, they will be relatively insensitive to the public interest. A trade economist has been quoted as saying, "In a free-for-all, we are part of the all." How can we expect moral acting in an economy that justifies social outcomes solely on the basis of an impersonal, competitive interaction between agents?

While many economists would admit that fairness is an important variable in an economy, they generally see little place for it in the science of economics because they believe that fairness is largely, if not totally, a matter of subjective opinion. One person's fairness is not another's, and there seems to be no objective way to decide such differences. Humanistic economics is able to see through this apparent dilemma.

Exploitation. The basis of this approach to fairness lies first in recognizing the existence of market or economic power as discussed in Chapter 2. Certainly one of the difficulties that conventional economics has in being able to deal with the concept of fairness is that it does not recognize the existence of power in the economy, that some economic agents or organizations are more powerful than others. Once we have a way of admitting the existence of power, the way is then open to objectively deal with fairness because we now have a definition within economics of the idea of exploitation.

Because there are needs, there is also power. If people's basic needs are not met, they cannot survive. Those who have a large command over economic resources have power over others who have a lesser command over economic resources and typically a critically limited ability to meet their needs.

This kind of power difference makes for the possibility that there will be exploitation, that some economic agents will be able to use their power advantage to exploit others. Unfairness, then, is the existence of exploitation, and fairness is its opposite—non-exploitation. The objective possibilities of dealing with fairness lie in this above analysis. We now have a working definition of fairness, which is non-exploitation.

In exploitation one agent is taking advantage of another or others. We already have a paradigm case of this occurring in a common economic topic that we have already discussed: the free rider. This problem is generally seen as arising in the context of public goods, such as roads, parks, and the like, where anyone can benefit from these goods whether they pay for them or not. Economists predict that individuals will not pay for benefits if they can allow other people to pay for their costs. The free rider is thus taking advantage of others, and in this sense can be seen as exploiting them. This principle, however, can be seen as not only applying in the matter of public goods but in any economic undertaking where there are joint benefits and costs—which is to say, most economic activity—since little of it is done in isolation and most of it is joint or social.

Certainly, any business enterprise or corporation comprises a number of people putting out a product as a result of their joint efforts. In this business activity certain individuals can be "free riding," or taking advantage of others if they reap a greater portion of the benefits than they are paying for by their efforts or other input. This would mean that one who receives too much income from their work does so at the expense of the one who receives too little income from theirs, since the product of the business is a joint product. Thus the one who is underpaid subsidizes the income of the one who is overpaid, and the overpaid individual free rides on the work of the underpaid individual. In its starkest form this certainly is what slavery is all about. We see, then, that the underpaid individual is exploited by the overpaid individual, or at least by "the system" in which there is underpayment.

If we generalize this argument one step further, we arrive at a very widespread example of exploitation. All of society can be seen as putting out a joint product—and that is what the GNP is. As an economist, I may teach in a university that was built by others, travel to it on roads built by others, eat in a school cafeteria staffed and provided for by others, and teach students who pay tuition achieved through the efforts of themselves or family members, and so forth, on and on.

What does it mean, then, that we have a class of people known as "the working poor?" These are people who work for a living, who contribute to the joint national product, but their incomes from this work still puts them below the poverty level. It turns out that if an individual works forty hours a week at the minimum wage, they would fall below the poverty level as we discuss in Chapter 11. If an individual works and still does not receive enough income to meet basic needs for a minimally adequate standard of living, is not that individual exploited? Are not those others who are receiving a more than adequate income for their work in some way achieving that living at the expense, either directly or indirectly, of those who are not receiving an adequate living from their work? From this argument we would conclude that the present minimum wage is exploitative, and thus unfair. Who would want to work by choice at an endeavor that does not earn one enough to live decently? The person in this situation seems clearly to be in an unfair position. There is very little that is subjective about this conclusion. It is shaped by the objective concept of standard of living. We find, then, that society through its power relationships is able to devise a situation where some of its members contribute to the joint product but receive an inadequate portion of benefits from that joint product.

The concepts of needs, power, exploitation, and in the case of wages, relative standards of living, show us how the principle of fairness enters into the study and application of economics. Our brief exposition of this principle here certainly does not answer all the questions raised by the topic, but is put forth to show how humanistic economics incorporates it into the study of economics. Later chapters will expound on these principles and attempt to show how fairness can be achieved. Now we will turn to another major catalyst, making for more moral choices.

The Basic Need for Security

More than a half century ago, John Hobson, a great economist in the humanistic tradition, articulated explicitly a basic insight in his book *Economics and Ethics* (1929):

> When moralists talk of altering human nature they are often misunderstood to mean that instincts and desires deeply implanted in our inherited animal outfit can be eradicated and others grafted on. Now no such miracles are possible or needed. But substantial changes in our environment or in our social institutions can apply different stimuli to human nature and evoke different physical responses. For example, by alterations in the organisation and government of businesses and industries, so as to give security of employment and of livelihood to workers, and some increased "voice" to them in the conditions of work, it seems reasonably possible to modify the stress of personal gainseeking and to educate a clearer sense of social solidarity in the discontent of modern workers, and it increases with an education that reveals the "social" cause of that insecurity in the absence of any reliable economic government. Security is, therefore, the first essential in any shift of the relative appeal to personal and social motives.[13]

Hobson stressed institutional security as a primary catalyst for overcoming our self-interested animal instincts and opening the way for a more socially responsible disposition. In this he anticipated by more than a decade Abraham Maslow's discovery that a satisfied security need paves the way to social and moral motivation.

With this basic realization, morality is brought into the pale of economics and social policy. But we need to point out that security does not guarantee morality, and neither is it necessary. All that we claim is that it has a facilitating influence by making moral choices less heroic. Such a claim we believe appeals to common sense, and not surprisingly we find it traditionally reflected in many institutional domains of our society.

To illustrate this, let us go back to the case of implicit contracts and the problem of designing institutions so that professionals, public servants, and others are not discouraged from following their professional commitments in spite of conflicting personal interests. Contending that all this was recognized by society at large, long before Hobson and Maslow, we should find the idea institutionally enshrined wherever the threat of conflict of interest problems loom largest: where the public needs to rely on the trustworthiness of professionals or civil servants to refrain from maximization and pursue excellence.

Not surprisingly, we find general provisions of relative job security in the employment of federal judges, university professors, and higher level civil servants. In the case of (federal) judges and university professors, the job security is in explicit terms of lifetime tenure.

It may be of interest to note that in the discussions over our Federal Constitution, such tenure provisions for the judiciary branch were never even questioned as long as a judge would be "in good behavior." The Virginia Plan and the New Jersey Plan, as well as the Pinckney Plan, all agreed in this fundamental respect; the only debate centered around the question of whether the executive or the legislative branch would appoint the judges. Moreover, Alexander Hamilton in the *Federalist Papers* explicitly recognized such lifetime tenure (called "the standard of good behavior") as "the citadel of public justice," and the key "to secure a steady, upright and impartial administration of the laws."

The provision of job security observed in such public institutions as the courts, the federal government and universities, is often, in a more informal and somewhat more limited manner, found in the private sector as well. Observe, for example, how bank tellers are induced to fully share their information with their trainees by in effect assuring them that the trainees, once trained, will not compete for their jobs.

Once we part with the deeply ingrained all-is-maximization presupposition of modern economic theory, the ground is cleared for enabling a more human economy that strives for excellence, not just in areas of law and academia but elsewhere as well.

A New Choice, in Theory and in Practice

Recognizing that human beings have a hierarchy of needs opens the way to seeing that our selves are dual, and thus we are confronted with the necessity, agony, and grandeur of choice.

Conventional economics not only misses all of this but obscures it as well. It sometimes presents itself as the "science of choice," but this choice turns out to be no choice at all. Economics has also done the same with other concepts, such as rationality and competition. It uses these terms but, as we have seen particularly in the case of rationality, presents us with an idiosyncratic and distorted version of what these concepts are supposed to mean. In the same way it has presented us with a distorted version of what the person is.

A hierarchy of needs implies two poles, and each of these poles corresponds to a different kind of self. Since the two selves are polar–let us say a north and a south or a higher and lower–one cannot go in both directions at the same time, and this is where a choice has to be made. That is what real choice is about. The mere calculating of values and then the "choice" of the highest value, as the idea of self-interest maximization proposes, is really not choice but only arithmetic. Real choice is qualitative, not quantitative.

It is interesting that an increasing number of economists talk about such concepts as enlightened self-interest (implying an unenlightened self-interest) and self-interest versus community interest, but do not yet realize that this means a dual-self, as we have shown in our discussion of the fallacy of overarching utility. We have already discussed the famous example of Lionel Robbins saying that the idea of self-interest does not exclude man from being an "ascetic," or a "sensualist," and Robbins concludes that "he is more likely a little of both," but does not see that you cannot be both at the same time, and thus cannot maximize across the two.[14] The two are incommensurable because they are opposite directions, and thus a choice has to be made. You cannot maximize between north and south.

The beauty of the dual-self concept is that while it takes in the complete compass of human nature and the human condition, it is at the same time a simple concept and at least quite as elegant as old man self-interest.

Economics, and to a large extent our society, has for hundreds of years now pursued the path of single self-interest maximization, and for a while the costs of this headlong rush were hidden. There was still an abundance of the meadows of trust, community, values, and ideals, not to mention the physical environment, that could absorb the detritus of this machine's smoke-spewing wheels. But those days are rapidly receding. The meadows cannot hold any more, and an increasing erosion of life and its qualities occurs. Meadowlands everywhere have been filled with fast food strips and their refuse–both socially and literally.

Economics can now take a new turn, and the dual-self theory provides the equipment to do this. It can bring back into our lives–or even forward into our lives–a clearing of the smoke, a clearing of the waste, a renewal of the meadowlands, and a place for us.

References

1. Gerald Marwell and Ruth E. Ames, "Economists Free Ride, Does Anybody Else?," *Journal of Public Economics,* 15 (1981), pp. 295-310.
2. George Stigler, "Economics, the Imperial Science," *Scandinavian Journal of Economics,* 86:3 (1984), pp. 304.
3. Werner Hirsch, *Law and Economics,* New York: Academic Press, 1979, p. xii.
4. Wilbur Long, "Altruism" in D. D. Runes, ed., *Dictionary of Philosophy.* Totowa, New Jersey: Littlefield, Adams, 1981, p. 10.
5. Harry G. Frankfurt, "Freedom of the Will and the Concept of the Person," *Journal of Philosophy,* 68:1 (1971), pp. 5-20.
6. *ibid.* p. 10.
7. Harvey Leibenstein, "A Branch of Economics Is Missing: Micro-Micro Theory," *Journal of Economic Literature,* XVII (June 1975), pp. 495-496.
8. James Buchanan, "Markets, States and the Extent of Morals," *American Economic Review,* 62:2 (1978), p. 366.
9. See Amitai Etzioni, "The Case for a Multiple-Utility Conception," *Economics and Philosophy,* 2 (1986), particularly p. 166.
10. Buchanan, *op. cit.*
11. Amartya Sen, "Rational Fools: A Critique of the Behavioral Foundation of Economic Theory," *Philosophy and Public Affairs,* 6 (1977), pp. 317-344.
12. *Guide to American Law.* New York: West Publishing, 1983, p. 143.
13. John A. Hobson, *Economics and Ethics.* London: D.C. Heath, 1929, p. 234.
14. Lionel Robbins, *An Essay on the Nature and Significance of Economic Science* [1932]. 3rd edition. London: Macmillan Press, 1984, p. 95.

Chapter 7

WELFARE ECONOMICS: BEYOND THE OLD AND THE NEW

As with the social sciences, modern economics prides itself as being a *positive* science, "positive" in the sense of merely describing, analyzing, and predicting what *is*. Therefore, any economics aiming at prescribing and telling us what ought to be is declared as "value-ridden" or normative.

This type of differentiation, veritably drilled into every student in an early chapter of almost any economics textbook, operates on the philosophical preconception that the two domains can be reasonably held apart. Yet when reading the ensuing chapters of the same text, the students will quickly discover that far from only describing what is, economic theory has much to say on what *ought to be* as well. They are taught that there ought to be less monopoly and more free competition, that there ought to be more free trade and less tariff protection, and that rationing is best done by market price. And students eventually find that prescribing is not improper after all, since alternative economic policies or institutions have to somehow be evaluated and government economic policies, one way or another, justified on theoretical grounds. In particular, the economist has a need to inform us when reliance on individual self-interest and free markets produces the "efficient" results and when it does not.

As indicated already in Chapter 4, we therefore have today an entire field in economics that deals with the way various economic arrangements and policies affect the welfare or well-being of all members of society; it goes under the name of *welfare economics*. For the humanistically inclined student, this field is of primary importance; not only does it deal with evaluations and values but it also focuses on the real world, its problems, and the ways to help bring about a better world. In fact, as we will see later, humanistic economics is really essentially a welfare economics with a human quality. At the same time, it is radically different from the standard welfare economics one encounters in the textbooks of the present time. In order to better appreciate the humanistic perspective, it is necessary to gain an understanding of the conventional alternative, where it came from, how it evolved, and to know more about its weaknesses and vulnerabilities, especially as pertaining to its application in real world decision making.

The Evolution of Welfare Economics

Although many contemporary textbooks end up inadvertently conveying the impression that welfare economics is something relatively new–a product of the twentieth century–it is generally agreed that the history of economics is also the history of welfare economics. It dates back to Adam Smith and even earlier. Let us first look at the kind of welfare economics that Smith inaugurated; an approach that was to dominate economics for almost a century.

The Classical Welfare Economics

In economics the classical period starts with Adam Smith's *Wealth of Nations* and extends up to the marginal utility revolution of the early 1870s. Besides Smith, it also includes such figures as David Ricardo and John Stuart Mill.

What unites the classical economists is a perception that the goal of any political economy is to enhance the wealth of nations, to secure a maximum growth of national income. For Smith that meant extending the market: increasing the division of labor or specialization, expanding free trade, rapid accumulation, and a growing labor force productively employed. Sound political economy was to serve the statesman in providing intelligent advice on what kind of policies enabled the most rapid growth of economic output. David Ricardo, too, addressed the same basic problem, but looked for solutions in the way the economic pie gets distributed. The more that goes to landlords, he theorized, the less that is available for the wealth-accumulating industrialists. His analysis demonstrated that tariffs protecting domestic agriculture from corn imports had a negative effect in this respect and his analysis was instrumental in the parliamentary repeal of the Corn Laws of 1846. The last of the classical economists, J.S. Mill, based his own political economy first and foremost on production and its technology, and only secondarily on exchange.

All these early economic theorists deemphasized consumption. Instead, they assumed that higher production would bring with it increased consumption and more welfare for all. They believed the road to growth to be paved with competition, a healthy dose of laissez-faire, and anything else that would enhance the productivity and size of the labor force. This emphasis on growth implied a long-run, dynamic point of view, where only land and natural resources were fixed, but everything else (including technology) was in constant flux and ready to be molded into a proper form by economic institutions or policy makers.

Neoclassical Welfare Economics

After the marginalist revolution of the 1870s, economists radically reconsidered the economic problem, or the goal of economics. The satisfaction of consumer wants now took center stage. Efficiency meant the best possible satisfaction of *given* wants and market demand with the *presently available* resources and technologies. The ticket to an efficient economy was once again a free market economy, but the highway to economic welfare was no longer the avenue of maximum growth. Instead, it was built on such idealized notions as "*perfect* competition," "perfect mobility of factors of production," "perfect information on the part of economic agents," and so forth. In short, economics became more of an abstract exercise, a game to be played on an increasingly theoretical level by academics eager to demonstrate their command of elegant formalism and logical rigor.

Against this new background, Alfred Marshall, the neoclassical economist of that period, felt that for the sake of practical use by the policy maker, a less formal and more pragmatically realistic type of theory was required to complement the highly abstract economics with its assumption of the various "perfections" for efficient resource allocation. This new theory we now call neoclassical welfare economics. It still accepted the general idea of free competition as a desirable framework, but now focused on various concrete *exceptions,* on cases where laissez-faire and private interests would *not* lead to the common good.

Henry Sidwick discussed cases where socially desirable goods and services (such as lighthouses and reforestation) are not in the individual private interest and as a result have to be provided by the public. Alfred Marshall used his analysis to suggest that efficiency might demand government subsidies to some industries exhibiting losses with economies of scale, e.g., utilities. These, and many more propositions of welfare, were intertwined with the more positive microeconomic price theory. It probably would have occupied a more extensive and prominent part had Marshall—who was very much concerned with development of human character and the healthy exercise of the higher human faculties through meaningful work—not also been occupied with the question of precise scientific measurement. And for that he preferred to center his economics around prices and the measuring rod of money. If economics was to be an exact science, it would have to confine itself to studying those desires, aspirations, and affections of human nature that express the material domain of existence and so relate to market prices. Not surprisingly, in his *Principles* (1890) the logic of price theory came to overshadow his more sporadic and more ad hoc contributions to welfare economics. The obvious task was for someone to present in a separate and integral way a unified theory of neoclassical welfare economics. And this was accomplished by Marshall's successor at Cambridge, Arthur Pigou, with his celebrated book, *Wealth and Welfare* (1912).[1]

The Triumph and Demise of Neoclassical Welfare Economics

Pigou's welfare economics can be seen as an attempt to generalize and complete the program started with Sidwick and Marshall. Also, his analysis steers away from formalist abstraction, logical rigor, and elegance, in favor of an orientation more suitable for practical applications. But as with Marshall, Pigou restricted his analytical focus to "that part of social welfare that can be brought directly or indirectly into relation with the measuring of money."[2] He called that component of human welfare the *economic* welfare."

A good part of Pigou's welfare economics is still very much alive today, such as his distinction between social cost and private cost: Very often, he pointed out, private cost/benefit calculations lead to decisions and actions that have "spillover" effects on third parties. For example, the dumping of toxic chemicals in a river may minimize private costs, but certainly not the cost to society. Since these spillovers are *external* to the market transactions, they are today generally called "externalities." Similarly, the private benefits accruing from some actions often involve benefits to others as well. Individual efforts aimed at education could be cited. Pigou concluded that such actions would not be sufficiently undertaken and it would be the government's task to provide additional incentives for their production or use. On similar grounds, Pigou advocated government subsidies for private research activity.

Pigou's welfare economics became much more daring and controversial when he discussed poverty and the distribution of national income. The center of the controversy is found in a chapter titled "Economic Welfare and Changes in the Distribution of the National Dividend" in his book, *Economics of Welfare*. There we read that "it is evident that any transference of income from a relatively rich man to a relatively poor man of *similar temperament,* since it enables more intense wants to be satisfied at the expense of less intense wants, must increase the aggregate sum of satisfactions."[3]

Here we have an interesting but straightforward application of the hierarchy of needs (or "wants" as social scientists of those days preferred to call it). The lowest survival needs are the most urgent ones. If we tax the rich who spend much of their income on luxuries, the loss in economic welfare to them will be less than the gain in providing more necessities to the poor. Such a claim is readily accessible to a common sense recognition of hierarchical needs, a concept almost universally accepted by the early economists from Smith to Marshall. It was precisely this self-evident hierarchy that provided the foundation of the law of diminishing marginal utility. All one had to do now was to apply it to the utility of the most general good: personal income. An extra dollar of income would generate more utility to a person who was flat broke than to one enjoying a high standard of comfort. Similarly, so it would seem, an extra dollar to the poor would provide much more satisfaction than an extra dollar to the rich. Such extension, however, has definite social consequences. It allows the scientific welfare economist to advocate income transfers to the poor, not in the name of compassion but, indeed, on the basis of cold economic efficiency. With Pigou, the economist now suddenly finds himself an advocate of redistribution, a social reformer.

This issue of income transfer between persons was not all that simple, however, even apart from any controversy surrounding its reformist implications. It would only be valid if two conditions held, both of which were explicitly recognized by Pigou. First, one has to be sure that such redistribution does not have the side effect of diminishing national income. If, for example, the taxed rich would respond by working less, there would be obvious and costly side effects. Whether this is so or not is an empirical issue and to a great extent depends on the amount and kind of taxation involved. Second, there is the possibility that the poor may not have the same *capacity* to derive utility from an extra dollar as the rich. Pigou alluded to this already when he compared people "of similar temperament" in the quotation above. Later on he elaborates: "It must be conceded, of course, that, if the rich and the poor were of two races with different mental constitutions . . . the possibility of increasing welfare by this type of change would be seriously doubtful." Even within the same race, the rich man "from the nature of his upbringing and training" can be assumed to spend his income more wisely. But he counters that, "after a time–more especially if the time is long enough to allow a new generation to grow up–the [poor's] possession of such [a higher] income will make possible the development in them, through education and otherwise, of capacities and faculties adapted for the enjoyment of the enlarged income." Accordingly, "the differences in temperament and tastes between rich and poor are overcome by the very fact of a shifting of income between them."[4]

Lionel Robbins' Attack: The Debate on Interpersonal Comparisons of Utility. Nevertheless, the assumption of equal capacity for happiness was directly assailed by Lionel Robbins, and his attack led to the first round in what is now called the debate over *interpersonal comparison of utility*. Robbins claimed that when talking about (and comparing) two different individuals and their utilities, we are bound to proceed unscientifically since satisfactions of others cannot be observed. Pigou's assumption of equal human capacities may be reasonable and convenient, but, said Robbins, "there is no way of proving that the assumption rests on ascertainable fact."[5]

Seven years later, in his 1938 presidential address to the prestigious British Economics Association, Roy Harrod reminded his colleague, Robbins, that the whole basis of *any* economic recommendations depended upon assuming comparability between individuals:

> If the comparability of utility to different individuals is strictly pressed, not only are the prescriptions of the welfare school ruled out, but all prescriptions whatsoever. The economist as an advisor is completely stultified, and, unless his speculations be regarded as of paramount aesthetic value, he had better be suppressed completely. No; some sort of postulate of equality has to be assumed. But it should be carefully framed and used with great caution, always subject to the proviso "unless the contrary can be shown."[6]

Of course, Harrod is advising caution, but he concludes nevertheless–equal capacity for happiness should be assumed, unless the contrary can be shown. And this, of course, would mean that application of the concept of diminishing marginal utility recommended moves towards the equalization of wealth.

Robbins immediately responded to Harrod in an article that appeared in the next issue of the *Economic Journal*, and his answer is revealing.[7] The crux of the problem of modern economics–the fact that it is committed to a certain set of values, whether consciously or unconsciously–is laid bare in Robbins' reply. There, in 1938, in one crystalline moment of clarity the issue was defined as perhaps never before or since. Let us look carefully at Robbins' argument in his article.

He begins by admitting that originally he had found Pigou's welfare proposition appealing, and felt that the approach of counting each person as one is "less likely to lead one astray." But then he came across an incident in a story he was reading that began to stir his doubts. The story involved a British official in India who was trying to explain the egalitarian meaning of Benthamism (utilitarianism) to a high-caste Brahmin. The Brahmin replied, "But that cannot possibly be right. I am ten times as capable of happiness as that untouchable over there." Although Robbins had no sympathy for the Brahmin's position, he was disturbed that there was no scientific way to prove the Brahmin wrong. This led him to conclude that the assumption of equal capacity for happiness was strictly a moral or value judgment, and was separate from the other propositions of economics.

But this separation did not leave him content: "For it meant, as Mr. Harrod has rightly insisted, that economics as a science could say nothing by way of prescription." Therefore, Robbins accepts the necessity for economics to make this value judgment: "I was bound to admit that what I was doing was simply to carry one stage further a very common and almost universally accepted practice. All economists recognized that their prescriptions regarding policy were conditional upon the acceptance of norms lying outside economics." Robbins recognized that in order for economics to be useful it had to take a stand one way or the other–it had to decide either with "Bentham" and "Saint Paul" that all people are to be considered equal, or with the "Brahmin" and "Hitler" that they are not. Robbins is quite clear where he stands with his choice: "I think that the assumption of equality comes from outside [of economics], and that its justification is more ethical than scientific. But we all agree that it is fitting that such assumptions should be made and their implications explored with the aid of the economist's technique."[8]

In coming to terms with Harrod and Pigou, Robbins almost seems apologetic for his previous criticism: "I confess I was very surprised. . . . All that I had intended. . . ." And in his conclusion he winds up on a note that is nothing less than humanistic:

> In the realm of action, at any rate, the real difference of opinion is not between those who dispute concerning the exact area to be designated by the adjective scientific, but between those who hold that human beings should be treated as if they were equal and those who hold that they should not.[9]

Equality as the Scientific Position.   Robbins, of course, now admits that he sides with those who hold that human beings should be treated as if they were equal. No caste-laden Brahmin, he, and certainly no Hitler.

While it is encouraging to see Robbins move away from his earlier position, we should not let the matter go at that. We quoted Robbins as saying something that many economists still believe, namely, that the "assumption of equality comes from outside (of economics), and that its justification is more ethical than scientific." But we think that this belief is wrong; the assumption of equal capacity of happiness *is* the scientifically more correct assumption. The other is the less justifiable, and the less scientific.

The reason is that the concept of a capacity for happiness, or capacity for feeling, comes from a mistaken analogy. With the idea of capacity of happiness, economists have drawn on the concept of human capacities and tried to apply it to the area of feeling. Now the notion of capacity is certainly meaningful and relevant in numerous areas of human activity and ability. These can include such things as intelligence, artistic ability, strength, and so forth. We certainly differ from each other in a multitude of ways, and we can look at these differences as variations in capacity. But–and here is the crucial point–*feeling* does not represent a capacity; rather, it is the essence of what being a person is. A person feels, and a person can be happy or sad. There is really no issue of a quantity of happiness. Such a concept would reduce the capacity for humanness.

This is very clear in the area of mental retardation. By definition a retarded person certainly has less mental capacity than a normal person. But no one who has any experience with retarded people would say that they have less feeling than anyone else. They show the same joy, the same pain as anyone else, although they may express it in a less intellectual and articulate way. It is for this reason that retarded people can easily be recognized as fully human, even though they have certain diminished mental "capacities."

So, to say that people differ in this regard, capacity for feeling, is to say that all persons are not equal *as* persons. Certainly this is a self-contradictory proposition, as well as being foolish. No science that is about people could be built upon this ground, and it is wise that Robbins backed off. Unfortunately, he did not recognize that it was necessary for him to do this if there ever was to be *a science* of economics.

But Robbins' point that we cannot compare people as feeling organisms, made in the name of science, is not only ill-advised for the social sciences; it is contradicted by the way we have to live in the real world. Imagine, for instance, the implications for our legal institutions and our penal code if we thought it incorrect to assume that all people have an essentially similar capacity to endure punishment of one kind or another. Following Robbins, we could not say that a $5 parking ticket to be paid by Mr. A is less of a punishment than a $500 ticket Mr. B got for driving under the influence. Could it not be, the scientific economist would ask, that Mr. B is a "highly efficient pleasure machine" (a phrase economists like to use to refer to someone's capacity to derive happiness from life)?[10] Has Mr. B. a very high capacity to feel, and does he tend to suffer much more than Mr. A under similar conditions? And if so, under the circumstances would it not be equally fair to fine Mr. B $5 for his OUI (operating under the influence) conviction and have Mr. A shell out $50 for the parking violation? Unless one can *prove* that this is not so, it might very well be true; we simply do not know. To treat everyone the same before the court, our scientific economists would maintain, is as arbitrary as treating people in a discriminating manner. As a result, he or she would like to conclude that we should dispense with the penal code and leave each case for the judge to decide.

Economic Subjectivism.   But such "scientific" reasoning is really foolish. The roots of such blindness stem from the underlying subjectivism with which modern economics chose to so thoroughly immerse itself.

Professor Robbins made his points by appealing to the need for scientific *observations,* and nobody can observe and measure other peoples' feelings. Such a skeptical assessment follows directly from the Austrian-type economic thinking that he introduced. That perspective, if you recall from Chapter 3, is one that denies the coexistence of separate *economic* and *non-economic* realms. Everything is self-interest. Furthermore, everybody has to live in time, and time is scarce. As a result, scarcity and "rational" human action are the relevant concepts for the modern economist. "Utility" to him means anything that satisfies a desire. In this Robbins echoed another subjectivist marginalist, Leon Walras, who observed: "From other points of view the question whether a drug is wanted by a doctor to cure a patient, or by a murderer to kill his family, is a very serious matter, but from our point of view, it is totally irrelevant. So far as we are concerned, the drug is useful in both cases, and may be even more so in the latter case than in the former."[11]

Walras' successor at Lausanne, the famous Vilfredo Pareto, made a distinction between utility (of truly useful things, useful for health) and ophelimity (of objects having only subjective value), and it is an important distinction.[12] The economic or "material" welfare school led by Pigou understood utility in the former sense. Material utility meant gratification of hunger and other necessities, not gratification of comforts and luxuries; it was not meant to apply to personal wants whose biological basis was much less obvious.

For Alfred Marshall, Edwin Cannan, and Arthur Pigou, economic or material utility *could* indeed be interpersonally compared, and it could be done on purely empirical grounds. If the lower needs of an individual are not met, we could quite easily observe the suffering person's health deteriorate. Nothing metaphysical about this. We do not have to have access to inscrutable other minds, all we have to do is to observe their bodies, the mounting physical deficiencies tormenting those in extreme poverty. An economy where we have to witness such deprivation on a massive scale is objectively an economy that lacks material utility and economic welfare. It is just common sense, as well as scientifically valid.

Economics' subjectivism, which it assumed was scientific, is really a philosophical fallacy. The question is not one of experiencing another's experience, which *is* impossible, but of taking another's *words* to essentially mean the same thing we mean by those words. So, when someone says he is happy or unhappy, hungry or satisfied, we know what that person means. To deny this is to deny the very basis of communication; that words, any words, have meaning. Therefore, we see that the subjectivist position reduces to its logical absurdity–solipsism, the belief that I alone exist. Certainly there is such a thing as the subjective, such as "I like raisins." But a preference for raisins as expressed in that statement should not be confused with the matter of each of us understanding the words–"I," "like," and "raisins." We know what it means to like raisins whether we ourselves like them or not. The neoclassicals of the material economic welfare school did not fall into the subjectivist fallacy because they relied on such observables as health and sickness.

Unfortunately, and certainly surprisingly, Robbins is seen in economics as ending the debate by scoring a rather speedy knockout. So, for example, Joseph Schumpeter could observe when writing in the 1940s that the "idea that satisfactions of different people can be compared and, in particular, summed up into the General Welfare of society as a whole" is one that "few economists will care to defend nowadays," and he refers to Robbins' 1938 article as an example of this rejection.[13] However, although it was seen as a victory in the name of positive science, many more socially conscious scholars nevertheless saw it as a loss. Back in 1953, Columbia's well-known economist, John Maurice Clark, summed up the state of modern welfare theory as follows:

> The form of theory which now bears the name can without real unfairness be described as welfare economics with the welfare left out, in a remarkably resolute attempt to meet the real or supposed requirements of economic science. Rejecting "interpersonal comparisons" this body of theory seems to end in rather complete agnosticism, aside from policies that increase the rational dividend without making anyone else worse off. But the existence of a single disadvantaged person acts as a veto on scientific approval of any policy—one cannot be scientifically certain that his loss does not outweigh the gains of many.[14]

The Rescue of Scientific Welfare Economics: The Idea of Compensation

Clark's disappointment merely echoes and reflects what both Harrod and Robbins had ended up agreeing on twenty years earlier. But there remains a puzzle: economists, after misreading Robbins' conclusion in the debate and deciding that interpersonal comparisons were invalid, have *not* remained silent on policy matters. They continued with business as usual, glorifying the efficiency of free trade, deploring the distorting effect of monopoly on resource allocation, and they still do so today in the name of science. In other words, what Harrod, Robbins, and Clark claimed could not be done, they were and are simply still doing. The puzzle might be easily resolved if we allow for the possibility of a new breakthrough, a new technique that would put the welfare back into scientific welfare economics. And this is indeed what appears to have happened.

The subjectivist impasse deplored by Harrod and Robbins was believed to have been overcome when in 1939 another great name of the period, Professor Nicholas Kaldor, proposed the new idea of a so-called "compensation test."[15] If there is a choice between two alternative states, let us say a tariff on Japanese shoes or no tariff, there are bound to be conflicting interests. Whatever we end up deciding, there will be losers and there will be winners. Now, *if* the group of people that gain from a policy change are able to fully compensate the losers, and have something left over besides, it ought to be seen as a good policy move that will enhance social welfare. So, for example, if we want to reduce tariffs and use part of the consumer gains to compensate the American shoe industrialists to the point where they no longer have any monetary reason to oppose the policy, then there would be no losers, only winners.

The new compensation test allows us to make scientific policy decisions without having to assume anything about interpersonal comparability of satisfaction. But the problem with it lies with the paying of compensation. The actual measurement and payment of this compensation would be far from a simple matter and rife with political conflict and controversy. Obviously, we would immediately be embroiled in endless and messy political battles. However, Professor Kaldor never meant to propose the resolution of policy issues by a political power play. He cleverly avoided that kind of problem by stipulating that *compensation need not actually be paid*. Rather than actual compensation, it is only *hypothetical* compensation that would serve as the acid test of scientific assessment and policy. If the compensation *could* be paid, because there was overall or aggregate monetary gain, then the policy was deemed to increase social welfare. Economists applauded; the Harrod impasse seemed washed away and welfare economics could proceed on the higher, more scientific ground, with no political problem.

But is this so? Not all economists agreed, the notable exception being William J. Baumol, a most respected American economist.[16] What troubled Professor Baumol was the hidden assumption behind the hypothetical compensation idea. If the compensation is not actually paid, and yet the economist approves of the policy–that in actual fact means that he is assuming the equivalent value or utility of a dollar for a rich person and a poor person, or between any of the parties who are affected by the policy. The reasoning is as follows.

Let us say a particular policy happened to increase the wealth of the rich by $5 per person and decreased the wealth of the poor by $5, and there were the same number of poor and rich involved. By the compensation test, the economist would be indifferent towards this policy. He could not say whether it would be bad or good. *Hypothetically*, the rich could pay the poor $5 and thus all parties would be back to where they were before. However, since the compensation is not actually paid, the poor remain $5 poorer and the rich $5 richer. To now accept this as neutral in overall welfare must be to assume that the rich get the same utility from their gain of $5 as the poor have lost from their decrease of $5, or namely, that a dollar for a rich person has the same value as a dollar for a poor person.

So, far from showing that we have been able to make a scientific determination without assuming the supposedly unscientific, unobservable assumption of equal capacity for satisfaction of rich and poor alike, the economist ends up operating on another and very strong assumption–namely, that the value of an extra dollar is exactly the same regardless of poverty or wealth. Thus Kaldor can be seen to have made a *different* judgment from Pigou comparing interpersonal capacity, rather than no judgment. And worse than any assumption of equal capacity for happiness, this is an assumption that is counter-intuitive and from a social point of view simply reactionary.

John Maurice Clark, when writing in 1952, seems to have had a point after all; the welfare had been taken out of scientific welfare economics only to be replaced by an inhuman and arbitrary surrogate pseudo-welfare. Unfortunately, Baumol's objections were ignored by the mainstream, although recently the issue had resurfaced.[17] Perhaps the economists' attachment to the trick of hypothetical compensation could be explained by the usually generous compensation involved when they themselves are employed to apply welfare economics in attempting to solve social and economic problems. Let us now look at just how the application of welfare economics works.

The Application of Welfare Economics

We have already seen that both Marshall and Pigou confined normative economics to satisfactions that can be brought into relation with the measuring rod of money. Let us first be clear what this entails, how utility or satisfaction are assumed to be objectively measured.

Value as Willingness to Pay

The value of an object is simply measured by the amount of money a person is prepared to offer for a thing. How much different objects are really worth to people can be measured by just how much they are willing to pay for them. Purchasing a Volvo rather than a VW Rabbit indicates not only that the Volvo is worth more to the buyer but also that it is at least worth as much as it costs, let us say $16,000, otherwise our buyer would not have agreed to buy it. The value is measured by *"willingness to pay,"* a conceptual standard that reveals the buyer's and seller's evaluation of the commodity. The economist can even go a step further and assume that $16,000 is not only the subjective minimum value to the buyer but–provided the purchase price is a competitive market price–can also be seen as an *objective* measure of what a Volvo is worth. However, one critical element is missing in the above discussion. What it is becomes apparent when we note that people without money, by this logic, will register zero willingness to pay and therefore lack any values whatsoever. Nothing has any value to them. Similarly, the successful business tycoon will manifest stronger values than a child with some meager allowance. The economist does not say that the tycoon–or a successful bankrobber, as the case may be–has *better* values than a financially indigent saint or a struggling student, but positively speaking, the former is said to exhibit a *greater* willingness to pay and "sacrifice" than the latter. To the scientific economist this suggests that they care more about their values, that their values are more deeply held. Similarly, the hard-nosed economist would also assert that a flat broke, unemployed beggar definitely values a can of sardines considerably less than a billionaire values a can of cat food for a pet.

Quite obviously, what the economist calls "willingness to pay" is really no different from "*ability* to pay," and once we choose to label it *that* way, any link with our common sense notion of what is value is radically broken. Why should anybody not value something just because he or she is too poor to buy it? Or, does not theft arise precisely because value is greater than ability or willingness to pay?

From a humanistic perspective, there are no good reasons why we should equate human values with the economist's objective willingness-to-pay criterion, *unless* everybody happened to have an equal ability to pay. The mainstream economist traditionally dealt with this problem by assuming something called the marginal productivity theory of income. People's ability to pay, i.e., their income, is an accurate reflection of the value of their product or work. In other words, in a perfectly competitive economy everyone gets paid exactly what he or she is worth. Therefore, income inequality is a measure of economic value in the first place, and not a reason at all to question willingness to pay as a measure of true value.

However, few economists today would take marginal productivity theory as an accurate account of how wages are determined, particularly in a modern economy where production is a joint effort involving large numbers of people. There are many other reasons for rejecting it as well.[18] Thus the marginal productivity defense of "willingness to pay" hangs on very nebulous grounds.

Assessing Alternatives: Cost-Benefit Analysis

Once one is willing to believe that market values are objective and respectable reflections of willingness to pay, economics can go one step further: why not use this objective value as a guide to measuring costs and benefits of contemplated changes in the economic system? So, for example, if one policy (e.g., subsidies to beef farming) would cut the price of pet food and so save pet lovers $100 million a year while another (e.g., subsidies for wheat farmers) would slash the price of bread to the tune of $80 million a year, and if the subsidy were the same in both cases, then we could deduce that the subsidy should go to beef farming and pet food. In other words, from this point of view market valuations can and should be used to guide public policy in calculating the costs and benefits of alternative policies. The project or policy with the highest net benefit would be, from a "positive" point of view, the one to implement. However, whenever we choose to do something, we change the nature of the game. There will be winners (e.g., pet food consumers, beef farmers) and losers (wheat farmers and bread eaters), but as long as we stick to the Kaldor criterion of hypothetical compensation, this is of no great importance. Using that criterion, the economist can wash his or her hands in innocence and declare that "society" is better off whenever benefit outstrips costs in an arithmetical way. This cavalier attitude is nicely expressed in the initial blessing given to the Kaldor criterion by Professor Hicks: "If A is made so much better off by the change that he could compensate B for his loss and still have something left over, then the reorganization [of production] is an unequivocal improvement." And he then concludes that the potential compensation criterion "is more useful than any other as a basis on which to establish maxims of *sound* economic policy."[19]

The history of this kind of cost-benefit analysis dates back to 1902 when the River and Harbor Act required the Army's Corp of Engineers to evaluate projects by their perspective commercial costs and benefits. But it was not until the 1930s after the Flood Control Act that the practice became more frequently used, not only by the Corps but other government agencies as well–the Bureau of Reclamation, the Social Conservation Service, and the Tennessee Valley Authority.

After many decades of applications, almost solely in the area of water resource development, cost-benefit analysis penetrated the Pentagon and from there the budgeting process of the Johnson administration, where the concept was pushed by budget director and economist Charles Schultz. Then came the application to economic, environmental, and health and safety (de)regulation, a function that was further strengthened by President Reagan's executive order signed in February of 1981. There it says that "Regulatory action shall not be undertaken unless the potential benefits to society from the regulation outweigh the potential costs to society."[20]

Today, we can hardly imagine government policy without cost-benefit analysis. Whether we like it or not, we have to contend with a deeply entrenched technique that determines a great deal of present-day environmental and social policy. And, of course, it is executed by technocrats acting under the intellectual leadership of economists. It is this kind of emancipation of positive economics that has lead to outcries such as this one by the late British sociologist Richard Titmus. He observed that economists, "after taking strong oaths of ethical neutrality, perform as missionaries in the social welfare field and often give the impression of personally owning a hotline to God."[21]

It is probably fair to say that economists advocating cost-benefit analysis are philosophers without knowing it, and the philosophy they are practicing is a modern variant of Bentham's utilitarianism, where questions of right and wrong, good and evil, are settled by a calculus that totes up benefits and costs of all proposed alternatives and seeks to maximize "value" as measured by willingness/ability to pay. We have already referred to one serious difficulty with these apparently sophisticated calculations: the resolution of the interpersonal comparison problem by means of Kaldorian hypothetical compensation. Let us take a look at some of the others.

First of all, especially in the area of social policy, we have to contend with the fact that many effects of a policy cannot be measured by market prices. If we build an airport near a city, there will be the cost of noise pollution, among others, borne primarily by people residing near the runways. But how do we measure these costs? Of course, we could ask the people involved, but economists never had great sympathy for such a pedestrian approach. In part, their aversion is to be explained by their distrust of interviews, an aversion well-grounded in their habitual assumption that everybody will respond "rationally," i.e., self-servingly. Instead, they have the cost-benefit analyst proceed differently: by *imputation* of the costs based on relevant market variables. They would analyze real estate values around airports in order to pinpoint the devaluation that can be attributed to the noise problem. That effect, once ascertained, is then entered into the calculus. Similarly, when contemplating relaxation of safety regulations in an industry, the prospective costs are estimated by looking at the higher wages for accident-prone jobs. To the degree that dangerous jobs have to pay more to attract and maintain a work force, to that extent the cost of additional accidents presumably can be estimated.

Obviously, there are serious problems involved in such an indirect estimation of costs to be imputed. For example, they incorrectly assume (1) that home buyers and workers are perfectly informed about what

they are buying or getting into, (2) that they can easily choose alternative opportunities, and (3) that the potentially affected homeowners and
workers are comparable to the individual already housed and working
in similarly affected situations. The latter assumption glosses over the
very real possibility that the hazardous industries may attract some risk-
loving workers and that the airports often attract people who are less
bothered by the absence of peace and quiet.

More seriously, if a contemplated move increases or reduces the
probability of fatal accidents, the cost-benefit technicians need to impute the benefit of a life saved or the cost of a life lost. Once again, this
is done by indirectly investigating what individuals themselves are willing to pay for reducing the chances of their own death. The economist
now asks: to what extent are people willing to work in jobs that carry
the potential of an accidental death? The estimates of the value of one
life, so generated, ranged in 1978 from a miserly $55,000 to a tab of $7
million.[22] Evidently, the range is more generous than the levels of the
estimates, but either way a number is generated that can be used to determine how many lives it is worth sacrificing.

Besides the problem of how to impute a value to non-market goods,
there remain other difficulties, particularly how to deal with aggregat-
ing effects that either occur over a span of time or at any point in time
across different groups of people. As to the first, it is obviously the case
that many costs and benefits of a project or a social policy will occur in
the future, say two, twenty, eighty years from now. In some cases, particularly those involving environmental policy, certain costs, such as
the clear-cutting of the Amazon rainforest, are irreversible and therefore to be borne by all future generations. Common sense would indicate that irreversible damage, given enough time, would also render the
costs infinite and therefore the idea unpalatable. Similar considerations
are involved when the extinction of a whole species is at stake, but we
do not have to focus on irreversibility to demonstrate the absurdity of
what results from the economist's well-intended way of dealing with
the general problem. The solution consists in discounting all future costs
and benefits to their present values. For that purpose an appropriate social discount rate has to be selected and it is not at all clear on what basis
to select such a rate. Not only are there many different interest rates but
they also vary over time. No one has to date been able to predict what
this so-called "social rate of time preference" will be ten, twenty, one
hundred years from now. Obviously, the higher the rate, the more we
have to discount (scale down) future benefit and cost effects and vice
versa.

Imagine now a policy that would save eleven lives fifty years from now. At a social discount rate of 5 percent this would be equivalent to only one life today. This policy would turn out to be inferior to any alternative which promises to save two lives today. But on what basis can we say that two lives saved this year are preferable to eleven fifty years from now or one hundred thirty two lives one hundred years from now? Why are present lives more valuable than future lives? What is so positive and objective about such an assessment? And one certainly has to wonder if future generations would not object to such a procedure. Similarly, as one scholar recently put it: "Is one person gazing in awe at the majesty of the Grand Canyon in 1990 to be regarded as having the same value, from the point of view of public policy, as 117 gazing visitors in 2040 or 13,777 visitors in 2090? Such equivalencies result from the use of a 10 percent discount rate," and he points to the relevance of all this to health and safety and environmental regulations where many of the most important benefits are likely to be felt, primarily after a considerable period of time, and to a large extent by those not yet born at the time decisions are made.[23] Once again, if all this is positive, objective analysis, so be it, but it is certainly not ethically neutral by any standard. Worse than that, it is extremely poor ethics as far as it goes. Definitely no hotline to God, this.

The other aggregation problem involves the distributional issue. What if a policy, such as, for example, the abolition of rent control, would benefit one group (e.g., landlords) at the expense of others (tenants)? Some cost-benefit specialists constituting the so-called "decision-making" school advocate that distributional consequences be integrated into the calculus, e.g., by assigning arbitrary weights to the net benefits of different groups. For example, if a policy adds a dollar to the poor, this is assigned an extra weight in the decision than if it were to add a dollar to the rich. Members of the "Conventional Approach" school, on the other hand, led by people such as Arnold Harberger, strongly reject such "tampering" with objective data based on the market price. To them, there is no objective method of determining the weights and the process is therefore arbitrary and unjustifiable. True, the conventionalists certainly are correct in pointing out the arbitrary, unscientific character of suddenly introducing non-market determined weights, but what they seem to overlook is the basic fact that they, too, end up assigning arbitrary weights, namely, the uniform weight of 1.0 implicit in the "willingness to pay" value criterion where a dollar is a dollar, regardless of whether it benefits a rich man or the poor. Such a weighting procedure seems no better when it comes to objectivity, its allegedly positive glamour in the field notwithstanding.

It is not our purpose to try to review in detail the entire apparatus of cost-benefit; space precludes such an enterprise and others have already done it.[24] We could have talked about the reductionist compulsion to boil everything down to a bottom line–a single number–how this leads to an overemphasis on readily measurable consequences, and how other specification-related problems lend themselves to political manipulation of the results. In fact, much of the current popularity of cost-benefit analysis can be explained by its nature of being a handy tool to give legitimacy to ideological preferences of government agencies. A good example of this problem can be found in the cost-benefit analysis that was to assess net benefits of additional flights to the United States by the Concorde supersonic passenger plane. The Environmental Protection Agency and the Council on Environmental Quality, together with the Federal Energy Administration, all found costs to exceed benefits, while the Federal Aviation Administration, NASA, and the State Department produced numbers suggesting the very opposite.[25]

There are other serious problems with cost-benefit analysis. The interested reader may, for example, consult the very humanistic critique of basic cost-benefit by Harvard's Steven Kelman.[26]

But enough has been said to indicate the limitations or "costs" of cost-benefit which more often than not will tend to outweigh the potential benefits. All this suggests that we better employ analytically minded and quantitatively inclined economists in other areas where their services are less wasted and also less potentially harmful.

Towards a Humanistic Welfare Economics

Little more needs to be said about the modern New Welfare Economics, its sterility and its antihuman nature, so now we turn to the humanistic alternative which claims to be grounded in a conception of social value that is both objective and operational. The remainder of the chapter will be devoted to an outline of this alternative perspective. The bedrock of any genuine human welfare school consists of four basic propositions:

Proposition 1: *There cannot be a value-free welfare economics.* This is true whether we are talking about "general welfare" or only "economic welfare." To pretend otherwise is simply to mislead the trusting student who unknowingly will gulp down many of the negative values implicit in so-called positive economics. So, for example, the New Welfare Economics, currently advertised as value-free or value-neutral, rests on a host of values. Let us take a closer look.

First, it is built on the premise that only the preferences of individuals are to count. In other words, there are no social values except
for what is desired by the aggregate of individuals in their market transactions. We have already discussed the inherent limitations in using
market transactions as indications of free democratic choice. Moreover,
it sounds more innocent than it is, since it takes the distribution of income underlying the wants *as given* and then proceeds to derive in highly abstract terms the *optimal* mix of consumer goods and inputs. Of
course, the nature or quality of an economy's income distribution is exactly where considerations of equity or ethics are central. And by
abstracting from this ethical question, by treating it as *outside* of the
economic optimum problem, one makes an *ethical* judgment that ethics
are to be kept out of the analysis. Just as a decision not to act is an action, so the decision to ignore ethics is also ethical.

More importantly, the value judgment to accept as given the distribution of income also totally sterilizes the practical import of the New
Welfare Economics. Although we may be able to pinpoint in theoretical terms a General Optimum, which allocates those resources of an
economy that best satisfy consumer demand, we cannot tell the
politicians how to get there. That is so because any change in the output mix will *ipso facto* change relative scarcity along with relative
prices, and also as a result the relative (real) incomes of the consumers.
Now incomes of people have changed and are no longer "given," and
the scientific economist would not have a basis for recommending any
such move or policy.

Similarly, the assumption that individual wants and their satisfaction constitute the goal of an economic system is predicated on the assumption of stable wants and demand. Otherwise, how would we
compare two situations—each satisfying wants—but, let us say, one
before a change, the other after the change. Here an ethical appraisal
cannot be avoided in deciding which constellation of wants is more
worthwhile. Nothing could be said, for example, about the benefits of
education since any effective education by its very essence changes
preferences. Thus, to insist on formulating the welfare problem on *given*
wants is a *philosophical* presupposition, and a deficient one at that. Marshall himself demonstrated a keen awareness of this when he reflected
that: "While wants are the rulers of life among lower animals, it is to
changes in the forms of efforts and activities that we must turn when in
search for the keynotes in the history of mankind."[27] Several decades
later, the American economist Frank Knight showed a similar awareness when observing that "the purposes of men are inherently dynamic
and changing," and that "the chief thing which the common sense in-

dividual actually wants is not satisfaction for the wants he has, but more and better wants," or even that "true achievement is the refinement and *elevation* of the plane of desire."[28]

Finally, we have already discussed the counter common sense value judgments that are involved in applying Kaldor's hypothetical compensation criterion in an attempt to avoid the (more humanistic and realistic) values underlying the work of Pigou and subsequently defended by Roy Harrod.

Once we fully realize that any welfare economics with any practical content is bound to be value-ridden, the task becomes to critically and philosophically evaluate alternative welfare-theoretical frameworks. It can be readily appreciated that a better welfare economics is one that rests on a better philosophy. Let us then further proceed to enumerate some of the basic propositions upholding the humanistic alternative.

Propositon 2: *There exist objective, absolute social values independent of existing individual preferences or market demand.* This criterion we may, following John Hobson, call the *"Human Standard."* It argues that the goal of any economic system, independent of market demands, ought to simply be the meeting of both the lower and higher needs of all its constituents. We may phrase this more explicitly by postulating:

Proposition 3: *The goal of an economy is and ought to be the basic material need satisfaction and dignity for all.* The content of our third basic proposition can be further analyzed in order to better appreciate its claim to objectivity.

First, basic human need satisfaction on the material level is, of course, fully objective in the sense that we can observe deficiencies arising from suboptimal levels of such goods as available water quality, nutritional calories, and unmet housing needs. In this we simply follow the time-honored approach of the neoclassical material welfare school, together with its equally humanistic affirmation of interpersonal comparability of welfare.

We add to this—and so leave the neoclassical behind—the higher need satisfaction as affected by economic activity, in particular the psychological need for self-respect and self-actualization, as, for example, being meaningfully employed. Here we focus on the higher self, not the material self. As a result, we have to move from mere empirical science to philosophy, more particularly a philosophy compatible with, and oriented towards, a higher self. As already discussed, one such philosophy was articulated by the eighteenth century German Immanuel Kant. He held that it is precisely the presence of a noumenal self that gives us intrinsic dignity as persons with inalienable (absolute) value. Kant differentiated "persons" from "things." Things are to be used, they are means with *relative* value (or price), while persons are ends with absolute and intrinsic value. It is absolute value that gives dignity.

Deeply intrinsic to our dual-self theory and Kant's moral philosophy is the objective claim of the value of the person and the human and civil rights that go with it. So, for example, our human dignity is violated if we are exploited by others; if we are not treated as equals by others; if we are prevented from exercising our right to democratic and free self-determination. Such a view of the person as an individual with inalienable rights clearly implies democracy, both in the political *and* the economic (or industrial) domain.

Freedom as self-determination, together with the right to a minimum living standard, constitutes the very bedrock of a humanistic welfare economics. It denies the legitimacy of any contracts, no matter how *apparently* freely entered into by parties, if the outcome would imply a contractual loss of that self-determination. Examples of such contracts are not only hypothetical agreements of voluntary slavery but, as we will see in the next chapter, the wage contract as well. Freedom to self-determination precludes being compelled to sell or rent oneself to the highest bidder in the marketplace.

We can see how the humanistic ideal recognizes personal rights of citizens and consumers, as well as those of workers. If as citizens we are to democratically elect our own administrators, as consumers we ought to freely choose our consumption bundles, and as workers we ought to freely (co)determine all the decisions affecting us, either directly or by explicitly delegating them to a freely elected administration. And we can also recognize that implicit in such a perspective is a general predisposition to decentralized, non-bureaucratic economic decision making. Obviously, such rejection of both centralized state socialism and corporate capitalism provides us with a foremost challenge to come up with a realistic third alternative, a task which much of Chapter 12 will address.

Already contained in our third proposition is a fourth one of practical policy significance:

Proposition 4: *Meaningful work is the primary avenue towards a fully human economic system.* It implies, first and foremost, the right to work at a remuneration compatible with a decent standard of living (i.e., full employment), and beyond that, the desirability of a kind of work that is neither degraded by an oppressive technology nor otherwise alienating. Any work that does not allow us to satisfy our social and moral needs of self-esteem has to be described as alienating and seen as negatively affecting character and preference. It should come as no surprise that alienation is widespread today. As the great humanistic economist John Hobson, a disciple of John Ruskin, put it seventy-five years ago, "A man who is not interested in his work and does not recognize in it either beauty or utility, is degraded by that work, whether he knows it or not."[29]

The late E. F. Schumacher, another great spokesman of the humanistic view, considered alienating jobs (with their adverse affect on human personality) the equivalent of *negative* education or an erosion of human capacities and skills. We may add that to the extent that particular technology affects the quality of our work life and our personality, this also denies the constant and "given" wants assumption underlying conventional welfare economics, both old and new. If so, the "positive" scientific welfare economists can no longer rigorously discuss the choice of technology, since technology and work affects wants. The humanistic economist, on the other hand, recognizes an *appropriate technology* as the very core of a meaningful *human* welfare economics–an economics, to paraphrase Schumacher, "where people matter."

A more specific and detailed listing of welfare prescriptions implied by our basic propositions will be undertaken in the following chapters. And in the spirit of humanistic economics, we will start doing so by discussing the organizational principles determining the meaningfulness of work.

References

1. Arthur Pigou, *Wealth and Welfare*. London: Macmillan, 1912. This book was considerably expanded and republished in 1920 under the title *Economics of Welfare*.
2. Arthur Pigou, *Economics of Welfare* [1920]. 4th edition. London: Macmillan, 1932, p. 11.
3. *ibid.,* p. 89 (our emphasis).
4. *ibid.,* pp. 91-92.
5. Lionel Robbins, *The Nature and Significance of Economic Science* [1932]. 3rd edition. London: Macmillan Press, 1984, p. 140.
6. Roy F. Harrod, "Scope and Method of Economics," *Economic Journal* (1938), p. 397.
7. Lionel Robbins, "Interpersonal Comparisons of Utility: A Comment," *Economic Journal* (December 1938), pp. 635-641.
8. *ibid.,* p. 641.

9. *ibid.*
10. See, for example, Milton Friedman, *Essays in Positive Economics.* Chicago: University of Chicago Press, 1953, p. 3.
11. Leon Walras, *Elements of Pure Economics* [1926]. Fairfield, New Jersey: Augustus M. Kelley, 1977, p. 65.
12. For a revealing treatment of this distinction, see Robert Cooter and Peter Rappaport, "Were the Ordinalists Wrong about Welfare Economics," *Journal of Economic Literature,* 22 (June 1984), pp. 507-530.
13. Joseph Schumpeter, *History of Economic Analysis.* New York: Oxford University Press, 1954, p. 1071.
14. John Maurice Clark, "Aims of Economic Life as Seen by Economists" reprinted in his *Economic Institutions and Human Welfare.* New York: Alfred A. Knopf, 1957, p. 59.
15. Nicholas Kaldor, "Welfare Propositions and Interpersonal Comparisons of Utility," *Economic Journal* (September 1939), pp. 549-552.
16. William J. Baumol, "Community Indifference," *Review of Economic Studies,* 14:1 (1946-1947), pp. 44-48.
17. Cooter and Rappaport, "Were the Ordinalists Wrong . . .?" *op. cit.,* pp. 507-530.
18. G. C. Harcourt, *Some Cambridge Controversies in the Theory of Capital.* Cambridge: Cambridge University Press, 1972.
19. John Hicks, quoted in I. M. D. Little, *A Critique of Welfare Economics.* New York: Oxford University Press, 1960, p. 92.
20. Quoted in James T. Campen, *Benefit, Cost and Beyond.* Cambridge, Massachusetts: Ballinger, 1986, p. 20.
21. Richard Titmus, *The Gift Relationship: From Human Blood to Social Policy.* London: Allen & Unwin, 1970, p. 199.
22. John D. Graham and James W. Vaupel, "The Value of Life: What Difference Does It Make?" in R. Zeckhauser, et al., eds., *What Role for Government Policy Research?* Durham, North Carolina: Duke University Press, 1983, pp. 176-186.
23. Campen, *op. cit.,* p. 60.
24. *ibid.*
25. *ibid.* p. 54.
26. Steven Kelman: "Cost-Benefit Analysis—An Ethical Critique" published in *Regulation* (January-February, 1981), pp. 33-40.
27. Alfred Marshall, *Principles of Economics* [1890]. 8th edition. London: Macmillan, 1952, p. 134.

28. Frank H. Knight, "Ethics and the Economic Interpretation," *The Ethics of Competition* [1935]. London: Allen & Unwin, 1951, p. 23.

29. John A. Hobson, *Work and Wealth: A Human Valuation* [1914]. Reprint, New York: Augustus M. Kelley, 1968, p. 88.

Chapter 8

RESTRUCTURING WORK: COMMUNITY IN ENTERPRISE

We now turn to one of the most important topics in a humanistic economics: work. Ironically, work occupies only a peripheral place in contemporary economics texts, where it is ordinarily referred to as "labor" and analyzed as one of several inputs (or "factors of production") in the making of consumable commodities and services. Moreover, from the point of modern welfare economics, the issue of work and its central place, not only in economics but in life itself, is almost totally absent. It is not seen to have any bearing on the matter of the welfare of society. Nevertheless, we can easily recognize that the concept of the quality of life cannot be separated from the quality of work. If there is not "quality" in the work experience, there cannot truly be an adequate quality of life. This points to the fact that income or "compensation" from work is only one of several rewards that working can provide, and in many cases not the most important.

It follows from this that in terms of human well-being we need to examine not only the existing systems of wage and work but also alternatives to these that hold high humanistic promise. Most of the present chapter will focus critically on the contemporary mainstream economic conception of work and an alternative proposed by economist David Ellerman. In Chapter 12 we will follow up this theoretical presentation with a remarkable case study in which these insights find detailed application in an ongoing economic development that has been very successful and promises great hope for the future.

The New Industrial Wage System

The wage system, which means people hiring other people, is not new. It probably stretches as far back into the history of mankind as slavery and serfdom. What is new, however, is the type of large-scale employment ushered in by the Industrial Revolution two centuries ago. Ever since, we readily identify capitalism as a modern economic system where capital employs labor for the sake of profits. Moreover, present-day market-oriented economics was conceived by Adam Smith at the same time that markets for hiring labor were becoming more widespread, suggesting an intrinsic link between the wage system and the market economy. Not surprisingly, anyone who would dare to question the wage system is automatically seen as either anti-capitalist or utopian, and certainly as a most questionable economist. This was already so during the first part of the nineteenth century when acceptance or rejection of the wage system separated capitalists from the new sect of idealistic socialists.

It was William Thompson who devoted an entire book, published in England in 1824, to challenging the economist's acceptance of wage labor as a natural, "unavoidable and necessary permanent" institution.[1] Taking off from the labor theory of value taught by Ricardo and the leading economists of his day, Thompson boldly concluded that "Labour is the sole parent of wealth." Capital is, as a result, not productive and capitalists' profits unjustified, being generated "at the expense of the labour of others." Decades later, Karl Marx elaborated and greatly refined Thompson's point of view, herewith giving birth to modern so-called "scientific" socialism.

In contrast, the new marginalist neoclassical economists defended the legitimacy of capitalists' profits and the productivity of capital. Workers were now seen as paid exactly in proportion to their individual productivity, and the returns to capitalists were also in proportion to the contribution of their provision of machines. Marshall, furthermore, talked of the capitalists' sacrifice of "waiting" as the counterpart to the workers' sacrifice of labor or effort. The capitalist could spend his or her wealth and thus reap the satisfaction of consumption, or else "abstain" from such indulgences and instead use his capital for investment. As a result of this investment, with the capitalist abstaining from consumption, the worker not only lives but in a modern economy presumably prospers, and thus capital is indeed as productive in its way as is labor. Therefore, the factors of production have come to generally be known in Western economics as land (resources), labor, and capital–or in Marshall's schema, land, labor, and waiting. But despite this fancy theorizing, the waiting doctrine and numerous others of its variety (i.e., entrepreneurial decision-making acumen, organizational skills, and the like) never did rest easy, and the question–Is capital productive?–still bubbles somewhat noisily in the background.[2] We will see that there is a radically new way to analyze this capitalist/Marxist dispute and to come up with an answer that brilliantly sidesteps the worn controversy and enables us to transcend the ideologies of both capitalist and Marxist.

Meanwhile, it is interesting to note that Marxists, in contrast to the earlier communists in England and France, pointed the accusing finger more at the private ownership of production than they did at the wage system. The latter would be acceptable, although not ideal, under a non-exploitative regime of state ownership. As a result, ironically, we find very few orthodox Marxists today who would question the appropriateness of the prevailing wage system in Eastern Europe or elsewhere in a socialist state. The wage system is a problem, they contend, only because of the private profits it generates. Eliminate these "fruits of exploitation" and there is not that much that is wrong with the paying of wages. There is, then, a strange common ground shared by the two rival ideologies of today: they both are committed to the institution of wage labor. It possibly tells us something about the key difference between capitalism and socialism: under capitalism man exploits man, under socialism it seems to be exactly the opposite!

The Humanistic Approach to Work: John Hobson

John Hobson (1858-1940) is perhaps the best known economist in the humanistic tradition of Sismondi and Ruskin. His primary goal was to remove the most inhuman aspect of everyday capitalist reality he himself had to contend with in the first half of the twentieth century. He wrote much about business cycles, imperialism, and above all, the quality of work.

With respect to work, he fought for "a secure weekly income, or for the conditions of employment which lead up to this."[3] He agreed that the goal of such a "living wage" may appear vulnerable for being too vague, but specifies that "a living wage is such a regular weekly sum as suffices to maintain the ordinary working family in health and economic efficiency." He also stressed, in great humanist tradition, the importance of security–a theme so central to our book that we may quote him at length here.

A weekly wage of bare efficiency with regular employment is socially far superior to a higher average wage accompanied by great irregularity of work. The former admits stability of modes of living and
ready money payments, it conduces to steadiness of character and
provision for the future without anxiety. Rapid and considerable fluctuations of wages, even with full employment, are damaging to
character and stability of standards: but *irregularity of employment
is the most destructive agency to the character,* the standard of comfort, the health and sanity of wage-earners. The knowledge that he is
liable at any time, from commercial and other causes that lie entirely outside of his control, to lose the opportunity to work and earn his
livelihood, *takes out of a man that confidence in the fundamental
rationality of life which is essential to soundness of character.
Religion, ethics, education, can have little hold upon workers exposed to such powerful illustrations of the unreason and injustice of
industry and of society.*[4]

It is a plea that cannot be easily ignored by anybody who is interested not just in seeing people satisfy their existing preferences, but in
developing "better preference structures," a more ethical society, or in
humanistic economic terms, a greater realization of their higher selves.

But Hobson, not remaining content with these matters, was above
all extremely concerned with the negative effects of excessive division
of labor resulting from a technology aimed at ever-increasing mass
production. "The [modern] conditions of labour," he observed, "are
realised as an invasion and a degradation of humanity, offering neither
stimulus nor opportunity for a man to throw himself into his work. For
the work only calls for a fragment of that 'self' and always that same
fragment. So it is true that not only is labour divided but the labourer.
And it is manifest that, so far as his organic human nature is concerned,
its unused portions are destined to idleness, atrophy, and decay."[5]

He observed that this type of human degradation and "alienation"
produced by meaningless work has its social costs in terms of human
personality and character. Moreover, such degradation is much more
common than many would like to admit. He puts it masterfully and
briefly: "A man who is not interested in his work, is degraded by that
work, whether he knows it or not."[6]

The real and effective remedy against such an alienation externality
is to give workers themselves a say in designing their work environment. For this reason, he not only advocated greater industrial
democracy, a "capitalism qualified by a large participation of labour in
management through profit-sharing and co-partnership," but also ex-
perimentation in what he called "a New Industrial Order." "Instead of
capital hiring labour at a fixed market rate, employing it to work up the

materials it owns upon premises it owns or hires, and marketing the product at a price which yields a gain, labour would hire the capital, both fixed and circulating, would be its own employer, market its own goods, and keep for itself the gains."[7] This idea he correctly saw as "the most radical of all the social-economic reforms" on the agenda. Not surprisingly, he was also decades ahead of its realization. Nevertheless, in raising this issue he beautifully capped his humanistic perspective of work with a grand vision. There is little, in terms of theory, that could be added to his pioneering work briefly summarized here. Whatever needed to be said to give substance to the vision of such a thorough socioeconomic reform, we believe has been accomplished by David Ellerman, in many ways a reincarnation of John Hobson's tireless spirit.

The Case Against the Wage System

The American economist David Ellerman moved against the wage system with an analysis both new and incisive. His analysis moves on two fronts. One is based on the philosophy of law labeled "the labor theory of property," the other emanates from a political theory of democracy. Ellerman's argument is placed within a framework of Kantian philosophy.[8]

Kant's entire moral philosophy is grounded in his well-known categorical imperative: "Act in such a way that you always treat humanity, whether in your own person or in the person of any other, never simply as a means, but always at the same time as an end."

As described in Chapter 6 on the dual-self conception of the person (also referred to in relation to human dignity in the last chapter), such a moral injunction is based upon the concept of persons having *intrinsic* worth or dignity, rather than being of merely *instrumental* use and commanding utility or a price.

Similarly, Ellerman, taking note of Kant's differentiation between *persons* (being ends-in-themselves) and *things* (functioning solely as means), reformulated the categorical imperative as: *"Act in such a way that you always treat human beings as persons rather than as things."* An essential quote from Kant allows us to see this person versus thing dichotomy:

> Beings whose existence depends, not on our will, but on nature, have none the less, if they are non-rational beings, only a relative value as means and are consequently called things. Rational beings, on the other hand, are called persons because their nature already marks

them out as ends in themselves–that is as something which ought not to be used merely as a means–and consequently imposes to that extent a limit on all arbitrary treatment of them.[9]

Being now equipped with such a norm we can proceed to examine carefully the employer/employee relation.

The employment relation, in contrast to the master/slave relationship, is not an ownership contract but a self-rental contract, where a person hires himself out for a limited period. As Paul Samuelson, a leading mainstream economist, put it so well: "Since slavery was abolished, human earning power is forbidden by law to be capitalized. A man is not even free to sell himself: he must *rent* himself at a wage."[10]

What Ellerman shows us is that even this self-rental, which all of us tend to accept as legitimate and part of unquestionable everyday reality, should be seen as a remaining and subtle form of medieval serfdom. But there is absolutely no need whatsoever for us to comprehend the truth of this radical statement in traditional Marxian terms. Rather, we will see how it follows as the outcome of the Kantian logic of human dignity and the concept of personal, inalienable rights.

Persons as Legally Responsible Agents

Ellerman puts forth what he calls the "parable of the hired criminal." Suppose that someone rents a U-Haul van and then hires an employee to do some general delivery services. Then let us imagine that this employer now decides that his new employee should use this rented van to rob a bank–a surefire thing, he persuades the employee. Furthermore, for the duration of the robbery the employee will remain under contract as a hired worker (but now with higher wages). Unfortunately for the two of them, they are caught and charged with the crime.

In court the employee advances the argument that he was not guilty, just like the U-Haul dealer who hired out the van. As with the dealer, he had merely rented the services of his "factors of production" to the employer–the U-Haul dealer sold the use of the van as he sold the use of his labor. Why should *he* be charged with the crime? Why not the U-Haul dealer as well? After all, the van was a necessary tool for the committing of the crime, as was his driving. He would quote from economics texts, "Labor service is a commodity," and argue that what use his employer or the entrepreneur makes of these commodities is the employer's business, not his.

Ellerman then properly notes that the judge, no doubt, would be unmoved by these arguments. He would point out that although all of the factors involved in the crime were productive or "useful," only the employee and his boss were *responsible* in the legal sense of having done it. Things cannot be responsible for anything; only humans by their intentional actions can incur legal responsibity. The judge would further maintain that a person can give up and transfer the use of an instrument, such as a van, and have no involvement in the subsequent purpose that the instrument is put to. But the worker could not, in fact, relinquish or transfer the use of his own labor, whether by contract or otherwise, without having subsequent involvement. In legal terms an employee is considered a servant to a master and the law in such master-servant relationships is as follows:

> All who participate in a crime with a guilty intent are liable to punishment. A master and servant who so participate in a crime are liable criminally, not because they are master and servant, but because they jointly carried out a criminal venture and are both criminous.[11]

Another way to put this is that the unique property of labor—responsible agency—is, from a legal point of view, not transferrable. The worker under criminal law cannot contract away his responsible agency. This is quite different in the case of the van owner. U-Haul can hire out the use of its tools or things, and not be responsible for their use. Ownership of such instruments of production as a van does not imply that the "fruits" of its use (here, negative) are automatically imputed back to the owner. In brief, a tool is not legally responsible for the product of its use, but a person is.

With the logic of this parable in mind, Ellerman then goes on to consider the case of normal or non-criminal production. Is there any more reason here why wage earners should suddenly give up their legal responsibility and become instruments like the van? The crucial answer is no. Regardless of the employment contract, they remain, in principle, fully responsible agents intentionally cooperating with any other members of the firm.

With this reformulation of the productivity question, by bringing in the critical element of responsibility, Ellerman can now shed new light on the old debate of whether or not capital is productive. The issue, he points out, is not whether capital is productive, but is it *responsible*? Who is really *responsible* for the production of net output, or the "whole product?" Even if capital (tools, instrument, machines) were more productive than labor, the fact remains that neither instruments nor any other things can be legally responsible for the results of their outputs. Things cannot be responsible for anything, only labor or human beings can be held responsible for what they produce.

This is Ellerman's "labor theory of property." In theoretical terms labor is responsible for what it does and is fully entitled to what it produces. Burglary tools, like a getaway van, can be very productive—even absolutely essential to the committing of a crime—but legally neither the tools nor their renters can be held responsible for their deed. Analogously, capital equipment can be extremely instrumental in producing output and profits, but neither the equipment itself nor their owners can be legally held accountable for the whole product; instead it has to be imputed to the human agents using those instruments.

Ellerman's focus on legal responsibility permits us to see why capitalist (or state) appropriation violates dignity. Persons are legally (or *de jure*) treated as things or nonpersons if they bear no legal responsibility for the results of their actions. This is precisely what happens in both a capitalist enterprise or a state-owned socialist firm: the employees suddenly are no longer legally entitled to own the output and net product they produce. Instead, the employer appropriates it all. The wage system evidently violates Kant's categorical imperative, it degrades persons into mere instruments of production, it treats them like oxen or circus elephants (the only difference there being that in the circus, payment for services rendered is in kind rather than in money).

Logically, the humanistic or Kantian enterprise is one where the people working in a firm are the firm, i.e., where the enterprise is labor-managed and those having joint actual responsibility for the net product are also the ones who can appropriate what is by legal reasoning theirs: the net product. In such a firm, everybody who participates in production (workers and management) is to equitably share the product of their manual and mental work. This, of course, implies also that anybody who does *not* work in the firm, such as absentee providers of capital, cannot share any responsibility for the whole product and therefore ought not to legally appropriate any part of its whole or net product, *other than a rental fee*.

The key principle of the labor-managed firm, in contrast to the standard corporation, is that in the self-managed firm *labor hires capital*, whereas in the standard corporation *capital hires labor*. In the labor-managed enterprise any outside capital is not *invested* in the firm but *hired* by the firm, just as our employer in the crime parable hired the van. This hiring price involves a certain fee, usually a contractually fixed return as with bonds, but the essential point is that the capital lender does not have any right to share in profits through dividends. Otherwise, it would be as if the van owner not only received a rental fee for the use of the van but also ended up being responsible for what was done with it.

Let us now go back to the Kantian framework and discuss a second reason why the wage system degrades persons into instruments or mere "means" instead of ends in and of themselves. This time we do not focus on the responsibility of agents, but ask instead how the person/thing distinction relates to decision making.

Persons as Decision Makers

Just as a "thing" cannot be responsible, so it quite obviously lacks the ability to make decisions. Accordingly, Ellerman postulates that persons are relegated to the legal role of "things" if they are not a legal party to the decisions made about the services they are to perform. Of course, this is exactly what happens in any rental contract, including the type of self-rental involved in the employment contract. When we rent a car, for example, we not only obtain the vehicle but along with it the legal responsibility and decision-making power to use it however we see fit. The rental contract will not specify whether or not we can drive to New York, visit a friend, or park in underground parking garages. The rental contract transfers decision making about the use of the car from the owner (let us say, Avis) to the renter. In legal jargon, then, the legal decision-making authority is conveyed to the renter and in the very process *alienated* from the owner.

Now apply the car rental logic to the self-rental of a worker to an employer. A man who must rent himself at a wage remains the owner of his earning power, but transfers decision-making power over that service to his employer, the renter. With his legal decision-making authority being transferred and alienated, he assumes the legal role of a thing rather than a person. Here we now have the second reason why the wage system disrespects Kant's categorical imperative by violating the claims of human dignity.

It is important to make a distinction between this surrender of decision-making power and delegating it. For example, when we delegate decision-making power to an investment broker concerning investment decisions about our money, we legally expect those funds to be managed in our name and in our best interest. Legally, the decisions so made are ultimately still regarded as our own decisions. Contrast that with the mere loaning of some money to a borrower who will make the investment decisions in his or her own name and interest. Quite obviously, an employment contract is not a delegation but an alienation of decision-making power. The employer will use the employee according to his own interests and in his own name.

A different and much more humanistic situation prevails in a worker-managed enterprise. Here we also tend to encounter a hierarchy in decision-making power, the top being occupied by the manager. But, in contrast to the conventional wage labor firm, the workers here explicitly delegate their decision-making power to management. The manager of such a "self-managed" enterprise exercises their decision making in the name of and for the benefit of those managed. Thus we have an equivalent to the political notion of self-government. That notion does not entail an absence of government, but rather a government "by the people and for the people," the kind we uphold as the very essence of democracy or self-rule. In the economic realm such democracy entailing self-management of all members of the firm is the distinguishing feature of a democratic enterprise. It is flatly incompatible with any outside provider or lender of capital entitled to a directorship or voting rights in management decisions, or other direct or indirect input in enterprise decision making.

The democratic or humanistic firm, in treating workers as persons rather than as things or mere instruments, conveys to its members the morally inalienable right to run the company. Such rights are *personal* rights rather than property rights. They are assigned to individual members who meet the qualifying function of being members just as voting rights in a township are assigned to the functional role of residing within the political boundaries of the town. As a result, they cannot be transferred to outsiders either through selling them or otherwise. As Ellerman observes, "a personal right may not be sold because the 'buyer' might not have the qualifying role and if the would-be 'buyer' did have the qualifying role, then he would not need to 'buy' the right."[12] (There is a simple but decisive test to establish whether a right is a personal or a property right. The former are automatically extinguished with the death of the bearer, the latter can be inherited.)

So much for the Kantian or dual-self case for Hobson's "most radical of all the social-economic reforms." It squarely puts worker-managed enterprises on the map, at least in theory, and does it so simply in the name of human dignity. But David Ellerman's insights do not end here; instead, they range over a wider realm that we will now explore. Let us first take a deeper look into the issue of democracy.

Capitalism and Democracy

Ellerman's radical claim that the conventional investor-owned corporation is incompatible with both workers' dignity and basic notions of democracy may come as an unwelcome surprise to many liberals who have long associated freedom of contract and capitalism with democracy.

The idea that the traditional capitalist firm was the democratic expression in economics goes back to the development of classical Liberalism as a social philosophy. The principle idea was that a person's rights and duties in society should be based on voluntary arrangements and not on inherited status. A classic statement of this basic liberal theme is Henry Maine's assertion that, "the movement of the progressive societies has hitherto been a movement from status to contract."[13]

Perhaps another reason for this capitalist=democracy equation comes out of what Ellerman calls the "either/or" mentality of the capitalism/socialism debate. Since capitalism is *the* only alternative to socialism, and since socialism is generally seen as undemocratic, then capitalism must represent democracy. In this context, however, let us emphasize that from Ellerman's perspective the dissociation of the idea of democracy from capitalism does not imply that the worker-managed firm is socialistic or that socialism is democratic. For Ellerman, the worker-managed firm is neither classically capitalist nor socialist; indeed it is a truly new form. With regard to the question of socialism and worker self-management, it is worth quoting him:

> It should be noted that I am using the word "socialism" in the dictionary sense of "governmental ownership and administration of the means of production." Some would argue that this refers only to "state socialism" or "governmental socialism," and that workers' self-management is the meaning of "true" socialism. But this is not the middle of the nineteenth century when the concept of socialism was ill-defined and open to competing interpretations. The history of the twentieth century has stamped an indelible meaning upon the word "socialism." That meaning is government ownership (at least as a "necessary condition"). Phrases such as "state socialism" or "governmental socialism" are simply redundant.

> Self-management is not socialism, and, indeed, it is diametrically opposed to the governmental ownership and control of industry. . . . Given the normal difficulties in political and economic communication, one can ill-afford sentimental attachments to private defini-

tions. If one doesn't mean governmental ownership, then one shouldn't say "socialism." Those who seek a new world should first find a new word.[14]

Those who equate capitalism with democracy generally assume that it is through shareholding in a firm that the democratic rights of the citizenry are exercised, and this is sometimes referred to as "shareholder democracy." Now it is mostly the case, and well-known, that in large public corporations the far-flung shareholders do not wield effective influence or control over either those with concentrated blocks of shares or the managers, who typically own a small portion of the shares. But even this practical reality can be set aside since it is not yet the critical one that prevents a capitalist shareholding corporation from being a democracy. Even if all shareholders actively voted their shares, and there was no concentration of share ownership, this kind of firm would still not be democratic. The reason is as follows.

The basic definition of democracy is that it is a system of government based on the consent of the governed. The problem with shareholder democracy is simply that the shareholders are not also the "governed" in a corporation. The governed, in fact, are all the members (employees) of the enterprise. To see a capitalist firm as democratic has no meaningful analogy in political theory. Ellerman describes the fallacious logic of this comparison as follows:

> It is as if the people in one country (the shareholders) joined together in a contractual association (the corporation) to elect a government (corporate management) to govern the people in another country (the corporate employees). The people in the second country (the employees) agree to another contract, a contract of subjection (the employment contract) to their governors. That would be the political analogue of a capitalist firm.[15]

Once again, the reader should be reminded that an alternative to capitalism is not bound to be socialism. In fact, we will see that a labor-managed democratic enterprise certainly does involve "private ownership of the means of production" rather than government (or state) ownership. The equity capital is privately owned by the membership, although through an ingenious twist to be discussed later in which capital is not allowed to affect the one-member, one-vote democratic principle. Similarly, a labor-managed enterprise can only function in a market system where, as any other business firm, it must make enough profits to remain in business. Finally, any group of private individuals, with or without community help, can always start up a new firm. If all this is not free enterprise, what is?

The democratic nature of the worker cooperative, however, will have to prohibit certain undemocratic options. Just as any political democracy cannot allow a permanent underclass of non-citizens, so it is also found to be true within an economic democracy. Thus anyone who is accepted as working in a worker-managed enterprise on a non-temporary basis (beyond a certain probationary period) should thereby automatically qualify for membership. In other words, the democratic nature of such an enterprise is not compatible with the "freedom" of hiring new employees as permanent non-members. That freedom, the freedom of labor rental, although legally permissible, comes to be seen as bogus, as Ellerman has shown in the following analysis.[16]

Liberty, Democracy, and the Employment Contract.   Could it not be asserted that the employment contract as an exchange of work for wages is a voluntary contract entered into by mutually consenting adults? And if so, would it not entail that capitalism simply extends that non-coercive freedom to the economic sphere? Is not such voluntary and deliberate cooperation of individuals the very opposite of the coercive totalitarian state and therefore the democratic alternative to such a system?

The answer to all these questions is not as clear and obvious as we would ordinarily believe. The reason is that the mere existence of a "contract" is not the relevant issue when it comes to the questions of freedom and democracy. What is crucially important here is the fact that there have long been two different types of voluntary contracts, one consistent with freedom and democracy and the other not. One is based on property rights, the other on human rights, which cannot be sold (or alienated) even with the supposed "free consent" of the bearers.

The property right-based tradition held by Hobbes and others is perhaps today best represented by the Harvard social philosopher Robert Nozick. He would like to permit contracts to sell oneself into slavery. In his prominent book, *Anarchy, State and Utopia* (1974), we can read: "The . . . question about an individual is whether a free system will allow him to sell himself into slavery. I believe that it would."[17] For Nozick, voluntary slavery *is* freedom, although seen by many others as the total abrogation of individual freedom and self-determination. This question is not merely academic: Shortly before the Civil War, a number of southern states passed legislation to explicitly validate self-enslavement contracts in order "to permit a free Negro to become a slave voluntarily."

In the same vein this alienist contractarian tradition as the basis of a political philosophy is a voluntary pact of submission (*"pactum subjectionis"*) of an entire people. More than three centuries ago, Thomas

Hobbes based his consent-based political thought on the idea of a voluntary contract of subjugation: "I authorize and give up my right of governing myself to this man, on this condition, that you give up your right to him and authorize all his actions in like manner."[18] The Spanish scholastic philosopher and jurist Francis Suarez was said to have argued just that in 1612:

> If voluntary slavery was possible for an individual, so it was for an entire people. . . . A natural rights theory defense of slavery became in Suarez's hand a similar defense of absolutism: if natural men possess property rights over their liberty and the material world, then they may trade away that property for any return they themselves may think fit.[19]

To illustrate this principle, if the United States Congress and the President would decide tomorrow to sell our right of self-determination to the Russian Supreme Soviet, then that would be entirely consistent with liberty and democracy. Obviously, such a hypothetical example is so extreme as to sound absurd, but it nevertheless serves well to illustrate that contracting is not the alpha and omega of self-determination. It helps remind us how questionable the automatic reaction of many contemporary defenders of self-rental contracts are. The "freedom" to rent oneself over a particular period is a self-contradictory freedom.

We should also take note that once any pact of submission is seen as legitimate, then it is easily assumed that such consent to submission need not be explicitly acknowledged by the ruled, but accepted by them implicitly. The American Reverend Samuel Seabury defended pre-Civil War slavery in this very manner when postulating, "Let the origin of the (slave) relation have been what it may, yet when once it can plead such prescription of time as to have received a fixed and determinate character, it must be assumed to be founded in the consent of the parties, and to be, to all intents and purposes, a compact or a covenant, of the same kind with that which lies at the foundation of all human society." And after asking the question, "Did your fathers ever sign it?", he answers, "No, it is a tacit and implied contract."[20] Again, the same could be asserted by defenders of the contemporary wage system, a bond uniting employer and employee to their mutual benefit and grounded in an implicit social contract.

Side by side with the property rights tradition there has long existed an alternative tradition which holds that there are certain natural or *human* rights which one can claim on the basis of being human. They cannot be transferred or alienated, even by voluntary consent or contract. The logic for this is: If we sell human rights, we are *legally* exchanging our humanness with a non-human status. Yet regardless of attempting such a contract we remain *de facto* (i.e., in reality) still human which implies that the contract of alienation can by its very nature not be fulfilled, rendering it therefore void on the grounds of natural rights.

Historically, such "rights of Man" were articulated three centuries ago by the English social philosopher Locke, and became the very underpinning of the Bill of Rights doctrines spreading through Europe. These included the inalienable right to life, liberty, and the pursuit of happiness of our Declaration of Independence and the individual rights recognized by the U.S. Constitution of 1789, as well as the United Nations Declaration of Human Rights (1948) ratified by both the United States and the Soviet Union. In contrast to written (or "positive") rights derived from the law of a particular political legislature, moral rights have always been rooted in natural law. The wage contract then, like the voluntary slavery of the nineteenth century, is a *positive* law, but in accordance with Ellerman's analysis it has to be seen as violating natural law and hence as morally wrong.

We may conclude this section with Ellerman's own words: "With the democratic revolutions and the abolition of slavery, that old liberal tradition of contractual subjection has descended to the present as *liberal capitalist thought*. With political autocracy ruled out, liberal capitalist thought praises the voluntarism of the economic *pactum subjectionis* of the workplace. With slavery abolished, liberal capitalist thought praises the freedom to rent oneself out or to rent other human beings. Such is the intellectual heritage of the old tradition which permits the legal alienation of basic rights by means of voluntary contracts."[21]

The Elusive Ideal of Worker Self-Management

The idea that workers should be the ones that make all the decisions affecting them, that instead of authoritarian bosses and absentee owners there could be self-rule or self-direction in enterprise, is, of course, not a new one. The idea arose alongside the factory and wage system and it will be, no doubt, a persisting ideal as long as these institutions prevail.

What better evidence is there for the pervasiveness of this ideal than to be able to quote a leading late-nineteenth century mainstream economist in support of the principle. We turn to J. S. Mill's *Political Economy* text of 1848 to read: "The form of association—which, if mankind continues to improve, must be expected in the end to predominate, is not that which can exist between a capitalist as a chief, and work people without a voice in the management, but the association of the labourers themselves in terms of equality, collectively owning the capital by which they carry on their operations, and working under managers elected and removeable by themselves."[22]

Among the most ardent philosopher-economists seeking to realize this idealistic vision was the Frenchman Pierre Joseph Proudhon. Already in 1852 he ardently advocated associations of workers as the new model to replace the joint stock companies of his day. But he also recognized that this ideal was totally unrealistic unless the questions of *finance* and *organization* form could be resolved. "The whole future of the workers depends on the answer to these questions. If the answer is in the affirmative, a new world will open out before humanity; if in the negative, then let the proletariat take warning. Let them commend themselves to God and the Church–there is no hope for them this side of the grave."[23]

We now know that his two questions could not be properly answered in the century that followed, and when Proudhon died in 1865 the New Humanity he had hoped for was still as much a dream as ever. This sobering state of affairs was to remain for almost a century.

The producer cooperative continued to be seen as "the child of sorrows and the darling of all those who expect the Cooperative Movement to produce something essential for the salvation of mankind."[24] The great philosopher Martin Buber in a survey of cooperative experiments before 1945 observed that "the development of the producer cooperatives can be represented as a zig-zag line which, on the whole, shows hardly any upward trend. New ones are always coming into being, but again and again most of the more vigorous ones pass into the sphere of capitalism; there is hardly any continuity."[25] Proudhon's New Humanity, predicated on Hobson's New Industrial Order involving the "most radical of all the social-economic reforms," remained in the nowhere land of Utopia. Instead, capitalism continued to mature with ever-larger and more powerful corporations as its very driving force. Even more disappointingly, socialism, seen by most as its only feasible alternative, grew under Stalin and his followers ever more centralized, bureaucratic, and brutal. Meanwhile, here in the United States and elsewhere, producer co-ops continued their marginal existence, unable to overcome the tendency to degenerate into conventional capitalist firms if successful, as mentioned by Buber.

American Case Studies.   Let us look briefly at two American case studies to illustrate the point.

First, there are the cooperative plywood firms which have existed for decades in the American West. The first of such companies began in 1921 when 125 Scandinavian immigrants near Seattle each put up

$1,000 for the initial twenty-five shares, and secured a bank loan for approximately $25,000. Shortly thereafter, the first sheets of plywood came off the production line of the Olympia Veneer Company, as the owner-workers named their company.

The initial investment entitled each owner to a job in the plant and a pro rata share of the profits. Each founder agreed to work initially without additional compensation and "to do any kind of work in or about the plant in a creditable manner. Not to work for his personal interest but for the interest of all concerned."[26] Company bylaws also stipulated total equality in profit shares regardless of skills or tasks performed. New stockholders could only be admitted by a majority vote of a worker-elected managing board. An owner could always drop out by selling his stock back to the company at a fair market value. So we can see that at its outset, Olympia Veneer operated with some very idealistic and democratic principles. But some problems began to emerge. The firm allowed itself the "freedom" to hire non-member workers (i.e., employees).

A year later the company was down to 118 stockholders and 100 non-stockholder employees. The process continued and by 1952 there were less than 50 working stockholders together with 1,000 non-owners. In 1954 the last 23 surviving stockholders voted to sell their plant to the United States Plywood Corporation. It is estimated that the 23 individuals received over $625,000 each, a handsome return on the original investment of $1,000, even counting inflation. Olympia's history came to an end at this point, but its status as a worker-owned producer cooperative had begun to erode almost from its beginning.

The economic success of the Olympia idea inspired the founding of many other cooperatives of a very similar character. In 1953 it was Anacortes Veneer, also in the State of Washington, the oldest plywood cooperative still in operation as of this writing. However, recent rumors have circulated that the stockholders, most of them near retirement age, were willing to sell their stock, so it appears that Anacortes will also eventually be absorbed by a larger, conventional corporation. (Recently, the plywood co-op membership shares were offered for $90,000.)

One scholar, C. J. Bellas, concludes from the experience of these twenty or so firms that "using the forty-year history of the plywood cooperatives as our best example of cooperative production, we must conclude that their organizational form is basically unstable." He goes on to explain that, "The owners, unwilling to dilute ownership, characteristically do not admit workers from an acquired firm to ownership. The democratic nature of the organization begins to deteriorate and it may eventually resemble a conventional corporation."[27] This, of

course, is exactly what the cooperative self-management idea was supposed to leave behind–a conventional, hierarchical organization with
hired wage labor.

A second case and a much shorter story is that of the Vermont Asbestos Group (VAG), which was formed in 1975 by its workers purchasing the assets from the GAF conglomerate. The business timing of
the venture was excellent since shortly thereafter the asbestos price rose
sharply enabling a 100 percent dividend the first year. Moreover, much
of the profits were reinvested allowing the book value of the shares to
increase from $50 to almost $2,000 within three years. Several other
companies and venture capital firms were prepared to make offers for
the stock, but the workers preferred to sell their shares to an interested
local businessman. And soon, having bought a controlling interest, he
handpicked a new board of directors and installed himself as the president and chairman of the board. Amen.

The Yugoslavian Example.   Meanwhile, in Eastern Europe a fascinating experiment with worker self-management that had started in
Yugoslavia in the early 1950s increasingly developed serious problems,
one manifestation of which was prolonged double-digit unemployment,
three-digit inflation, and a stagnating growth rate. Analysts have been
coming up with all sorts of answers trying to explain the crisis.

Economists of the new "property rights school" attribute much of
the blame to the fact that Yugoslav worker members have little incentive to reinvest profits in their own firm, particularly in the financing of
assets that are depreciated over a long time period. The reason is that
individual workers have no claim to the increased value of the firm; all
he or she gets is the increase in profits generated by the assets, but not
the value of the asset itself. Investment in long-term projects means
committing hard-earned dollars to a common property that benefits the
more senior workers the least and the youngest the most. Newly hired
members, for example, would share the benefits of the capital accumulated in the past by retiring workers they replace. Such a lack of any
recoupable claims in retained earnings was also believed to be a real
bias against admitting new members and in favor of labor-displacing
technology, both contributing to ever-increasing slack in the Yugoslav
labor market.

It did not take much for such conservative free-enterprise
economists as Svetozar Pejovich, Michael Jensen, and William Meck-
ling to extrapolate their negative picture of the Yugoslav worker-
managed firms to all worker cooperatives in general. The very concept
of democratic worker management was identified with this intrinsic

flaw in the capital structure. From there it was a small step for the experts to conclude that democratic worker cooperatives may be good philosophy, but bad economics.

The picture so far painted does indeed look rather bleak. The few successful producer co-ops sooner or later turn undemocratic and capitalist, and if legal constraints successfully prevent this, as in Yugoslavia, the democratic firm is bound to suffer serious dysfunctional economic side effects. In short, popular sentiment seemed confirmed: worker cooperatives are not a viable or economically promising institution. Therefore, successful business can only be conducted in the modern capitalist corporation, and if one does not like that fact, then nationalized, bureaucratic firms with their paradigmic inefficiencies are the only realistic alternative.

History and civilization have come up with corporate capitalism and bureaucratic socialism; choose one or the other, get ready to rent yourself and perhaps forget such niceties as dignity and industrial democracy!

It is at this juncture that we can reach out and touch upon yet another of David Ellerman's landmark contributions.

Structuring Democratic Enterprise for Success

Ellerman has recognized that corporate stock ownership, which we think of as conventional property, is really a bundle of three different types of rights. They are (A) the *voting rights* to elect the board of directors and through it the management of the firm. Then there is (B) the *right to share in profits* in the form of dividends. Finally, the ownership right attached to stock ownership we may call (C) the *right to net worth,* i.e., the difference between the corporation's total assets and liabilities. The capitalist ABC consists of these rights, all tied together as a package. They are property rights which can be transferred, inherited, bought, and sold (alienated). Figure 8.1 illustrates this discussion.

This works well for capitalist firms, but not for the type of industrial democracy we have referred to. As we have seen, democratic self-government on the firm level necessitates a one-member, one-vote principle incompatible with either outside shareholders having votes or by anyone buying more votes by buying shares. We have seen how employee-owned VAG was a very short-lived experience precisely because of this problem. The same disturbing reality pertains to any other conventional worker-owned firm based on regular stock held by its worker owners. What we have here is still an investor-owned corporation, only now the investors are also the employees. Since shares are

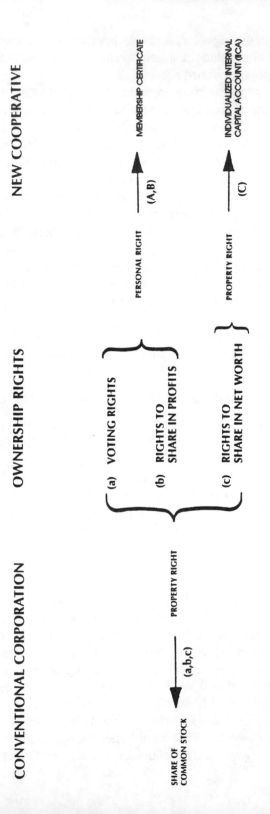

Figure 8.1

THE STRUCTURING OF OWNERSHIP RIGHTS:
CONVENTIONAL CORPORATION VS.
NEW COOPERATIVE

transferrable, there is nothing to prevent employees from selling their shares to outsiders or buying additional ones from co-workers. As soon as that happens, the Kantian principles are violated: (1) some workers will be owners with decision-making power and others will be merely renting themselves to their wealthier partners, and (2) some workers will not share in the whole product that they helped generate.

There is yet the other problem that does not relate to the issue of democracy, but instead explains the tendency of such an employee-owned enterprise to degenerate into a capitalist firm. It arises from the fact that the ownership shares also carry the net worth. After years of accumulation, the net worth of the company is bound to rise just as it did in the successful plywood cooperatives. We have noted that in recent years some had a value of approximately $90,000. The workers can only capitalize on these rights to accumulated net worth by selling their share(s). The more successful the firm, the higher the price a new worker-member would have to pay, and if the price is prohibitively high no new employee-owners may be found. As a result, the owners are tempted to hire mere wage workers or to sell their shares to the highest investor bidder. Either way spells an end to the notion of a democratic and employee-owned enterprise. To avoid all of these predicaments, nothing short of restructuring the traditional ownership rights will do. This involves the following: the tied-up package containing the three rights has to be untied, partitioned, and restructured.

The first step is to separate the (A) voting and (B) profit rights from the (C) right to net worth. In the process a new carrier for the voting and profit rights has to be created in the form of *membership certificates*. For the sake of democracy, these membership certificates have to be *personal* rights attached to the worker's functional role of being a member of the enterprise. Since these certificates are not sellable property rights, it automatically guarantees the one-person, one-vote democratic principle. This is comparable to the personal or political right of being a resident in a certain area. By being a resident (member) you have the right to vote. You can exercise it as long as you live there, but you must give it up if you leave. Also, and most important, you cannot sell the right to someone else. One automatically gets the right by being a resident.

Now to the matter of (B) the right to a share in the profits. In a conventional firm these are the dividends. In a worker-member cooperative there is no separation of owners and workers since they are the same persons, and thus salary and dividends in a conventional firm reduce to the same kind of payment in a cooperative. However, since worker-members need to receive income on a regular basis like anyone else, quarterly income is broken up into two parts, a regular monthly salary and a residual quarterly profit share.

The term "patronage income" is used to refer to a co-op worker's income since it is neither salary (paid by owners to workers) or dividend (paid by owners to self after extracting labor and other costs). This regular paycheck is often called an advance of patronage income. This sum—either an addition if there is a profit or a reduction if there is a loss—is made to the worker-member's individualized Internal Capital Account (IICA) to be discussed shortly. The amount of this sum is in proportion to the individual worker-member's contribution to the net profits (or losses) of the firm, this proportion based upon that individual's relative pay or relative hours worked.

What about the regular paycheck itself (to be seen as an advance of patronage income)? How is that determined? Since the firm is a democratic worker-member cooperative, the relative pay for each role or job in the firm is based on membership, job analysis, discussion, and ultimately voting. These considerations will also naturally be subject to the general job market prevailing for each type of job, so that payment for work will be at a minimum in line with what this position pays elsewhere.

In brief, we can say that conversion of a firm to democratic worker-ownership allows each member as a person, rather than a utilized thing, to participate in firm decision making and at the same time obtain the whole product of their labor.

So much for the voting and the profit rights; now we still have to address the question of what happens to (C) the right to net worth. Ellerman repackages it in the form of a system of individualized quasi-savings accounts, the IICAs made out to each member of the firm. A newly hired worker, after some probationary period, deposits his or her membership fee into such an account. Each fiscal year the employee's balance on patronage income (annual profit share) is added to his or her account. The money accumulating in that account is his or her own property; in a sense it is loaned to the firm for reinvestment in return for annual interest which is also added to the account. Of course, losses to the firm are similarly debited to all its members' IICAs. When the worker-member retires or for legitimate reason leaves the firm, he will be paid the accumulated earnings shown in his or her capital account. All this may sound complicated, but it is really quite simple. What is difficult about it is its radical newness, we are simply not used to this kind of reinterpretation of the traditional ideas of ownership rights.

Let us now see what this ingenious invention of IICAs accomplishes. It does several things, but above all it avoids the kind of pitfalls of the plywood cooperatives as well as the Yugoslav producer co-ops. (Needless to say, the institution of membership certificates already takes care of the Vermont Asbestos Company's problem.)

Remember the problem with the plywood cooperatives? They could not find worker-members capable of laying out $60,000 to $90,000 for a share to become a co-owner. The easy way out was to sell all the shares to the U.S. Plywood Corporation. Now, imagine that the Anacortes Veneer cooperative had the Ellerman-type IICAs. What about each of the more senior worker-owners showing $90,000 in their accounts? If they are to retire, they can pocket the money that is in their accounts waiting for them, but the new workers replacing them do not have to pay $90,000 each to join the club. All they need to join is the small membership fee to open an IICA of their own. The senior workers do not have to consider selling out to a capitalist competitor as the only way to capitalize their accumulated hard-earned incomes. The plywood-type degeneration problem herewith disappears.

What about the Yugoslav lesson? What about that intrinsic flaw in the capital structure of worker self-management? Happily, there is no more problem here either. Why should Ellerman's model workers be reluctant to invest and reinvest their profits? Everybody can take out exactly what he or she put in during their job tenure at the firm. There is simply no longer any problem here because there is no longer the common pool into which one's profits are poured. Instead, each member has his or her own private IICA, registering exactly one's contribution to the firm over all the years. The senior workers now have a common interest with everyone else: invest so as to maximize the (present value of the stream of annual) returns to the enterprise. There is now no more tendency to abstain from accepting new applicants, no longer a bias to replace them with machines, and no longer a bias towards weakening labor demand and the labor market.

This is the essence or theoretical bone structure of the new cooperative conception. It is also summarized in Table 8.1 above. We will flesh it out when considering its real world implementations in Chapter 12. But enough has been said to convey the message: the radical breaking up and reassembly of the traditionally bundled property rights yields a new and perhaps fundamental improved solution. This solution may very well be the basis for John Hobson's "most radical of the social reforms" ushering in, after much delay, his New Industrial Order and preparing the way for Proudhon's New Humanity. But, regardless of whether it is the beginning of a new reality or just another recurrence of an old dream, it certainly makes for an interesting economics, an economics that explicitly respects human dignity.

Meanwhile, conventional economic theory has continued to be a force tending in the very opposite direction. Not only does it continue to hold in contempt anything or anybody refusing to bow to its stand-ard-bearer, Rational Economic Man, but it has also started to export its gospel of one-dimensional man with missionary zeal to other dis-ciplines and ways of thought. The invasion started with sociology, but now also threatens law and other disciplines. The next chapter will at-tempt to survey this new "imperialist" tendency.

References

1. William Thompson, *An Inquiry into the Principles of Distribution of Wealth Most Conducive to Human Happiness, Applied to the Newly Proposed System of Voluntary Equality of Wealth*. London: Longman, Hurst, Rees, Brown & Green, 1824.
2. The question of the productivity of capital resurfaced in the 1960s during the famous Cambridge controversy. For a detailed account see E. K. Hunt and J. G. Schwartz, eds., *A Critique of Economic Theory*. Baltimore: Penguin Books, 1972.
3. John A. Hobson, *Work and Wealth* [1914]. New York: Augustus M. Kelley, 1968, p. 196.
4. *ibid.*, p. 199 (emphasis added).
5. *ibid.*
6. *ibid.*, p. 88.
7. John A. Hobson, *Incentives in the New Industrial Order* [1922]. London: Hyperion, 1980, pp. 109-110.
8. David Ellerman, "The Kantian Person/Thing Principle in Political Economy," *Journal of Economic Issues,* XXII:4 (December 1988), pp. 1109-1122.
9. Immanuel Kant, *Groundwork of the Metaphysics of Morals*. H. J. Paton, trans. New York: Harper Torchbooks, 1964, p. 96.
10. Paul Samuelson, *Economics*. 10th edition. New York: McGraw-Hill, 1976, p. 52.
11. Francis Batt, *The Law of Master and Servant*. 5th edition. London: Pitman, 1967, p. 612.
12. David Ellerman, "On the Labor Theory of Property," *The Philosophical Forum*, XVI:4 (Summer 1985), pp. 293-326.
13. Henry Maine, *Ancient Law* [1861]. Reprint. London: Dent, 1972, p. 100.

14. David Ellerman, "The Employment Contract and Liberal Thought," *Review of Social Economy,* 44:1 (April 1986), pp. 14-15.
15. *ibid.,* p. 25.
16. *ibid.,* pp. 13-39.
17. Robert Nozick, *Anarchy, State and Utopia.* New York: Basic Books, 1974, p. 331.
18. Thomas Hobbes, *Leviathan* [1651]. Reprint. Indianapolis: Bobbs-Merrill, 1958, p. 142.
19. Quoted in Ellerman, "The Employment Contract," *op. cit.,* p. 29.
20. *ibid.,* pp. 35-36.
21. *ibid.,* p. 37.
22. John Stuart Mill, *Principles of Political Economy (with Some Applications to Social Philosophy)* [1848]. 5th edition. New York: D. Appleton, 1891, book IV, chapter 7, section 6, pp. 357-359.
23. Pierre Joseph Proudhon, quoted in Martin Buber, *Paths in Utopia.* Boston: Beacon Press, 1949, p. 29.
24. Buber, *op. cit.,* p. 71.
25. *ibid.*
26. K. V. Berman, *Worker-Owned Plywood Companies (An Economic Analysis).* Pullman: Washington State University Press, 1967, p. 86.
27. C. J. Bellas, *Industrial Democracy and the Worker-Owned Firm (A Study of Twenty-One Plywood Companies in the Pacific Northwest).* New York: Praeger, 1972, p. 96.

Chapter 9

ECONOMICS IMPERIALISM AND THE NEED FOR ITS CONTAINMENT

The term "imperialism" is generally understood to mean a nation-state's intentional practice of extending its control and dominion over other nations, to rob them of their independence by forcefully turning them into colonies. What usually comes to mind are the days of the Roman Empire or, in more recent history, the British Empire. In such a conceptual framework the term "economics imperialism" would simply imply the attempt of one powerful economy or economic system to control and dominate other economies for its own accumulation of wealth. John Hobson, being the first economist to study such phenomena, vividly described it as "a social parasite process by which a moneyed interest within the state makes for imperial expansion in order to fasten economic suckers into foreign bodies so as to drain them of their wealth in order to support domestic luxury."[1] Hobson wrote this almost nine decades ago when the imperialist movement was in full swing with all major powers trying to outdo each other in establishing new colonies over the globe. Only the drastic event of World War I put an end to that remarkable epoch in history, although many economists of a more Marxist-Leninist persuasion believe the capitalist imperialist forces are in full bloom even today.

Whatever the history and present state of this type of economics imperialism, this is *not* what this chapter is about. Instead, we now turn our attention to a very different type of imperialism: the expanding domain of the theory of economics that started to manifest itself in the

1960s and is still gaining momentum today. Unlike the kind Hobson observed, which relied on brute military power, this one is of a far more subtle kind; it conquers analytically minded scholars striving for greater rigor and respectability in whatever discipline they happen to find themselves. It is an imperialism of the mind, seeking to "liberate" other minds by advocating a new, *economic* approach to conventional issues and social problems.

One of the very first economists to recognize and name this new phenomenon was Kenneth Boulding, who in his presidential address to the American Economic Association, December 1968, referred to "economics imperialism" as the attempt on the part of economics to take over all other social sciences.[2] This is a movement to change the way we think, to export the economic way of thinking, pioneered by Gossen and the Austrians and popularized by Wicksteed and Robbins more than a half a century ago. Economics by their view, we recall, is not properly defined by its subject matter (commerce, market behavior, GNP, budget deficits, etc.), but instead as the scientific method studying all human behavior and social interaction believed to be described by the rational choice model discussed in Chapter 5.

Ironically, the modern imperialist movement started at the University of Chicago where most of the pioneers still teach. It is there where we meet its most outspoken prophets, Gary Becker, Robert Fogel, George Stigler, Ronald Coase, and Judge Richard Posner. We say "ironically" because earlier one of the founders of the Chicago school, Frank Knight, emerged as an outspoken opponent of such an approach. In 1951, for example, he wrote:

> It is characteristic of the age in which we live to think too much in terms of economics, to see things too predominantly in their economic aspect; and this is especially true of the American people. There is no more important prerequisite to clear thinking in regard to economics itself than is recognition of its limited place among human interests at large.[3]

Not so long after this warning was sounded, imperialism got started by applying economic reasoning to such fields as education (human capital theory) and economic history (cleometrics). Next was sociology, in particular new theories about sexual behavior, marriage, love and affection, child production, lying and cheating, divorce, and crime. Soon came other spheres relating to the entire gamut of life: the most economical suicide, the most economical way to die, as well as economic insights about life after death. At the same time, interest grew in exploring such traditional issues of political science as voting behavior, presidential elections, riots and panics, and government in general. Similarly, the economic approach was also used to explain the behavior of rats, birds, snails, and even such microscopic animals as the *stentor corruleus,* whose behavior was found to be "simple-minded but still rational."[4] More recently, a new area was invaded, the domain of law and legal theory.

Space precludes a meaningful survey of all these missionary ventures, but at the risk of some oversimplification we do want to make the following observation. The extension of economics into animal behavior is certainly warranted and has produced more significant results than elsewhere. Moreover, the intrusions into political science, although marked by a strongly cynical flavor, do shed some valuable light on certain questions. When it comes to sociology and the economics of life and death, most of the work done by Gary Becker and others may strike the reader as somewhat silly or at least as far-fetched; nevertheless, the harm it does is relatively minor. As an example, we quote a paragraph from *The New World of Economics* which concerns itself with the rational way to die:

> It is only human for one to feel sympathetic toward the person who dies with everything going wrong: a malfunctioning liver, arteriosclerosis, a defective kidney, ulcers, respiratory problems, and waning eyesight. However, such a tumultuous exit may indicate that the individual involved has more thoroughly enjoyed life than the person who dies with only a failing heart and everything else in perfect order. If this is the case, the sympathy may be misplaced. The fact that all of one's organs are malfunctioning at the time of death may indicate that one has fully utilized his organic capital assets in the pursuit of utility; the person who dies with a perfect liver may have foregone a number of drinks during the course of his life that could have contributed significantly to his own welfare: a liver in good order is useless if the heart goes first.[5]

Turning to the economic analysis of law, on the other hand, we are dealing with a very different matter; here the extension of economics is positively dangerous. It is for this reason that we will have to economize our resources by focusing only on that particular brand of imperialism. First, let us look a little closer at the common element and driving force of imperialist intrusion.

The Heart of Economics Imperialism

The idea of economics imperialism naturally derives from the economist's notion of what is rational human behavior. If economists study human choice and behavior on such a basis, then why narrow itself to consumption and production in formal markets? Decisions and choices are not only made by consumers and businessmen and workers interacting in the marketplace. The very same agents who decide what to buy and where to work *also* decide when to marry, whom to vote for, when and how to rob a bank, and, in the capacity of a judge, come up with a ruling on which party is entitled to certain property rights. Once we grant that rationality is not confined to explicit market transactions, but rather a dominant aspect of social behavior in general, then it would seem to follow that the conceptual apparatus constructed by economists to explain market behavior would also explain non-market behavior. Personal decisions and choices can be thought of as being either rational or else emotional or arbitrary. This seems to be the bottom line of the imperialist logic. The *only* domain or territory that is not (yet) claimed is the emotional. This is nicely brought out in the following passage of Richard Posner's: "I happen to find implausible and counterintuitive the view that the individual's decisional processes are so rigidly compartmentalized that he will act rationally in making some trivial purchase but irrationally when deciding whether to go to law school or get married or evade income taxes or have three children rather than two or prosecute a lawsuit. But many readers will, I am sure, intuitively regard these choices, important as they are–or perhaps because they are so important–as lying within the area where decisions are emotional rather than rational."[6]

Modern economics, Chicago-style, makes assumptions about individual human behavior and also attempts to make predictions about such individuals in social interaction; in other words, it can be seen to study reflected, non-emotional social behavior wherever it happens to occur. By maintaining that such concepts as utility, maximization, opportunity cost, rational choice, competition, scarcity, and the law of demand are general and open-ended, it paves the way for expansionism. As Posner put it, such concepts "make a work of scholarship 'economic' regardless of its subject matter or its author's degree."[7] Once economics is so "defined logically" there is "nothing that makes the study of marriage and divorce less suitable *a priori* for economics than the study of the automobile industry and the inflation rate."[8] Or, to quote Gary Becker, it is "the combined assumptions of maximizing behavior, market equilibrium, and stable preferences, used relentlessly and unflinchingly, [which] form the heart of the economic approach."[9] So we once again meet our old friend Rational Economic Man for another round of description and critical evaluation. It is he who is behind the imperialist expansion of economics into the traditionally non-economic domains of sociology, political science, criminology, anthropology, and law–and as Jack Hirschleifer recently noted, "with more to come."

Ironically, all this is going on just as many leading economists, such as Amartya Sen, have come to see the epitome of a rational actor as a "rational fool," an emperor with no clothes. (It is indeed puzzling how such a social dunce could be so immensely successful in empire building!) But it is not a joke. Quite the contrary, it is serious business, leading even more restrained economists such as Jack Hirschleifer to admit that "there is only one social science," and that "economics really does constitute the universal grammar of [such] social science."[10]

Some see the end to economics imperialism to be just a matter of time, but even such predictions are anything but reassuring. Ronald Coase, for example, speculates:

> If the main advantage which an economist brings to the other social sciences is simply a way of looking at the world, it is hard to believe, once the values of such economic wisdom are recognized, that it will not be acquired by some practitioners in these other fields. This is already happening in law and political science. Once some of these practitioners have acquired the simple, but valuable, truths which economics has to offer, and this is the natural competitive response, economists who try to work in the other social sciences will have lost their main advantage and will face competitors who know more about the subject matter than they do.[11]

To us this sounds more like a projection of ultimate victory than a hopeful note envisioning the decline of the empire. In any event, one can only hope that both Hirschleifer and Coase are wrong, that social scientists will have the courage and ability to mount a more successful resistance to the line of economic reasoning. Anything we as economists can offer to that end will help–and this book, in part, is meant to be a humble contribution to such purpose.

The Economic Analysis of Law: From Coase to Posner

Let us now proceed to illuminate the most dangerous thrust of the imperialist movement, the one aimed at conquering legal theorists, lawyers, and judges. The beginning of this agression can be precisely dated; it started with Ronald Coase's landmark October 1960 article titled "The Problem of Social Cost."[12]

In order to understand the concept of social cost we recall that in Chapter 8, dealing with welfare economics, we discussed the problem of externalities, particularly external costs. Costs of this nature arise when one self-interested agent engages in activities that impose costs on others. The classic case is, of course, the external costs of pollution, for example, factory smoke in the midwest that causes acid rain and with it agricultural damage in the eastern part of the United States. As a classic solution to such problems, economists, following Pigou, have been advocating some kind of government intervention, one that would ideally compel the polluters to take into account the pollution damage resulting from smoke emission. This could be done by an emission charge. If the discharge fee is properly set, then all the damage done by the polluting activity would be "internalized" and private profit maximization would once again operate in the name of the social good.

Ronald Coase and the Problem of Social Cost

Ronald Coase in his celebrated article seeks to demonstrate that there is another way to handle the problem of external costs. Moreover, the alternative is considered preferable since it relies on private exchange rather than on public taxation. He demonstrates the new approach with several examples, one of which goes as follows. A commercial farmer (F) and a commercial cattle rancher (R) are operating on neighboring properties. If there is no fence protecting the farmer's crops, then R's cattle will stray across the border and damage F's crops, and, of course, the more cattle that are raised, the greater the damage to his neighbor F.

Here we obviously have a classic example of an externality. The conventional approach and the one that may seem to be sanctioned by common sense, would be to have R bear these costs one way or another. One way would be to make R liable for the damages. Let us say that the damage to F's crops is $1,000, but that it only costs $500 to build a fence. Under such circumstances we would expect the rational rancher to build the fence himself and save $500 in the process.

Professor Coase, however, proposes a new and perhaps intriguing slant on the problem. He also considers additional costs that the fence imposes on R. Since his cattle can no longer feed on his neighbor's crops, they will fatten slower and as a result he incurs, let us say, another cost of $300 on that score. Nevertheless, given such cost estimates, a fence is still in his interest and he will end up saving $200. Obviously, fencing would no longer be in his interest if its costs were substantially higher, or if the crop damage to F were significantly lower.

Coase goes further. He suggests that for the sake of analysis let us assume now that in the original situation the farmer would have *no* right to keep his neighbor's cattle out. In other words, the rancher is not liable for the damage done to the crops. F now has a choice; he can build a fence and prevent the $1,000 damage or save the $500 fencing cost and endure the crop loss of $1,000. Obviously, he will build the fence, even if he would have to compensate R for the $300 that the fence would impose on the rancher by curtailing his feeding area.

In other words, regardless of whether the farmer is entitled to see his property undisturbed by his neighbor or whether the rancher is entitled to let his cattle roam freely, a cost/benefit calculus suggests that the fence will be built, herewith solving the problem of external cost. From the standpoint of the fence getting built there is the intriguing discovery that it makes no difference which one of the two paries has the entitlement (property right).

In this analysis by Ronald Coase it is possible to dispense with government intervention in terms of the externality problem. All we need are well-specified property rights. As long as there is no fence and therefore an externality problem, it is in the interest of either party to approach the other and make a deal under which both are better off. Each party will attempt to buy the entitlement held by the other, assuming, of course, that the price is less than the cost to be borne if they fail to reach a private contract. Similarly, the bearer of the entitlement will have an incentive to sell it if he can so make more money than he could by retaining it. As a result, we have an allocation of productive resources that will maximize the total market value of the parties' joint product (that is, their individual products added together).

Of course, the initial allocation of entitlements will affect the *distribution* of business costs and profits. So, if the farmer had the rights initially, the outcome would leave him better off than if the rancher had the rights. This is a fundamental problem for Coase and his followers which we will return to.

Now, it may be that the fence costs $2,000, herewith fundamentally altering the calculus. Under such a circumstance, it would not be worthwhile for either party to erect it. It comes down to this for Coase: what is not worthwhile for each from an individual perspective is also not a good idea from a social point of view, simply defined here as the quest for maximum market values in the *combined* beef and crop production, ignoring distribution.

Take another famous example. Suppose sparks emitted from a railroad steam engine burn crops growing alongside the tracks. Whose fault is it? Who is liable? What should be done about the problem? In a

Coasian world it is a joint problem: both the railroad's engine and the farmers' corn field are seen to have "caused" the fire. To prevent the problem we could require the railroad to install a spark-guard or the farmers to leave the land near the tracks fallow. Either way the consumer pays, either in higher railroad rates or a higher price for agricultural crops, such as corn. Let the parties themselves find a solution. Let them strike a deal. Again, the optimal combined outcome should be equivalent to one where either the farmers or the railroad initially owns the primary property rights, and it does not matter which one.

Other examples involve dirty factory smoke interfering with the functioning of a laundry, the building of a tall schoolhouse in front of a windmill, and so forth. Coase tells us that by leaving it to free exchange, and provided the relevant property rights are allocated to someone, there is no externality problem, no need for Pigouian taxes, no need for welfare economics.

If all these results seem strange and counterintuitive, it is only because we are accustomed to thinking in terms of inherent or natural rights, whether in the form of personal rights or property rights. We intuitively take such rights as given and proceed from there. Not so in this part of the newly expanded economic empire. Here all rights are seen as merely instrumental, as serving the purpose of consumer wants. If something enables economic maximization, it *is* the right. We should add, however, that at least in the pioneering work of Coase all these conclusions pertain to the business world of commerce where all the actors are businessmen. As we will see, things will appeal even less to common sense when we turn to another missionary agent of the empire, Judge Richard Posner.

The wonderful world of Ronald Coase described so far rests, however, on two important assumptions relating to (1) zero (or insignificant) transaction costs and (2) zero (or insignificant) redistribution costs. If either of these two assumptions does not hold, the entire analysis begins to unravel.

Transaction costs measure the actual or prospective costs involved in making and enforcing a deal. They include the costs of locating and getting together with the other party, the time spent in arriving at an agreement, and the efforts necessary to exclude third parties from sharing in the benefits on a free rider basis.

It can be argued that the types of examples Coase discussed seem at first sight reasonably consistent with the zero transaction cost assumption, except perhaps in the case where a railroad may have to deal with a large number of farmers. However, self-interest (or in the language of the field, so-called "strategic behavior") may quite considerably complicate things. The problem arises if the parties cannot agree on how to divide up the savings generated by the bargain, and this is especially true in the absence of a benchmark market price. Each party has an incentive to bargain for the lion's share of the surplus by disguising one's true intentions, bluffing, threatening non-cooperation, all in order to "free ride" as much as possible on the other. It seems reasonable to assume that all this haggling can be prohibitively time-consuming. Transaction costs now emerge as quite significant, suggesting that the two parties may not be able to reach a bargain that otherwise would be in their interest. This would be a prisoner's dilemma outcome. One way to show this is to witness the arms race between the two political superpowers. In the previous fence example, such transaction costs will have an equivalent effect as did the increase in the cost of the fence construction. And now in a world of stategic behavior and prohibitive transaction costs, it would suddenly seem to matter whom the courts entitle with the property right.

What is the law to do in situations such as the above where transaction costs are indeed significant? The answer to this question was already implied in Coase's article and is now referred to as the *Coase Theorem;* it has the courts assign entitlements to the party who values them most–the highest bidder, so to speak. It is with this type of thinking that Coase has prepared the way for the much more controversial Posner and followers.

There remains, however, the other necessary assumption–no significant redistribution costs. If assignment of entitlement significantly benefits the rich, there will be a worsening of distributional equality which would need to be offset by appropriate redistribution. But all such redistribution schemes (taxes, subsidies, and the like) will have distortive (i.e., costly) effects. If, for example, you levy a higher income tax on the rich, they would have a tendency to work less than they otherwise would have. As a consequence, we will hardly escape the brute fact that the apparently unavoidable costs of redistribution will seriously undermine the welfare effect promised by a Coasian solution to the externality problem, and this is particularly so when the courts assign important entitlements to the party exhibiting the greatest willingness (and ability) to pay.

The cases discussed by Coase focus on a specific and relatively confined area in law, the one dealing with incompatible land uses which goes under the heading of nuisance law. It typically involves two private parties where the victim seeking remedy brings the dispute to the judge. Following a basic approach similar to Coase, Guido Calabresi applied the same idea on a broader spectrum to the so-called law of torts dealing with unintentional harm one party inflicts on another, such as in car accidents.[13] The law involved here is no longer restricted to (judge-made) common law, but also applies to the enforcement of statutory law made by legislators. In these cases it is usually the government that seeks to enforce the law. From there, it was only a small step to apply Coasian justice to other areas, such as product liability law and air pollution law. The stage was set for the appearance of a new super missionary who would be able to stretch the new idea so as to cover the entire landscape.

Richard Posner, being the right man at the right time, emerged to fill this role. He was at the Chicago Law School in 1968 where he studied economic price theory under George Stigler. He soon obtained a Ph.D. in Chicago-type free market economics, and in 1973 published his landmark textbook entitled *The Economic Analysis of Law,* which not only pushed the ideas of Coase and Calabresi into the mainstream of legal scholarship but argued that the economic approach to law could be more developed and expanded to include just about any legal notion, including constitutional law. As the *Washington Post* observed more than a decade later: "Posner's textbook became a legal bestseller and provided an army of recruits with basic training in 'law and economics.'"[14] Moreover, in 1972 he became the founding editor of the *Journal of Legal Studies,* a post he held until 1982 when he was appointed to the Seventh Circuit Court of Appeals in Chicago. Today he remains a top contender for a future position to the Supreme Court. To make things even more spectacular (and, as we will argue, more dangerous), he has inspired several other top contenders for that post, among them Ralph Winter, Frank Easterbrook, Douglas Ginsberg, and the celebrated nominee rejected by the Senate, Robert Bork, not to mention the successful contender Antonin Scalia.[15] When we keep in mind that four of the current Chief Justices as of this writing are in their eighties, making for a strong likelihood of several vacancies in the near future, it becomes readily apparent how potentially all-powerful the new Posner-led extension of the economics empire into law really is. But more of that later; first, we will have to examine what that approach at its very least implies.

Richard Posner's Approach to Law and Economics

The type of economics that Posner learned so well at Chicago reflects the line developed by Wicksteed and Robbins. "Economics," Posner tells us right at the onset of his famous textbook, "is the science of human choice in a world in which resources are limited in relation to human wants." And he continues, "It explores and tests the implication that man is a rational maximizer of his ends in life, his satisfactions—what we shall call his 'self-interest.'"[16] It is all there. Economics is not a fixed subject matter with a predefined domain. It is not about money, commerce, shopping, or work. It is not confined to market behavior, but instead encompasses all rational behavior and the capacity to make good decisions wherever they have to be made.

The reader is now ready to be introduced to the concept of "efficiency," which is said to result from self-interested free exchange. Through such interactions, the resources (land, labor, capital) are permitted to gravitate to their highest valued uses. So, for example, if farmer A and farmer B reach an agreement to sell land from one to the other, it must mean that the buyer can extract more use value or satisfaction from the land than the seller could. More specifically, the new owner will be able to shift the use of the land to growing those products that consumers are most willing to pay for, and so in the process automatically maximize the value consumers attach to the land use. When resources are being used where their value is greatest, they are said to be employed *efficiently*.

The problem as Posner himself realizes is that "value," and with it efficiency, are determined by what is called *willingness to pay,* which not only measures the relative urgency of a want but also a potential buyer's *ability to pay* regardless of the desire or need—in other words, his or her level of wealth. Quite obviously, a particular efficient allocation of resources is determined by the distribution of purchasing power and wealth in an economy. Redistribute that wealth and we can expect different demands, different levels of willingness to pay, different values, and a different efficiency allocation. It follows that if economists advocate efficiency in resource use, they are also implicitly making a value judgment that the existing distribution of income and wealth is perfectly just, and that consumer demand is and ought to be the dominant value of society.

Posner, far from hiding these considerations and qualifications, informs his readers about them and logically seems to suggest with restraint: "The economist's competence in a discussion of the legal system is limited to predicting the effect of legal rules and arrangements on value and efficiency, in their strict and technical sense, and on the existing distribution of income and wealth."[17]

But wait, just as the reader starts feeling more relaxed and inclined to drop his or her defenses, the tune suddenly starts changing. In the very next section dealing with the relevance of economics to law we read: "Economics turns out to be a powerful tool of normative analysis of law and legal institutions—a source of criticism and reform."[18] Apparently, the economist is now suddenly licensed to tell society that one course of action is more valued than another, particularly "since efficiency is a widely regarded value in our world" anyway. Just as a mathematician can tell us which solution to an equation is true, or an engineer can tell us which type of bridge is the safest, so the economist (together with like-minded judges and legal scholars) can tell us which type of legal rule is best for society.

Efficiency as Wealth Maximization.   The simplest type of efficiency that economists talk about is "Pareto efficiency." It implies that as long as we can make somebody better off without making anybody worse off, we are improving efficiency. When that is no longer possible we have reached the most efficient allocation. Although this may sound somewhat abstract, such Pareto efficiency can be easily conceptualized. In a private voluntary contract between two parties, economics claims that any exchange will be enhancing efficiency in the Pareto sense since nobody would choose to hurt him- or herself by consenting to a deal. This is the basic assumption already critically examined in Chapter 2.

Let us assume for the sake of this discussion that we accept this principle. However, things begin to unravel should there exist so-called "third party effects," where the effects on other individuals are to be taken into account. Now we would have to compare benefits of the trading partners with potential costs to others. Here we meet once again the nasty problem of interpersonal utility comparisons that has long been a source of endless grief for utilitarians and economists alike. One way to solve it, recalling our discussion in Chapter 8, was to use the Kaldor hypothetical compensation criterion. (In contemporary literature the Kaldor principle is often called the "Kaldor-Hicks" criterion to honor another inventor of the same idea. We will use the labels interchangeably.) It asserts that if the gains from a potential move could fully compensate the losers and have something left over, it is an efficient move regardless of whether the losers are actually compensated or not. In Chapter 8 we demonstrated in the context of that discussion that it implied the counterintuitive and completely unfounded assumption of an extra dollar being worth exactly the same to a billionaire as to a poor beggar. Only if that were indeed an accurate picture of the constitution of human beings could we say that the greater utility of the gainer has not more than offset the utility loss of a policy's uncompensated victims. Otherwise, we simply are at a loss to tell whether social welfare has increased or not.

Now, we can avoid this troublesome difficulty by changing the language from "utility" or "welfare" to "wealth." We seem unable to assert that the passing of the Kaldor-Hicks test increases total utility and welfare, but we are able to claim that *wealth*–defined as the output of all tangible and intangible commodities multiplied by their market values– will indeed increase. It is not clear what is truly gained by such seemingly linguistic manipulation, but its appeal is strong enough for Posner to interpret efficiency in terms of wealth maximization rather than utility maximization.

At this stage, it should be pointed out that wealth in the Posner fashion is *not* equivalent to GNP since it includes intangible commodities "traded" in non-market exchanges occurring within households and elsewhere. An example would be a greater allocation of time to child care within a family houshold. More importantly, his definition of wealth does *not* use market *prices* as weights for output but market *values* instead. Within this framework prices and values are not the same. Take water, for example. Bottled drinking water may have a market *price* of less than $1 per gallon, but its market *value,* according to Posner, would include the value as measured by a willingness to pay for all of the bottled water on the market. So, if an Arabian king would be willing to pay $10,000 per gallon of bottled water, but actually could obtain it for only a dollar, we would have to add to his "value" also $9,999 and then add his total value to all other values accruing to the consumers and producers of water. In economic terminology this simply means that wealth is not just market price times quantity transacted, but the total consumer and producer surplus defined by supply and demand.

The limitations of equating a measuring value with *"willingness to pay"* have already been pointed out in our earlier discussion of cost-benefit analysis. Most economists are well aware of these limitations and problems intrinsic to the concept, and they are therefore reluctant to openly advertise its use too much. Not so Mr. Posner, who proudly makes willingness to pay the very bedrock of his wealth-maximizing efficiency. In a relatively recent book titled *The Economics of Justice* (1981)–and by "justice" he means nothing other than wealth maximization–we read: "The individual who would like very much to have some good but is unwilling or unable to pay anything for it–perhaps because he is destitute–does not value the good in the sense in which I am using the term 'value.'"[19] The only preferences that have ethical weight in his system of wealth maximization are the ones backed up by money. Later, he further elaborates that people who lack sufficient earning power to support even a minimum decent standard of living are entitled to nothing at all, except perhaps private charity. And he sounds even more cruel when asserting that if someone "happens to be born feeble-minded and his net social product is negative, he would have no right to the means of support."[20]

With Posner, the willingness/ability to pay principle is now allowed to openly penetrate legal decisions. Witness the following example which he offers to illustrate application of his wealth-maximizing efficiency: Imagine a case where "someone of monetary means broke into an unoccupied cabin and stole food in order to avert starvation." Posner asserts that this is right and just since transaction costs for a bargain with the distant cabin owner were prohibitive and there "would be reason to believe that the food was more valuable, in the economic sense of value, to the thief than to the owner."[21] In other words, the thief would have been able to pay the owner for the food. What emerges as an important element here is that the desperate burglar was "someone of monetary means." Otherwise, we have to surmise that the same act triggered by the same need was inefficient, and therefore to be severely punished.

It is indeed so that Posner's wealth maximization has some advantages over ordinary utilitarianism, although the weighing of preferences by income and wealth is not one of them. One advantage is that utilitarianism may condone rape because the offender may derive more pleasure than the victim experiences pain. But by defining efficiency as wealth maximization and provided that transactions costs are tolerably low, Posner does stress the importance of mutual consent which underlies market transactions, as well as more civilized non-market human relations. If a rapist cannot evoke such consent, it has to be assumed that rape is not wealth maximizing. This emphasis on consent, Posner tells us, reflects an ethical criterion "congenial to the Kantian emphasis on treating people as ends rather than means."[22]

A problem arises, however, when either free market developments, a government policy, or a legal rule in pursuit of efficiency impose costs on others who, true to the Kaldor-Hicks criterion, will not be compensated and therefore can hardly be assumed to eagerly muster consent. Here Posner comes up with another clever idea, the concept of "ex ante" compensation. Just as a person buying a non-winning lottery ticket could be seen to have "consented" to the loss, so with an entrepreneur who loses money as a result of a competitor's development of a superior product. Rational individuals are supposed to know the risks and so implicitly consented to the possibility of their loss.

As a "parallel but more difficult case," Posner also mentions the worker who loses his job when the product he helps make is no longer competitive. But here the hired worker would not be responsible for the product no longer being competitive, as Ellerman pointed out in Chapter 8 (that is management's responsibility). To have him or her suffer the consequences of job loss with no compensation precisely treats the worker as a means and not an end. So Ellerman's analysis, also relying on Kant, shows us that Posner's appeal to Kant should in fact undercut Posner's own argument.

Posner's logic would also seem to apply to catastrophic injuries occurring in a high-risk occupation. No compensation would be required here as well since the worker had implicitly consented to the tragedy when making that unhappy job choice. The social and legal implications of such imputed consent would obviously be far-reaching.

Perhaps most dehumanizing is Posner's view of personal rights. Slavery is wrong for one reason only: it is inefficient. By the same token, a woman ought to own the rights to her body since it can be shown that she alone can most efficiently decide when and where to rent it or otherwise use it. Similarly, Posner's world is one of almost complete disregard for intrinsic human rights and human dignity as the following example indicates: "Let there be 100,000 sheep worth in the aggregate more than any money value that can reasonably be ascribed to a child: is a driver [who swerves to avoid the sheep] therefore a good man when he decides to sacrifice the child? The economic answer is yes."[23] Although we might add that things would not be so clear for Posner if the parent would be someone "of monetary means."

By now the reader should be reasonably acquainted with the nature and ethics of wealth-maximizing efficiency. It is thus important to note that one can easily think of other and more meaningful efficiency concepts. Let us for the record mention two others, *social welfare maximization* and *social justice maximization*. The former is highly sensitive to distributional concerns and would only approve of changes if the distributional consequences would be tolerable or favorable towards the poor. The latter allows for social values not only as they pertain to distribution but also as they recognize personal rights. Other law-and-economics scholars, such as Calabresi, have at one time or another explicitly made room for the fact that rational agents may have preferences for such "public" or societal goods as principles of right and social justice. He, for example, has summoned such "moralisms" (as he labels them) to account for certain legal doctrines, such as the unenforcability of enslavement contracts.

Economic Efficiency and the Law

The efficiency concept can be applied to law, both positively as an explanation of what it is and does and normatively as a guide to legal policy of what it should be and what it should do. With respect to the positive and explanatory role, much of the analysis has traditionally focused on the economic theory of the common law, the kind of law made by judges rather than by legislature and constitutional conventions. Analysts such as Posner approach such law as a set of rules which imposes costs or benefits (subsidies) on the activities involved. We know that by changing the rules one changes incentives and so affects behavior.

The economic theory of the common law is, in the words of Posner, "that the common law is best understood not merely as a pricing mechanism but as a pricing mechanism designed to bring about an efficient allocation of resources in the Kaldor-Hicks sense of efficiency."[24] This type assertion is not only radically new, it is bound to make little sense to judges, most of whom have no background in economic theory and not surprisingly do not ordinarily refer to economic concepts in their legal opinions. Posner resolves the economic abstruseness as follows: "The true grounds of decisions are often concealed rather than illuminated by the characteristic rhetoric of judicial opinions. Indeed, legal education consists primarily of learning to dig beneath the rhetorical surface to find those grounds. It is an advantage of economic analysis rather than a drawback that it does not analyze cases in the conceptual modes employed in the opinions themselves."[25] In other words, Posner's theory of law tries to deduce judicial outcomes from general propositions not stated in the courts' opinions. The judges are seen as moved by principles which they hold unconsciously and unaffected by the principles they consciously believe to hold. Or, as Robert Cooter put it, "If judicial decisions can be explained without reproducing the opinions, then the reasons given in the opinion are not the real reasons for the decisions; [and] if the real reasons are latent and not manifest in the opinions, then the opinions are diminished in dignity and stature."[26] It is not only the opinions but the judges themselves who look rather diminished and degraded by such a claim.

Let us now show how the normative arises from the positive. Imagine that Posner's tests have convinced legal scholars that the positive theory of law has been strikingly successful, that there is indeed a pervasive tendency for law to aim for wealth-maximizing efficiency. How, under such circumstances, are we now to regard a particular ruling or doctrine that violates the alleged regularity? Posner often uses words

such as "unsound," "legalistic," "specious" to label such misfits in contrast to the "proper" and "correct" decisions which accord to wealth
maximization. We can now appreciate how easy it is to slip from the
positive "is" to the normative "ought." As one critic, Frank Michelman
of the Harvard Law School, puts it, "If the actual law is generally but
imperfectly efficient, why not make it perfect? If we can perceive an
organic economic unity in the corpus juris, detect an inner logic cours-
ing through the law, why not tidy up, cast off the excrescences, ration-
alize the whole, assist the law in realizing its Idea?"[27]

Using another example by Michelman, consider a judge who consciously holds a theory of what judges are supposed to do that is at odds
with the economic efficiency criterion for law. Can we persuade that
judge to abandon that theory in favor of wealth maximization by arguing that the law will gradually work itself out to the most efficient level,
no matter what the judge does, so he or she might as well do his or her
part to help things along their inevitable course? Once again, it is easy
to get carried from a positive analysis to a normative conclusion. And
in the case of law and economics, it is, of course, that particular type of
efficiency (wealth maximization) and not the social welfare and social
justice kind that will pop up in legal policy studies. Concerns relating
to redistribution and intrinsic rights will have by then already disap-
peared from the scene. So we are told the only thing that objectively
matters is concern for one's own consumption of commodities.

An Application of Judge Posner's Contribution: Selling Babies

There is perhaps no more telling example, illustrating where
Posner's ideas lead, than to turn to one of his publications dealing with
the legal institution of adopting infants. It certainly shows how wealth
maximization emerges as the powerful tool of normative analysis and
institutional reform that Posner claims it to be.

The paper, published together with Elisabeth Landes in 1978, could
be understood as just another stone thrown against what was in those
days perceived, at least by some, as excessive government regulation
of economic and social life.[28] Its subject, however, pertains not to such
pedestrian issues as air transportation, banking, new drugs, and asbestos, but now concerns "excessive" government regulation of child adoptions. More specifically, the topic is centered around the baby shortage
in white infants, where couples often have to wait three to seven years
to receive a baby. Since the number of illegitimate births have continually been on the rise since 1957, the problem is not caused by availability

of contraception and abortion, but rather lies in the fact that fewer of the babies born out of wedlock are given up for adoption. According to Posner, it is a supply problem where the chief supplier, the adoption agency, is legally prevented from operating as an efficient profit-maximizing organization. Rather, the agency should be legally empowered to offer a high enough compensation to parents who can conceive. The regulated price is generally limited to the direct medical costs related to pregnancy and birth, a far cry from the free market value of a child. This type of skimpy compensation certainly does not provide great incentives to forget about abortion and breed more babies, and so to supply all those 130,000 married couples who would be prepared to enter the baby market as potential buyers every year.

What about the competition? Why, authors Posner and Landes ask, are not more babies adopted through independent or private agency adoptions? The answer is "government" regulation again, particularly the limitation on the fees that may be offered to prospective or actual mothers. True, the compensation there is slightly more generous, but still insufficient by failing to include such items as (1) covering the opportunity cost of the biological mother not working, (2) the disutility of pregnancy and delivery, (3) any value the biological mother attaches to keeping the child rather than giving it up, and (4) the transaction costs of finding a broker (usually an obstetrician or lawyer) who would locate and bring together buyers and sellers. Under such circumstances, women, especially the not-so-well-to-do, will prefer abortion or raising the child to "selling" it to an interested party.

Now, because it is not easy to monitor compliance with the regulated fees and since we are dealing "in a highly individualized commodity" exchanged in an unorganized setting, a certain fraction of the 17,000 independent adoptions end up being black market adoptions with prices ranging from $9,000 to $40,000 per infant. To a large extent the high costs simply reflect the expected penalties the illegal supplier might face and the additional search costs entailed by operating in a clandestine market. As a result, such black market babies are overpriced and it would be inappropriate to take them as evidence for estimating a legal free market price for babies. Posner assures us that the cost of freely bought and sold babies would be considerably lower, "perhaps no more than the cost of an automobile."

Posner concludes the analysis by suggesting that "the baby shortage and black market are the result of legal restrictions that prevent the market from operating as freely in the sale of babies as of other goods. This suggests as a possible reform simply eliminating the restrictions."[29] Here we have a notable example of Posner's legal policy analysis and the type of recommendations it produces. Posner and Landes are, of course, aware that public opinion is against them, that "many people believe that a free market in babies would be undesirable." Posner then tries to show that these objections are misguided, often deliberately manufactured by "well-organized interests opposed to an improvement in social welfare"[30]–the bureaucratic adoption agencies and their professional staff who are fearful of losing their profession under a new regime featuring a baby market.

Let us look at the way Posner and his co-author treat two of the misguided objections. The first is that rationing baby supply by price may be in the best interest of both contracting parties, but not necessarily calculated to promote the welfare of the infant. He concedes that this point cannot be dismissed as foolish since in economic theory there is no presumption "that the satisfactions of the thing traded" are also maximized.[31] In other words, what is true for soybeans and shoes may not hold for human commodities as well. But, he answers, the question is really "whether the price system would do as good a job as, or better than, adoption agencies in finding homes for children that would maximize their satisfaction in life."[32] He then offers indirect evidence that children adopted through private agencies (which were generally placed with a minimum of screening) score virtually identically on IQ and other achievement tests with children raised by their biological parents, or in Posner's words "natural" children. After noting in passing that such adopted children did not perform so well in certain psychological tests, he proceeds by ignoring that negligible point and concludes that "if children adopted without the screening process seem nevertheless to do about as well as natural children, then one is entitled to be skeptical of the need for or the value of the screening."[33] Moreover, beyond a baby's need for love, warmth, food, and shelter, one cannot "read from the face of a newborn" whether he or she will be intelligent, athletic, musical, or artistic, hence agencies cannot be presumed to match these qualities with the qualities of the adoptive parents any more than the market can. Finally, and above all, Posner reassures us that willingness to pay money for a baby would seem an overwhelmingly important factor from the standpoint of child welfare. Is not it true, he asks, that "few people buy a car or a television set in order to smash it?" Why would anybody rational adopt a baby in order to abuse it or make a slave of it?

Another objection relates to the concern that baby selling may logically and inevitably lead to baby breeding. True, Posner says, "any market will generate incentives to improve the product as well as to optimize the price and quantity of the current level of product." But, he counters, why not stress the aspect that under a regime of market baby production "there might be efforts to breed children with a known set of characteristics that could be matched up with those desired by prospective adoptive parents," and so on.[34] This, of course, is true if a baby is a thing, a possession to be used (but not abused) just as a motorcycle or a dog. In a sense, the efficiency problem reduces here to making sure that the fast bikes go to the racers and the hunting dogs to the hunters. If that can be accomplished, the world has been made a slightly better place for all. Certainly consumer satisfaction is up. The basic humanistic principle that babies and children, as well as people, are different from objects, things, and commodities, that they have an intrinsic worth and a dignity rather than a price, appears totally beyond Judge Posner's moral grasp, despite his harkening to Kant.

It is a sad chapter in human history that we have come to the above. Civilization has evidently not only brought us a deeper appreciation of humanity but also the kind of ideas espoused by Posner and his economics and law movement. For us, it demonstrates the moral bankruptcy of the imperialist agents.

The Need to Halt the Empire

By now many readers, perhaps even some economists, may feel pretty alienated by Posner's approach to law and its institutions. It raises the question as to what response has such writing evoked in the academic community. As for the political community, we can safely assume that Posner's appointment to the Court is an expression of plenty of support, at least of an executive that feels at home with wealth maximization. Whether he will also be rewarded with a seat in the Supreme Court remains to be seen.

Interestingly enough, just about all of the academic criticism, some of which has been very penetrating as in the case of Professor Frank Michelman, has come from legal scholars. Economists, on the other hand, have had a tendency to approve or else pretty much ignore the entire matter. One exception is the Berkeley professor Robert Cooter who, starting with his Ph.D. dissertation, has voiced some restrained criticism of Coase and Posner.[35]

Perhaps the strongest criticism has come from another imperialist who has recently even been awarded a Nobel Prize for economizing politics: James Buchanan. He was quick to point out in an article titled "Good Economics–Bad Law," that our own system of government is based on maintaining a separation between the collective decision-making process–involving *legislation* by constitutional and political bodies–and the institution of law as such, which is to adjudicate conflicting claims within a set of rights and rules.[36] Posner, of course, seeks to apply the same extra-legal economic principle, wealth maximization, to both domains. In his scheme the individual common law judge would be abandoning his role of jurist for that of a legislator. Yet, Buchanan warns us, the basic structure of our constitutional democracy is predicated on keeping interpretation and enforcement of laws independent and distinct from the making of laws. We will turn to Buchanan's own work in Chapter 10.

This prepares the stage for specifying a meaningful alternative to wealth maximization as a guiding principle of law. Werner Hirsch, another economist who has written the book *Law and Economics*, gives us a clue about the distinct nature of law by drawing our attention to the concept of "Reasonable Man" underlying legal matters. We already pointed him out in Chapter 6, but it is worth repeating that "he is a person who is not only protective of his own rights, but also has a fair regard for the welfare of others." And Hirsch continues: "For example, the law holds that a person whose acts deviate from the standard of the 'reasonable' can be found negligent and held liable. Economics, on the other hand, is built around the concept of the 'rational man,' who in the extreme is totally self-serving, seeking only to maximize his self-interest."[37]

The Reasonable Man, then, in contrast to the Rational Man, is concerned with justice and fairness, in other words with equity rather than efficiency. He behaves in a reasonable, prudent manner responding to the needs of others. To him, just as with the humanistic person, the goals of private benefit often conflict with the attainment of societal objectives of what is fair and right. Justice and fairness, both acknowledged to be alien terms to economists and their narrow abstraction, Rational Man, need to dominate considerations based on economic efficiency. Hirsch warns us that although efforts at reducing complexity for analytical purposes are commendable, such pretending at simplicity can be "gravely misleading." Rather, we have to instead face the simple fact that justice-maximizing efficiency often requires trading off resource allocation against distributional and equity concerns. Now, in explaining such trade-offs, the interaction of law and economics has much to offer, "particularly in the areas of applying microeconomic theory and econometric methods to the estimation of the effort of laws, both existing and proposed."[38] And that is exactly the task Hirsch pursues in his often insightful book. But, this is quite different from the imperialist reduction of law to economics aimed at by Posner and his followers.

To fight against the reduction of reason to instrumental rationality, to make room for a Reasonable Man besides Rational Man, is precisely what humanistic economics is about. True, both economic conceptualizations of Man have relevance when it comes to explaining conduct, whether occurring in a formal market or otherwise. But when the aim goes beyond explanation and prediction to the guiding of socioeconomic policy, we hold that Reasonable Man is the one and only touchstone for improving humanity and society, as well as the economy.

More importantly, we see in remedial government policy, and especially in law, the only active antibodies to the frequent destructive greed of the unregulated marketplace. As we will show in the next chapter, government, too, seems increasingly infected with the germ of private-interest maximization and as a result less and less capable of performing its vitally important corrective function. This leaves us with the last domain of freedom and autonomy: the law. Obviously, the aim of economics imperialists and their conservative political supporters is to do whatever they can to also infect the very immune system of the social organism. So it appears that in a very real sense, economics imperialism, Posner-style, is the academic equivalent of AIDS. If we allow him and his followers to continue such reckless and illicit intercourse, the future will be characterized by an accelerated social sickness with unprecedented consequences.

References

1. John A. Hobson, *Imperialism: A Study* [1902]. Ann Arbor: University of Michigan Press, 1965, p. 367.
2. See also Kenneth Boulding's, *Economics as a Science*. New York: McGraw-Hill, 1970, p. 131.
3. Frank Knight, quoted in A.M. Polinsky, "Economic Analysis as a Potentially Defective Product: A Buyer's Guide to Posner's Economic Analysis of Law," *Harvard Law Review,* 87, p. 1658.
4. Most of these issues are covered in a text by Lionel McKenzie and Gordon Tullock titled *The New World of Economics*. Homewood, Illinois: Richard D. Irwin, 1975. The book has since gone through five or six editions.
5. *ibid.,* p. 124.
6. Richard A. Posner, *The Economics of Justice*. Cambridge, Massachusetts: Harvard University Press, 1981, p. 2.
7. *ibid.*
8. Richard A. Posner, "The Law and Economics Movement," *American Economic Review,* 77:2 (May 1987), p. 2.

9. Gary S. Becker, *The Economic Approach to Human Behavior.* Chicago: University of Chicago Press, 1976, p. 4.
10. Jack Hirschleifer, "The Expanding Domain of Economics," *American Economic Review,* 75:6 (December 1985), p. 53.
11. Ronald H. Coase, "Economics and Contiguous Disciplines," *Journal of Legal Studies,* 7 (June 1978), p. 210.
12. Ronald H. Coase, "The Problem of Social Cost," *Journal of Law and Economics,* 3 (October 1960), pp. 1-45.
13. Guido Calabresi, "Some Thoughts on Risk Distribution and the Law of Torts," *Yale Law Journal,* 70 (1961).
14. *Washington Post* (National Weekly Edition), October 29, 1984, p. 23.
15. *ibid.*
16. Richard A. Posner, *The Economic Analysis of Law.* 2nd edition. Boston: Little, Brown, 1977, p. 1.
17. *ibid.,* p. 5.
18. *ibid.*
19. Posner, *Economics of Justice, op. cit.,* p. 61.
20. *ibid.,* p. 76.
21. *ibid.,* p. 17.
22. *ibid.,* p. 89.
23. *ibid.,* p. 83.
24. Posner, "Law and Economics Movement," *op. cit.,* p. 5.
25. Posner, *Economic Analysis of Law, op. cit.,* p. 6.
26. Robert Cooter, "Law and the Imperialism of Economics: An Introduction to the Economic Analysis of Law and a Review of the Major Book," *U.C.L.A. Law Review,* 29 (1982), p. 1266.
27. Frank I. Michelman, "Norms and Normativity in the Economic Theory of Law," *Minnesota Law Review,* 62 (1978), p. 1031.
28. Elisabeth M. Landes and Richard Posner, "The Economics of the Baby Shortage," *Journal of Legal Studies,* 7 (1978), pp. 323-348.
29. *ibid.,* p. 339
30. *ibid.,* p. 346.
31. *ibid.,* p. 342
32. *ibid.*
33. *ibid.*
34. *ibid.,* p. 345.
35. See, for example, Robert Cooter's article, "The Cost of Coase," in the *Journal of Legal Studies,* 11 (January 1982), pp. 1-33.
36. James Buchanan, "Good Economics–Bad Law," *Virginia Law Review,* 60 (1974), pp. 483-492.

37. Werner Hirsch, *Law and Economics*. New York: Academic Press, 1979, p. xii.
38. *ibid.*, p. xiii.

Chapter 10

GOVERNMENT AND THE MARKET:
THE VITAL LINK

The attitude of economists towards government has its roots in the laissez-faire beginnings of economics with Adam Smith. Smith was inspired in his economics during his 1760s' travels to France, where he encountered an early group of economic thinkers called the physiocrats ("the rule of nature"). These French social thinkers were campaigning against the dominant economic doctrine of the day that was known as mercantilism. Mercantilism developed out of the monarchies of feudal Europe which held that the purposes of trade, as well as economic activities in general, were to add to the wealth of the crown. When King Louis XV's finance minister, Jean-Baptiste Colbert, asked a group of merchants how the crown could help them bring greater wealth into the country, they responded by saying "laissez nous faire" (let us alone). Thus this phrase was born into economics, to be shortly afterward popularized through the work of the Britisher Adam Smith.

From its origin then, not only was economics unsympathetic to government action but it came into being as a doctrine whose explicit mission was to call again and again for the limitation of government in social welfare, trade, and industry. Perhaps the endpoint of this belief system—coupled with a good dose of self-interest theory—is James Buchanan's "Public Choice" conception of government, discussed later in this chapter.

Economists then, especially in their microeconomics, have been natural allies with attempts by conservative politicians to limit the role of government. When President Reagan took steps to demote the position of economists in his government in late 1984 due to what he felt was bad advice he had received from them, the *New York Times* commented, "On its face, the eclipse of the high-powered Washington economists seems somewhat at odds with the Reagan administration's philosophical concern about restoring the power of the marketplace, which is a proposition close to the heart of any economist."[1] Economists defend their stance, which Heyne admits "often treats proposals for reform of the economic system so unkindly," by claiming that they are realists, not conservatives. Heyne continues, saying that "realism is not necessarily conservatism, but it often looks quite similar. And there is a sense in which knowledge does promote conservatism. Even physicists have been accused of hopeless conservatism by would-be inventors of perpetual-motion machines."[2]

What about this "realism"? Our survey of economics and of economic history in earlier chapters has referred to the dangers and the failures of pure laissez-faire economics. The greatest historical lesson in this regard is undoubtedly the Great Depression, when the early laissez-faire advice of the economics profession was finally rejected by Roosevelt, probably without a moment to spare, and only after much hardship and misery had already occurred. But if the Great Depression is the most prominent example of the failure of pure laissez-faire, it is far from an isolated instance. As a matter of fact, almost from the beginning of the industrial age there has been a series of government enactments that have had an important and significant ameliorative effect on problems arising in the socioeconomic system. The claim of the "realist" economist would generally be that such enactments were unwarranted or would make matters worse, and given those circumstances, advised against them. And yet, each of these policy initiatives was advanced in periods when social and economic disasters had already occurred and it took reform action to stem the tide of further devastation, restore stability, and adequately provide for society's needs. In his important and significant book the economic historian Karl Polanyi[3] makes the case that social and government policy was absolutely necessary at critical times to prevent an unrestrained market from overriding society and wreaking havoc. Furthermore, the market itself would not be able to perform its beneficial and socially productive functions without the active involvement and maintenance of the government and legal system. Far from being an embodiment of a self-regulating system of nature, the market as a man-made institution took constant human vigilance and care to maintain its proper functioning.

Regulatory Legislation in Historical Perspective

Early examples of the intrinsic necessity of government in a market economy are the series of Poor Laws enacted in England to deal with the problem of commoners displaced from the land by the enclosure movement. These included the Gilbert Act of 1782 and the establishment of minimum wage supplements in 1795.

Also in England, the most developed industrial country in its day, we find the Factory Act of 1833 establishing a system of inspectors to prevent child and female labor from being abused. Similarly, the Ten Hour Act of 1847 set a limit on how many hours of work an employer may demand from his workers. In 1844 the large English industrial city of Manchester found it necessary to pass housing and sanitation standards to deal with the filth and disease that continued unchecked. A national board of health was established in 1848 to monitor the Sanitary Acts.

This environment of government regulation was not only found necessary in the areas of worker and public health and safety but, as already indicated, in the very structure of business itself. Joint-stock companies in England, the forerunners to our own present-day corporations, produced a series of financial disasters before the establishment of the 1844 Limited Liability Act and the development of state corporate chartering that outlined a framework of rules and regulations for large companies. Similar incorporation legislation was enacted in other industrial countries. In time, these proved insufficient, and the combining of large, monopolistic business enterprises led in the United States to the passage of the Sherman Anti-Trust Act in 1890, which was then again strengthened by the Clayton Anti-Trust Act in 1914. And all this in the largely unrestrained "golden age" of laissez-faire capitalism. The Great Depression was still to come.

The area of banking and the regulation of money and credit has a very long and involved history with government regulation. The Bank of England had been set up in 1696, but in the late 1800s it was to be "the lender of last resort" in financial panics. The United States resisted national banking, but after a series of banking panics and the depression of 1907, reluctantly set up the Federal Banking System in 1913. This was greatly expanded and developed in the 1930s after the Great Depression. Also in the 1930s, the Securities and Exchange Commission was established in the United States to regulate the issuing and selling of securities. Its size and scope of activities have greatly expanded since then. Now it is dealing with the issue of how to regulate the financial activities of American companies in their overseas transactions.

Under the philosophy of laissez-faire, it was somehow assumed that merchants and businesses were to be free to do whatever they wanted to, but not workers or employees. Attempts on the part of labor to join their numbers and organize in order to resist the economic power of large-scale enterprises were widely and routinely opposed, not only by the private police forces of companies but the military forces of the state as well, often joining ranks with company police. This came to an end in the United States with the passage of the National Labor Relations Act of 1935 which specifically recognized the right of labor to organize.

In addition to some of the above-named legislation, the 1930s in the United States saw the passage of the act establishing Social Security. This, along with unemployment compensation, work-injury insurance, the minimum wage, and other human welfare benefits, had already been established in most of the industrial countries in Europe. In the next chapter we will look more closely at these developments.

The Early Origins of the Attitude of Economics Towards Government

Let us return again to Adam Smith to examine the social and political setting in which Smith lived and wrote.

In doing this we first note a most striking fact. It is that Smith himself, as prominent a public figure and as economically middle class as he was, was not able to vote for the British Parliament–he did not own enough property![4] This enables us to recognize that government in Smith's day was a very limited exercise in democracy, still largely under the rulership of the land-holding aristocracy. It was not until the so-called Glorious Revolution of 1688, only thirty-five years before Smith was born, that the aristocrats of Parliament finally asserted their power over the English kings. However, it was only after the death of Adam Smith in the 1800s that Parliament began to assume its present form as a representative democracy. This was largely initiated by the Great Reform Bill of 1832 which still preceded the concept and establishment of universal suffrage. In Smith's day, apart from the early Poor Laws, Parliament had passed almost no social legislation as we know of it today. It very much represented the interests of the nobility and wealthy upper classes.[5]

Thus we see that the whole meaning of government for Smith, as well as for the French physiocrats, was very different from today. Government then was largely the instrument of the wealthy and the powerful, the remaining feudal command mechanism of the Middle Ages. The idea and practice of government as a democracy representing the interests of the population at large, "for the people and by the people," was largely unknown. The irony in regard to Smith is that the way in which the improvement in the lives of the common man could be obtained—Smith's humanistic aim—was precisely by reducing the influence and control of this aristocratic body in the economic affairs of the common Britisher.

According to Smith, England was more notably "a nation of shop-keepers" than the province of the landed gentry. Nevertheless, he warned of the dangers of this new class unduly influencing government: "To found a great empire for the sole purpose of raising up a people of customers . . . is, however, a project altogether unfit for a nation of shop-keepers; but extremely fit for a nation *whose government is influenced by shopkeepers*."[6] Despite this caution, after Smith's death the rising new class of "shopkeepers" found in his work the theoretical justification they needed to block the first government attempts to remedy the appalling and scandalous social conditions in England.

Three Stages. In light of the above account we see the history of the relationship between government and market proceeding in three historical phases. First, we have mercantilism which represented the economic rulership of the crown and the nobility. This is followed by Adam Smith's laissez-faire stage which aimed towards obtaining freedom and well-being for the commoner by protecting his economic activities from the rulership of the crown and the aristocracy. Third, we have the stage of democracy in which the government is now a forum for representing the interests of the population at large, and is no longer an instrument of the ruling aristocracy.

Economic theory as we see it is still largely mired in stage two, laissez-faire, and has not adequately come to grips with the realities and potential of stage three—democracy. Humanistic economics is the economics of democracy rather than of laissez-faire, and makes the case that inappropriate laissez-faire attitudes and policy will keep substantial portions of a population in economic impoverishment and human non-fulfillment. Of course, the positive lessons of economics' laissez-faire past are to be retained and appreciated.

Government: Special Interests or the Public Interest?

For the economist, Economic Man is a creature of an infinite array of wants and preferences. This conception has historical roots in the British philosopher David Hume, who not only wrote about economic matters himself but was a friend with direct influence upon Adam Smith. For Hume, the self was a "bundle" of preferences. This term, which became famous and is carried down through the present day in economics, very well captures the picture of a self whose needs have no hierarchical order and exist as an unlimited collection of random and independent elements.

For the person, so for the government. If the person is a bundle of preferences, then the government, being a representative collection of persons, also represents various bundles of preferences. Therefore, the job of government is to mediate between these preferences or provide an arena where some of these preferences override the others. Here is how it is put by the economist Robert Mundell: "Government is easy when the governed have similar preferences. . . . The problem becomes difficult when the governed have divergent preferences; this poses innumerable problems and requires either compromise or the exercise of authority."[7]

From this point of view, compromise or authority are the only options for government. Now it is certainly the case that compromise and power play a large role in political and governmental activity, but we should recognize that from the mainstream perspective these are the only roles that are possible.

Humanistic economics shows us another possibility. Since an individual is really not just a one-dimensional, utilitarian bundle of preferences, but someone with a higher self, thus having the possibility of acting out of truth, justice, fairness, and morality, then government also has those possibilities. In fact, government is that institution which is the agency for the expression of this human capacity.

By definition, the market through its very structure and function was never meant to be a vehicle for such capacity. Indeed, it can accurately be said that in general the market is amoral. Actors in the market *may* express higher values. They may be concerned with quality for the sake of quality and not only for profit, with the well-being of others and not just their own economic advantage, with maintaining a clean environment, with socially conscious investing, and so forth. In other words, economic actors may choose to act in a "tuistic" way, despite

Wicksteed's preachments to the contrary. Yet there is nothing in the market *as market* that calls for this. But government by nature, structure, and purpose is supposed to make ethical choices. This is possible because the individual has the capacity to be moral, and the government is that institution which can express this capacity on the level of social decision making.

This allows us to realize that the government is not just the place for the balancing of special interests or the assertion of authority of one special interest over another–but that there is a true common interest, and the government can be an expression of that. Government in its highest form, in its most fulfilled and realized function, is just that. *When government fails it loses this sense of common interest and descends to the lower sphere of only mediating special interests.*

The common interest of a society is its expression of its higher self. This means that when a society moves to provide, for example, a greater ability for the disadvantaged to meet their needs, it is not merely responding to one special interest over another. Although provisions for the poor are only utilized by the poor, everyone in the society falls under their protection because anyone may become poor. Therefore, it is in the common interest of a society to promote the well-being of the needy and to overcome exploitation. This also comes out of Kant's categorical imperative and the golden rule. The human capacity for acting justly is what makes this possible. If there were no such capacity, if all were just self-interest, then the disadvantaged would be nothing other than another special interest group (and exploitation becomes a meaningless concept).

Today we have largely lost the sense of what is the common or public interest, and conventional economics has played its part in this loss. It supports the portrayal of the disadvantaged and needy sectors of our society as another special interest, just like banks and insurance companies. But the fact that the public interest includes the upliftment of the poor is revealed by the *"pro bono publico"* provision that almost all professions have in their codes of ethics. The translation of this Latin phrase is "for the *public* good," and it calls for the professional to render some portion of his or her services to the poor for free. The poor that are served this way are not conceived of as a "special interest" with yet another hand in the till of the public coffers, but as precisely *the public* in the phrase, *pro bono publico,* which the professional is called upon to serve.

Market and Power

The reason why government needs to promote the public good, and why this property of government is so vital, is that by itself the market will lead to exploitation by the wealthy and powerful over the poor and the weak.

In Chapter 2 we showed the disadvantage that a weaker trader has in a market composed of unequal traders, which reflects the difference in market power between someone who trades for needs and someone who trades for wants. As a general tendency, the unrestrained market will increase income discrepancy and power differentials between these traders.

The necessary corrective for this is regulation of these inherently exploitative natural tendencies of the market, and this is what government does or is supposed to do. In a well-functioning society it is these qualities or values that a government expresses, and in so doing operates to correct the thwarting of anyone's basic needs. Therefore, what humanistic economics shows is that from the standpoint of economic theory there is always the need for government to regulate the economic environment within which the market operates. Mainstream economics is intrinsically a theory of economics without government. Humanistic economics acknowledges government as fundamental to the economic process if social well-being is to be secured.

Government and the Dual-Self

We have seen that a one-self conception of Man as a total theory of human action is not only incomplete but self-contradictory and self-destructive. We have also seen that the market system taken as a total institution will necessarily fail to meet human needs, and in so doing will create a lopsided sense of human values. Thus the market taken by itself will not produce an adequate and just social order.

In practice, this has been recognized from the beginning, and society has always either maintained or developed other institutions outside of the market system to meet the needs that the market by itself cannot meet.[8] The problem has been that economic theory has not been able to recognize this for the reasons we have presented, so that what society in its wisdom achieved on a practical level, economics had no place for on a theoretical level.

From a dual-self standpoint we can recognize government as the institution in which society expresses its higher values or second order preferences. This does not mean that government is always an expression of these values. All too often it is not, but what we are showing is that in theory the government is that institution that specifically has this capacity and purpose. We also need to go further and say that from the standpoint of economic theory, the good society always has the need for government action to interact with and complement market allocation.

The Market as Contest

When one leaves economics textbooks behind and turns instead to the world of business, there one finds the competitive language of competition as contest. There are constant and widespread references to "market dominance," "competitive advantage," "predatory pricing," "defensive position," "outdistancing competitors," "a balanced playing field," and so forth. Only one overly trained in the theories of *perfect competition* can fail to see that the language of business in fact very accurately describes what the market is. The market is best seen as a contest or a competitive game with winners and losers. As Frank Knight emphasized, "In perfect competition there is no competition."[9]

As in any such activity, there need to be rules and a referee. In an economic system these are provided by the government. Since the game is a dynamic one whose style of play is always changing, the rulemaker and enforcer have to be constantly changing as well. The object of government regulation of the market is that the game should be played as fairly as possible. That is what anti-monopoly legislation was meant to be all about. A further object is that no one should get injured in the game, and that is what welfare and unemployment legislation is about. The goal or purpose of the game, which it is the responsibility of the government to maintain, is that the well-being of the whole society is furthered by the game. The players in the game cannot be expected to be players and referees at the same time. As players, their goal is winning. We are very happy if they also wish to play "a good game," but as Adam Smith himself told us long ago, do not count on it. It is therefore the responsibility of the referee to make sure that the overall purpose of the game is maintained and not destroyed under the pressure of the contest.

In our competitive game both the players and the referees are members of the same society, and in fact may be the same person in different roles, or in different jobs at different times. Their "player" aspect represents their competitive, material self—perfectly natural and, indeed, a part of human nature, as conventional economics is never tired of pointing out. However, their "referee" aspect is also a part of human nature—in this case their higher, socially conscious self—and this is what humanistic economics emphasizes. As we have shown, it is what makes humanistic government possible, which is to say, government in its evolved and fulfilled form.

Freedom Revisited

In a market with power imbalances, those who are trading to meet their basic needs–that is, they trade in order not to be worse off–cannot be said to have a truly free choice. They are compelled to trade by the pressure of their needs even if they do not like the terms or conditions of trade. Literally, they must either trade or die. This means that their choices in the market are coerced. They are coerced by their needs into trading. And we should note that all coercion, even at the willful hands of another party, works by putting pressure on the human need system, such as through the exaction of pain.

Thus we find that when government action enables a population to meet its needs it enhances human freedom *in the market*. The more that traders are in the position in regard to market choices where they can take it or leave it, the more their behavior represents free choice. Traders in the market with assurance of having their basic needs met are no longer coerced, and they no longer are forced by survival to submit to unfavorable market conditions or, put another way, to sell out. They are not forced by the market to compromise their integrity.

A somewhat different way to look at this is that the more individuals are capable or assured of "self-sufficiency" relative to the market, the more effective the market will be in promoting the good society. It is therefore the necessary and proper role of government to promote the self-sufficiency of those individual traders, and in so doing bolster the humanistic efficiency of the market. Self-sufficiency should be understood as the ability to meet one's basic needs without having to rely on exploitative exchange.

The Need for a Correspondence Principle

In order to achieve the above it is necessary to restrict the economic force of the market so that its domain does not overreach the socioeconomic and political jurisdiction of government. The jurisdiction of government has to correspond with the domain of the market. It is only through such a *correspondence principle* that such higher self values as justice can be honored and maintained.

Examples of government entities lacking the ability to effectively control their economy are readily found, for example, in the areas of taxation and pollution control. If one of the fifty states of the United States should seek to increase its revenues by means of raising the corporate income tax, we would expect many potentially affected corporations to move their operations to states where similar taxes are much lower. It happens automatically through competition between the states. It is the threat of losing its industry that deprives the state government of much power to set taxes at the level it seeks.

Similarly, if a state like Maine wants to protect its rivers by significantly raising pollution control standards, the response may very well be plant closures and relocation with concomitant job losses. Once again, the state only has the power to control its industry as long as it has industries left to control. In both cases it is the federal government which has the power to regulate taxes and environmental variables, assuming, of course, industry cannot escape the controls by moving abroad.

Another basic issue illustrating the need for correspondence arises in macroeconomic management. As long as decisions controlling the currency are made outside of a state, inflation cannot be controlled inside that state. And as long as that state is part of a larger national economy, it cannot use Keynesian stabilization instruments to control its GNP. But once again, at the federal level we will have correspondence and as a result the ability to control much more effectively what eludes state legislative bodies.

All of this is, of course, rather elementary economics and has long been recognized as the very foundation for federal taxes and legislation pertaining to the economy. Yet it is important to remember the very same need for correspondence as we contemplate greater economic integration at the global level, a topic relating intimately to the free trade controversy to be discussed in Chapter 13.

Ensuring the Proper Functioning of Government: The Need to Separate Money and Politics

In order for government to exercise its proper function which we have been describing, its operating motives must be as free as possible from lower-self economic motives. That is, the motives of market actors must not become the motives of government actors. To the extent that these two orders of motive are kept in their separate spheres, then government is able to regulate and compensate for market power as we have described. When these two spheres overlap, when market power is also influential in the governmental sphere, then the proper function of government is compromised. To put it most directly and succinctly, money must be kept out of politics. When it is not, or to the extent that it is not, then government action will correlate with and reinforce market power, rather then regulating and compensating for it.

Another way to describe this issue is through the contrasting concepts of consumer sovereignty and political sovereignty. As we have previously seen, consumer sovereignty in the market is a matter of "one dollar-one vote," so that market power operates through wealth. The more dollars one spends, the more "votes" one has in the market. Political sovereignty or democracy, on the other hand, operates through the principle of one person-one vote, so that political power is equivalent to persons, not money. When wealth is allowed to spill over into the governmental sphere, we have the situation of one dollar-one vote modifying one person-one vote, or consumer sovereignty limiting and distorting political sovereignty. This really reveals the ugly face of economic imperialism in practice. When this happens, government cannot or will not be allowed to *govern* the economy. We can even say that in this case the economy governs the people (the political body), rather than the people governing the economy.

Thus we see that derived from humanistic economic theory are policies that support a separation between the political sphere and the market sphere, or the separation of politics from economic power. This separation can never, of course, be complete and final because the self-interested ego will naturally continue to try to use its power to promote its special interests in government (and we note in passing that these interests are the real special interests). But it is the task of a healthy society to continually keep on guard against the tainting of the democratic process by monied interests. This is a form of Jefferson's "the price of liberty is eternal vigilence."

The Alliance Between Government and Economic Power: Lobbying

In American society a source of the tainting of the democratic sphere by the market sphere is the existence of what is known as lobbying, or the lobbying institution, and it is revealed in the revolving-door interchange that operates between the government regulatory agencies (such as the Federal Trade Commission and the Federal Energy Association, and the like) and the industries they are supposed to regulate. In an old but still relevant study by Common Cause in Washington, D.C.–itself a lobby–it was shown that one-half of all federal regulators shuttle between jobs in the government and in the same private sector their agencies regulate.[10] These ties between government regulators and industry show up in the sources of influence on government activity. For instance, logs kept by the Federal Energy Administration for a six-month period showed that 80 to 90 percent of the top officials' contacts and communications with outside interests were with the energy industry, and "only a scant 6 percent" were with non-industry interests such as consumer and environmental groups.[11]

We have mentioned that Common Cause is a lobby. It is ironic, and a commentary on the current tendencies towards devolution of American government, that there is a need for a public interest *lobby*. The public itself was supposed to be precisely what was embodied in the establishment of representative government. The existence of corporate and special interest lobbying, however, has become so extensive and pervasive that the lobbying institution has increasingly colored and shaped the processes of government. Therefore, in order for the public to attempt to enter back into the picture, it has to do so through the back door of lobbying.

The existence of lobbying came about through an interpretation of the First Amendment in the Bill of Rights which states that people have the right "to assemble, and to petition the government for a redress of grievances." When Jefferson put forth the Bill of Rights, he did so to protect the rights of individuals from the powers of the federal government which was identified with powerful commercial and financial interests. Among the Federalists (those who supported a strong federal government) "was the almost unanimous opinion," according to the historians Charles and Mary Beard, "that democracy was a dangerous thing, to be restrained, not encouraged, by the Constitution, to be given as little voice as possible in the new system, to be hampered by checks and balances." Elbridge Gerry, a member of the Constitutional Convention, declared that "the evil the country had experienced flowed from the 'excess of democracy'. . . . Arguing in favor of a life term for Senators, Hamilton explained that 'all communities divide themselves into the few and the many. The first are rich and well-born and the other, the mass of the people who seldom judge or determine right.'"[12]

The great loophole occurred, which Jefferson certainly did not foresee, when corporations were granted the legal status of individuals, thus being able to take advantage of the Bill of Rights. The effect of this "personification of the corporation" is described by Thurman Arnold, former Attorney General under Roosevelt: "The ideal that a great corporation is endowed with the rights and prerogatives of a free individual is as essential to the acceptance of corporate rule in temporal affairs as was the ideal of the divine right of kings in an earlier day. . . . So long as men instinctively thought of these great organizations as individuals, the emotional analogies of home and freedom and all the other trappings of 'rugged individualism' became their most potent protection." As a result of this, Jefferson's intent with the Bill of Rights was undermined: ". . . the great corporation actually worked to monopolize completely the mantle of protection designed for the individual."[13]

So, the Bill of Rights became an entryway for the institution of corporate lobbying in which vested economic interests could exert a powerful influence on legislation. And it also seems to have had an effect on the economic status of the people who make up our legislative bodies. The Senate has been referred to as a "Rich Man's Club." For example, out of the one hundred senators in the 1976 Senate, twenty-two were millionaires, and a few others were well on their way.[14] In the general population, whom the senators are supposed to represent, .03 percent are millionaires. We might add that in 1987 there were only two women in the Senate. So, at the top law-making level a very exclusive strata of the population (male millionaires) are extremely well represented.

PAC Money.   The most significant effect of money in politics through the 1980s is the increasing impact and influence of Political Action Committees or PACs in providing money to the campaign funds of various congressional and senatorial candidates. A PAC can be set up by any group, such as a corporation, a trade association, or a labor union, to solicit donations from individuals above the amounts that individuals are allowed to contribute to a campaign in their own name. (We note here the irony of corporations being treated as a group rather than an individual in this case.) In the 1982 off-year elections there were nearly five times as many PACs as in 1974, and the average successful candidate for the House of Representatives received nearly a third of his campaign funds from them.[15] By 1986, the figure had risen to 50 percent for over half of the elected House members.[16] From the campaign period of 1985 to October 1986, PAC contributions jumped around 30 percent over the 1981-1982 campaign period, with 80 percent of this money going to incumbents.[17] In that election, 98 percent of House incumbents seeking reelection won.[18] It should also be noted that under current law there are no limits on how much wealthy candidates can spend on their own campaigns. For example, John Rockefeller spent $12 million, including $10 million from his own deep pocket, to win a West Virginia Senate seat.[19]

Does this money buy influence? You bet. After all, why are all these increasingly huge sums of money being contributed? Long-time Democratic representative Dan Rostenkowski, chairman in 1986 of the House Committee that rewrote the federal income tax code, was reported as saying that he was "nauseated" by the influence that PAC campaign money seemed to have on some members of the committee. Republican William Frenzel of Minnesota, a longtime supporter of PACs, said his enthusiasm for them had waned: "Republicans have been concerned or enraged or whatever by PAC contributing performances." Republican Senator Barry Goldwater complained that "it is not 'we, the people' but political action committees and moneyed interests who are setting the nation's political agenda and are influencing the position of candidates on the important issues of the day."[20]

The campaign of Common Cause to extend public funding of political races to the House of Representatives and the Senate (whereas of 1987 it still only covered the election of the President) would be a prime example of the kind of policy that follows from the theory of economics as seen from a humanistic perspective. Most economists adhering to some form of mainstream perspective would not realize that the support of the Common Cause position should follow directly from economic theory, and either would tend to view the issue as a purely political one upon which economics has nothing to say, or may even take the position that an economist ought to oppose what Common Cause is trying to do. The power of humanistic economics is shown again in this context, in that it demonstrates *the economic relevance* of the issue of public financing of political campaigns.

The "Public Choice" Theory of Government

The humanistic conception of the role and place of government stands in contrast to the position taken by a substantial segment of the economic profession, as this chapter has extensively pointed out. However, we have not yet dealt with the most well-known exponent of applying the Economic Man way of thinking to government–James Buchanan who has won a Nobel Prize for his development of what is known as the Public Choice theory of government. We are already familiar with the essential arguments of this position, and much of our analysis has attempted to show its shortcomings. Our discussion here of Buchanan's position will serve as a review of the whole issue. We will conclude this section with a critique of Buchanan's "contractarian" philosophy.

Buchanan's basic assumption is that the human being is still an Economic Man whether he or she is operating in politics or in the market. In his Nobel Prize address[21] Buchanan describes the three-pronged foundation of his theory: "Methodological individualism, homo economicus, and politics-as-exchange."[22] Then he says, "The differences in the predicted results stemming from market and political interaction stem from differences in the structures of these two institutional settings rather than from any switch in the motive of persons as they move between institutional roles."[23] Finally, "Politics is a structure of complex exchange among individuals, a structure within which persons seek to secure collectively their own privately defined objectives that cannot be efficiently secured through simply market exchanges. In the absence of individual interest, there is no interest."[24]

Our criticisms of Buchanan's position are as follows, which we present as a series of numbered although interrelated points:

1. If individuals do not shift Economic Man motives when they move from the market to politics, does this also apply to persons as they operate in academia? Namely, does it apply to Buchanan himself as a theorist? If so, then we ought to conclude, following his logic, that Buchanan's argument has no relation to what is true; he only writes whatever will advance his own self-interest. In this he appears to have done very well.

2. Buchanan recognizes that he has a problem in his theory. He has theorized that since politics is free exchange, this means that the establishment of government and its institutions must have come about voluntarily. And yet, he sees government as coercive. He notes, "the observed presence of coercive elements in the activity of the state seems difficult to reconcile with the model of voluntary exchange among individuals." He then asks himself the question, "why must individuals subject themselves to the coercion inherent in collective action?" "The answer is evident," he concludes, ". . . Individuals acquiesce in the coercion of the state, of politics, only if the ultimate constitutional 'exchange' furthers their interests. . . ."[25]

But here a contradiction is revealed. To "acquiesce in coercion" does not make any sense as language. We cannot acquiesce to coercion if these words are to mean what they are supposed to mean. Either we acquiesce (which means we agree) and then there is no coercion, or if there is coercion, we are forced to submit and that is not an acquiescence. The source of Buchanan's problem is his belief that coercion is inherent in collective action. He is not able to see that collective action comes out of the possibility of cooperation and there is nothing coercive about cooperation. His difficulty is further revealed in a later statement: "The political analogue to decentralized trading among individuals must be that feature common [to] over all exchanges, which is *agreement* among the individuals who participate. The unanimity rule for collective choice is the political analogue to freedom of exchange of partitionable goods in markets."[26] By the unanimity rule he means that for politics to be analogous to market exchange, there should be unanimous agreement on all political decisions.

3. Buchanan tries to get himself out of trouble. He recognizes that in practice the unanimity rule for political agreement is far too "restrictive," and a government could not function with it. So his prime contribution is to move the unanimity rule to a previous stage or phase of political action—instead of the present day-to-day operation of politics. Politics in the present may be "coercive" but that is now all right, according to Buchanan, as long as the previous phase is not coercive. That phase is the choice of rules, or the stage of deciding on a particular political constitution. Here the individual "may rationally prefer a rule that will, on particular occasions, operate to produce results that are opposed to his own interests." He will do so, Buchanan argues, if the individual "predicts that on balance over the whole sequence of 'plays' his own interests will be more effectively served."[27] In other words, in order to support his theory of government, Buchanan is led to make a distinction between an individual's short-term and long-term interests. And here he is in even deeper trouble.

4. Buchanan apparently does not realize that short-term and long-term interests are incommensurable and here, in effect, he is really positing a dual-self theory. We have previously referred to this issue in Chapter 6 when we referred to Buchanan in the context of our critique of "overarching utility." This is the economists' attempt to explain how individuals decide between two different utilities (or interests) by the economist assuming that utility is the basis for the decision. As we pointed out there, it is a contradiction and it does not work. The decision between two self-interests (such as short- and long-term) can only be made on a different basis from self-interest. By indirectly positing a dual-self theory, Buchanan contradicts his initial starting point of assuming *homo oeconomicus*. However, he lends great support to humanistic economics.

5. Where Buchanan goes with his theoretical apparatus is to conclude that we need to reassess the Constitution or even have a new constitutional convention. In that reassessment or convention Buchanan confidently assumes that people will rationally decide on rules that out-

law deficit spending and "intergenerational transfer programs characteristic of the modern welfare state,"[28] by which we presume he means
either Social Security or AFDC or both.

As to deficit spending, Buchanan as an economist lets himself lapse.
He apparently equates a government deficit with a consumer household
deficit, as politicians are wont to do. However, a government deficit can
just as well be a producer deficit, or an investment promising future
returns. It would seem to us to be the legitimate role of economists to
point out this distinction rather than to obscure it.

In regard to Social Security we only need point out what politicians
of all political persuasions have discovered, that Social Security is one
of the most popular government programs ever developed and is hardly likely to be voted out. We will discuss government welfare programs
in Chapter 11.

Contractarianism

In Buchanan's call for reconsidering the Constitution or the
American social contract, he expresses his logic that all fairness resides
in the social contract or contractual agreement. Here is an expression
of his position: "A rule is fair if players agree to it. It does not say that
players agree because a rule is fair. That is to say, fairness is defined by
agreement; agreement does not converge to some objectively determined fairness."[29] This is the contractarian logic of reducing everything
to social convention or agreement. It holds that there are not external
values "out there"; everything is subjective and confined to feelings
within individuals. A philosophical position of this kind is *nominalism,*
which maintains that all things exist simply because we have created
them and have given them an identity–a name. Nominalism is a first
cousin to subjectivism, already discussed in Chapter 7. It is usually contrasted with *realism,* which holds that universal concepts do, in fact,
exist, and our minds–far from having created them–merely refer to
them. Obviously, the kind of humanistic philosophy portrayed in this
book is in sharp contrast to the nominalism and subjectivism of conventional economics, and espouses philosophical realism.

Let us see what is implied in the notion of Buchanan's contractarian
fairness, where he assumes that fairness is what agents agree on. Like
subjectivism, it is a fallacious conception. How can we really argue that
all matters of principle can be reduced to social agreement? How do
people agree in the first place? By majority vote? By dictatorship of the
blue-eyed? By unanimity? The contractarian would say: they would settle *that* question by agreement. But now the question is, how is such
"agreement" to be reached? What is the procedure for the procedure?

It is a problem of infinite regress, unsolvable *unless* we break the contractarian chains and are willing to recognize that there are objective and fair ways to decide that precede agreement or exist *a priori*. Here we have to plant ourselves firmly on humanistic soil, which holds that there are fundamental personal, human rights existing prior to a particular social contract. These rights are objective and are often expressed in the concepts of natural law, such as articulated in the Declaration of Independence.

For the humanistically inclined, the moral principles that flow out of the higher self are not culturally relative, but are transcultural in that they are not created by cultural processes. The confusion over this point arises out of the obvious fact that unless a community agrees with and supports moral principles, they will be violated. But this should not be taken to mean that the community *invents* those principles.

Conclusion

The Buchanan position and the Economic Man way of thinking provide a supposedly objective and "scientific" basis for what is, in effect, the undermining of government. In this, they are very far from being neutral, non-judgmental, and non-evaluative as Buchanan and others would like to claim. Their recommendations generally point towards a narrowing down of the scope of government and an expansion of the private interest sphere. We have seen through our analysis that this tends to be a support for the economically powerful over the economically weak.

Humanistic economics sees this conclusion as wrong-headed. We predict that the outcome of putting its suggestions into effect would be an even more rampant commercialization of society, an increasing monopolization in industry and business, continuing and increasing erosion of our natural environment, an increase in poverty, and a corresponding increase in crime and vice.

From the standpoint of our economics, the problem is not government but the need to further develop democracy so that government is increasingly democratic. This does not mean so much the limiting of government but the limiting of the influence of money in government. This is the preservation of the democratic political principle of one person-one vote against the imperialistic encroachment of the market principle of one dollar-one vote. As of the end of the 1980s, the prime recommendation that comes out of this is not a new constitutional convention but the increasing implementation of public funding of political campaigns.

There must be principles that precede any constitution or contract. For the humanistic economist these principles are those of individual human dignity, implying the provision of basic human rights which include economic rights. It is hard for us to imagine these universally being secured without a democratic political system. But such a democratic system does not in itself define and decide what dignity is. Rather, we know it when we see it. We do not need a vote to tell us whether a sunset is beautiful. Market and government in proper balance is beautiful. Out of balance, it produces the very ugliness which the science of economics should exist to correct.

References

1. *New York Times*, January 13, 1985, section 3, p. 28.
2. Paul Heyne, *The Economic Way of Thinking*. 4th edition. Chicago: Scientific Research Associates, 1983, p. 454.
3. Karl Polanyi, *The Great Transformation* [1944]. Boston: Beacon Press, 1957.
4. Robert L. Heilbroner and Lester C. Thurow, *The Economic Problem*. 6th edition. Englewood Cliffs: Prentice Hall, 1981, p. 23.
5. Robert L. Heilbroner, *The Worldly Philosophers*. 5th edition. New York: Simon and Schuster, 1980, p. 67.
6. Milton C. Myers, *The Soul of Modern Economic Man*. Chicago: University of Chicago Press, 1983, p. 123 (emphasis added).
7. Robert A. Mundell, *Man and Economics: The Science of Choice*. New York: McGraw-Hill, 1968, p. 170.
8. Polanyi, *op. cit.*
9. Quoted in James Buchanan, "Markets, States, and the Extent of Morals," *American Economic Review*, 68:2 (May 1978), p. 364.
10. "Study Finds Financial Conflict in Bureaucracy" in *Christian Science Monitor*, October 21, 1976.
11. "Lobbying." Four articles by Peter Stuart. *Christian Science Monitor*, October 8-10, 14, 1975.
12. Charles A. and Mary R. Beard, *The Rise of American Civilization*. Vol. 1. New York: Macmillan, 1931, pp. 315-316.
13. Thurman Arnold, *The Folklore of Capitalism*. New Haven: Yale University Press, 1937, pp. 189-191.
14. *Christian Science Monitor*, January 28, 1978.
15. *New York Times*, September 11, 1983 (Book Review), p. 12.
16. *New York Times*, June 7, 1987, section 4, p. 5.
17. "Hill Anticipates Campaign Finance Reform," *Congressional Roll Call*, November 20, 1986.

18. "PACs: Keeping the House in Cash," *Washington Post,* April 8, 1987, p. A19.
19. "Out of Control? Even Some Beneficiaries Upset by System of Raising and Giving Campaign Money," *Wall Street Journal,* July 18, 1986, p. 10.
20. *ibid.,* pp. 1, 10.
21. James M. Buchanan, "The Constitution of Economic Policy," Nobel Acceptance Address, *American Economic Review* (June 1987), pp. 243-250.
22. *ibid.,* p. 243.
23. *ibid.,* p. 245-246.
24. *ibid.,* p. 246.
25. *ibid.*
26. *ibid.,* p. 247.
27. *ibid.,* p. 248.
28. *ibid.,* p. 250.
29. James M. Buchanan, "Fairness, Hope and Justice" in Roger Skurski, ed., *New Directions in Economic Justice.* Notre Dame, Indiana: University of Notre Dame Press, 1983, p. 56.

Chapter 11

BEYOND THE WELFARE STATE: FULL EMPLOYMENT

In Chapter 2 we presented the idea that the market by itself will not sufficiently and adequately be able to meet human needs. We showed why this is true in theory, so it should not be surprising that this is also found to be true in fact. This fact is reflected in the development in modern industrial societies of what is generally known as welfare, and the description of some of these societies as welfare states. Let us take a look at how the institution of welfare has developed in the United States.

The Development of Welfare in the United States

The New World was the land of opportunity because it had an abundance of good land. Those in England who were looking for a new life, a fresh start, could look towards the Colonies as a place where this was possible. For most of the early history of the United States, poverty was therefore not a large problem. Private relief agencies could do the job, and these were mostly needed by the newest immigrants.

But by the early 1800s private relief and charity began to prove inadequate and conditions for the poor deteriorated. A report to the New York State legislature in 1824 is reminiscent of conditions that we have observed in England. It noted that the poor were farmed out, with little distinction in treatment between them and criminals. As a result, the state created a control agency that was a forerunner of today's welfare agency. Other states followed New York, and by 1929 only Mississippi, Nevada, and Utah did not have such an agency.

We mention 1929 specifically because that was the year of the stock market crash which was soon followed by the Great Depression. The bread lines of the 1930s marked the breakdown of the then-existing social welfare system.

The establishment of a new welfare system in the United States echoed what President Roosevelt had called the "Four Freedoms": freedom from want, freedom from fear, freedom of speech, and freedom of religion. The Roosevelt reforms included the Federal Emergency Relief Act (which provided grants to states) and the Civil Works Administration (which later became the Works Project Administration [WPA]) and finally the Civilian Conservation Corps (CCC), creating public works jobs through federal funding. These acts were passed in 1933. Finally, in 1935 there was the passage of the Social Security Act which became the basis of our present welfare system. The main programs of this Act were the establishment of pensions (old age and survivors' benefits), unemployment benefits, and Aid to Families with Dependent Children (AFDC). Because AFDC is state-administered and partially federally funded, there is wide variability in state levels of support.

Other developments in the United States welfare system since Roosevelt included the Medicare program, which was initiated in 1965 to pay for a portion of hospital and doctor bills for the elderly and disabled. In 1974 Supplemental Security Income (SSI) was created to establish a uniform nationwide minimum income for the blind and the disabled to replace the wide variations in different states' provisions for these persons. Medicaid is a program to help finance medical expenses for those who have qualified for either SSI or AFDC.

There is also the Food Stamp program that provides eligible low income families with monthly allotments of coupons that can be redeemed for food (and a few other supplemental food programs, such as school lunches). Later on in this chapter we will see to what extent the above programs meet the basic needs of United States citizens.

The Modern Welfare State

The term *welfare state* derives from the concept of welfare economics, as used and developed by Pigou and Hobson and discussed in Chapter 7. It has its fullest realization in the various nations of northern Europe. The philosophy of the welfare state is that the government should modify the play of market forces so that the nation moves in more socially desirable directions. This is a concept that sees the state, in economist J. F. Sleeman's words, "as a positive agent for the promotion of social welfare. In this it can be contrasted with the laissez-faire ideal of the state acting rather as a policeman or arbiter." He continues, "Not only should the government provide social services, such as social security, medical treatment, welfare facilities, and subsidized housing, but these should go beyond the provision of a bare minimum towards ensuring that all have equal opportunity, so far as the country's resources allow."[1]

The welfare state pursues active policies to promote full employment and sees the right to a job as one of the basic rights of citizenship. This goal contrasts sharply with the typical American image of the welfare state as encouraging idleness, although, as we shall see later on, this perception in America of the role of government in welfare seems to be changing.

The philosophy of the modern welfare state is echoed in Franklin D. Roosevelt's 1937 Inaugural Address, despite the fact that the U.S. has not really become a welfare state in these terms:

> ... we knew that we must find practical controls over blind economic forces and blindly selfish men.
>
> We of the Republic sensed the truth that democratic government has an innate capacity to protect its people against disasters once considered inevitable–to solve problems once considered unsolvable. We could not admit that we could not find a way to master economic epidemics just as, after centuries of fatalistic suffering, we had found a way to master epidemics of disease. We refused to leave the problems of our common welfare to be solved by the winds of chance and the hurricanes of disaster. ...
>
> In that purpose we have been helped by achievements of mind and spirit. Old truths have been relearned, untruths have been unlearned. *We have always known that heedless self-interest was bad morals; we now know that it is bad economics.* Out of the collapse of a prosperity where builders boasted their practicality has come the conviction that in the long run economic morality pays.[2]

We should note that in most European countries the basic rights of citizenship that are part of the welfare state are incorporated explicitly into their constitutions. This is reflected in the fact that most modern Western industrial societies have higher social welfare expenditures than the United States as demonstrated below.

Table 11.1

SOCIAL EXPENDITURES*
IN SEVENTEEN COUNTRIES, 1981
(as % of Domestic Gross National Product)

1.	Belgium	37.6	10.	Norway	27.1
2.	Netherlands	36.1	11.	Finland	25.9
3.	Sweden	33.4	12.	United Kingdom	23.7
4.	Denmark	33.3	13.	Canada	21.5
5.	Germany	31.5	14.	USA	20.8
6.	France	29.5	15.	Japan	17.5
7.	Italy	29.1	16.	Switzerland	14.9
8.	Ireland	28.4	17.	Greece	13.4
9.	Austria	27.7			

*Social expenditures=government expenditures on education, health, pensions, unemployment compensation, maternity benefits, child allowances, etc.

Source: OECD, *Social Expenditure 1960-1990,* Paris: OECD, 1985.

The Poverty Level in the United States

How well does the United States meet the freedom from want (i.e., need) that is one of Roosevelt's Four Freedoms, and how well have we mastered "economic epidemics"? The answer has to be that in comparison to other modern industrial Western societies, not well. There is the observation of the eminent Swedish economist Gunnar Myrdal that "the United States is that country among the rich countries that has the most and worst slums."[3]

Each year since 1964 the United States government has estimated a level of income that constitutes what is known as the poverty level–people and families whose income is below this level are formally defined as living in poverty. The level was estimated in the following way. The Department of Agriculture devised a "minimal food plan" (budget) for "emergency and temporary use when funds are low." The cost of this food budget, say, for a family of four, was calculated on a year's basis. The Department then turned to the findings of a study that was done in 1955 which showed that the average poor family spent about one-third of its total income on food. Therefore, by multiplying the calculated minimum food budget by three, the government arrived at the minimum overall budget that a family of four needed to live on. This amount of income defined the poverty line. The number of families who had a lower income than this were called the *poor*. By adjusting for changes in the cost of the minimum food budget in different years, the number of poor could then be calculated for years previous to 1964, as well as the years since.

By this method, for example, the poverty line for an urban family of four in 1985 was $10,989, which amounted to 14 percent of the population or a little over 33 million Americans living in poverty.

Table 11.2

TRENDS IN POVERTY, 1960-1986
(Selected Years)

Year	% Population	Number of Poor (millions)
1960	22.2	39.8
1965	17.3	33.1
1970	12.6	25.4
1973	11.1	22.9
1975	12.0	25.9
1980	11.6	25.0*
1985	14.0	33.1
1986	13.6	32.2*

*These figures are approximations.

Underestimation of the Numbers.   The above data and comparisons reflect official United States Government statistical procedures. However, these procedures have come into serious question and there are strong indications that they underestimate the number of poor in the United States.

The method of calculating a minimal food budget developed in 1964 is based on careful and precise, essentially computerized, budgeting—so that *just* the right amount of potatoes are bought, (say 5.7 pounds) and just the right amount of milk, and so forth. It is easily recognized that this is not the way people really buy their food, rich or poor, and thus the minimum food budget is not realistic and is set too low. A poor family lacks the necessary information and knowledge to live on this minimal amount of food. However, even with this method of estimating the food budget, the poverty line level of food expenditure, according to 1973 figures, was a meager thirty-three cents per meal per person.

Second and most important, the estimation that a poor family spends one-third of its income on food depends upon the assumption that increases (or any changes) in food prices over the years since 1955 are in proportion to price increases in other commodities, such as housing. If these other costs have increased at a faster rate than the cost of food, then the multiplication of three becomes an underestimate. This, in fact, has been the case. Professor David Gordon has estimated that to take this differential cost increase into account we would need to update the 1973 figures, for example, by multiplying the food budget by a factor of four rather than three. (He estimates that food costs as of 1973 amounted to only one-fourth of a poor family's budget.) Using this estimate, the poverty line moves upward and roughly 18 percent of the population falls below it, not the 11.1 percent the table shows.[4]

In summary, if we use Gordon's adjustment and note that the number of poor has increased since 1973, we arrive at the observation that there has been relatively little decline since 1960. With all these considerations we conclude that the official estimates of poverty are underestimates, and the decline in percentages in the table may be largely exaggerated. The inadequacy of the income figures set for the poverty level is expressed in the words of the Commissioner of the Massachusetts Department of Public Welfare, who is quoted in 1986 as saying, "The poverty level for a family of three is $9,100 a year. I couldn't live on $9,100, much less raise two children."[5]

Further indications of the underestimation of the official poverty data comes from a Gallup poll conducted in 1986 which asked the question, "Have there been times during the last year when you did not have enough money . . . to buy food . . . [and] clothing your family needs . . . [and] to pay for medical or health care?" More than one in four Americans answered yes to this question.[6] Whatever the statistical validity of this kind of very summary figure, it is certainly higher than the 13.6 percent that the government gives as the number in this country who experience poverty.

This is not to say that there has not been some real decline over the years in the number of poor. Certainly, since the Depression years of the 1930s this has been the case. In President Franklin Roosevelt's famous 1937 Inaugural Address he said, "I see one-third of a nation ill-housed, ill-clad, ill-nourished," a figure which economic studies have supported. By today's statistics we can make the broad estimate that roughly 20 percent of our population is living in poverty, which is a decline from the 1930s. But, the impression of a continuing and constant elimination of poverty that some analysts suggest does not seem to be supported by a careful look at the data.

The Income Gap Between the Rich and the Poor

Our analysis has shown that the market is least effective as an institution promoting truly voluntary exchange when there are wide income and wealth gaps between different segments of the population, that is, between the rich and the poor. Again, we can quote Roosevelt who expressed on a popular level what humanistic economics has found to be true in theory: "The test of our progress is not whether we add more to the abundance of those who have too much; it is whether we provide enough for those who have too little."[7]

Data show that this gap is currently widening, and this has been referred to as "the shrinking middle class." We find that from the 1970s to at least the mid-1980s, the income of the middle-income members of our society has been declining, and that of the poorest of them declining even further. Mean family income in general between 1973 and 1985 declined 6.6 percent. At the same time, the mean family income of the poorest 20 percent of families declined 32 percent.[8]

These changes reflect a widening wealth and income gap between the rich and the poor. This turns up no matter at what level the percentages are cut. In 1982 the richest 1 percent of American families had 27 percent of the wealth. Five years later this increased to 36 percent of the wealth.[9] In 1973 the richest 20 percent of the population had seven times the income of the poorest 20 percent. In 1985 this difference had increased to ten times the income. In 1984 the top 40 percent of American families had 67 percent of the income and the lowest 40 percent of American families had 15.7 percent of the income, and that was the lowest percentage since 1947.[10]

Children and Their Mothers.   Of these poor, a disproportionately large number are children. For example, in 1985 one out of every five children under the age of eighteen lived in poverty, and one out of four under the age of six.[11] These children in poverty are also disproportionately from minority groups. In New York City, for example, two out of five Hispanic children and three out of five black children live in poverty.[12]

This high proportion of children in poverty reflects the precariousness of the American family. Many of these children live in single-parent families, usually headed by their mothers. Thus we also find that a high proportion of the poor are also women. In 1984, 27 percent of all white households headed by a female were below the poverty level. Fifty-one percent of all black households headed by a woman were below the poverty level.[13] This development has led to the use of the descriptive phrase, "the Feminization of Poverty."

The fact is that millions of women are only a divorce away from poverty. Others are only a job layoff away, an illness, or the death of a wage-earner. In one study of this problem, individual stories included that of a married New England woman with several children whose income went from $70,000 a year to $7,000 when her husband left her. A former welfare worker in the Bronx became a welfare mother when her husband became addicted to heroin. Widows in California who were once affluent now count their pennies to buy food as their fixed incomes fall further behind a rising cost of living.[14]

Homelessness.   With this increase in poverty we find an increase in homelessness. In 1974 the typical father of today's children spent 14 percent of his pay on housing costs. In 1984 the typical expense for housing costs was 44 percent of pay.[15] In 1974 there were 14 million low-rent housing units available. In 1983 this number had actually declined to 12.9 million units. Meanwhile, the number of households needing low-rent units keeps increasing, from 8.9 million in 1974 to 11.9 million in 1983. It is projected that by the year 2003 there will be 17.2 million households needing low-rent units, which is many millions more than the 9.4 million low-rent units expected to be available.[16] The increasing problem of homelessness in America is so embarrassing that when the United Nations showed a film on New York as part of their observance of the 1987 Year of Shelter, the United States pressured the U.N. to drop the footage showing homelessness in New York.[17]

Hunger.   A Harvard-based physicians group called the Physicians Task Force on Hunger has done a survey of the extent of hunger in the United States. The group made a survey of 150 rural counties where more than 20 percent of the residents live on incomes below the poverty level. The group concluded in 1985 that "hunger was getting worse, not better." The chairman of the group, Dr. J. Larry Brown of the Harvard School of Public Health, reported that up to 20 million Americans go hungry at least two days a month, a figure the group obtained by adding the 15 million or so people below the poverty line, who nevertheless do not receive food stamps, to the 5 million or so people just above the poverty standard, who also do not receive food stamps. The group referred to the problem of hunger as "an epidemic."[18]

Health Insurance. Along with a severe problem of hunger that seems to be on the increase, there is also the problem of widely inadequate health insurance and health coverage. In the Gallup poll referred to above, 21 percent of the population reported that they could not meet their health care needs during the course of the year. This figure was 31 percent for blacks and 24 percent for women. The estimate is that 37 million Americans, one in six, have no health insurance. Some are laid-off workers, but the vast majority are employed people and their dependents. Some of these people are ineligible for employer-paid health benefits because they work on a part-time or temporary basis, while others are self-employed or work for small businesses that do not offer workers health insurance benefits. Republican senator David F. Durenberger, Minnesota, said that "although it seems impossible in this day of artificial hearts and organ transplants, 37 million Americans are without the insurance coverage necessary to pay for a broken arm, appendicitis, or the birth of a baby."[19]

From Welfare to Workfare

The welfare solution to poverty was the hope of Western industrial economies from the rise of the welfare state at the end of the nineteenth century. Figure 11.1 shows the development of welfare programs. Each of the lines shows a particular type of welfare program: work injury compensation, old age security, sickness, maternity insurance, unemployment compensation, and family allowances. The vertical and horizontal axes show how many countries have adopted the program and roughly in what year. For example, if we take unemployment compensation, the first countries adopted it around 1905. By 1920 about seven countries had it, and by 1960 about seventeen countries.

The figure shows that an increasing number of countries have adopted each of these social programs, and that it took between fifty and eighty years for any such program to be adopted by most of the countries. What we seem to have here is an evolutionary development across national and cultural lines. However, it appears that this development may have reached a historical turning point towards much slower growth following the "OPEC oil shock" in the 1970s. This effect was described in the Organization of European Community Development report (OECD) of 1981 as "the welfare state in crisis." With the slowdown of productivity and growth in the Western economies, and the corresponding increase in economic interaction between these economies—namely, in the combined forms of international competition and interdependence–a significant body of opinion developed in many of these countries that they did not want or were not able to finance welfare programs to the same level of growth as in the past.[20]

Figure 11.1

THE DIFFUSION OF WELFARE PROGRAMS

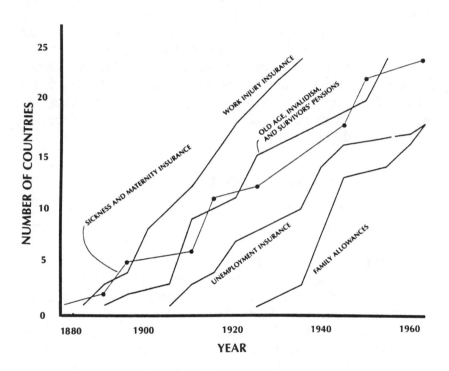

While the above may be seen as the negative side of recent developments in the concept and implementation of welfare, in that it spells a curtailment in society's effort to meet the basic needs of all its members, there is also a positive side: Increasingly, Western economies are now pointing in the direction of providing employment as an alternative to welfare, and here lies the key to the solution of the problem of poverty.

The welfare state concept was not just based on the idea of income transfers and government grants to those who were not able to meet their basic needs, the so-called welfare as a "safety net" concept. There was also the idea, as Sleeman's statement indicated earlier, of developing jobs or employment capabilities so that the poor would be able to meet their needs by the opportunity to work, rather than through "hand-outs."

This shift of emphasis from the safety net concept of welfare to the employment development concept is reflected in the current interest in the U.S. in what is known as "workfare" as a replacement for welfare.[21] Workfare is the idea that welfare recipients, in order to receive their benefits, be involved in some kind of work or in a job training or education program.

The Level of Unemployment

Many economists, humanistic or otherwise, find it distressing that the level of unemployment, despite small periodic ups and downs, has been steadily ratcheting upward since the 1950s as shown in Figure 11.2[22]

Figure 11.2

THE RISING TREND OF UNEMPLOYMENT

(Average Annual Unemployment Rate)

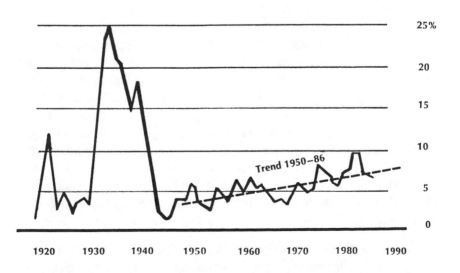

Some blame the rise in unemployment on the "seductive cushion of unemployment insurance."[23] This explanation is belied by the fact that unemployment insurance has actually fallen to a historic low. In 1986 less than one in three workers received benefits.[24] Thus, far from being a seductive cushion, unemployment insurance is increasingly ceasing to be what it was intended, protection against extreme need when one has been laid off from a job.

The percentage of the labor force unemployed, as given by the Bureau of Labor Statistics (BLS), has some curious and questionable features that lead many observers to believe that, just as in the case of the poverty data, it substantially underestimates the number of unemployed. To see this, let us understand how the BLS arrives at its official unemployment rate.

Each month, a survey is done of a representative sample of American households, recently approximately 60,000. A series of questions are asked of the members regarding which of them are working, unemployed and looking for work, not looking for work, and so on. First, and probably most distorting, those household members who are working part-time, regardless of whether they would like a full-time job or not, are counted as fully employed. Second, those who are classified as "discouraged workers," and who say they have given up looking for work because they believe no jobs are avaliable, are considered not to be in the labor force at all, and so the unemployment percentages do not include them. This group runs between 1 and 1.5 million people.

"Discouraged workers" are part of a still larger category of those not in the labor force who want jobs. This numbers approximately 5 to 6 million people. It includes single-parent mothers who are not able to earn enough in the job market to afford childcare, students, and others who say they would take a job if they could find one. Whatever the reasons for their being unemployed, these persons have not looked for a job within a four-week period immediately preceding the survey. Looking for a job during that time period is a necessary condition to being included in the BLS-defined labor force. The Bureau does not, therefore, count them as unemployed. In the below Table 11.3 such individuals are referred to as "Civilians Not in the Labor Force Who Want Jobs."

Figuring the Jobless from Official Data. The BLS does gather data that give a basis for estimating these additional numbers, although these numbers are not part of the official unemployment statistics and are rarely if ever reported in the press. In Table 11.3 an indication is given of the impact of differing definitions of employment/unemployment based entirely on Bureau of Labor Statistics data. The first adjustment

Table 11.3

UNEMPLOYMENT RATE FOR CIVILIAN LABOR FORCE BASED ON FULL-TIME EQUIVALENT EMPLOYMENT
(Figures in 000's)

	1977	1978	1979	1980	1981	1982	1983	1984	1985	1986	1987
BLS Labor Force	100,665.	103,882.	106,559.	108,544.	110,315.	111,872.	113,226.	115,241.	117,167.	119,540.	121,602.
Resident Armed Forces	1,656.	1,631.	1,597.	1,604.	1,645.	1,668.	1,676.	1,697.	1,706.	1,706.	1,737.
BLS Civilian Labor Force	99,009.	102,251.	104,962.	106,940.	108,670.	110,204.	111,550.	113,544.	115,461.	117,834.	119,865.
BLS Civilian Employment	92,017.	96,048.	98,824.	99,303.	100,397.	99,526.	100,834.	105,005.	107,150.	109,597.	112,440.
Official Unemployment Rate	**7.1%**	**6.1%**	**5.8%**	**7.1%**	**7.6%**	**9.7%**	**9.6%**	**7.5%**	**7.2%**	**7.0%**	**6.2%**
Adjusted Civilian Labor Force Based on Full-Time Equivalent Employment	91,940.	95,046.	97,575.	99,614.	101,044.	102,661.	104,204.	106,231.	107,933.	110,147.	111,728.
Combined Full-Time and Full-Time Equivalent Employment	83,667.	87,511.	90,095.	90,412.	91,001.	89,674.	90,982.	95,510.	97,546.	99,818.	98,900.
Full-Time Equivalent Unemployment Rate	**9.0%**	**7.9%**	**7.7%**	**9.2%**	**9.9%**	**12.7%**	**12.7%**	**10.1%**	**9.6%**	**9.4%**	**11.5%**
Discouraged Workers	1,026.	863.	771.	993.	1,103.	1,568.	1,641.	1,283.	1,204.	1,121.	1,026.
Adjusted Labor Force Including Discouraged Workers	92,966.	95,909.	98,346.	100,607.	102,147.	104,229.	105,845.	107,514.	109,137.	111,268.	112,754.
Full-Time Equivalent Unemployment Rate Including Discouraged Workers	**10.0%**	**8.8%**	**8.4%**	**10.1%**	**10.9%**	**14.0%**	**14.0%**	**11.2%**	**10.6%**	**10.3%**	**12.3%**
Civilians Not in the Labor Force Who Want Jobs	5,775.	5,446.	5,427.	5,675.	5,835.	6,559.	6,503.	6,070.	5,933.	5,825.	5,714.
Adjusted Labor Force Including Civilians Not in the Labor Force Who Want Jobs	97,715.	100,492.	103,002.	105,289.	106,879.	109,220.	110,707.	112,301.	113,866.	115,972.	117,442.
Jobless Rate	**14.4%**	**12.9%**	**12.5%**	**14.4%**	**14.9%**	**17.9%**	**17.8%**	**15.0%**	**14.3%**	**13.9%**	**15.8%**

Source: Ward Morehouse and David Dembo, *Joblessness and the Pauperization of Work in America: Background Paper.* New York: Council on International and Public Affairs, February 1988. (Based on U.S. Department of Labor, Bureau of Labor Statistics, *Employment and Earnings*, various issues from 1978-1987 and Monthly Employment Situation News Release, April 3, 1987.)

made is to eliminate the armed forces, which have been included as employed in the BLS definition of the U.S. labor force only since January 1983. Without excluding the armed forces (the inclusion of which has the net effect of decreasing the official unemployment rate by one- to two-tenths of a percent), comparisons with earlier time periods are distorted.

As we have discussed, one of the striking changes in recent years has been the growth of part-time employment. This is particularly noteworthy in the case of part-time employment for those who want full-time work but are unable to find it. Such part-time employment has more than doubled since 1970. The official unemployment rate is based on a definition of employment that counts anyone who worked as little as one hour a week during the reporting period in the same manner as those who are employed full time. Therefore, the unemployment rate for the civilian labor force has been recalculated based on full-time equivalent employment in Table 11.3.[25] As would be expected, by so adding approximately 5 million workers this pushes up the unemployment rate so that in 1987 it stood at 11.5 percent instead of the official BLS figure of 6.2 percent. When part-time employment was proportionately a smaller element of the total labor force, the BLS practice of treating full-time and part-time employees the same made relatively little difference in the official unemployment rate. But as this category of the labor force has grown, especially during the recent recession, the difference between the official rate and a modified rate based on equivalent full-time employment has increased.

The next adjustment made is to include officially defined "Discouraged Workers." This is an adjustment that has assumed increasing significance in recent years, as more and more persons previously in the labor force have lost their jobs and given up looking for another because they believe none exist. By adding the 1 million discouraged workers to the calculation of unemployment, we find the rate for 1987 increases still further from the official unemployment rate of 6.2 percent and an unemployment rate based on equivalent full-time employment of 11.5 percent to 12.3 percent. As in the case of the adjustment for part-time employment, the discrepancy between this method of calculating the unemployment rate and the official rate has grown in recent years.

When the further adjustment is made for the large group of the "Civilians Not in the Labor Force Who Want Jobs" (excluding our previous addition of the officially defined "Discouraged Workers"), the jobless rate for 1987 jumps from the official unemployment rate of 6.2 percent to 15.8 percent, almost 2 1/2 times as high.

What this analysis shows is that the official unemployment rate, which has shown the numbers dropping steadily from a high of 9.7 percent in 1982 to 6.2 percent in 1987, overlooks or even hides a huge, almost equivalent number of those who are not counted as being in the labor force by the Bureau of Labor Statistics. The *New York Times* refers to these persons as "America's Army of Non-Workers."[26] These millions of non-workers and marginal workers are among the more than 30 million Americans officially living in poverty.

The Rise of the Working Poor

Despite the very large number of unemployed, from 1973 to 1984 the U.S. added nearly 20 million new jobs to the economy while most of Europe had virtually zero employment growth during the same time. As a result of this, again despite the large unemployment problem, America has been termed "the great jobs machine." However, when the types of new jobs that have been created are examined a sobering picture emerges. A study for the Joint Economic Committee of Congress by economists Barry Bluestone and Bennett Harrison in 1986 leads to the conclusion that since 1973 there has been a significant restructuring of the American economy under way.[27] The United States seems to be proliferating low-wage jobs and possibly shifting towards an increasingly polarized labor market structure between higher paying and lower paying jobs. This can be seen as an important reason underlying what we have previously referred to as the shrinking middle class. The following table shows Bluestone and Harrison's data indicating this change in jobs.

Table 11.4

EMPLOYMENT LEVELS AND EMPLOYMENT SHARES
(All U.S. Workers)

	Number of Employees (mil)			Shares of Net New Employment (%)	
	1973	1979	1984	1973-79	1979-84
Low Stratum	29.6	32.0	36.7	19.9	58.0
Middle Stratum	48.1	55.9	59.7	64.2	47.5
High Stratum	15.4	17.4	16.9	15.9	-5.5
Total	93.2	105.3	113.4	100	100

The change presented in this table is substantial. Whereas only 19 percent of the new jobs created between 1973 and 1979 were in the low stratum, a whopping 58 percent of the new jobs created between 1979 and 1984 were in that stratum. This correspondingly led to a decline in the middle stratum of incomes: 64 percent of the new jobs between 1973 and 1979 were in the middle stratum and only 47 percent of the new jobs were in the middle stratum between 1979 and 1984. Corresponding with this, Bureau of Labor Statistics data have consistently shown a sharp reduction in both average real weekly earnings and average hourly wages in the economy. Mean earnings peaked at $340 a week in 1973 (in 1984 dollars). By 1985 they had fallen to $291. Real hourly wages have declined by only a slightly smaller percentage, from $9.21 to $8.28.[28]

There is the possibility that this decline in average work income, and the huge creation of low-wage jobs compared to high-wage jobs, is due to the entrance into the economy of the large numbers of younger workers from the baby boom generation. Bluestone and Harrison tested this hypothesis and they found that both younger and elder workers experienced the same kinds of trends, although, to be sure, the low-wage trend was much more severe among younger workers. But even among those thirty-five and older, more than one-third of net new employment after 1979 yielded an average wage of only $7,000. Rather than being the result of an influx of a large number of younger workers, this shift from higher paid work to lower paid work corresponds to a loss of jobs in the manufacturing sector of the economy and the continued growth of the service sector of the economy (which includes fast food chains, convenience stores, bank tellers, and other low-wage and low-benefit work that is typically not unionized).

There has been some criticism of the validity of the Bluestone and Harrison study, particularly by conservative economists of the supply-side school.[29] This criticism includes the claim that a great percentage of new jobs creation was in the salaried sectors of the population which include managers and professionals, and this is excluded in an analysis that only looks at wages. Since the conclusions about the shift in the economy are so far-reaching and basic, it seems clear that in a relatively short order, experience will show whether Bluestone and Harrison are essentially correct.

The Minimum Wage.   As we have noted previously, when a family only has one wage earner working at the minimum wage, the families' income is below the poverty level. For example, in 1986 full-time work at the minimum wage–$3.35 an hour–yielded $6,968 a year. That is 20 percent less than the poverty level–$8,738–for a family of three.[30] We also find through the mid-1980s a decrease in value of the minimum wage. It has traditionally been set at the level of half the average private wage, but by 1986 was at least a dollar below that.[31]

The above analysis should lead us to crucially realize that in order for an employment program not to be a further exploitation of the poor, it needs to produce wages that lift the worker's family above the poverty level.

"Natural" Unemployment?

A humanistic economy needs to be one that provides full employment. Full employment means simply what it ought to mean in common sense terms: everyone who wants to work can work.

This concept runs counter to a common notion in and out of economics that there is a perfectly acceptable level of unemployment. This is sometimes referred to as the "natural level" of unemployment. All of this is unacceptable from the standpoint of humanistic economics because each person counts totally. Each has an infinite worth. Another way to put this is that each person counts not as one, but as *the* one. When economists or others talk about acceptable unemployment, they are undoubtedly always referring to the next person, not themselves.

It is interesting to note that even on technical grounds the concept of a natural level of unemployment, or at least a rising natural level of unemployment, fails. Economist Richard Krashevski conducted a study which concluded that natural unemployment is "a myth that needs to be laid to rest."[32] The argument that has been advanced in economics for increasing the so-called natural unemployment rate to 7 percent from the 4.5 percent in the 1960s rests on the idea that new groups of people entering the labor force–baby boomers, working women, and various racial and ethnic groups–many of these with lower skills, make it harder to reduce unemployment much below 7 percent without bringing about inflation.

Krashevski tested the above idea by calculating what the unemployment rates would have been over the two decades previous to the mid-1980s if the labor force had the same composition of these new entries into the labor force. While unemployment rose from an average of 4.8 percent in the 1960s to 6.2 percent in the 1970s, Krashevski's analysis indicated that labor force changes explain only slightly more than a fourth of this rise. What is more, although joblessness rose again to an average of 8.1 percent in the 1980-1985 period, demographic factors are responsible for an even smaller increment in that rise.[33]

"Rational Unemployment."   Along with acceptable or natural unemployment, there are other concepts about unemployment which exist
in economics that are at least equally as objectionable from a humanistic standpoint, and certainly even more strange. The most notorious of
these is the well-known concept of "rational unemployment." According to this idea, people become unemployed by their own rational choice
as a voluntary and optimal decision. Economist Jacob Mincer first applied this concept to women by explaining that wives participated in the
labor force for only a fraction of their adult lives because they decided
rationally to drop out when wages were low (when unemployment increased), and they reentered as employment picked up and wages
rose.[34] Rather than suffering involuntary unemployment, Mincer argued that these women were in fact actually optimizing their allocation
of time between leisure and work. Later, such theorists as Milton Friedman extended this theory of optimal substitution between leisure and
work to all labor groups.[35] Still a further step was to view unemployment as an individual's voluntary investment in his or her future work
through job search or preparation, and the like. In other words, unemployment was characterized in this theory as a rational occupation:
a worker compares the returns from unemployment to the returns from
alternate ways of spending time.

At this point in this chapter and in this book, it should be apparent
that such a theory as rational unemployment suffers from what we might
call the intoxicating enchantment that some economists experience with
the concepts of rationality and choice. Even though we have previously
seen various problems and shortcomings with these concepts and in
their use, the theory of rational unemployment probably pushes this in-
toxication to its ultimate heights. The plain foolishness of this position
cannot be long enjoyed, however, because the theory of rational unemployment has made effective inroads in economics. It has led to the
belief that unemployment is unimportant.[36] Unemployment was now
shifted in economics from a macroanalysis of the economy's insufficient demand for workers to a microanalysis of unemployment as an
individual's choice.

Combating Unemployment with Profit Sharing:
Martin Weitzman

Not all of economics is under the sway of the above-described in-
toxication, and hopefully not even a majority of the field is. Consequently, many economists have studied the question of full employment and

have advanced plans for obtaining it. One of the most currently discussed, and one which draws a lot of interest, is Martin Weitzman's concept called the "Share Economy."

Weitzman presented his idea in a 1984 book that is written with rare enthusiasm, and promises a great achievement. Witness his concluding paragraph:

> Those who clamor for an "industrial policy" to improve capitalism need look no further than a change in the way workers of large industrial corporations are compensated. Just let labor be paid on a share system–and turn loose the dogs of competition. That simple change will unleash more powerful forces for economic prosperity and social progress than are to be found in the wildest visions of national planners or cultural revolutionaries.[37]

Martin Weitzman claims to have discovered a new road to non-inflationary full employment that works through changing the conventional wage system into one where employees share in the profits. But it is a very special type of profit sharing Weitzman has in mind. It has little to do with the idea that workers, by psychologically identifying with management, would become more motivated and productive. Instead, there is a different force involved which Weitzman compares to a "vacuum cleaner effect."

To understand this principle, imagine a business employing door-to-door salespersons who work on commission, such as with Avon or Amway. Let us say they get to keep a certain proportion of the company's net revenue, but everybody is paid the same, the average of all commissions. Furthermore, the employer has total liberty as to how many salespersons are to be hired. Obviously, as long as a candidate is expected to sell *anything,* the profit motive demands that he or she be hired. Naturally, the employer will want to maximize the number of employees; the more salespeople, the better. Like a vacuum cleaner, he would scan the territory searching nooks and crannies for extra workers willing to work. But the vacuum cleaner works literally at the expense of the already hired workers, who find their income increasingly diluted with every new employee joining the payroll.

It is this type of industrial sharecropping that Weitzman would like to see introduced in corporate America. Workers and their unions would have absolutely no say as to how many are employed by the now labor-hungry owners and their representatives in management. Quite likely, *everybody* would get a job under this circumstance, but only by beating wages down to much lower levels.

After all the unemployed are sucked up, Weitzman's theoretical model promises a permanent situation of prevailing excess demand for labor in the sense that employers would like to hire even more people at the going levels of compensation. He believes that this "gives dignity to the working man and woman, in the sense of being significant, useful members of society."[38] Also, when workers are scarce and employers want them, working conditions will be improved. To this one critic comments: "Thus labor acquires its newfound 'dignity' by becoming a flex-price commodity always in demand as opposed to a fixed-price commodity which was only hired up to a point."[39]

Very few people dispute that Weitzman's scheme will promote full employment, and will do so *not* with inflation *but* with wage deflation instead. The more important question becomes–Is it fair? We believe not, although the plan would tend to benefit some groups in society, particularly the hard-core unemployed. But this would create resentment on the part of existing employees towards the new ones hired, thus poisoning the job climate prevailing in the companies–hardly helpful to greater productivity.

There are many other faults with the entire idea, but our summary sketch is not meant to provide a detailed examination. One critical point, however, we do need to conclude with: Weitzman's share economy puts all the risk on workers without giving them any control. This goes against firmly established and accepted principles. Common stock carries the most risk and provides the most control, preferred stock has less of both, and bondholders least. As Ellerman noted, "Profit-sharing without ownership tries to reallocate the risk-bearing function without reallocating the concomitant control rights . . . ."[40]

Meaningful profit sharing requires ownership sharing also, and here we have to go beyond Weitzman to the type of worker cooperative described in the next chapter.

Seeking Full Employment by Legislation

For humanistic economics, the unconcern about unemployment generated by a theory such as rational unemployment marks one of the most serious failures of the economic way of thinking. Not only does humanistic economics find unemployment important, but it sees it as the major focus of economics–that and the corresponding elimination of poverty ought to be the core goals of economic theory. With these problems addressed all other economic issues naturally fall into place.

In order to bring about full employment, we have devised a program that we offer as an act of political legislation, and we call it the Full Employment Development Act or FEDA. Before presenting the act, we will describe its historical background.

The Historical Background

With the end of World War II economists realized, or at least believed, two interrelated things: that government or macroeconomic policy is needed to eliminate real unemployment, and that macroeconomic policy *could* eliminate unemployment. This belief or recognition led in 1946 to the passage of what was called the *Employment Act*.[41] This act set as the official objective of government "to promote maximum employment, productivity, and purchasing power," and, of course, to do so within the framework of the principles of the American economic system. Under this law the President was to submit to Congress at least yearly an Economic Report prepared with the advice of an expert Council of Economic Advisors, whose purpose it was to review the existing economic situation with regard to the objectives of the Employment Act.

Today, over forty years later, we still have the Economic Report of the President, as well as the Council of Economic Advisors, but we seem somehow along the way to have lost the objective of maintaining full employment, the whole point of the act in the first place.

In this spirit an attempt to overcome the limitations of the 1946 Employment Act was made in the 1978 "Full Employment and Balanced Growth Act,"[42] also known as Humphrey-Hawkins after its congressional proponents. Humphrey-Hawkins was seen to "affirm in law, for the first time, the right of every American willing and able to work, to useful employment, paying decent wages," as noted by the congressional Human Resources Committee when they reported the act out of Committee. It set as goals the achievement of 3 percent adult unemployment and 3 percent inflation rate within five years after the act's passage, which came due in 1983. However, it allowed the President in his Economic Report to revise those goals upward if it was deemed necessary, and, needless to say, all presidents since then have done so.

If the easy use of that option is one of the weaknesses of the act (and there are others as well), another provision is quite strong and has yet to be adequately appreciated. The act states that "policies and programs for reducing the rate of inflation shall be designed so as not to impede achievement of the goals and timetables specified . . . for the reduction of unemployment."

Humphrey-Hawkins had critics on two sides. There were those who believed that the act would wreak havoc on our economic system, especially with its presumed softness towards inflation. The other side believed that the act was essentially meaningless, since the target goals were given no specifically mandated means of implementation. The Human Resources Committee rightly and dryly noted in its report that "both points of view could not be correct."

We are now well past the act's target year. Not only was the unemployment rate in 1983 not less than the 6.0 percent rate at the time of the act's passage, but at 9.6 percent it was over three times the original target goal of 3.0 percent. At the same time, the inflation rate in 1983 was almost at the target rate of 3.2 percent. Thus we know that at least one side of the act's critics was correct.

A cynic or a disillusioned optimist may read in this legislative and economic history the conclusion that full employment is indeed not something to be attained by humankind; the failure of the occasional political stirrings in this direction reveals this to be the case.

We believe, however, that this history is a part of a very different picture and has a different meaning. The 1946 Employment Act, the Humphrey-Hawkins Act, and other such efforts and sentiments can be seen as the evolutionary *beginnings* of a profound concept whose time is still to come, a concept that will increasingly come to be recognized as an important criterion by which a modern society earns the right to call itself civilized.

What we are calling the Full Employment Development Act (FEDA) brings together two already existing and implemented principles. Out of their combination this new act emerges, as if, after the lens of a projector has been given a few turns, a picture leaps into focus. The two principles are (1) universal education (as presently established in our public school system); and (2) occupational counseling and training, now narrowly implemented in the United States Job Service, CETA, the Job Training Partnership Act, and similar programs.

The Full Employment Development Act (FEDA)

The concept of the Full Employment Development Act is stated in the following two paragraphs:

As with education, our society now assumes the responsibility of employment for every one of its eligible citizens. This means that when any citizen actively seeking work finds themselves unemployed he or she can turn to their government for whatever assistance is necessary in finding suitable employment. This can include job search, counseling, retraining, education, relocation–whatever is needed to effectively assist the citizen in becoming employed again.

While the unemployed citizen is involved in the program, he or she receives unemployment compensation, public assistance, and whatever social service supports are currently available and needed for personal maintenance. These benefits are naturally terminated when the individual becomes employed or prefers idleness to newly available work opportunities.

The Implications of FEDA. The philosophical underpinning of FEDA comes out of education. We now provide for universal education. One of the major functions of education is to prepare the citizens of our society for successful occupational and vocational participation. What FEDA does is to logically extend our commitment to educating all our citizens when the individual is no longer in school, in effect assuring that this commitment to education is followed by an equal commitment to lifelong occupational preparedness and support. In this way our society continues to invest in the development of human occupational potential and "human capital" throughout a person's working life and not just up to the age of eighteen. In addition, it puts welfare and income maintenance programs into a coherent and rational framework for perhaps the first time. And this is all done in a way that is, on a conceptual level, remarkably simple and straightforward.

This is the evolution of a new sense of government accountability–employment accountability–in which a society no longer leaves individuals alone to fend for themselves in an employment environment whose main determining forces lie beyond the control of the job seeking individual. In this evolution the government of a modern industrial or post-industrial society can be seen as moving from its emphasis on welfare to that of employment.

Under this act, unemployment compensation, public assistance, and other income maintenance programs become subsumed under and directly related to employment and employment development. We move from the welfare state to the employment state. This does not mean that we remove welfare supports from people, or that we are creating demeaning workfare. Not at all. What it does mean is that so-called welfare is being directly related to matters of employment, where it should be in the first place.

In addition to the whole conception and purpose of FEDA, a specifically humanistic feature of it is its emphasis on the individual. FEDA envisions its implementation through the upgrading and further development of an increasingly important social role, the Employment

Counselor. This is someone with whom the unemployed individual has a one-on-one ongoing relationship until that individual is successfully reemployed. It is the function of the employment counselor to specifically assess the unemployed individual's particular needs, his or her strengths and weaknesses, and to provide the resources necessary to help this person get back to work. This will include all those options mentioned earlier, including retraining. At the same time, the counselor's responsibility consists in making sure that the individual is not unreasonably turning down available job opportunities. The employment counselor is the contact point between government's employment accountability, as called for in the Act, and the unemployed individual seeking work.

But not all good things in life are free. FEDA has a price tag, too. If we assume 15 million unemployed, and a necessary personal client/counselor relationship with a ceiling of fifty unemployed per counselor, we must be prepared to finance 300,000 counselors, let us say, each drawing a $20,000 salary. This alone will cost $6 billion. Add to this sum the costs for office space, secretarial and janitorial personnel and material, the cost of an arbitration system, the cost of worker training, and, initially, the cost of training the counselors, and we are talking about a program that could amount to as much as $40 billion, or 1.2 percent of GNP. Quite obviously a lot of money, some of which could come from reduced welfare and law enforcement budgets, but most of the rest would have to come from elsewhere, preferably by trimming our defense expenditures by 5 to 10 percent.

Up to this point, we have not talked at all about where the jobs come from, and whether the individual becomes reemployed in the private or the public sector. Those considerations fall outside of the intended scope of FEDA. Decisions about these matters can be included in the act, or amendments to it. FEDA also, at this stage, does not specify what level of financial input can go into an individual's counseling, retraining, and education. The idea is that it should be sufficient to enable the individual to go back to work. What FEDA does specify is that the job-seeking individual is entitled to unemployment benefits, and the like until he or she is reemployed. This is the incentive for the government to get people back to work. Similarly, FEDA, through a determination of the counselor, can withhold such benefits from potential freeloaders. This is the incentive for the individual job-seeker. (Since disputes about counselors and their judgments are likely to arise, we would also need an appeals procedure by which such disputes could be resolved.)

One area in which FEDA will perform very well is in the placement of people in available but unfilled jobs, and in matching people to jobs. But the question comes up which we just alluded to: Are there enough jobs? The answer to this falls in the domain of government macro-economic and monetary policy. FEDA is not a substitute for that policy but a complement to it. What it says is that it should be the responsibility of a society not to allow millions of unemployed people to flounder around in economic and vocational limbo while we await a hoped for long-term correction of current economic problems.

FEDA puts the responsibility on the government for creative economic policies that lead to employment, but unfortunately creativity cannot be prescribed by law. This creativity need not take on the mantle of public service jobs, and this is not a public service job act. When Hubert Humphrey introduced his original full employment act to Congress in 1974, it contained a critical provision that public service jobs were to be created if unemployment reached a certain level. This was the most controversial part of the legislation, a focus of debate for a number of years, and in the end was removed from the act before it was finally passed in 1978. With these "teeth" of the bill removed liberal critics saw the new legislation as amounting to very little. As indicated before, subsequent events would seem to have proved these critics right. This does not mean, however, that the Full Employment Development Act as presented here needs to reinstate the original public service job provision of Humphrey-Hawkins. But we think the question of whether a modern society like ours can provide and sustain full employment, without an adjustable and flexible public employment program, is one that needs to be carefully considered. One of the benefits of the proposed act would be that it provides us with a framework and vantage point to effectively answer this question.

Full Employment Through Government-Business Partnership

Numerous creative economic solutions are coming to the fore, often on a state or even a regional level, which point to a direction that could be taken on a federal level to meet full employment goals. Many of them involve new partnerships between government and private enterprises. Robert Reich in his book has referred to this whole area as "the next American frontier."[43]

An interesting and successful example of this new partnership is a Massachusetts initiative called the Bay State Skills Corporation (BSSC).[44] This is a quasi-public corporation which was created by the

Massachusetts legislature to meet the problem in that state of jobs that were open and available, but without enough individuals in the state with the necessary skills and training to fill those jobs, although there were plenty of people without work. The relatively small sum of $3 million was provided for the start-up of BSSC in 1981, earmarked for training and education programs to be run jointly by a business (or businesses) and a public or non-profit educational institution, such as a university or a community college. The heart of the program is a 50/50 matching provision, where the participating business matches BSSC funds on at least a dollar-for-dollar basis. The incentive for the company is that half of their training fees are paid for by the government, and the gain for the state is that the unemployed go back to work, get their skills upgraded, and the whole economy is given a boost.

An example of the program was a contract in which Data General Corporation and the Digital Equipment Corporation joined with Northeastern University to establish a program to teach electrical engineering and computer sciences to women. The BSSC grant of $52,721 was more than matched by $72,000 from the two participating companies. BSSC money was used to pay for some of the start-up costs associated with the program. While the original program served only seventeen women, it has now become a permanent part of the University's curriculum with long-term benefits for future students and the high-technology industry.[45]

The BSSC concept was recently evaluated by ABT Associates, a respected program and policy research organization. ABT concluded that "an unusually high proportion of the local grant programs are not only sound ideas but also are operational successes."[46] As of August 1982, they had awarded grants to over fifty educational institutions and worked with 185 businesses and medical facilities, with 3,400 individuals in training. This was accomplished in Massachusetts when the impact of a national recession was being experienced and many businesses were pulling back instead of reaching out.

Programs like BSSC, producer cooperatives (such as that pioneered in Mondragon, Spain—see Chapter 12), or special tax abatements for locating a plant in a poverty area are just some of an open-ended range of economic policy options that is only limited by our creativity and imagination. These options could go a long way in providing the jobs and productivity our society needs. The Full Employment Development Act places the reponsibility on the federal government (where it necessarily belongs) to stimulate and promote this kind of activity, and to break out of the deadlock and mentality of laissez-faire neoclassical economics that still remains with us like a stale and devitalizing ghost.

Conclusion

We have seen in this chapter the vast extent of poverty and unmet needs that exists in this society, until 1985 one of the richest in the world. Even mainline texts describe the situation as being one of "poverty amidst plenty."[47] According to the humanistic analysis, this condition is an inevitable consequence of a market society, and most particularly the labor market. These deficiencies can only be corrected by government action.

Until quite recently, that action was conceived in order to supply income and in-kind payments to the poor so that they could meet a minimum level of their basic survival needs. Now there is the growing recognition that this action should be directed towards providing the means and conditions for adequate employment. If every job seeker could find employment, there would be much less need for welfare. In the model Full Employment Development Act described in this chapter, we showed how the concept of universal education, which almost everyone accepts, could be extended one step further to universal employment.

The appeal for social programs is usually made on self-interest grounds, no doubt under the influence of conventional economists and their belief that there is only self-interest. So it is stated that welfare leads to less crime, less political unrest, is cheaper in the long run, and so forth. This is the best argument that we can usually expect. At the other extreme of conventional economists are those of a more Austrian persuasion, such as adherents of the Public Choice school, who construe the concept of self-interest to mean that social programs indeed ought to be significantly trimmed or even eliminated.

From a humanistic perspective, we believe the appeal of social programs is most correctly made on the grounds of the higher or common self. When one person suffers we all suffer; when one is hungry we are all hungry. It is simply a shame to experience, as Pigou put it, "the sordidness of mean streets and the joylessness of withered lives."[48] There is a lower-self human tendency to block out this experience because it is painful. This blocking out is a denial process, and so distorts reality. Let us remind ourselves that the root of the word empathy is the word pathos—to suffer—so that empathy means "to suffer with." That is also the same root for the word passion; compassion and passion go hand in hand. Our economics has tended to be cold and bloodless, an economics of denial. Now it is time for it to become an economics of reality, an economics of passion.

References

1. J. F. Sleeman, *The Welfare State.* London: Unwin University Books, 1973, p. 4.
2. Reprinted in E. Will and H. Vatter, eds., *Poverty in Affluence.* 2nd edition. New York: Harcourt, Brace & World, 1970, pp. 7-8 (emphasis added).
3. Gunnar Myrdal, *Against the Stream.* New York: Random House, 1972, p. 284.
4. David Gordon, ed., *Problems in Political Economy.* 2nd edition. Lexington, Massachusetts: D.C. Heath & Co., 1977, p. 297.
5. "Harvard Group Ponders Poverty Toll," *New York Times,* September 7, 1986.
6. "When Ends Don't Meet," *Washington Post,* National Weekly Edition, April 6, 1987, p. 37.
7. Quoted in *New York Times,* April 27, 1986 (Book Review), p. 13.
8. Barbara Ehrenreich, "Is the Middle Class Doomed?," *New York Times,* section 6, p. 54.
9. James Hightower, *New York Times,* June 21, 1986, section 4.
10. Ehrenreich, *op. cit.*
11. "The Children Who Live in Cars," *Washington Post,* National Weekly Edition, June 24, 1985, p. 8.
12. Hightower, *op. cit.*
13. *Economic Report of the President.* Washington: USPGO, 1986, p. 286.
14. Ehrenreich, *op. cit.*
15. *ibid.*
16. *New York Times,* July 12, 1987, section 4, p. 5.
17. *Bangor Daily News,* December 30, 1986, p. 1.
18. "The Hunger Epidemic and Its Symptoms," *New York Times,* March 3, 1985, section 4; and "Hunger in U.S. Is Widening, Study of 'New Poor' Reports," *New York Times,* April 20, 1986, section 1, p. 1.
19. "The Millions Without Health Insurance," *Washington Post,* National Weekly Edition, July 21, 1986, p. 9.
20. *Christian Science Monitor,* April 12, 1985, p. 13; and "The Global March to Free Markets," *New York Times,* July 19, 1987, section 3, p. 13.
21. *Monitor,* October 21, 1986.
22. "Our Unemployment Quandry," *New York Times,* November 30, 1986, section 3, p. 1.
23. *ibid.*

24. Sar Levitan, "A Weaker Net Under Workers," *New York Times,* September 1, 1986.
25. This calculation has been carried out by a rather sophisticated methodology and explained by Ward Morehouse and David Dembo, *Joblessness and the Pauperization of Work in America: Background Papers.* (Quarterly Publication.) New York: Council on International and Public Affairs.
26. *New York Times,* September 27, 1987, section 3, p. 1.
27. Barry Bluestone and Bennett Harrison, *The Great American Job Machine: The Proliferation of Low Wage Employment in the U.S. Economy.* A study prepared for the Congressional Joint Economic Committee, December, 1986.
28. *ibid.,* p. 21.
29. "A Logy 'McJobs' Economy? One Analyst Pooh-Poohs View," *Christian Science Monitor,* January 9, 1987, p. 19.
30. "Rewriting the Social Contract for America's Have-Nots," *New York Times,* April 12, 1987, section 4, p. 5.
31. Levitan, *op. cit.*
32. *Business Week,* December 22, 1986, p. 13.
33. *ibid.*
34. Jacob Mincer, "Labor-Force Participation and Unemployment" in R. A. Gordon and M. S. Gordon, eds., *Prosperity and Unemployment.* New York: John Wiley, 1966, pp. 73-112.
35. Milton Friedman, "The Role of Monetary Policy," *American Economic Review,* LXIII (March 1968), pp. 1-17.
36. Clair Brown, "Unemployment Theory and Policy, 1946-1980," *Industrial Relations,* 22:2 (Spring 1983), p. 171.
37. Martin Weitzman, *The Share Economy.* Cambridge, Massachusetts: Harvard University Press, 1984, p. 146.
38. *ibid.,* p. 121.
39. David Ellerman, "The Ownership-Sharing Firm: Profit-Sharing Based on Ownership-Sharing," unpublished manuscript, March 1987, p. 5.
40. *ibid.,* p. 6.
41. *Public Laws.* Chapter 33, February 20, 1946.
42. "Full Employment and Balanced Growth Act of 1978," *Public Laws,* October 27, 1978, pp. 95-523.
43. Robert Reich, *The Next American Frontier.* New York: Times Books, Random House, 1983.
44. "How Government, Business, and Schools Can Team Up to Fill Jobs," *Christian Science Monitor,"* May 9, 1983, p. 7.

45. "Annual Report, 1982," Bay State Skills Corporation, 1 Ashburton Place, Room 2110, Boston, Massachusetts 02108.

46. *Business Training Partnerships in Action: An Evaluation of the BSSC Program.* ABT Associates, March 15, 1983 (55 Wheeler Street, Cambridge, MA 02138).

47. Campbell R. McConnell, *Economics.* 8th edition. New York: Mc-Graw-Hill, 1981, p. 93.

48.   Quoted in Robert Cooter and Peter Rappaport,"Were the Ordinalists Wrong about Welfare Economics?" in *Journal of Economic Literature,* 22 (June 1984), p. 519.

Chapter 12

HUMANISTIC ENTERPRISE: THE CASE OF MONDRAGON

The time has now come to flesh out our humanistic conception portrayed in Chapter 8 of a successful enterprise that is in keeping with the humanistic spirit and the recognition of a dual-self. For this purpose we now turn to Spain, more specifically its Basque provinces located in the mountainous northeastern corner of the country. There for the last three decades a new type of enterprise has been evolving and growing. Today it constitutes one of the largest and most dynamic firms in Spain. Its importance, however, reaches far beyond the Basque mountains and the Spanish border. In fact, we now believe that what has been taking place there may affect profoundly the future course of economic developments elsewhere as well.

All this by way of introduction. The story we are about to tell is a story of a simple parish priest working with average working men and women in a small town, Mondragon. Let us take a brief look at the historical context of what was about to happen in the mid-1950s.

Father Arizmendi Comes to Mondragon

Mondragon was a sleepy town of 8,000 inhabitants in the Basque province of Guipuzcoa, located about thirty miles from the Atlantic Coast in the Cantabrian Mountains. Its name derives from "Tail of the Dragon" due to the ragged shape of a mountain ridge right above the town. (The Basque name of Mondragon is Arrasate.)

Since the 1950s it had one major industrial plant employing several hundred workers: the Union Cerrajera producing locks and similar items. Most of the old town was clustered around its old church. It had been prosperous in the late Middle Ages when local iron ore resources were forged into high-quality swords and other weapons. But Mondragon essentially remained a small rural town very much on the periphery of the late nineteenth century industrial revolution sweeping through the coastal areas of the Basque country. Even worse, after the bloody Spanish Civil War and the extra reprisals of the revengeful Franco dictatorship, Mondragon, like the rest of the Basque area, struggled with an economic collapse and almost hopeless poverty. Almost half of the people in Mondragon were unemployed.

It was in this desperate situation during the year 1941 when we note the arrival of a twenty-five-year-old curate sent there directly from the seminary by his bishop. His name was Don Jose Maria Arizmendiarietta; in short, Don Jose or Father Arizmendi. He saw his mission as being the counselor and advisor of the local working people, particularly the young.

Shortly after arriving, he encouraged the boys in his youth group to join together and, using community contributions, create a badly needed technical vocational school. With small donations from a quarter of the Mondragon families, and with Father Arizmendi's dedicated leadership, the school opened in 1943 with an enrollment of twenty. Some of these students went on to study for an engineering degree at the University of Zaragoza. Eleven graduated five years later in 1952. Out of these eleven, five young men were to become the nucleus of the Mondragon experiment. With their engineering degrees these highly motivated young men worked in supervisory positions for private companies, trying at the same time to be a force for a more democratized workplace. Father Arizmendi recollected their frustrating experience when interviewed many years later:

> With total selflessness and integrity they worked in the hub of many companies, hoping to be able to promote their evolution and change, at least to the extent to which the various antagonistic elements could live together and engage in a dialogue. By one side they were called colleagues; the other side tolerated them less with each day that passed, forcing them to clash with attitudes that were inflexible and intransigent, even in matters that were peripheral to the structure of the enterprise and to its fundamental development—a phase that lasted until 1954.[1]

In response to this unsatisfactory situation, in November 1955 they purchased a bankrupt paraffin cooker business in the neighboring town of Vitoria, accomplished by pooling their savings and raising more than $130,000 in over 200 small local contributions. The new enterprise, which started up in 1956, was to be a vehicle to put into practice their idea of the dignity of work and democratic enterprise. They called it ULGOR, an acronym of the initial letters of their names. Initially, operations were carried out informally, without bylaws, as a small self-managed firm. Soon a new and bigger plant was built at Mondragon in order to produce a space-heating stove.

Meanwhile, Father Arizmendi searched for a legal and financial structure that would allow ULGOR to formally operate according to the principles of solidarity and democratic self-government. As he recalled his endeavors later, a formula had to be found by which the enterprise could be brought into line with Spanish law and yet enable the first industrial cooperative to exist and flourish. "To do this, we had to overcome more than legal difficulties. . . . from the beginning we bore in mind the needs of modern enterprise, and a formula was adopted which would make its development viable from all points of view: economic, technical, social and financial; not as a second ranking entity suitable only for a limited field of activity, but one which would be appropriate across a wide sector of the economy."[2]

ULGOR's organizational structure was skillfully adapted so as to be compatible with a 1941 Spanish law of cooperatives, originally designed and passed for agricultural co-ops. The fact that ULGOR was an industrial and not an agricultural co-op created a risky situation, making it vulnerable to potential sanctions by the hostile Franco regime. It is for this reason that the founders of ULGOR kept as low a profile as possible, a policy that lasted until the fascist dictatorship came to an end with Franco's death in 1975. Although ULGOR started its Mondragon operations in 1956 with twenty-four worker-members, its pathbreaking new legal structure was neither much written or talked about until the early 1970s. The first English language description had to wait until 1973–an article by Robert Oakshott appearing in January of that year in the British paper *Observer*.

ULGOR soon began to produce butane gas stoves under a license granted from an Italia company (Fargas Spa). They built a new factory and launched the brand name FAGOR. By 1959 there were 170 worker-owners. Other new co-ops were created, particularly through a combination and conversion of two previously conventionally organized foundaries, later to be called Ederlan.

The new cooperatives were off to a great start, in part thanks to a very favorable economic climate prevailing at that time in the protected Spanish market. At the same time, Father Arizmendi was plotting again. In the late 1950s he had a new idea: the formation of a cooperative bank much like a credit union in the United States. This time even his disciples at ULGOR were hesitant. We are told by one of them about their reaction to the proposal: "We told him, yesterday we were craftsmen, freemen, and engineers. Today we are trying to learn how to be managers and executives. Tomorrow you want us to become bankers. That is impossible."[3]

But Father Arizmendi researched the idea and, convinced of its soundness, arrived at ULGOR's next board meeting with all the paperwork done and ready for signatures. His followers were surprised but persuaded. In July of 1959 its new statutes were formally approved and the bank began operating in 1960. The new Caja Laboral Popular (CLP) provided a badly needed source of outside capital for the expanding co-ops. Families in Mondragon deposited their savings, enjoying not only one-half percent of interest more than elsewhere but also secure in knowing that their savings would have to be invested among the cooperatives associated with the bank, rather than flowing outside the Basque area.

The new bank was also to assist in the formation of new co-ops and to provide and administer funds for a cooperative social security system. The Mondragon workers under Spanish law are considered self-employed, and so are not protected under the national system.

In order to be able to benefit from the financial resources and services of CLP, every co-op was to sign a Contract of Association, articulating principles that would regulate economic and operational relations among the associated member enterprises. More specifically, in signing the Contract of Association the co-ops commit themselves to uniform principles pertaining to capital ownership, employment creation, earnings differentials, distribution of surplus, and democratic organization. It is for this reason that we today talk about the Mondragon co-ops as a group rather than as individual enterprises.

The Caja Laboral Popular, as the center of the group, expanded rapidly. After ten years it featured 54 branches all over the Basque region. In 1986 the number was 171 with an overall staff of 1,223. We will talk about it further when discussing the entire organizational structure of the co-ops.

Meanwhile, in 1964 ULGOR joined together with three other cooperatives to form a group called ULARCO. The group expanded from 1,350 members in 1964 to 6,700 in 1980. Similarly, under the active leadership of the bank four to five new industrial co-ops were created every year; by 1986 all industrial co-ops together had almost 18,000 working members. A new consumer co-op, EROSKI, was set up in 1968. Today it has about 150,000 consumer members, a staff of 1,400, approximately 100 supermarkets spread all over the Basque region, and annual sales of $300 million. It is also Spain's eighth largest outfit selling consumer goods.

A social security services co-op, LAGUN-ARO, was set up in 1970 and provides its 50,000 associated members with comprehensive health and pension benefits.

In 1977 a separate research and development cooperative, IKER-LAN, was established to ensure that the enterprises of the Mondragon group remain competitive in terms of newest industrial technology.

More recently, a cooperative business school, IKASBIDE, was opened to help the member co-ops better respond to new challenges of increasing international competition.

Father Arizmendi died in 1976; he always remained a simple curate riding his old bike through the hilly neighborhoods of Mondragon. But he left behind a veritable industrial empire which today is one of Spain's most important and dynamic enterprises. The cooperatives together have a work force of 20,000 men and women. And it all happened in just three decades with no outside help. The legacy of Father Arizmendi is no longer confined to the success he had in the Basque area. Today economists and politicians from all over the world are studying this fascinating experiment, specifically his novel ideas pertaining to the organization of a brand new type of enterprise which is neither capitalist nor socialist. Its legal and economic structure borrows the best from each system and then goes beyond both of them.

Let us now take a closer look at exactly how Mondragon operates, how successful it has been, and how its structure can be exported elsewhere.

Mondragon Co-ops: Organizational Highlights

There are basically three new ideas that can be singled out as providing the very key to Mondragon's success. They pertain to how the cooperatives are managed, how they are financially and legally structured, and how they are supported by the cooperative bank. We will discuss these three institutional innovations in turn.

The Management Structure

The very concept of "worker self-management" almost always provokes the automatic image of every staff member and worker actively trying to decide every aspect of the enterprise. Such a vision of organizational chaos only serves too well in rejecting the whole idea out-of-hand.

However, the association of self-management with uninformed, amateur, and crippling management is similar to imagining that American Telephone and Telegraph (AT&T) is managed by thousands of pension fund managers together with the hundreds of thousands of "widows" holding stock in the company. Of course, the fact that AT&T is owned by its stockholders does not mean that it is also managed by them, and the same applies to a democratic worker cooperative. In both cases there is management by delegation; in both cases there is hierarchy and a chain of command starting in the executive suite and reaching down to the shop floor. Where a worker cooperative is different lies in the fact that their executives manage in the name and interest of all the cooperative members, rather than in the interests of absentee stockholders. They do this because the executive is appointed by a board of directors, which in turn is elected by the firm's members. Nevertheless, many cooperatives have indeed suffered from mismanagement primarily due to a lack of discipline with respect to shop floor workers ignoring management orders.

The potential of this type of problem was clearly recognized by Father Arizmendi and he sought to prevent it by creating a management structure that would provide executives a lot of elbow room and shop floor discipline. Paragraph 3 of ULGOR's "Internal Code of Rules," worked out by Father Arizmendi, reads:

> Human work must be subjected to discipline and its performance as a team effort requires order and thus authority. The members of this cooperative, once they have elected those most suitable for government, must show spontaneous and rigorous respect for the order of those who hold positions of command within their internal structure.

What Father Arizmendi sought and found was a hierarchical structure that allows managerial efficiency and power, but prevents illegitimate power, arbitrary action, and abuse. The managers in Mondragon are appointed for a four-year term by the co-op's nine-member *Supervisory Board*. The permanent members of the Board, consisting of the chairperson, vice chairperson, and the secretary, meet with the manager several times during a month on the so-called

Management Council, but these are primarily advisory and consultative meetings where a proposed move by management can be criticized rather than vetoed or otherwise interfered with. Similarly, members of a *Social Council* elected by the firm's various departmental units directly represent their shop floor interests, but, again, only to report to management about such traditionally union matters as job description, salary scales, grievances, and safety matters. As long as management stays within the general guidelines set by the bylaws and the Supervisory Board, they can attend to day-to-day business as seems fit. Of course, repeated ignoring of Supervisory Board suggestions may cost their reappointment when the four-year term is over.

Nevertheless, the participatory role of the rank and file co-op member is essentially constrained to their electing every year two members to the Supervisory Board. They do so by majority vote in the *General Assembly* which ordinarily convenes once a year. Besides voting two of the six electable members of the Supervisory Board for a three-year staggered term, the General Assembly also has to decide to accept the annual business report and vote on some basic matters like the internal rate of interest to be charged on equity accounts and the level of threshold payments for new members.

The chart in Figure 12.1 illustrates the organizational elements of a Mondragon cooperative structure.

Arrangements such as these appear well-suited to reconcile the so often conflicting demands of managerial efficiency and worker democracy. These institutions also explain why Alastair Campbell, an expert on Mondragon, can observe: "Managers in the Mondragon co-ops are notably enthusiastic. They clearly suffer no discouragement from being 'controlled by the workers.'"[4]

The Legal Structure

Father Arizmendi's second and even more ingenious organizational innovation consists of structuring the legal and financial aspects of the enterprise in a radically new way. It is the invention theoretically discussed towards the end of Chapter 8: the explicit recognition of members' rights to a fair share in the net book value of the firm (assets minus liabilities) by means of the new *individualized internal capital accounts* (IICA).

When a new person joins the co-op, and successfully completes a probationary period of several months, he or she becomes a member. Membership entails a threshold payment, the level of which changes every year as determined by the General Assembly. Currently, the level is about $5,000. Normally, one-fourth of this sum has to be paid at the

Figure 12.1

THE ORGANIZATIONAL STRUCTURE
OF A MONDRAGON COOPERATIVE

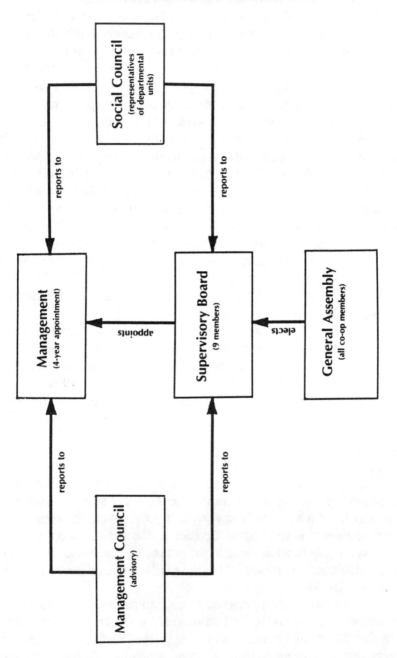

start, the remainder can be paid out of a salary deduction over a two- to four-year period. Fifteen to 25 percent of the threshold payment represents a non-refundable contribution to the cooperative's financial reserves, but the rest is used as an initial deposit on the newcomer's IICA. Each year the value of the account is adjusted upwards to compensate for inflation. After this is done, the owner is also entitled to a 6 percent annual interest on the total amount of capital contributed (loaned) by him or her. These adjustments come before net surplus (i.e., profit) is computed.

Each year a large part of profits (called "net surplus") is divided in proportion to patronage, measured primarily by salary (called "advanced surplus"). The resulting profit share is automatically used to augment the balance in the IICA. In a sense, it is retained or borrowed by the firm until the member retires or otherwise leaves the firm. In case a member transfers to another co-op he simply transfers his or her account. But if a member goes elsewhere, the co-op usually holds on to 20 percent of his or her balance "for educational services rendered."

The distribution of net surplus into three components is strictly regulated by some formula, but Spanish law requires that 10 percent go into a *social fund*, financing schools and retraining facilities for the community at large. Under ordinary circumstances, 20 percent of net surplus is allocated to enterprise collective reserves. The remaining 70 percent is then allocated to members' IICAs. In years of very high net surplus the proportion between collective reserves and IICAs is more like 50/50. Similarly, if net surplus is negative, i.e., there is a loss, 30 percent comes out of collective reserves and the rest will have to be debited to everybody's IICA. Such depreciation of the accounts happens only rarely, but it may have occurred in the midst of the deep depression that hit Spain in the early 1980s. Apart from such distressful but rare events, the Mondragon enterprise automatically retains 90 percent of its annual profits, a fact which gives it great financial advantage in competing with conventional corporations in the marketplace. And, as discussed in Chapter 8, under this type of legal structure workers generally have little interest in wanting their take-home income to grow at the expense of reinvestment of profits.

Today, the average member of a Mondragon co-op enjoys an IICA balance of more than $25,000; many who entered only during the last fifteen years have less than that, but the figure for some senior members may be considerably higher.* The sum of $25,000 earns an annual interest of 6 percent–$1,500–which is paid out to the account holder during the month of December. But the principal, annually augmented by profits and an inflationary adjustment, has to remain in the IICA until the worker-member retires or leaves. (It should be noted that because of the annual inflation-related appreciations of the balances shown in the IICA mentioned on the previous page, the holders in fact rake in a handsome 6 percent *real* (not nominal) return on their investment.) Meanwhile, it can be used to serve as collateral for pre-retirement expenses, such as buying real estate or a new automobile.

The novel idea of such individualized capital accounts as carriers of the firm's net book value can be seen as introducing a bit of capitalism into the democratic cooperative institution. But it is a very special capitalism, more akin to proprietorships or partnerships rather than the investor ownership characteristic of the corporation. Perhaps a "coproprietorship" expresses best the type of business involved. It is an extraordinary enterprise that merely allows each working member of the cooperative to claim and eventually to capitalize his or her own contribution to the value of the firm. Moreover, as long as each member has such a considerable financial status in his or her enterprise, we can expect a very positive incentive effect facilitating the generation of a highly motivated work force.

In contrast to the quasi-capitalist institution of IICAs, the monthly earnings structure of the range of worker-members is fairly egalitarian. Jobs are evaluated according to skill, effort, and responsibility required, on a scale ranging from 1 to 4.5. In other words, the highest paid senior executive jobs are never paid more than 4.5 times the lowest paying ones. Since the lowest paying or "entry jobs" are based on the going or "competitive" rate in the Basque area, it works out that managers get paid considerably less than their counterparts in rival investor-owned corporate enterprises. Of course, some part of this income deficiency is made up by the IICAs.

---

* The $25,000 figure is an estimate based on the experience of the Caja Laboral Popular staff holdings which, according to its bylaws, is to reflect the general situation prevailing in the associated cooperatives.

The contrast with the U.S. corporate world is sharp. According to a recent survey published in the *Wall Street Journal* (April 10, 1987), senior executives of larger U.S. corporations get a salary of $100,000 to $300,000, figures that do not reflect the other 40 percent of their total compensation, including bonuses and stock option plans. Compared with the minimum wage, this would imply an earnings ratio of something like 50 to 1 between highest and lowest paid.

Once again, all this serves to illustrate the unique make-up of a Mondragon cooperative, its blends of "capitalist" efficiency with "socialist" ethics. Nothing illustrates this better than Mondragon's cooperative bank, the Caja Laboral Popular, which has emerged as the very brain center of the cooperative empire. Besides management autonomy and the internal capital accounts, it represents the third pillar supporting this humanistic success story.

The Cooperative Bank

As already noted, the Caja Laboral Popular (CLP)–literally "The Working People's Bank"–was set up in 1960 as another brainchild of Father Arizmendi. It may have been the most important. It certainly has been a towering figure over the institution without which the future of Mondragon would not look nearly as rosy as it does. Its outstanding features consist in (1) how it operates as a bank, and (2) the way it has been ceaselessly spawning new cooperative enterprises. One function has been carried out in its banking division, the other in its entrepreneurial services division. Most recently, the entrepreneurial services division has been split off as an independent second tier cooperative with a staff of more than 100 members. It is about to move into a brand new building located behind the bank. Let us first take a look at the former.

The Caja Laboral Popular's Banking. The CLP is today less than thirty years old and yet, thanks to an extraordinarily rapid growth, it is already among the two dozen largest banks in Spain. Its assets have grown from 500 million pesetas in 1965 to more than 200 billion pesetas (almost $2 billion) today. Such phenomenal growth can be primarily attributed to its ability to attract deposits by means of an aggressive policy to open several new branches all over the Basque region every year. The number of branches is about to reach the 200 level. Obviously, the bank has been most attractive to depositors and savers who value the extra one-half percent interest that Spanish credit union-type banks can offer, together with the assurance that all of their money will be invested in new cooperative enterprises and jobs located in their own region. (Recently the Spanish government has given its permission for the CLP to also invest a fraction of its loans in non-cooperative enterprises.)

The CLP then turns around and invests the funds in short-, medium- and long-term loans to the associated co-ops as well as in legally required government securities. So, for example, in the year 1985 the CLP held 28 percent of its assets in cash or liquid forms, kept 19 percent in

Figure 12.2

THE CLP AS SOURCE OF COOPERATIVE FINANCE, 1965-1985
(million pesetas)

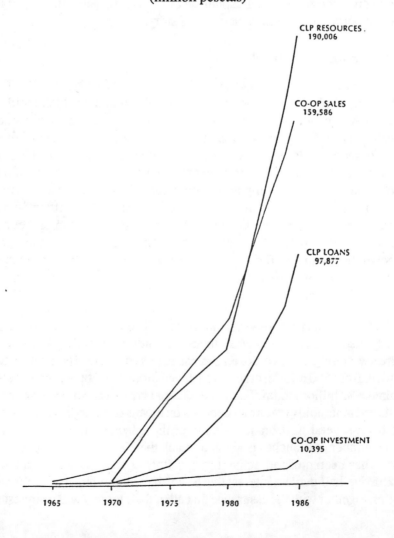

government securities, and invested 41 percent into the discounting of (inventory-related) bills and loans. The last two categories amounted to 77 billion pesetas of which 47 billion (or approximately $400 million) went to finance associated cooperatives. All this was easily made possible by 147 billion pesetas in deposits and by the 18 billion pesetas of "own resources" consisting of 4 billion pesetas capital (IICAs of the staff) and 14 billion pesetas of different kinds of reserves.

Figure 12.2 above illustrates in summary fashion the growing finance power of the bank during the last twenty-five years.

It is readily apparent that the CLP has recently been bursting with funds. In fact, in 1986 its owner equity and deposits exceeded total investment and sales(!) of all associated worker cooperatives by $160 million.* At the same time, its own resources alone would have been sufficient to loan twice the money to the co-ops than they actually did.

This astonishing picture of rapidly growing cooperative finance power is likely to continue at an accelerated rate, herewith promising a reassuring future to the entire Mondragon group, even if the depressed state of the Spanish economy should continue for many more years. It certainly provides an impressive counterexample to the conventional wisdom, deeply rooted in 150 years of belief, that worker cooperatives will always be severely handicapped when it comes to securing external sources of finance.

Of course, the bank has been highly profitable. Even during the recession years, 1982-1985, its net surplus relative to its assets has been two to three times higher than net profits on the assets for American banks over the same period.[5] But that does not mean that the bank's staff is wallowing in ballooning IICAs. In 1986 a total of $2 million was deposited in the internal capital accounts of the 1,223 staff members, adding on the average $1,635 each. Since CLP bylaws require that the bank staff can only allocate an amount that corresponds to the average net surplus level allocated to the IICAs of all associated cooperatives, most of the profits ($19 million in 1986) are put into bulging reserve accounts, thus enriching the entire Mondragon community. In addition, another $2 million was spent on retraining group members.

All this is well in keeping with the basic purpose of the bank: community job creation through generating economically viable new enterprises. This now brings us to its Entrepreneurial Services (ES) division.

---

* The currency conversion used here is 127 pesetas per U.S. dollar.

The Entrepreneurial Services Division.   Located until 1988 in the headquarters of the CLP and now in a separate newly built facility near-by, more than 100 staff members engage routinely in such far-flung activities as launching new enterprises, studying new markets, and financial restructuring of what might be called "chapter 11" bankruptcy cases. It functions like a benevolent investment banker specializing in high risk ventures.

For our purposes, we will attempt to convey an idea of what it primarily does by a hypothetical example describing some of the steps involved in launching a new cooperative.

Imagine three young Mondragonians, fresh out of school and eager to "go into business." One has graduated from the cooperative engineering school, the other two just have high school diplomas.

They make an appointment for an initial interview at The Entrepreneurial Services Division (ES) to talk about their plan. ES listens and forms an opinion about the commitment of the three. If they form a favorable impression, a "partnership contract" is signed. The contract commits both parties to go ahead. Each of our three aspirants are obliged to kick in a threshold payment, double the ordinary size. Today this means roughly $10,000 each, but most of the money can be borrowed from the CLP at favorable rates.

ES, on the other hand, commits itself to provide the rest of the financing. It also provides an office, complete with secretary, to the group's spokesman (now called "the promoter") who is expected to work there full time for eighteen months. His or her salary is paid by a bank loan with deferred interest. ES also assigns one of its experts, lovingly called "godfather," on a full-time basis to guide and assist the promoter.

The first order of business is to search for a suitable product, and for that purpose ES already has ten to twenty pre-researched products in its periodically updated "product bank." These usually include a heavy proportion of high tech-oriented product ideas, such as computers, robotics, high precision plastics, laser technology, and the like. Our promoter may have ideas of his or her own, and if the godfather finds them promising, they go ahead with it. Either way, a painstakingly detailed three-volume feasibility study is prepared where the promoter has access to an impressive array of technical services.

So, for example, the Marketing and Export Departments will assist with questions of the forecast of sales. The Production Department can help plan the production layout. For designing the factory the Industrial Building Department is ready to engage its activities. The Personnel Department helps with questions pertaining to manpower training and

oversight during loan period / keeping
social control of loan

hiring, while the Legal Department assists with all the legal work involving incorporation procedures, the obtaining of licenses or patents, and related matters. Finally, there is the Administrative/Financial Department to turn to for setting up the accounting system.

After eighteen months, and with the detailed feasibility study completed, ES has to make a decision whether or not to fund the project. In case it does not, another product is selected and the process repeats itself. Almost always, however, ES will give the green light provided an environmental impact statement is satisfactory too.

Once the co-op is launched, ES provides a seven-year loan based on the assumption that the co-op will turn profitable after three years. The interest on the loan is initially zero, but increases after two years to 2 percent and reaches 15 percent in the last year. During that period ES carefully monitors week by week the financial developments. It immediately intervenes if there is trouble on the horizon, either by providing new finance or, in more drastic cases, by replacing the promoter/manager or even the entire product line. If all goes well, our three Mondragon entrepreneurs will soon find themselves securely on board, as manager, chairperson, and vice chairperson, together with a host of newly admitted co-workers. And so Mondragon can boast yet another associated enterprise.

What is important to note is that once the initial partnership contract is signed, ES steps in until the new enterprise is *successfully* launched. Although the creation of new enterprises is a risky line of business—in the United States nine out of ten new firms fail within five years—the Mondragon success rate is practically 100 percent. (Of the 100 new co-ops, three failed for unrelated reasons. In two cases converted bankrupt capitalist firms were dropped when its management decided that the future held too little hope. They themselves wanted out and ES wished them well.)

Of course, not all 100 co-ops were set up from scratch. Often, ordinary co-ops in the Basque area ask to join the group, and after legal and financial restructuring are also admitted. Sometimes whole sub-units of an existing co-op are spun off and set up as independent new associate firms. Whatever the process, ES plans to launch at least four or five new co-ops every year to keep its dozen padrinos ("godfathers") busy, and to provide new jobs—the explicit "bottom·line" goal of the Mondragon group.

Not surprisingly, job creation has been impressive: almost 20,000 new members since the early 1960s! And all this with little or no help from the central government in Madrid, but primarily by means of local

community self-reliance instead. This, in a nutshell, is the success story
of humanistic enterprise par excellence! But let us evaluate now more
carefully the performance of the Mondragon experiment.

The Performance of Mondragon

Ever since its original inception, job creation has been held to constitute the primary goal of the Mondragon co-ops. It seems fitting, therefore, to first take a good look at this aspect of performance.

Table 12.1 below summarizes the data quantifying the growth in
worker-members since 1956.

Table 12.1

WORKER MEMBERS AT MONDRAGON CO-OPS:
1956-1988

Year	Worker Members
1956	24
1960	395
1970	8,543
1975	13,189
1980	18,733
1985	19,161
1988	22,000

The job creation was excellent until 1980 when the Spanish
economy went into a severe depression lasting four years. Basque unemployment approached the 20 percent level. Between 1975 and the
low point of 1983, the Basque economy lost over 60,000 jobs. According to a study commissioned by the World Bank, "had Mondragon's
membership paralleled employment growth in the Basque economy
over 1976-83, by 1983 the number of overall members would have fallen to 12,956, only 69 percent of its actual level."[6] The same study estimated that only 1 percent or 160 members unsuccessfully tried to
transfer to another job within the cooperative group. Yet, those unfortunate members received 80 percent of their previous pay for a two-
year period, or until they found work outside Mondragon. In addition,
they were assured that if they could not find work, they could return to
Mondragon after two years. Meanwhile, the crisis blew over and membership at Mondragon has grown by some 900 since 1983.

The reason why Mondragon could so successfully resist layoffs when hit by slumping sales is, of course, their ability to adjust compensation. Once again, the World Bank study is revealing here. While Basque wages remained more or less fixed between 1980 and 1983, it was employment that remained fixed at Mondragon. Instead, its members voted a 10 to 12 percent reduction in their overall compensation, enough to prevent any losses. (Meanwhile, the Basque profit rate was strongly negative, averaging -8.1 percent between 1980 and 1983.)

There were four studies done in the 1970s showing that Mondragon is more efficient than even the most successful Spanish capitalist firms.[7] Similar data for the 1980s do not exist, but there are qualitative reasons to suggest that the cooperatives still have the edge over their conventional counterparts.

For one, studies indicate that workers are more motivated to follow the directives of (their) management and that they tend to encourage each other towards a greater work effort. As a result, fewer supervisors are required to get a job done. Another competitive advantage comes from the fact that normally 90 percent of net profits are annually reinvested in the firm, enabling the co-ops to finance their expansion at more favorable rates than conventional capitalist corporations that had to rely on bank loans and other sources of external finance.

Another reason why Mondragon could adjust more easily was its ability to sell its products outside the glutted Spanish market. For example, at Fagor, its largest component unit, domestic sales fell by about 10 percent in real terms between 1980 and 1982. Yet that reduction was more than offset by a sharp increase in export sales. Generally, exports have slowly but surely grown in importance, from 10 percent of sales in 1970 to 23 percent in 1985. At Fagor the ratio is currently almost 50 percent.

This brings us to another prime indicator of Mondragon's performance: growth in its industrial and agricultural sales. Table 12.2 below provides the data on this dimension.

As the table clearly indicates, sales growth was unusually rapid until 1980. Since then it has slowed down considerably, especially when we correct for increases due to inflation. Now that the Basque economy is recovering, we expect Mondragon to resume its sterling performance. But it will not be so easy since Spain entered the Common Market in 1986. Firms such as Fagor will have to fight for a growing market share in household appliances against such European giants as FIAT of Italy and Siemens of Germany. The initial reports are not discouraging, but the real test of market performance is still ahead. So, for example, during 1986 export sales of consumer goods declined by 9 percent, a result explained to some extent by the weak dollar and the financial crisis in South America. Moreover, employment in that sector decreased by 105 worker-members, a decline associated with a record level investment program aiming at boosting competitiveness through automation.

Table 12.2

SALES OF MONDRAGON GROUP: 1960-1986

Year	Overall Group Sales (index form, 1980=100)	Overall Group Sales at Constant Prices (index form, 1980=100)
1960	.3	.02
1970	10.2	42.1
1975	28.5	66.7
1980	100.0	100.0
1985	204.1	114.6
1986	240.4	124.1

Finally, when evaluating the performance of the co-ops, it should not be forgotten that they have achieved their continued growth with an exceptional degree of equality, as guaranteed by the 4.5:1 pay distribution rule mentioned on page 262.

In conclusion, it is fair to say that Mondragon has performed exceedingly well. But it was able to do so in a general economic climate favorable to growth. This is no longer true. Today, the cooperatives are playing in a higher and more competitive league. Whether or not they will continue to do well is more of a question than an assumption. Much depends on the state of the world economy in the years to come. However, whatever happens in terms of its sales during the next few years, we need not be concerned about its immediate future. The reason is, of course, its financially powerful bank that stands ready to lend a helping hand should the news from the sales front turn out to be disappointing. Only time will tell if this will end up being necessary.

The Replicability of Mondragon-Type Co-ops

How exportable is the Mondragon idea? Could it work elsewhere? Is it a specific result of the particular cultural context in which it was conceived more than thirty years ago? How important is the political situation that divides the Basque people from the Spanish and so creates an us-against-them type of bonding, a willingness to overcome individual aspirations and considerations of benefit for the sake of one's people?

All the above questions will legitimately continue to be raised until they are satisfactorily answered one way or the other. We will sidestep the cultural issue, however, because we maintain that what makes Mondragon work is not only the community spirit that obviously prevails; it is also the novel economic institution of individualized internal capital accounts which we see as a brand new alternative to both corporate capitalism and bureaucratic socialism. In Chapter 8 we saw that this insight appears to overcome most, if not all, the theoretical reasons that have been conjured up in order to explain the historical failure and contemporary problems of ordinary worker-managed producer cooperatives.

From a purely economic theory-oriented perspective, Mondragon can be expected to work elsewhere, at least as well as or better than capitalist and socialist firms have been working. And, of course, the social and humanistic features of such well-formed cooperatives are so overwhelmingly positive that the question of replicability imposes itself as one of utmost importance and increasing relevance.

One way to answer these questions is to actually try it elsewhere and see what happens. This is beginning to be done here in the United States and only time will tell what kind of wisdom can be gained from these recent experiments. Before addressing some of these developments, it may be appropriate to discuss three particular problems that might be expected to arise. They pertain to the questions of labor mobility leading to capital payout of the company, the question of trade union attitude, and, more generally, the problem of running Mondragons in an economy fully open to international competition. Let us take a brief look at each of them.

The Question of Labor Mobility. Co-op members in such a community as Mondragon exhibit a relatively low inclination to change jobs, particularly if this would imply leaving town. Two reasons come readily to mind: there is a high degree of community identification and a relatively integrated but localized social welfare system. In quitting and moving one risks losing on both counts.

Now, imagine a Mondragon-type enterprise by itself in a large city, such as Madrid or Boston. Initially, there will be no group, no other enterprises of the same kind to which one could switch by transferring one's capital account built up over some time. So why join such a firm in the first place? And if one joins, for the sake, let us say, of landing a job, why not move on relatively soon as long as there is little in one's

IICA? Dispositions and inclinations such as these can be readily expected, and within the context are quite understandable. Yet they pose a threat to the very viability and integrity of a democratic, well-formed cooperative. If commitment to the cooperative principles is lacking, if attrition is high, our city Mondragon will suffer constant and excessive decapitalization, with no friendly bank to turn to for greater reliance on external finance.

Fortunately, the problem is not quite as bad as it may at first sight appear. The reason is that the very system of IICAs allows for some automatic screening where workers joining only for a job will be kept out. The primary screen is the initial entry fee, currently some $5,000. Most unemployed will lack the means or the necessary credit record to make a strong effort to join. And those who, despite this handicap, decide to seek membership at whatever sacrifice it might entail are tried out for a six-month period in which their social skills or their cooperative attitude and commitment are closely scrutinized before they are entitled to join the cooperative as full members. Through mechanisms such as these the enterprise will be able to avoid problematic members with a short-run job focus. Instead, they will draw new members that exhibit a lower propensity to quit whenever a slightly better pay opportunity comes along. Although this would go some ways in solving the threat of constant decapitalization, it also has a negative social aspect: the workers that are in greatest despair, who need a job more than anybody else, would not normally be able to become members in our humanistic enterprise.

Meanwhile, it seems reasonable to anticipate that a Mondragon-type co-op can be more successfully replicated in a community setting, especially a town dominated by a single employer, where workers threatened with plant closure might unite to buy that company. Similarly, wherever we have a semi-autonomous region with its own culture, such as the Basque people in Spain and France, the Albanians in Yugoslavia, the French Canadians in Quebec, and the like, the Mondragon idea may fall on especially fertile grounds.

The Position of Labor Unions.   Mondragon workers began their enterprises when trade unions were outlawed by the Franco regime. Only in 1977 was the ban lifted, but until this day there is not much interest in organizing a trade union. Why should they? The managers are ultimately under worker control and perform their duties on behalf of everyone. There are no outside interests to which management may cater or which may conflict with what the workers need most. Americans need no institution or paramilitary to defend them against Congress, the White House, and the courts. Similarly, genuine industrial democracy seems to void the need for trade union involvement. In Mondragon many of the tasks typically assigned to a union local are carried out by the social council.

But the entire issue is somewhat more complex than it would first appear. First of all, by the concept "trade union" we refer to the traditional type of union which has, in one form or another, dominated the industrial landscape for a century. For such more antagonistic unions there seems to be no need in a democratic cooperative; but at the same time, unions in general are not necessarily incompatible with Mondragon-style industrial democracy. There is also the distinct possibility of envisioning a somewhat reformed trade union that might even have an important place in a self-managed cooperative. David Ellerman from the Industrial Cooperative Association has long argued for such a new role which he sees as one of "legitimate opposition," akin to the opposition party in the British Parliament.[8]

This new breed of trade union may also be instrumental in organizing new buy-outs by providing interested workers with a mechanism and procedure for legal matters and a sophisticated feasibility analysis. Remember, a Mondragon-type of cooperative outside the Basque country has no Caja Laboral Popular with an Entrepreneurial Division to rely on. It is conceivable that a progressive national or international union may be able to take over some of these important tasks.

The question of the role of trade unions is rather crucial. As long as unions see Mondragon as a threat to their existence, they will seek to nip its very growth in the bud. And without trade union tolerance, if not support, replicating Mondragon elsewhere may have to remain a dreamy vision for a distant age.

The Issue of Foreign Competition.   In discussing replicability it should be clear that even if it would be entirely possible to transplant the Mondragon idea to other places, the problems do not end there. In other words, a democratic worker cooperative is not a cure-all for the industrial ills of our time. Specifically, when exposed to the destabilizing infection of cheap foreign imports it is as vulnerable as a conventional firm. Of course, its internal governance structure will allow it to lower its wage rates (anticipated patronage income) to meet such competition, but that meeting may have to occur at income levels that, although they would be ample to sustain life in South Korea or Indonesia, would not do so in Europe or North America. The only successful shields against such low-wage competition may be tariff walls and other measures incompatible with uninhibited and free trade on a global scale. We will discuss this problematic more in Chapter 13, but we already need to point out here that democratic cooperatives, conceived and organized humanistically, are not easily compatible with an excessively liberal economic philosophy of free trade. It is possible that we will have to choose one or the other.

Nevertheless, Mondragon-type enterprises contribute less to the problem since by definition they cannot and will not invest in other firms abroad. It follows that if we had an entire economy dominated by such cooperative firms, there would be little or no capital moving abroad to capitalize on lower labor costs. These firms, of course, would still be subject to wage-lowering competition from foreign firms (whether the foreign firms are cooperatives or not). This problem will be addressed in the next chapter.

Whatever the future developments might turn out to be, it is somewhat academic to worry about it all here and now. What Mondragon has to first of all demonstrate is that it can live and prosper in the harsh winds of the free-trade European Economic Community. Only after that should we turn to the worst-case scenario, the tornados and hurricanes prevailing in a free-for-all, open global economic system.

The American Way to Mondragon

After its first "going public," it did not take long for the Mondragon idea to cross the Atlantic and move some inspired Americans to advocate its organizational principles as early as 1977. The occasion was a printing company—Colonial Press in Clinton, Massachusetts—which had closed down only hours after then-President Carter's nationally televised "town meeting" in that community. The plan was to have workers re-open it with a Mondragon-type set-up. They obtained interim financing from a private source, bought equipment, and soon started operating, while postponing the establishment of individual capital accounts until the legal formalities were worked out. But that day never came. The enterprise lost large amounts of money every month until the private loan dried up. Soon thereafter the company closed its doors for good. The example showed that as long as workers do not have a capital stake in the firm, they are not sufficiently motivated to care about mounting losses. To a large extent, Colonial Press failed because it had postponed the individual capital contributions.

Some small firms were set up during the following years, one of which was the Solar Center in San Francisco. The first larger-scale experiment involved a meatpacking firm (Rath Packing Company) in Waterloo, Iowa, where more than 2,500 workers decided in 1979 to buy the plant to prevent it from going bankrupt. It used a modified Employee Stock Ownership Plan (ESOP) model to restart the plant only to fall victim to unfavorable hog prices and other problems five years later. Yet the organizational form developed at Rath and the Solar Center became the models for subsequent attempts to establish large democratic worker-owned firms in the United States, the latest and currently most successful being Seymour Specialty Wire Company in Seymour, Connecticut. They all rely on the basic model of an ESOP, but with an alteration that allows the one-member, one-vote principle to take hold. In order to get an idea of this method it is necessary to first understand the ESOP model.

Organization of an Employee Stock Ownership Plan (ESOP)

The father of this novel concept is Louis O. Kelso, a San Francisco lawyer, who in 1967 wrote about establishing "universal capitalism" by attempting to turn 80 million workers into share-owning capitalists on borrowed money. But it was not until the 1970s, when the powerful Senator Russell Long of the Senate Finance Committee pushed the idea in Congress and was able to secure significant tax concessions subsidizing the concept, that the ESOP movement became significant.

Since we are dealing with a type of employee pension plan, the legal context is highly complex and strictly regulated. But for our purposes we may describe the operation of the plan as follows:

A company sets up an ESOP and negotiates a large loan from a bank to the ESOP, which in turn loans the money to the company in return for the company's stock. The ESOP now holds the stock in trust for the employees. It is voted by trustees for "the sole benefit of the employees," meaning normally according to the recommendation of management.

The ESOP now has to repay the bank loan and does so out of payments from the company sufficiently high to cover both interest and principal. Here is where huge tax savings come in. For tax purposes, the company can fully deduct its payments to the ESOP as "deferred labor compensation." The ESOP turns around and now pays back the banker who must only–at another big tax savings–pay 50 percent of that interest income in income taxes. As a result, the bank is usually willing to offer financing to ESOPs at substantially reduced rates. As the loan is paid off, the ESOP shares are vested in (i.e., allocated to) the employee accounts. But the employees only acquire direct ownership of the shares when they retire or otherwise leave the firm, and not when they are working in it.

The simplified picture sketched here primarily applies to large employee "buy-outs" of investor-owned corporations, the best known examples of which are South Bend Lathe, Weirton Steel, and Bates Fabric. Two years ago it was estimated that sixty such buy-outs have saved approximately 50,000 jobs.[9]

Such large ESOPs are generally 100 percent worker-owned on paper, although the ownership rights cannot be directly exercised. Nevertheless, provisions prevent the existing employee from taking stock but require that the firm pay the departing members in cash. As a result, any absentee stock ownership is successfully prevented. Similarly, the stock contributions to employees are based on relative salary, a measure of labor contribution equivalent to "patronage." In other words, workers' individual contribution to their company's net worth are reflected in their stock ownership, functionally somewhat similar to Mondragon's individualized internal capital accounts.

On the other hand, such ESOPs fall considerably short of humanistic ideals on several counts. First, trustees vote the stock following recommendations of management, *not* employees, at least until the bank loan is paid off. And even if repayment should materialize, the voting will be according to accumulated numbers of stock, not according to the democratic one-person, one-vote formula.

Second, establishment of such ESOPs normally implies the forfeiting of the previous regular pension plans. Instead of holding stock in a diversified portfolio where stock in the employer's company cannot exceed more than 10 percent, the workers are now beneficiaries of a much more risky plan where all stock is held in one's company.

Third, in the case of an annual loss no stock can be taken away from the individual ESOP allocations. Instead, the value of stock simply gets reduced, implying that senior workers with more stock get a greater loss allocation than junior members. In other words, unlike Mondragon's humanistic allocation according to labor input (patronage), the allocation here would be according to capital.

The last two flaws are intrinsic to the substitution of stock shares for Mondragon's internal capital accounts and cannot be avoided. But the first problem relating to democratic worker control can be corrected by an important modification of the ESOP.

The Democratic Modification of an ESOP.   There are essentially two ways to democratize the type of ESOP so far discussed. Both succeed in substituting worker democracy for indirect worker-ownership.

One arrangement establishes a two-tiered voting scheme. The employee-owners simply vote on a one-person, one-vote basis on how to instruct the trustees to vote the shares. This is the basic principle used by Rath Packing Company and still underlying the Solar Center, the Atlas Chain Company, and Seymour Specialty Wire. The last few examples demonstrate that it can and does work. Recently, this scheme has been explicitly recognized and legalized in new legislation relating to ESOPs.

The other alternative creates two classes of stock, one voting and one non-voting. Each employee gets one voting stock, the remaining shares would be non-voting and serve the Mondragon-type IICA function. The legal status of this scheme is a little ambiguous at this stage since current ESOP legislation requires that ESOP shares have voting rights. Such "general voting power" language is intended to protect ESOP participants from receiving stock with inferior voting power. Yet the two-class arrangement could be seen to protect these voting rights since every participant also receives stock with the maximum voting power. Under this circumstance it is not clear whether the courts would still consider that the non-voting stock violates the interest of the regulations. Provided that this problem can be cleared up, we can expect modified ESOPs in the future to be constructed according to this two-classes-of-stock schema. It is as close as we can come to instituting a Mondragon-type humanistic enterprise within the shell of a modern American investor-owned corporation.

The Significance of Mondragon

Since it began in the 1950s, the Mondragon group of cooperatives, including enterprises, banks, consumer outlets, schools, and other institutions, has become an almost incredible success story in bringing the ideals of democracy and full human dignity into the workplace. It raises the very tangible hope that the vast social problems raised by the industrial revolution have finally found their solution in the form of the co-op as conceived by Father Don Jose Arizmendi and implemented by the undaunted people of the Basque region of Spain. Currently, we find the co-op idea growing elsewhere as well, and it is being taught and fostered in such organizations in the United States as the Industrial Cooperative Association in Somerville, Massachusetts, Co-op America in Washington D.C., and Workers Trust Incorporated in Eugene, Oregon.

The Mondragon co-op model shows us that the problem of capitalism was not the market itself, since worker self-management and decision making can only happen in a market economy. Rather, the problem was in the labor-rental contract where capital hires labor. In the democratic enterprise labor hires capital. The traditional labor-hire form creates absentee ownership, and therein is the essence of the problem. Absentee ownership is the logical antithesis of what we can call self-ownership. In absentee ownership someone somewhere else makes decisions as to what you do and what happens to you. That absentee owner can decide to shut down a plant and relocate it, thus devastating the local community. A community enterprise cannot do that, unless, of course, it decides to relocate the whole community (as consisting of the worker-owners and their families). An absentee owner does not have to live with the pollutants created by a plant somewhere else, and thus is not directly or personally concerned about pollution. However, the members of the worker-owner community do have to live with their pollution, and therefore have a direct incentive not to pollute the environment where they live and work. And this applies to all forms of externalities, such as land use, social conditions, schools, housing, and so forth. Absentee owners do not personally face the consequences of their decisions regarding these, but enterprise members who live and work in the community do. In effect, the democratically owned co-op transfers all of these externalities into a very real and present form of internality. We can see in this analysis that the externality problem is largely a consequence of the labor-hire contract and its allowance for absentee ownership.

It is interesting to note that the ideological cast of traditional Marxist theory appears to have misled the Yugoslavs in their attempt to create what they called market socialism, as we have described in Chapter 8. They considered the problem to be ownership rather than the labor-hire contract. Therefore, when they introduced worker self-management, they made it mandatory that all capital investment made by the firm was owned by the state rather than the firm itself. This, as it turned out, has been disastrous for the necessary economic incentive to invest in the capital base of the plant, and thus for productivity. (This is not to say that a portion of company surplus should not go to the larger community, be it the state or even the planet, but this is a taxation issue to be decided by democratic political decision making, and should not be a matter of ideology.)

Finally, the whole discussion above raises the interesting question of what a society or economy of all cooperative enterprises would look like. While this question is totally speculative and refers to a world that does not and may never exist—perhaps should not—it is not a useless question because it is a way of trying to gauge the social effects and meaning of the co-op form. In attempting to answer this question, we find that it generates a host of subquestions. For example, would a fully co-op society lead to fundamental changes in the market system so that it would no longer be recognizable as we know it today? In other words, would producer interests and consumer interests increasingly blend and meld together so that they would no longer be recognized as two separable economic roles? Would the same thing happen between enterprise and government as the cooperative spirit became the emergent social attitude? Would the bioregion become the relevant political unit rather than the state?

What all of these questions seem to have in common is the theme of integration, or perhaps reintegration. We live in a world today that is atomized, bereft of community, and lacking in the milk of human togetherness. This state of affairs is in an intrinsic way connected to the forces that made for the industrial revolution. The mainstream theories of economics, with their glorification of competition and self-interest, reflect this monumental and historical occurrence. The work of Father Arizmendi and countless others of like spirit and mind have created a basic economic form which has cooperation as its guiding vision. Perhaps this is the healing balm that economics itself can bring forth to make whole again the rifts of an all too divided human community.

References

1. Quoted in Terry Mollner, et al., *Mondragon: Beyond Capitalism and Socialism*. Philadelphia: New Society Publishers, forthcoming, chapter 5.
2. *ibid.*
3. Quoted in Robert Oakshott, *The Case for Worker Co-ops*. London: Routledge & Kegan, 1978, p. 175.
4. Alastair Campbell, *Mondragon 1980*. Leeds: Industrial Common Ownership Movement Ltd., 1980.
5. The U.S. performance pertains to all FDIC insured commercial banks, as reported by *Business Week* (April 6, 1987, p. 76). The CLP data are taken from its recent *Annual Reports*.
6. Keith Bradley and Alan Gelb, *"Mixed Economy" Versus "Cooperative" Adjustment: Mondragon's Experience Through Spain's Recession*. Report No. DRD122. Washington, D.C.: World Bank, 1984.
7. Henk Thomas and Chris Logan, *Mondragon: An Economic Analysis*. Boston: George Allen & Unwin, 1982, chapter 5.
8. David Ellerman, "The Union as Legitimate Opposition in an Industrial Democracy," unpublished staff paper, Industrial Cooperative Association, Somerville, Massachusetts, 1979.
9. See the cover story in *Business Week* (April 15, 1985).

Chapter 13

TOWARDS A NEW WORLD ECONOMY

The road to a human economy is neither straight nor always clear. Long stretches of it elude us and some of them still need construction, a task that will occupy many future would-be travelers. But the measures discussed so far, a government insulated from corruption, a full employment economy with democratic industrial enterprises, provide a giant move in the right direction. Yet it is also true that what is wise and noble is not always viable, even if there is no lack of political will.

Many of these reforms would appear to have a very real price tag, an opportunity cost as economists are so painfully aware. Will our full employment state be practically sustainable or will it drag down productivity and so dull our competitive edge that we may not want it after all? More specifically, assuming that we have diverted resources to humanistic ends but other countries have not, can we afford to pay a minimum wage of $4 or $5 per hour if other countries pay their manufacturing labor force less than $1 per hour? Can we afford to raise the standard of living of the poor and provide greater respect for individual human dignity if other countries are, for whatever reasons, not about to pursue such a goal? Similarly with worker cooperatives. Assuming the ideal of an economy of cooperatives can be realized, can it also be sustained? Can it also compete against enterprises located abroad that operate with labor costs amounting to a mere fraction of the cooperative incomes?

All of these troubling questions relate to the international context we find ouselves in. Increasingly, a humanistic economy cannot be discussed outside of such a context. It is for this basic reason that we will now turn to some of the more basic issues intrinsic to the global economy. Among these we will focus on four: the time-honored doctrine of free trade, the problem of Third World poverty, the debt crisis, and a new model for humanistic development.

Free Trade Doctrine in Humanistic Perspective

We have seen how economics from its very beginning can be viewed as the science of self-interest and as an intellectual defense of laissez-faire capitalism. Whatever the truth of these self-interest assertions, they seem to gain credence when we turn to the topic of international economy. Here, more than anywhere else, modern economic theorists and policy makers, whether in business, government, or academia, speak almost with one voice: the basic teaching of the science, all agree, is that a regime of free international competition and free international trade benefits all countries, rich and poor alike. Except for some special cases involving so-called infant industries or considerations of defense, *the less* national governments try to regulate trade flows through legislation or tariffs, *the better.* Even those economists who have long questioned the alleged unalloyed goodness of unrestricted laissez-faire within a national economy are unwilling to question the doctrine of laissez-faire when it comes to trade between countries. In fact, it very much appears that, at least in our modern age, a strong faith in such global scale laissez-faire constitutes the ultimate acid test of who belongs to the distinguished brotherhood of Western economists. It is for this very reason that one has to look long and hard in order to find any textbook or scholarly work that approaches the free trade doctrine with a critical attitude. Hopefully, our observations here will mark the beginning of an era where students learn that the issue is by no means as clear-cut as generally assumed.

The Argument for Free Trade

We will start with a brief textbook type of explanation of why free international trade is in the common interest of all nations. In the process we begin with an abstract example similar to the one used by David Ricardo more than 150 years ago.

Imagine two countries, Portugal and England, each producing two commodities, growing wine and manufacturing cloth. Furthermore, they are both produced by labor only. Now suppose that one week of labor produces more wine in Portugal than in England, while England is better at producing cloth. Naturally, it would follow that to the extent that Portugal specializes in wine and England in cloth, trading the surpluses would allow for more production and consumption of both goods in both countries. This is an example of one country having an *absolute* advantage in one good, the other in another. Obviously, common sense would dictate specialization and trade.

But now suppose, and here Ricardo had a brilliant analytical insight, that Portugal has an absolute advantage in *both* goods. It can produce both wine and cloth with less labor time, i.e., at a lower cost. More specifically, assume that it can produce cloth 20 percent cheaper and wine 600 percent cheaper. Ricardo now proceeded to prove that both countries will *still* gain if Portugal specializes in wine making and England specializes in the spinning and weaving of cloth. The reason is that Portugal has a *comparative* advantage in wine production while England has a *comparative* advantage in cloth.

To see this, let us take another example. Imagine you are a junior executive in a bank doing high caliber work. The bank also employs a secretary who is a sloppy typist and understands little about banking. You happen to be, in fact, better and faster on the word processor than he is. In other words, you have an absolute advantage in both jobs. Even so, it would be foolish if you decided to do your own typing at the expense of being involved full time in the more essential banking business. Because the secretary is even poorer in running a bank than in running a word processor, he has a comparative advantage in typing, while you have a comparative advantage in attending to the more intricate banking affairs.

Since every country, regardless of absolute advantage, has a comparative advantage in the production of some commodities, it follows that it will gain to specialize in producing those commodities which it can do best, to export them, and then to import what they themselves cannot do as well. Thus free trade and international specialization are seen to be always in everybody's interest.

In Ricardo's example–specifying greater productive efficiency of Portugal's labor and inferior efficiency of the English workers–we can assume that since labor is the only input, wages will be considerably higher in Portugal, both in the wineries and around the weaving looms. Would not Portuguese workers be apprehensive of the prospect of having to compete with the cheap foreign labor of England? They probably would. Similarly, the English might be reluctant to face competition with the much more productive Portuguese. Yet the principle of comparative advantage assures us that such feelings are unfounded. When trade is opened between the two countries, workers in both countries will be able to profit through the higher real wages that accompany higher productivity brought about by this international division of labor.

So much for the essence of the story told in all the modern textbooks. It opens the student's mind to an analytical economic perspective and softens any earlier apprehensions about the alleged benefits of a country, such as the United States, heavily importing cheaper merchandise from abroad.

Nevertheless, regardless of these soothing theoretical assurances, somehow more and more politicians all over the world do not seem to get the message. Although a recent OECD study confirms that tariff protection for industrial goods has been (with the exception of Australia) falling strongly between 1965 and 1980 and is expected to fall further,[1] the same study also notes that non-tariff trade barriers, such as quotas, voluntary export restraints, and the like, have been strongly on the increase since the late 1970s. For example, the proportion of manufactured exports to Europe and North America from Japan, Korea, Taiwan, Hong Kong, and Singapore that were subject to such restrictions grew from 15 percent in 1980 to 32 percent in 1983.[2]

Similarly, protectionist sentiments have been getting stronger in Congress in spite of the irritation and frustration of economists. One has to wonder why real world decision makers are not taking advantage of the Theory of Comparative Advantage. Could it be that they know something that has been eluding the economists?

Towards a Critique of the Free Trade Doctrine

To begin with, the Ricardian argument presented earlier, asserting the greater efficiency of free trade, rests on two particular assumptions that need to be spelled out. As usual, efficiency is presented in terms of maximum consumption of goods (and services), and the intrinsic satisfaction people get from performing certain types of work ("producers utility") is ignored. In this context it is worthwhile to quote one less orthodox economist, M.I.T.'s Lester Thurow:

> Although it is true . . . that one can show that free trade maximizes consumption, free trade does not necessarily maximize producer's utility. If the French love to be a farmer or see farmers, it may be rational to protect French farmers with tariffs and quotas. What is lost in terms of extra consumption utility is more than gained in extra producers utility.[3]

Of course, all we need to do to apply this pertinent observation to Ricardo's example is to replace England by Thurow's France. But more than that, Thurow's illustration is clearly highly relevant for defending protective measures designed to enable the survival of the family farm, which, of course, is another excellent example of a humanistic enterprise. In spite of this, economists everywhere are increasingly crying for dismantling agricultural tariffs in the name of global economic efficiency. It is not clear whether they do so in naive ignorance of the basic point observed above, or whether they, alienated from country life, are deliberately trying to push urban middle class interests.

As for another implicit assumption, we also have to remind the reader of the basic fact that efficiency is measured by consumer demand rather than by human needs. So it was perfectly efficient for pre-revolutionary Cuban college students in the 1950s to "specialize" in dermatology and law in order to attend to the wants of sunburned tourists and property-buying foreign investors. They did, but only by ignoring "wasteful" or "inefficient" specialization in preventive medicine that would have benefited the penniless, landless laborers.

But let us not quarrel about these qualifications concerning psychic externalities and the nature of true efficiency, regardless of how important and relevant they may be. Instead, we will now, for the sake of argument, proceed into the ballpark of conventional international economics. As we shall shortly see, there may very well be something else that is fundamentally wrong with the free trade doctrine in general, and the theory of comparative advantage in particular.

Economic Doubts About Free Trade.   The theory of comparative advantage sketched above has mesmerized economists for almost 200 years. Until recently, it also held sway among most politicians, whether they consider themselves left, center, or even right of the political spectrum. Whatever opposition there has been traditionally tended to come from beleaguered trade union economists and their corporate counterparts, who are crying for "protectionism" to save their own skins by keeping their foreign competition at bay.

Yet there is at least one academic economist, John M. Culbertson of the University of Wisconsin, who has recently been given quite a lot of media attention precisely because he dares to oppose the free trade doctrine. Such opposition to free trade is based on a growing and strong conviction that the low-wage imports of the newly industrializing countries (NICs), including Korea, Taiwan, Hong Kong, and Singapore, will indeed dangerously undermine our standard of living.

Professor Culbertson is, of course, fully aware of the time-honored doctrine of comparative advantage, but he denies its relevance, especially in the contemporary socioeconomic situation. The classic example of England trading cloth for Portuguese wine is declared as being both hypothetical and highly misleading. It postulates two countries, two governments striking a bilateral agreement that is essentially a non-monetary, or barter, deal. As such, it automatically makes two assumptions: that both nations benefit, otherwise they would not freely consent, and that some goods are exchanged for an equivalent amount of other goods. The latter implies that the trade automatically *balances out* between the two nations.

In contrast, real world economy trade agreements are not negiotiated by nations, but by individual companies. Neither "England" nor "Portugal" has any role in determining the transactions that freely cross their borders, and as a result we cannot assume that either country necessarily benefits. A particular transaction may benefit the particular company greatly, but hurt most everybody else in the economy.

Similarly, individual unregulated trade also does not at all guarantee balanced trade. It may be somewhat plausible in the textbook examples, where climatic factors alone tend to favor agricultural specialization of one or another commodity, to assume that every country will be able to specialize in some exports in order to pay for its imports. But this is much less the case when we are dealing with manufacturing in today's world of multinational corporations, low transport costs, and efficient communications networks. Culbertson stipulates that no country can claim anymore to have a special advantage in production technology and management techniques. As a result, the country with the lowest labor costs can manufacture *everything* cheaper and will certainly want to do so as long as it has a surplus population and labor force.

In such a world a country like the United States will see its corporations setting up new efficient plants abroad, not just in one or two industries where it lacks a "comparative advantage," but everywhere where it has *absolute* cost disadvantage. The result will be a massive trade deficit with those parts of the world where labor costs are much lower. For example, a recent OECD study shows that direct and indirect labor costs to produce a pair of men's jeans or women's coats are one-fifth of U.S. costs.[4] Similar relationships hold in other exported goods involving more sophisticated machinery and other capital equipment.

The only way in which such a trade deficit can be balanced would entail exporting some goods that we can produce cheaper than is now possible in Taiwan, Korea, Hong Kong, and Singapore. Ultimately, this would have to imply that we are "competitive" in terms of the labor costs involved, meaning our wages would have to decline to their levels. All this assumes, of course, that there are no offsetting labor productivity differentials in favor of the United States.

According to Culbertson, then, the bottom line of the comparative advantage doctrine in action always boils down to wage competition: trade will be imbalanced until labor costs are "balanced" or equalized, in other words, until American workers are paid no more in real terms than they are in today's NICs. Even worse, if China and India get into the act, their almost unlimited labor supply, fed by rapid population growth, will tend to pull our wage levels down to near nineteenth century levels.

Now, even economists would grant that, according to their so-called "factor price equalization theorem," uninhibited free trade will tend to equalize wage rates across countries. But, in contrast to Professor Culbertson, they expect real wage levels in the NICs to rise to our levels, and they point to the postwar experience of first Europe and then Japan catching up with the United States as hard evidence. Culbertson, on the other hand, expects our real wages to be significantly reduced during this equalization, a process that he expects to last much longer since the ample labor supply of the NICs is not similarly constrained by a slow population growth.

By this disconcerting analysis, then, the United States will be deindustrializing by exporting jobs in exchange for all kinds of products "made in Asia." In the process our industrial landscape will be increasingly marked by plant closings and job losses in industries as diverse as boots and shoes, steel, automobiles, and semiconductors.

True, some of the unemployed will find work in the service industries, sheltered from foreign competition, as well as such import-related jobs as dock workers or clerks in branches of foreign banks. We have already seen in Chapter 11 just how the American job machine has been doing its job during the last decade and how our real wage levels have stagnated at 1973 levels. It is, of course, also true that Americans as consumers can, at least in theory, profit from buying cheaply imported VCRs and Korean automobiles, provided they can still afford it after losing their blue collar manufacturing jobs.

In the process of this deindustrialization the domestic demand of Americans will slump, recessions will discourage investment in research and new technology, and if we will no longer be able to afford expensive formal education, on-the-job training in the cutting edge industries will take place in Asia. All these will work to our further disadvantage, while the economic boom in the East will tend to fuel their population growth and so further expand the pool of low-wage workers.

But, the economist will reply, what about the adjustment process of shifts in the exchange rates? With a trade deficit, will not the value of the dollar simply fall until balance is restored? Culbertson counters that a falling dollar is precisely one way in which our standard of living is cut.

> Economic textbooks commonly depict changes in exchange rates as an "adjustment mechanism," in a way that implies a painless adjustment, through which international trade brings benefits to each nation. A nation with a trade deficit, for example, accepts an adjustment in its exchange rate, and all is well. But the reduction in the international value of the dollar, for example, is not a means by which the United States "adjusts" to a deficit in its foreign trade *without pain or cost.* Quite the contrary. It is a means by which the painful and costly "adjustment" of a reduction in its wage rate and standard of living–to bring them in line with the nations with which it is being economically integrated by international trade–are brought about![5]

Currently, a dollar is roughly 670 Korean wons. Possibly, once the dollar is much closer to parity with that country's currency, the problem will cease. But a dollar would then only buy a handful of rice, and a short spring vacation to the Bahamas or elsewhere would have to be earned with a year or two of hard work at the going wage levels.

However, here is another problem that textbooks usually ignore. What if the NICs do not allow the dollar to adjust, by simply pegging the value of their currency to ours. Exchange rates since 1980 suggest that this is pretty much what has happened. While the Japanese yen did indeed appreciate since then by almost 50 percent, the currencies of Hong Kong and South Korea have shown a strong tendency to lose, not gain, against the U.S. dollar during the last ten years–and this in spite of the mounting trade surplus with the United States. It looks as if the necessary "adjustments" will have to happen by means other than exchange rates. (One way is for the NICs to progressively buy our assets, our real estate, and our factories, herewith further weakening our position to face the future.)

What is the solution for this ongoing erosion? John Culbertson, for one, is not against international trade, only against unregulated *free* trade. Instead, he advocates a more *balanced* trade, where our government assures through bilateral trade agreements that our imports from the NICs are so controlled that they no longer outrace our exports to them. Such regulated trade appears superior to across-the-board tariffs that make no distinction between lower prices, resulting from genuine economic efficiency (involving real savings in resources by turning out the same goods with less labor or material), and lower prices based on poverty wages.

Of course, it is precisely the erection of such selective non-tariff barriers for which concerned politicians have increasingly been fighting. Under the influence of traditional economics, such non-tarriff barriers are still opposed by a large majority of economic experts both here and abroad. What is at stake are the jobs of millions of Americans, Canadians, and Europeans. The cost of saving these jobs may be high, but we believe it is still lower than losing them, especially when the would-be victims are primarily rural or unskilled workers with nowhere to go. It also needs to be pointed out that the various estimates of costs per job saved are so dependent on the particular investigator's underlying assumptions that they differ widely. Some studies calculate that limiting Japan's export of cars increased U.S. prices by 3 percent, others 25 percent.[6] Just because we often *could* compensate along the lines of Kaldor for their lost work does by no means guarantee that sacrificing jobs at the altar of free trade would also serve humanity and social justice.

The Need of Re-Linking Market and Government: The Correspondence Principle

Only time will be able to tell how accurate Culbertson's critique of the free trade doctrine really is. There is, however, a more general reason why free international trade violates a basic canon of humanistic economics. It relates to the vital necessity of linking market and government. Earlier in Chapter 10, we postulated in the context of a closed national economy that any meaningful political self-determination is predicated on the ability to restrict the economic market forces so that their domain does not overreach the political jurisdiction. In other words, there has to be correspondence between the two domains. The same principle applies to an international economy as well.

International free trade readily expands the economic domain to a global level, yet the sociopolitical control of a country's economy cannot reach beyond its own borders. Having lost its political sovereignty over the economy, a nation can no longer effectively control it. If, for example, it should decide to significantly raise business taxes, we can expect an immediate outflow of capital and a loss of jobs. Similarly, if the national objective is to stimulate the economy through an expansive monetary policy, interest rates will fall, herewith draining capital. In other words, each country becomes hostage to the coldhearted pull in international capital. The former president of Mexico, Lopez Portillo, spoke from experience when he lamented in 1982:

> We have been a living example of what occurs when that enormous, volatile, and speculative mass of capital goes all over the world in search of high interest rates, tax havens and supposed political and exchange stability. It decapitalizes entire nations and leaves destruction in its wake.[7]

Or take another example: when a country wants to stimulate its level of employment by means of an expansionary fiscal policy. A globally integrated national economy cannot prevent most of the additional purchasing power from leaving the country through a substantial boost of imports. Once again, a fully open economy will be frustrated in its attempt to control unemployment.

In other words, Keynesian fiscal and monetary policy will no longer deliver. John Maynard Keynes himself was fully aware of this when he wrote back in 1933:

> Ideas, knowledge, science, hospitality, travel–these are things which should of their nature be international. But let goods be homespun wherever it is reasonably and conveniently possible, and, above all, let finance be primarily national. We do not wish, therefore, to be at the mercy of world forces working out, or trying to work out, some uniform equilibrium according to the ideal principles, if they can be called such, of laissez-faire capitalism. We wish . . . to be our own masters and to be as free as we can make ourselves from the interference of the outside world.[8]

To Keynes, the gains of a successful full employment policy more than compensated for whatever diseconomies that might result from a failure to fully pursue international specialization.

We may add another more speculative observation at this point. If it is true that countercyclical government policy would have to be sacrificed on the altar of unregulated free trade, then it seems to follow that we are back in the pre-Keynesian world described by Count Sismondi, John Hobson, and perhaps more decisively by Karl Marx. It is a gloomy world pregnant with instability, crisis, and other surprises, the most frightening of which could be a rebirth of the Marxian laws of motion with the predicted consequences.

There is, of course, another solution to the correspondence problem, at least in theory. If national social control cannot be attained through self-sufficiency, a re-linking of market and government could also occur by globalizing government. Only a world government will be able to once again control and guide global economic activity. But it has to be a government that represents all people according to established democratic principles rather than ability to pay. As such, it would be in stark contrast to the new post-war international political structures, such as the World Bank and the International Monetary Fund, which have to be seen as operating on the old economic principle of one-dollar, one-vote. An international economic order government on such un-democratic principles can only be expected to function by means of coercive power, exploitation, and brute force, as we shall have to witness below.

Meanwhile, lacking any realistic prospects for a meaningful new world government, a move to greater self-reliance seems most preferable. Like Keynes, we "sympathize with those who would minimize, rather than those who would maximize, economic entanglement among nations."[9]

Third World Poverty

A decade ago, Robert McNamara, the former president of the World Bank, prefaced the first *World Development Report* with the following paragraph:

> The past quarter century has been a period of unprecedented change and progress in the developing world. And yet despite this impressive record, some 800 million individuals continue to be trapped in what I have termed absolute poverty: a condition of life so characterized by malnutrition, illiteracy, disease, squalid surroundings, high infant mortality, and low life expectancy as to be beneath any reasonable definition of human decency.[10]

A significant portion of the report discussed this poverty problem and projected better times ahead. Assuming a GNP growth rate of 4 to 5 percent for the poorest thirty-eight countries, and assuming no pronounced changes in their income distribution, the report projected that the proportion of absolute poor in these countries will decline from 52 percent of the population to 27 percent by the end of this century. Even so, that would still imply 600 million absolute poor by that time. These figures seem discouragingly high, but at least indicate steps in the right direction. Unfortunately, they increasingly turn out to have been much too optimistic. Five years later, in the 1982 report, the figure of the absolute poor was estimated to be "close to one billion," and by all indications it is likely to be still higher today.

What is going wrong? Why are the poor getting suddenly poorer? The search for the reason(s) leads us down a complex trail of a number of factors, but the contribution and interrelationship of each of the elements is becoming clearer. The end of the trail seems to run suspicious-ly close to the doorstep of the International Monetary Fund (IMF).

We will begin with economic stagnation. The poorest countries have not been economically growing at the predicted annual rate of 4 to 5 percent, but at 2 to 3 percent instead. Since population growth has been 2.5 to 3 percent annually, most of the poor countries have made only insignificant gains in GNP/capita and some even lost ground, par-ticularly during the last six years. For example, the approximately 100 million inhabitants of Zaire, Madagascar, Ghana, Mozambique, Zam-bia, Somalia, Senegal, Uganda, and Chad have seen their standard of living deteriorate over the last two decades, while others, such as Bangladesh, Ethiopia, Nepal, Togo, and the Central African Republic, have shown little or no economic growth. Contrast this with the twen-ty-one richest industrialized countries which have managed to have their GNP/capita boosted at an annual rate of 2 to 3 percent during the last two decades, a standard of performance only approached by China, Burma, Pakistan, and Sri Lanka.[11]

It is hard to deny the basic fact that the war on global poverty has so far been a losing battle. Yet the problem of persistent and destitute Third World poverty remains the most important economic problem we face today as social scientists, social philosophers, and humanitarians. It has been described and illustrated in many places. Let us take note of some of the dire statistics as presented by Oxfam:[12]

- Fifteen to twenty million people die each year of hunger-related causes, including diseases brought on by lower resistance due to malnutrition. Over 40 percent of all deaths in poor countries occur among children under five years old.

- At least 100,000 children in Asia and Africa go blind each year from vitamin A deficiency caused by inadequate diet. More than 500 million people in poor countries suffer from chronic anemia due to inadequate diet.

- In the wealthy countries 20 to 25 percent of the average fami-ly "income" is spent on food. In most poor countries the average rural family must spend as much as 75 to 85 percent of its in-come on food.

- In 1974 less than 10 percent of the grain which rich countries fed to their cattle would have entirely eliminated the grain shortages of the poor countries for that year.

- In the forty lowest income countries, fewer than 30 percent of the people have access to safe drinking water.

- In eighty-three countries of the world, 3 percent of the land-owners control almost 80 percent of the land. In Argentina, for example, 2 percent of the landowners own 75 percent of the land.

- Less than 60 percent of the world's cultivatable land is current-ly under cultivation. Less than 20 percent of the potentially cultivatable land in Africa and Asia is under cultivation. Most of that land is controlled by large landowners or is open country.

The facts, meant to picture the situation prevailing in the early 1980s, speak for much of the 1960s and the 1970s, and probably for the 1990s as well.

Third World Debt

The disappointing story of lack of change in the world poverty situation is reflected in other drastic changes that directly relate to the plight of the poor. During the last fifteen years there has been a monumental development: the explosion of Third World indebtedness. The overall debt owed by developing countries has risen almost tenfold and now approaches $1 trillion. Although the bulk of it is owed by Latin American countries, it has also emerged as a crushing burden for the poorest economies, especially in Africa.

A summary of the situation prevailing in 1985 for three continents is presented in Table 13.1 below. The figures speak for themselves, especially for countries such as Bolivia, Jamaica, Costa Rica, Senegal, Zambia, Liberia, and the Ivory Coast, where the debt/capita exceeds the annual per capita income. Not only have countries like Zambia and Senegal not grown since 1965, but they have also now been burdened with an enormous debt draining their resources for decades to come. Similar horror stories could be told for Bolivia, Liberia, and Jamaica. And the situation is not that much better for the others. In other words, while twenty years ago most African and South American countries were poor, they are now poor *and* almost hopelessly in debt.

Table 13.1

THE EXTERNAL DEBT BURDEN FOR
TWENTY-EIGHT SELECTED COUNTRIES, 1985

	External Debt	GNP/c	Debt/c	Debt/c GNP/c
Latin America				
*Bolivia+	4.0	470	625	1.32
*Jamaica	3.8	940	1727	1.83
Peru +	13.7	1010	736	0.72
Ecuador ++	9.2	1160	978	0.84
*Costa Rica ++	4.1	1300	1576	1.21
Chile ++	14.0	1430	1157	0.80
Brazil ++	106.8	1640	787	0.47
Mexico ++	97.4	2080	1236	0.59
Argentina ++	48.5	2130	1590	0.74
Venezuela ++	32.0	3080	1849	0.60
Asia				
Burma	3.1	190	84	0.44
India	35.4	270	46	0.17
Indonesia +	35.7	530	220	0.41
Philippines+	26.2	580	478	0.82
Malaysia ++	18.0	2000	1153	0.57
Korea +	50.0	2150	1216	0.56
Africa				
*Mali	1.5	150	200	1.33
Malawi	1.0	170	125	0.73
Zaire	5.0	170	163	0.95
Kenya	4.2	290	205	0.71
Tanzania	3.6	290	162	0.55
*Senegal	12.5	370	378	1.02
Ghana	2.0	380	157	0.41
*Zambia	4.5	390	671	1.72
*Liberia	1.2	470	545	1.15
*Ivory Coast +	8.5	660	841	1.27
Nigeria +	18.3	800	183	0.22
Cameroon	2.9	810	284	0.35

* highly indebted countries where debt exceeds annual GNP
+ indicates that over 50% of debt is in variable interest rates
++ indicates that 20-50% of debt is in variable interest rates

Source: World Bank, *World Bank Development Report, 1987*. New
    York: Oxford University Press, 1987.

There is much debate these days over whether the debt is at all payable. The issue does indeed look grave if we remember that the debt is a hard currency debt; in other words, it can only be repaid through exports to the industrialized capitalist countries and their financial institutions. In 1984 the *Wall Street Journal* reported that for the Ivory Coast and a dozen Latin countries, the serving of the total long-run and short-run external debt exceeded total export earnings.[13] In the case of Argentina the servicing would have necessitated twice the revenues gained in exports. Obviously, for these countries the only way to repay their debt has been to borrow more and more. In Africa, too, many countries, such as Sudan, Zimbabwe, Zaire, Ghana, and Nigeria, had debt servicing/export ratios between 50 percent and 100 percent. For the more recent year of 1986 the Overseas Development Council estimates that the cost of servicing the African debt was $12 billion, roughly one-half of their combined export earnings in that year. Unless exports can somehow be significantly boosted in those countries, the prospect there, too, is for mounting crisis.

The Causes of the Debt Crisis.   In order to explain the extraordinarily heavy amount of international borrowing, there had to be a generous source of investible funds and eager lenders. Both became available during the 1970s, the decade of growing eurocurrency markets. Eurocurrencies are funds deposited in London, Paris, and Zurich, coming from all over the world, but specifically from Saudi Arabia and other newly rich OPEC oil exporters. International superbanks, such as the English Midland Bank, Chase Manhattan, and the like, then sought investment opportunities among promising Third World nations who would guarantee the loans. The interest rate was typically a couple of percentage points higher than the American prime or the London LIBOR rate, or else, with shorter term loans, the interest rate was to be renegotiated when loans became due and "rolled over."

The stage for the monsterous debt crisis was set when various events coincided in the early 1980s. Conservative monetary policies in England, the United States, and elsewhere began to drive interest rates to record levels. It was estimated that the rise from 10 percent to 16 percent during those years added a hefty $41 billion to the debt burden of developed countries. Brazil, Mexico, and the others had to borrow more to meet that obligation.

At about the same time, the United States and its European trading partners went into a steep recession, drying up export opportunities for the Third World. Prices of such commodities as oil, coffee, sugar, and copper tumbled to record low levels. Once again, a large number of

Third World countries were forced to ask for new loans to bolster their shrinking export dollars.

To make things even worse, most of the world debt was denominated in U.S. dollars, a currency which then rose to record heights during the first half of the 1980s. So, for example, if Brazil exported coffee to western Europe, its export earnings lost purchasing power in terms of servicing its dollar debt.

Together, these events impacted so strongly on the borrowing countries that the only way to keep them afloat was for international bankers to reluctantly lend them more. The problem was further aggravated by persistent capital flight from the Third World to safer bank accounts abroad. The Morgan Guaranty Trust Company of New York estimates that between 1976 and 1985 about $200 billion escaped from their home countries, more than a half of that from Mexico, Argentina, and Venezuela alone. It concluded that without this capital flight, Argentina, Venezuela, and Mexico would have been virtually debt-free in 1985![14] Meanwhile, capital flight continues, but some of the other pressures have eased. Interest rates declined in 1983 and 1984, the industrialized economies started to recover (allowing Third World exports to pick up), and the U.S. dollar started to fall towards record low levels. For these reasons, the debt problem appears somewhat less threatening than it did three or four years ago. But now that interest rates have started to move up again, dangerous instability is likely to reignite, as recent problems with Brazil have demonstrated. In 1987 Brazil stopped making payments on two-thirds of its $108 billion debt.

The nature of the debt among the poorest and African nations has been somewhat different from that of South America. Most of the African external finance has come from Western countries or through international agencies (such as the World Bank) and is granted at very low and fixed interest rates. There are some notable exceptions to this general situation. Countries like Malawi, Zambia, and particularly the Ivory Coast (a leading coffee exporter) and Nigeria, supplemented the concessional loans they received with heavy borrowing from private sources, and to that extent they too were highly vulnerable to increases in international interest rates. The Ivory Coast, for example, has almost half of its external debt in variable interest rates. Not surprisingly, it also has announced that it would not pay the $1.2 billion due in 1987 on its $8 billion debt. Similarly, we can expect Nigeria to get into deep trouble soon if interest rates rise and oil prices fall.

More generally, the average low-income Third World country, whether in Africa or South America, suffered primarily from balance of payment deficits due to the recession in the Western industrialized countries and unfavorable weather patterns (droughts), reducing the opportunity and ability to export and often necessitating more imports. That such international commodities as petroleum, copper, tin, and bauxite fluctuate heavily in their prices is widely known. It explains to a large extent the trouble an oil exporter like Nigeria has been having recently. Similarly, the plunge in mineral prices has hurt Zaire and Zambia. But what is less known is that even agricultural crops tend to suffer from large price fluctuations and have, perhaps more importantly, tended to exhibit a strongly negative trend since 1970. Table 13.2 below illustrates this basic problem.

Among the selection of countries, Tanzania and Mali have been most hurt by such counterproductive changes in the terms of trade. The data indicate that those two countries almost had to double their exports in order to be able to buy the same amount of imports. This development just by itself sets the stage for a mounting balance of payment crisis. This now brings us to another principal actor in the debt crisis, the IMF or International Monetary Fund.

The International Monetary Fund as a Source of Finance

Created in 1947 as an offspring of the Bretton Woods Conference, the final structure of the IMF was essentially conceived by the U.S. Assistant Secretary of the Treasury Harry White. It reflected primarily U.S. interests and to a lesser extent British and Canadian ideas. The United States still dominates the IMF through a system of weighted voting, where votes are assigned according to the relative economic size of member countries. The board has six permanent members from the United States, Britain, West Germany, France, Japan, and Saudi Arabia. Since any change in rules requires almost a three-fourths majority of total member votes, the United States' commanding 19 percent of votes results in a virtual veto power. Most Third World countries are members, but few of them are ever even invited to participate in high level policy discussions.

The IMF is designed to "facilitate the expansion and balanced growth of world trade" and do so via the prime avenue of free trade. Its purpose is to assist countries in short-run financing of their balance of payment deficits, and in the process to impose stiff policy conditions on the would-be borrowers designed to compel them to bring their financial house in order. The medicine it prescribes usually consists of the following conditions:

1. devaluation of the currency;

Table 13.2

TERMS OF TRADE FOR AFRICAN EXPORTS
OF FOOD AND OTHER CROPS[*]
(index form 1970=100)

	1970	1975	1980	1985
Mali (cotton, peanuts)	100	83	76	62
Malawi (tobacco, peanuts, cotton, corn)	100	94	72	73
Tanzania (coffee, tobacco, cashews, sisal, cotton)	100	63	63	57
Ghana (cocoa)	100	86	95	86
Kenya (coffee, tea, pyretium, cotton, corn)	100	123	116	109
Senegal (peanuts, cotton)	100	120	76	75
Cameroon (cocoa, coffee, cotton)	100	74	91	84
Ivory Coast (cocoa, coffee, cotton, palm oil)	100	79	81	76

*Excludes oil and mineral exporters. Terms of trade ratios measure a country's index of weighted export prices to that of import prices. The figures here pertain to the so-called "net barter terms of trade." The data here are in essence based on a selection of countries featured in Table 31 of World Bank, *Accelerated Development in Sub-Saharan Africa,* Washington, D.C., 1981, p. 174. Omitted from that list are Togo's Zambia and Upper Volta, which are mineral producers primarily, as well as oil-producing Nigeria. Statistics were updated by data from the World Bank *World Development Reports* of 1982 and 1987.

2. spending cuts in public expenditures;

3. elimination of state subsidies for basic food staples bought by urban residents (typical examples are bread, rice, and cooking oil subsidies);

4. decrease in real wages through wage controls; and

5. elimination of government controls on foreign exchange.

The immediate result of such an "austerity program" is almost always a combination of (1) heavy inflation not compensated for in wage increases, (2) layoffs of public servants and workers in state enterprises augmenting unemployment, and (3) a shocking loss of purchasing power of the urban masses who tend to be pushed below the subsistence minimum diet they have learned to get by on. But belt-tightening has its limits too, especially when only 20 percent of the population can afford to wear belts. When the cash-starved governments have no other choice than to approve the IMF conditions in order to borrow, the resulting loss in purchasing power–threatening the very means of existence of the impoverished urban masses–triggers strong and violent opposition. General strikes are often accompanied by so-called "IMF riots." Since 1977 they have been happening around the globe–in Egypt, Peru, Bolivia, Sudan, Zambia, and in Tunis, Tunisia. Probably one of the bloodiest occurred in 1984 in San Domingo, the capital of the Dominican Republic, where sixty lost their lives in the violence. It led the *Wall Street Journal* to observe that for that impoverished country the debt is not denominated in dollars alone, but also in blood.[15]

Very often the threatened governments manage to soften the blow by rolling back some of the price increases on basic food items; sometimes they end up abrogating the IMF accord altogether, as in the case of Zambia during the winter of 1986/87.

More rarely, strong leaders have the ability and strength to confront the IMF and successfully bargain for less unfavorable conditions. That happened when the former Tanzanian president Julius Nyerere turned to the IMF for help in 1979. His country had just experienced a strong deterioration in terms of trade and spent an estimated $575 million, much of it in hard currency, to defeat the invading army of Idi Amin from neighboring Uganda. (It should be added that the cost of the war exceeded the value of one year of exports. Moreover, the war against Idi Amin was very much encouraged by the Western countries who also loaned more money for the purpose.)

The IMF was ready to help out, provided Tanzania devalue its currency, freeze wages, alter its import credit and retail pricing policies, and curtail health and educational expenditures in favor of large invest-ments in export crops. Nyerere in turn declined, accusing the IMF "of trying to intervene in Tanzania's international affairs and of acting on behalf of industrial countries that were hoping to confine Tanzania to its colonial rule as an exporter of primary products."[16] He further ex-plained:

> We expected [the IMF's] conditions to be nonideological, and related to ensuring that money lent to us is not wasted, pocketed by political leaders or bureaucrats, used to build private villas at home or abroad, or deposited in private Swiss bank accounts. . . .
>
> Tanzania is not prepared to devalue its currency just because this is a traditional free market solution to everything. . . . It is not prepared to surrender its right to restrict imports by measures designed to en-sure that we import quinine rather than cosmetics, or buses rather than cars for the elite.
>
> My government is not prepared to give up our national endeavor to provide primary education for every child, basic medicines and some clean water for all our people. Cuts may have to be made in our na-tional expenditure, but we will decide whether they fall on public ser-vices or private expenditures. Nor are we prepared to deal with inflation and shortages by relying on monetary policy regardless of its relative effect on the poorest and the less poor.[17]

Negotiations were broken off and resumed ten months later when a compromise set of conditions was worked out and later implemented.

Whatever the approach of the impoverished country, whether it is a casting out of the entire IMF-dictated reform policies or the adoption of a tough stance supported by rhetoric, the basic problem remains that there is really nowhere else to turn. The only other way out is to declare a moratorium on the servicing of part of the entire debt. The latter solu-tion has been tried by Peru and Bolivia and more recently by Zambia and Brazil. Such a policy, threatening the entire international banking community, is no doubt quite popular politics, particularly where hos-tility towards the IMF is deeply ingrained in popular consciousness, as it had been in Brazil. Already in the mid-1960s the refusal of President Goular to bend to the IMF brought about an authoritarian military coup. In the Portuguese language IMF is spelled FMI, which to Brazilians stands for "Fome, Miseria, Inflafao," or "Hunger, Misery, and Infla-tion."

Apparently, critics of the IMF are correct in perceiving it as an agent that represents almost exclusively the interests of the industrialized world. Its strong-arm tactics in dealing with the poor robs nations of the choice to pursue a more rational self-reliant development strategy. Even

worse, its insistence on free trade, free capital flows unhampered by
currency laws, does much to encourage capital flight and, in the process,
balance of payment difficulties. From a humanistic perspective, its
presumed basic mission to bring about financial adjustments for
countries with balance of payment problems does make sense. But why
not insist that countries importing too much curtail or eliminate imports
of luxury consumer goods? Why not encourage policies that inhibit
capital flight? The answer in both cases is the same—such remedies are
not in the interest of the rich countries and their representatives.

As long as the current international economic order is dominated
by such institutions as the IMF, effective poverty relief in the poorest
countries will remain an almost unattainable goal. But prospects for a
changing of the rules are equally bleak. The only way out, so it would
seem, is to refuse to play ball altogether. In the last section of this chapter we will explore some of the necessary steps for a more self-reliant
development strategy.

Relief from the Debt Crisis?

Returning to the trillion dollar debt, much of it owed to private
bankers by Mexico, Argentina, Brazil, and Venezuela, experts debate
whether this debt is really payable or not, and the various ways to reduce
it. So far, no clear solution seems to have been offered. The conventional idea that debtor countries may eventually outgrow the debt by accelerated export-led growth strategy continues to lose credibility.
Meanwhile, the now chronic ailment is dealt with by a wait-and-see attitude. However, it is clear that we need not wait much longer to see
what the future holds if a combination of events should occur.

Any significant upward pressure on interest rates will have an immediate detrimental effect on the Latin debtor, as indicated earlier in
Table 13.1. Also, any downward pressure on oil prices will make most
vulnerable the $200 billion debt owed by Mexico, Venezuela, Equador,
Indonesia, and Nigeria. Moreover, any repeat of the 1982-84 global
recession in the industrialized countries will tend to push a number of
Third World exporters of raw materials over the brink. Similarly, a
growing protectionism among the capitalist countries will seriously
weaken some of the heavily indebted countries that have so far stayed
away from the brink: Malaysia, Korea, and other newly industrializing
countries. Finally, should the U.S. dollar rise back to the record levels
of 1985, there would be serious trouble ahead for all non-oil exporting
debtors. Now imagine just two or three of these events coinciding and
it becomes readily apparent how little is needed to make the debt bub-

ble burst. Only by assuming the best possible scenario of no major recession before the turn of the century, low and stable interest rates, no increase in protectionism, moderately higher oil prices, and a U.S. dollar at continued record low levels, can we hope to keep the now chronic disease from getting worse.

Whatever happens, one thing is certain: As long as the existing power relationships are able to maintain control over the world economy, hundreds of millions of economically destitute people are likely to remain poor for generations to come. There are simply no magic solutions to the debt and poverty problems, although new ones are continuously being thought up. The list is long, ranging from exchanging loans for bonds, exchanging loans for equity, capping interest rates, debt repudiation, to demands for a New International Economic Order. Meanwhile, there are also real rays of light and hope, as the following account demonstrates.*

Cutting Debt by Saving Trees. In 1987 Bolivia eliminated almost a fifth of its total external debt by agreeing to preserve 200 million acres of its Amazonian rain forest and prohibiting clear-cutting on another ecologically important 200-million-acre tract. This new type of debt-for-nature swap was recently initiated by Conservation International, a Washington-based non-profit organization. Already, Peru, Brazil, Chile, Costa Rica, Guatemala, and Mexico have indicated considerable interest in following Bolivia's example.

There is a close and deadly link between the alarming rate of deforestation in the Amazons (estimated to currently proceed at a rate of 75,000 acres a day) and the debt crisis. According to Peter Seligman, the president of Conservation International, "the global environmental crisis has been accelerated by tremendous pressures on the developing countries to service its debt."[18] One way for a Third World country to come up with the hard currency dollars to pay interest to the international creditors is to resort to an exploitation of timber and other natural resources at an accelerated pace. It is almost as if we all have to choose between keeping the debt serviceable and intact by sacrificing whatever

---

* For the sake of being original, we may add another. How about privatizing the debt? Thus, for example, every Brazilian would owe about $700. In a democratic and individually free fashion each citizen could then decide whether to pay the debt or else seek relief in the bankruptcy court of his or her district. This may be one area where privatization would seem to hold some promise when little else appears to do the trick.

is left of the precious Amazonian rain forests, or ultimately canceling the debt and keeping the forests. From a humanistic and environmental point of view, the solution to this "dilemma" is clear. But what makes the Conservation International/Bolivia deal especially attractive is that it works on both sides of the equation: it cuts the debt by saving the trees.

The $650 million debt relief involved pales against the background of a $400 billion Latin American debt, but if the idea catches on, we may have finally found a truly enlightened way out of the crushing debt crisis.

Attempting to Outgrow Poverty the Socialist Way

In our discussion of the debt crisis we chose to ignore the communist countries, although many of them also are deeply indebted. In the early 1980s Poland almost collapsed under the weight of its debt burden which in 1985 was still $29 billion. The debt problems of Yugoslavia and Hungary are considerable as well. But when it comes to communist Third World countries, such as Cuba, Vietnam, Cambodia, and China, there simply does not exist a debt problem. China's debt, for example, may in absolute terms be comparable to Ecuador's, but at the same time its population is 100 times and its national income 20 times larger.

Perhaps more noteworthy and ideologically more controversial is the fact that the poverty problem also gets greatly diminished after a communist takeover. Comparisons between China and India are usually invoked to support such a claim.

Let us take the example of Cuba. Before the socialist revolution in 1958 the country was, with a GNP per capita of $374, by no means among the poorest. However, in the rural areas the same statistic average was $91, and for many Cubans it was close to zero. A 1974 World Bank study stated that "unemployment was some 16 percent in 1956/57, poverty was widespread, with a large fraction of the population illiterate and undernourished."[19] Inequality of wealth and income was extreme. In land, for example, 9 percent of owners held 73 percent of the land.[20] The study continues, "in the first few years after the revolution dire poverty and unemployment were virtually eliminated."[21] Assets, particularly land, were redistributed and, through public financing, virtually every Cuban can now obtain free health care and free education. Moreover, basic necessities (food, clothing, and shelter) have been made available to all Cubans through government subsidies and rationing.

A 1982 study on the Cuban economy, prepared for the Joint Economic Committee of the U.S. Congress, lists among the accomplishments "a highly egalitarian redistribution of income that has eliminated almost all malnutrition, particularly among children."[22] More recently, a feature story in the *Boston Globe* reported: "With free health care and schools, cheap rationed food, job security for all and a television set in eight of ten homes, Cuban living standards rank among the highest in the Third World."[23] All this is particularly impressive if we compare Cuba with its capitalist neighbors, Haiti, the Dominican Republic, and Jamaica, all of which are not only poverty stricken but also strangled by a huge per capita debt.

Nevertheless, there is a cost to the type of development strategy pursued by Cuba. In exchange for a modest standard of living, a secure job, universal health care, and education, the citizen must relinquish significant political and civil rights. These include freedom of speech, the press, association, and movement, as well as realistic aspirations for true economic democracy.

During the short months of the Prague Spring of 1968, a former editor of a leading Czech newspaper expressed the basic trade-offs very well:

> He [the worker] has no say whatever in the political functioning of the society, not even in deciding policies in his locality, not to mention being excluded from participation in matters of production, conditions of employment or anything else at his place of work. The outcome is a kind of unspoken agreement, which on the worker's side might run something like this: "I have handed over to you all my prerogatives and civil freedoms. In exchange I demand job security, a decent living standard, minimal expenditure of my labor power and adequate free time."[24]

Despite this lack of individual liberty, the Soviet model has understandably looked quite attractive to many politicians in underdeveloped countries. It does provide a sure and relatively fast avenue to abolish within one generation the basic problem of poverty. But it ends up doing so within a bureaucratic, authoritarian, collective straitjacket that is no better suited for full human development than the capitalist alternative it seeks so forcefully to replace. The communists manage to give everybody a piece of bread, but they too often forget that man only lives by bread alone if he has no bread. It is for this reason that we must look for a satisfactory solution outside the capitalist/communist dichotomy. What is needed is a brand new set of ideas which are practical and untarnished by ideology. We need to conquer poverty within a framework of liberty. Such an alternative does already exist and is well rooted in humanistic economic thought. It owes most of its impetus to the Indian philosopher and statesman Mahatma Gandhi.

Outgrowing Poverty the Humanistic Way: Mohandas K. Gandhi

Gandhi was born in India in 1869. At eighteen years of age he was sent to England where he completed his education as a lawyer. Soon thereafter his outlook changed radically, a development apparently triggered by his reading John Ruskin, the British humanist. Gandhi, in his autobiography, tells us that Ruskin's *Unto This Last* (1866), where he criticizes British political economy, was "the one book that brought about an instantaneous and practical transformation in my life."[25] The new Gandhi soon emerged as one of the best-known disciples and practitioners of humanistic thinking that the world has seen.

Gandhi fought ceaselessly but non-violently for the humanization of India, and he saw the first step to be the country's independence from England. Since his death in 1948, Mahatma Gandhi has been honored as "the father of the Indian nation," but today we know that he has been considerably more than that. He has been the father of a new idea, an idea that has worldwide application and promise, the idea of humanistic economic development.

In a sense he paralleled John Hobson's attempts to infuse economic activity with the ideals of John Ruskin. Hobson addressed the problem of work in an industrialized market economy. Gandhi, on the other hand, applied the humanistic ideals to the problems of undeveloped India and implicitly to the current problems of the Third World. Like Ruskin and Hobson, he deplored the divorce of economic activity from human and ethical norms. Economic activity should be geared to the human welfare for all *(sarvodaya)*. The goal of an economic system, he wrote, "is human happiness combined with full mental and moral growth."[26] Beyond the provision of the basic necessities of life (food, clothing, shelter) the economic system has to produce in accordance with the basic human needs and values of equality, non-violence, and creative labor.

Much of Gandhi's speeches and writings on development can be briefly summarized as follows: He foresaw, as soon as the British had left the country, an ongoing social and economic "revolution," a restructuring of the colonial economy that would emphasize self-reliant, egalitarian village economies in the rural areas. In contrast to Marx and Lenin, revolution had to be non-violent. Its aim was to change the social relationships. Work, both agricultural and industrial, had to be brought to the unemployed rural masses. It was the function of machines to serve, not replace, people.

> I am not fighting machinery as such but the madness of thinking that machinery saves labor. Men "save labor" unless thousands of them are without work and die of hunger on the streets. I want to secure employment and livelihood not only to part of the human race, but for all. I will not have the enrichment of a few at the expense of the community. At the present the machine is helping a small minority to live on the exploitation of the masses.[27]

To be compatible with the decentralized, village-based economy, industry had to be small scale and traditional, employing a non-violent, non-alienating technology that would allow labor and laborers to acquire a maximum of human dignity and moral substance.

Fate, however, did not permit Gandhi to see his economic ideas implemented. He died in 1948 by the bullet of an assassin. His successors first postponed the reform plans and then shelved them altogether. Inequality widened, the land tenure and education reforms never materialized, and the bulk of the rural population has remained in poverty.

Gandhian Economics Reformulated: Amritananda Das

Gandhi's economics may sound to many overly idealistic, perhaps somewhat naive, and no doubt simplistic. But it need not be that, and it has been given analytical strength by means of a marvelous study by Amritananda Das published in 1979.[28]

Das argues for a selective reinterpretation of the Gandhian development strategy, one in which Gandhian thought is translated into the vocabulary of contemporary development analysis and so related to the conceptual-analytic framework of the modern theories of development planning. Such scientific reinterpretation, "with little resemblance to the ethico-mystical mish-mash usually represented as Gandhian economics," will yield illuminating insights into the development policy problems of poor nations.[29]

The goal of Gandhian basic development strategy is to increase the proportion of labor-intensive activities in the investment mix in order to reduce urban unemployment and rural underemployment. Any improvement in the job market hinges on the creation of new opportunities for employment and self-employment exceeding the growth of the labor force.

How can this be done? Das analyzes the problem from a dual economy perspective. There is the "modern sector," relying more on machines than labor and yielding relatively high profits, thereby generating a reinvestible surplus that is necessary for growth. Alongside the urban-based modern sector, we also have the "traditional sector," which operates with little capital but much labor, and which not only dominates the vast rural areas of a Third World country but operates in urban areas as well.

The question now is where to allocate the available investment funds. If we put them all into the modern sector, they will grow the most, but with little extra employment. If, on the other hand, we channel it all into the traditional sector with its village economies and small shops, they will most effectively create new jobs but little else. More than likely, the investible capital will tend to dissipate, leaving little to expand employment in future periods. The long-run consequences of both alternative allocations are the same: a tendency for structural unemployment to get worse.

Faced with a choice of this type, the conventional development doctrines, whether neoclassical or neo-Marxian, have been strongly predisposed to invest and reinvest in the urban modern sector. The result, at least in the pro-Western market economies, has been a population and labor force growth that year after year exceeds the growth in new employment opportunities. Mounting structural unemployment, immiseration of the traditional sector, stagnation or evaporation of domestic purchasing power, and massive out-migration of desperate job seekers crowding into suburban shanty towns are some of the well-known manifestations of the conve l ategy. Today they can be easily witnessed everywhere in the Third World.

The Das Investment Strategy.   Instead, what is needed is some sort of formula avoiding both horns of the dilemma, and that is exactly what Das proposes with his rule: reinvest enough of the savings in the modern sector so that the same investible surplus is assured year after year, and move all the remaining savings each year into the labor-intensive traditional sector. A simplified example may help clarify what he means.

Assume a modern sector that can produce on a sustained basis an investible surplus of 10 percent annually herewith increasing total savings by the same percentage. Also assume that the labor force in the entire economy grows at an annual rate of 3 percent. Das' rule now implies that we (re)invest 3 percent of total savings in the modern sector, while (re)allocating the remaining 7 percent of savings to the traditional sector. We are now assured that the growth of investible surplus exceeds the growth in the labor force every year, causing structural unemployment and rural poverty to decline steadily. The humanistic impact of such a strategy seems promising: slowing migration to the city and revitalizing the village economy–thus providing greater economic security by means of more intact (extended) family relationships and increased domestic purchasing power.

The basic investment strategy outlined above needs to be complemented by specific government programs. For example, the labor-intensive, traditional sector needs help in marketing its products more effectively. It needs better access to credit through an effective cooperative banking system, and it needs government assistance in terms of technical expertise. The modern sector, on the other hand, has to be discouraged from producing goods that compete with the traditional sector. Its primary purpose is to produce intermediate goods (fertilizer, electricity, transportation equipment, and so forth) that is needed by the traditional sector. Insuring compliance with such guidelines may mean either preventing multinational control of this sector or some form of nationalization.

The Question of Foreign Trade.　　The opportunity to export and import allows the modern sector to accumulate more investible resources than otherwise possible. However, if it imports goods that are already manufactured in the domestic traditional sector, even if produced at a higher cost, the accelerated growth in savings will be at the expense of significantly increased structural unemployment. For a poor country already suffering insufficient job creation, such a policy will be "a prescription for disaster on an unimaginable scale of human suffering."[30]

In contrast, the Gandhian approach will examine the opportunities of trade with an eye to accelerating job creation, not national income. As we have seen earlier, Ricardian conventional economics has taken pride in demonstrating how maximum use of foreign trade will increase domestic national income. A true Gandhian will not be impressed. To repeat, the only really relevant question is how foreign trade might positively affect the level of employment. As soon as we look at trade from this vantage point, its alleged benefits cannot be taken for granted. Most likely, some type of trade will worsen structural unemployment and hurt the rural economy, while another type will improve matters. The goal is to know which kind of trade does which.

On the other hand, by following a conventional strategy, Third World countries would choose to speed up the rate of overall growth and accumulation and tend to prefer a state-of-the-art technology in producing capital-intensive goods for export. In exchange, they would import consumer goods, some luxuries, and other goods that replace those produced in the labor-intensive traditional industries. In both cases, the transfer of savings to the traditional sector suffers, thereby promoting more urban and rural unemployment and more human suffering.

In stark contrast to this type of growth-oriented trade policy, the Gandhian approach deemphasizes the production of more capital-intensive investment goods. Instead, it would try to import them at lower costs. As a general rule, then, it would rather import machines, chemicals for fertilizers, and the like, in exchange for exports of *labor*-intensive goods produced in the *traditional* sector. In the process the overall capital/labor ratio of domestic production would tend to decrease, implying more jobs.

Equally important, however, is that a Gandhian strategy starts out by looking *within* to assure maximum employment year after year, and only after such optimization will it explore trade for potential additional gains compatible with its employment goals. More specifically, Das recommends the following approach. First, the sectoral investment mix has to be planned optimally assuming no foreign interaction whatsoever. As pointed out earlier, this implies allocating the reinvestable surplus to a maximum possible extent to the traditional sector, *provided* the necessary minimum to the modern sector has been accomplished. After reaching this initial goal, we then inspect in an incremental fashion the potential for additional employment gains that some foreign trade may bring about. For most commodities, the secondary strategy will consist in producing an exportable surplus within the traditional sector in order to import more and cheaper capital-intensive investment goods. But for some specific commodities it may prove rational to pursue an accumulationist strategy, particularly if it is much cheaper to obtain substitutes of domestic labor-intensive goods through capital-intensive exports. For example, we may want to import cheap sugar from the Dominican Republic in exchange for certain machine tools.

But, again, all these potential gains from trade are only explored as incremental departures from the initial closed economy starting point, and they will only be pursued as long as there is a positive overall impact on employment. This incremental trade policy is in sharp contrast to the conventional approach that determines trade from the beginning to maximize profits, accumulation, and growth. Quite obviously, the importance of trade in general and *unregulated* trade in particular is greatly diminished in a Gandhian economy seeking to revitalize the traditional sector and the village economy.

Explaining the Lack of Gandhian Development. What we have so far described is a reasonable and also an entirely feasible and practical development strategy that promises to effectively combat Third World poverty. Yet it is clearly not happening. Why?

According to Das, the problem rests with the leadership, the "elites" of a Third World country. Such elites have a predisposition to the conventional accumulist approach, pushing the growth of the modern capital-intensive urban sector industries. In part, this can be explained by the educational and urban background of the techno-managerial class. But more importantly, it is due to the historical interdependence with the international economic system geared to meet the needs of advanced industrial nations and their institutions.

The international terms of trade as they have been evolving over decades–almost centuries–encourage exports of processed or manufactured goods, not raw materials. Typically, in order to compete successfully, the manufacturing sector needs to be modernized and made technologically comparable with the manufacturing sector in the developed nations. This will immediately create pressure for a capital-intensive, modern development of manufacturing within the underdeveloped country. This modern sector, then, comes to be seen as the true engine for growth. At the same time, such growth starts to feed on itself. More state-of-the-art technology has to be imported, and better port facilities, modern airports, and high-rise hotels have to be constructed to interrelate more effectively with the international economic system. Needed resources for such infrastructural development will have to be taken from the traditional sector through tax policies and artificially depressed agricultural prices subsidizing the urban population.

The need for social contact with the international trading elites from other countries also affects the lifestyle of the domestic elite. They increasingly demand air-conditioned offices in high-rise office buildings, penthouse flats and Western-type consumer goods that the traditional sector cannot effectively provide. Imports of luxuries produced abroad, ranging from toothpaste to whiskey to limousines, command an increasing proportion of available reinvestable surplus. And these Western consumption patterns soon become a source of envy and emulation for the rest of the urban population. All this is likely to strain the balance of payment and will tend to lead straight into the debt trap and/or into the hands of the IMF. Moreover, it all happens at the expense of the traditional sector, fanning the fires of poverty, rural underemployment, and unemployment. Whatever remains of the original vision of a more humane society goes up in smoke.

To his credit, Gandhi foresaw from the very beginning the dynamics of this process. More than that, he also envisioned a possible breaking of this vicious cycle through appealing to the nationalistic spirit of the elites. They had to be made to understand that their country was exploited by the international system and the powerful developed economies, and that what was needed would be a policy of maximum possible self-reliance and economic independence. Only if the elites could be persuaded to pursue such a policy would there be any hope for a reform of development strategy. What Gandhi could not foresee was that the contemporary debt crisis constitutes a paradigm example of a trap that compels national elites to pursue policies not at all designed to meet the basic needs of the masses. On the other hand, it also offers a badly needed opportunity for a new nationalistic reidentification that might speed up the long-awaited realization of a radically recast attitude in leadership and an equally radical reorientation of the world economy.

References

1. OECD, *Costs and Benefits of Protection*. Paris: OECD, 1985, pp. 27-28.
2. *ibid.*, p. 36.
3. Lester Thurow, *Dangerous Currents*. New York: Vintage Books, 1984, p. 121.
4. OECD, *op. cit.*, p. 119.
5. John M. Culbertson, *International Trade and the Future of the West*, Madison, Wisconsin: 21st Century Press, 1984, p. 144.
6. OECD, *op. cit.*, pp. 139-140.
7. Lopez Portillo in a speech to the United Nations, September 1, 1982.
8. John M. Keynes, "National Self-Sufficiency," *The Yale Review* (1983), p. 758.
9. *ibid.*
10. World Bank, *World Development Report 1978*. New York: Oxford University Press, 1978, p. iii.
11. World Bank, *World Development Report, 1987*. New York: Oxford University Press, 1987, Table 1, pp. 202-203.
12. From *Facts for Action* (Oxfam American Educational Publication #1). Boston: Oxfam, n.d.
13. *Wall Street Journal*, June 22, 1984.
14. Morgan Guaranty Trust Company, *World Financial Markets*, March 1986, pp. 13-15.

15. "Debt Crisis Is Inflicting a Heavy Human Toll in Dominican Republic," *Wall Street Journal,* August 20, 1987, p. 1.
16. R. Yaeger, *Tanzania: An African Experiment.* Boulder, Colorado: Westview Press, 1980, p. 88.
17. From Teresa Hayter and Catharine Watson, *Aid: Rhetoric and Reality.* London: Plato Press, 1985, p. 56.
18. Quoted in the *Wall Street Journal,* January 20, 1988, p. 1.
19. Chenery Hollis, et al., *Redistribution with Growth.* London: Oxford University Press, 1974, p. 263.
20. *ibid.,* p. 264.
21. *ibid.,* p. 263.
22. Laurence Theriot, "Cuba Faces the Economic Realities of the 1980s," Bureau of East-West Trade, U.S. Department of Commerce, 1982, p. 5.
23. *Boston Globe,* October 6, 1985, p. 87.
24. A. J. Liehm, "The Prospects for Socialist Humanism" in K. Coates, ed., *Essays on Socialist Humanism.* Nottingham: Spokesman, 1972, p. 117.
25. Mahatma Gandhi, *An Autobiography.* Ahmedabad: Navajivan, 1927, p. 22.
26. Quoted in R. Diwan and M. Lutz, eds., *Essays in Gandhian Economics.* New Delhi: Gandhi Peace Foundation, 1985, p. 67.
27. Quoted in G. R. Madan, *Economic Thinking in India.* Delhi: Chand, 1966, p. 134.
28. Amritananda Das, *Foundations of Gandhian Economics.* New York: St. Martin's Press, 1979.
29. *ibid.,* p. viii.
30. *ibid.,* p. 37.

Chapter 14

A FINAL WORD

As we said at the beginning of this book, humanistic economics is neither an economics of the left nor of the right. But this does not mean that it is an economics of compromise, an economics that is a middle-of-the-road amalgam of socialist and conservative ideas. Far from it. Humanistic economics would appear to represent a radical new direction in economic thought. We do not believe this to be the case, as we will soon point out. However, if it is radical, it is not in the ordinary political sense of either right or left, but in the sense of seeking changes at the core or root of economics, as well as in basic socioeconomic structures.

For us, this core is the conception of the person or the self. Traditional economics, as we hope we have shown, has never gotten away from its root concept of self-interest. Let us recall here that this central idea to economics was advanced by another group that were known as radicals in their time—the Philosophical Radicals as they were called: Jeremy Bentham and the Utilitarians. So, if we are radicals, it is because we must go back to that same root and do some digging up and replanting.

The reason for this work of replanting is not just because of gaps and errors in academic theory, but more importantly because economics is important and its implementation affects everyone. We believe that many of the social tragedies of our time in part (although not all, of course) result from these errors in economic thought. This statement should be taken as a testimony to the significance of economics, and as an indication of the critical work that needs to be done to shape economics into a form compatible with the true nature of the human being. We hope that this book is a signpost and an encouragement for others who also see the need to embark along this path.

If the political stance of humanistic economics is neither classically left nor right, it is also not really new. Its historical roots go back to the humanistic side of Adam Smith, as does the protest against his non-humanistic side. This protest was first mounted in a significant theoretical way as far back as 1819 when the Swiss Count Jean Charles Leonard Simonde de Sismondi formulated his *New Principles of Political Economy*. But the masters of orthodoxy have always felt uncomfortable with the humanistic critique and preferred to pretend that it did not exist. Not surprisingly, Sismondi is one of the few economists whose principal work has never been translated into English. The alternative economic constructs of John Ruskin and John Hobson were also ignored by economists, even though they were written in English.

More recently, the situation was perhaps different with E. F. Schumacher's *Small is Beautiful* (1973). This classic turned out to be a veritable bestseller, and as such, it probably is the first humanistic economics book that has passed the cherished test of the academic economist, the test of the marketplace. Schumacher seems to have struck a sensitive chord, a silent force that is ready for action. After 200 years of the (increasingly musty) economics of the traditional kind, after almost a century of being blessed with the stale welfare criterion of Vilfredo Pareto in its modern dress of the Kaldor-Hicks compensation test, we believe that we are ready for a change.

If there is a unique contribution of the present book, besides bringing the tradition of human economy up to date and relating it to present issues and developments (such as the new ideas in worker cooperatives), it is in supplanting the one-self economic principle of self-interest with a dual-self model. In doing this we both highlight the inadequacy of the one-self model and bring in the concept of a hierarchy of incommensurable or qualitatively different needs. Economics then becomes able to deal with such fundamental socioeconomic concepts as a conflict of interest.

The Economic Problem: Yesterday and Tomorrow

When we survey our present society from the perspective of humanistic economics, we are drawn to the historical antecedents of this present situation. In Smith's day the economic problem was the problem of production, how to transform the amply available resources into material wealth. Towards this purpose Smith and his followers relied on the concept of the invisible hand. They said, in effect: Let us not be concerned with the issues of morality and justice *in our economies,* because if each person pursues their own self-interest the public good will ultimately be served. However, there was a critical presupposition in Smith's argument. He assumed the existence of moral concerns and sentiments which served as the protective and guiding social framework within which material self-interests were allowed to operate. This assumption of an existing moral framework was appropriate for the times. Capitalism, in its infancy, had inherited substantially intact the whole religiously based structure of trust and fairness that was the code of feudal (pre-capitalist, pre-industrialist) life. But this situation did not endure.

Economic Integration and Social Disintegration

What Adam Smith did not foresee two centuries ago was that the implementation of his economic proposals, such as increasing the division of labor and enabling ever-widening markets, would lead to moral erosion which threatened to destroy the very framework of the marketplace itself. James Buchanan himself has acknowledged concern with such a problem (although his solution for dealing with it is quite different from ours). In brief, Adam Smith was assuming a peaceful coexistence of two seemingly complementary social forces, self-interest and moral sentiments, yet history suggests that the former will gradually eliminate the latter if given free rein. To use an analogy, it seems that there is a Gresham's Law in socioeconomic relations as well as in the circulation of coins. Gresham's Law (promulgated by the sixteenth century English financier Sir Thomas Gresham) is an old economic axiom which states that bad money (e.g., coins of low silver content) will tend to drive good money (e.g., coins of high silver content) out of the market. The law apparently applies to the social side of economics as well; low economic values tend to drive higher economic values out of circulation.

Whatever the drawbacks, in feudal days people knew their neighbors. Moreover, they knew the people with whom they exchanged goods. Economic exchange was guided primarily by considering the basic human needs of the community. People knew each other and cared for each other. The use of money played a peripheral role at best. During the "economic revolution," markets started to replace traditional barter and money started to circulate and become an important commodity in its own right. Yet in these early days of economic change people still had a feeling of community. When buying bread at the baker's, the exchange was not merely economic but also social. Imagine in these days, a smalltown father rushing to the bakery to get some bread for the next day's breakfast only to discover that the bakery had closed early that afternoon. We would expect that the initial feeling of disappointment and frustration could be to a large extent mitigated by finding out that the baker had taken a much-needed afternoon off to spend with his family in leisure. Now compare this situation with a modern supermarket or a bank that closes twenty-five seconds ahead of the actual closing time. We are furious; there is absolutely no consideration for the staff inside, neither do they really care about the angry customer outside. People do not matter because in the marketplace they no longer know who they are dealing with.

Ever since increasing mass production has destroyed the traditional local economy, markets have grown in scope and size. Today we are on the threshold of an integrated world economy. We can expect an economic system of even greater complexity and integration in the near future. And indeed we are told that this is going to be good for us.

Yet such an "evolution" will move people even more into the background. Interpersonal relations will give way even more to relations between things. We do not know who produces what. The market is silent; it does not care and neither can we. All we do know and care about is the nature of the commodity and its price. People become means, and commodities become new ends. Humanistic social values give way to pecuniary calculation and materialism. With this continuance human welfare would be at a low point.

And the trend is continuing. Marketization of society now is chewing away on the last human need-oriented economy: the nuclear family. Increasingly, either involuntarily or by choice, family members follow job opportunities and careers incompatible with the social values of belongingness, loyalty, and family stability.

We have to keep in mind that marketization and materialism are two sides of the same coin. Both cater to the desire for things or the lust for power, rather than to the need for interpersonal relationships. And society becomes increasingly atomistic.

This moral and social erosion cannot go on forever. Ironically, the market needs a moral framework to function properly. In the words of the late Fred Hirsch, social and moral norms "are needed not for the optimistic objective of attaining some wholly good or fully rational society, but for the more modest and limited purpose of maintaining some key underpinnings of our existing contractual, market society."[1] By eroding higher human need satisfaction, the market increasingly becomes the victim of self-inflicted wounds. With the social and moral framework eroded and defunct, rules and regulations are necessary to ensure the working of the system—and more and more rules to enforce those rules so that we arrive at the present point where so much of society is encased in huge bureaucratic frameworks. Modern business today is more and more the process of making and enforcing contracts and subcontracts. Anybody who visits the headquarters of a large corporation will be overwhelmed by the presence of lawyers everywhere. Elsewhere in the book we have referred to the outcome of this as economic gridlock.

Rules and regulations cost money, above all tax dollars. Yet it is precisely taxes that members of an increasingly materialistic and atomistic society are more and more reluctant to pay. As a result, individual self-interest, originally seen as freeing an economy from feudal constraints, not only eventually succeeds in stitching together its own kind of straitjacket. It is progressively cutting its own throat as well.

Towards a Reformulation of the Economic Problem

During the second half of the 1800s, the economic problem changed in England. There was increasing concern that they would run out of coal, and that continual and unlimited growth would come to an end. It was at this time that Jevons defined economics as the science of the allocation of scarce resources. Thus the problems of distribution and consumption rose to the forefront. Earlier, J. S. Mill envisioned what he called a stationary state economy: he was one of the first who accepted, even welcomed, such an economic goal. Let us refer to the famous quote by Mill in order to demonstrate how remarkably pertinent and relatively humanistic his analysis was:

> It must always have been seen, more or less distinctly, by political economists, that the increase in wealth is not boundless: that at the end of what they term the progressive state lies the stationary state, that all progress in wealth is but a postponement of this, and that each step in advance is an approach to it . . . if we have not reached it long ago, it is because the goal itself flies before us (as a result of technical progress).

> I cannot . . . regard the stationary state of capital and wealth with the unaffected aversion so generally manifested towards it by political economists of the old school. I am inclined to believe that it would be, on the whole, a very considerable improvement on our present condition. I confess I am not charmed with the ideal of life held out by those who think that the normal state of human beings is that of struggling to get on; that the trampling, crushing, elbowing, and

treading on each other's heels, which form the existing type of social life, are the most desirable lot of human kind, or anything but the disagreeable symptoms of one of the phases of industrial progress. The northern and middle states of America are a specimen of this stage of civilization in very favorable circumstances; . . . and all that these advantages seem to have yet done for them (notwithstanding some incipient signs of a better tendency) is that the life of the whole of one sex is devoted to dollar-hunting, and of the other to breeding dollar-hunters.[2]

These perceptions and prescriptions of Mill were avoided by the discovery and use of a new energy supply—oil. Growth would go on unimpeded after all, and the problems of distribution and consumption need not be faced.

But now in the late 1900s all of our petrochemical resources are running short, along with numerous other resources, and we find ourselves back almost at the same point as the farsighted Mill. The technological optimists expect that a new energy source will come forth, just as it did in the late 1800s. Many expect it to be a more potent kind of nuclear power. However, by this time we should be able to see how shortsighted such a hope is, regardless of which side of the nuclear safety issue one lands on. The discovery of oil gave the economies of the world (or the world economy) a reprieve, but did not gainsay an infinite supply. Today, amidst our increasingly strained social and physical ecology, we must look backward to Mill for the road that carries us to a rational future. The economic problem for the foreseeable future now becomes the attainment of a controlled-growth or steady-state economy.

What this brief historical survey shows us is that at each stage of formulating the economic problem, the ignoring of the higher self has led us into trouble. The big push towards development did not bring us the promised social harmony. Furthermore, the vanishing moral foundation of human society has demanded that an increasingly complex, stifling, and inhumane system of rules and regulations be put in its place. Through the same ignorance we have developed an economy with an insatiable appetite that threatens to eat away the thin mineral crust of the earth's surface out from under us. It is thus folly to separate the Economic Problem from the human problem, as if we can have separate means without consideration of the ends. At all points and at all times, the approach to an economic question must be undertaken in the light of the ultimate purposes of human life, the *summum bonum* of classical Greek philosophy, or (higher) self-realization as advocated in the present book. What this means in the context of the steady-state economy is that the issue of economic justice must be explicitly taken as part of the economic problem. We have seen that reliance on the market by *itself* not only will not solve this but will most likely make it worse.

The Goal of Humanistic Economics

The needs of our times, both in practical socioeconomic matters and in terms of theory, call for a more generous definition of our science. We need a new economic vision that does not limit itself to observing and explaining market behavior or to theoretical speculations about how to best satisfy a society composed of computer-like Rational Economic Men. Instead, what we need is a science that treats people as holistic individuals with a structure of basic needs and an inborn potential to grow towards higher levels of being and more meaningful lives. Injecting life into the mechanistic core of economics is a challenging and desperately needed task; it is the challenge of human economy.

As social scientists we can no longer afford to ignore the social context when analyzing the behavior of atomistic individuals. This implies a need to introduce fairness and the question of ethics. What good is a social science if it does not enable us to find a better society, a more preferable quality of life for everyone?

In a humanistic economics of the type we propose, much of the conventional theory would appear as a special case, a special case where individuals are inherently insecure and "locked into" the material world of the jungle fighter. But there is nothing intrinsically "natural" or human about such a human nature. It can and should be changed, not by authoritarian imposition from above but by democratic realization from below. One must choose either the role of an apologist for materialism and ever-worsening social decay on the one hand, or that of a promoter for a better world on the other. In short, we have been sounding the trumpet for a new welfare economics where "welfare" does not mean simpleminded material abundance, but human dignity and well-being.

Psychology, for the most part, contradicts the economist's notion of "given" individual tastes and preferences. Thus, it is time to go deeper and to tackle the question of *how* individual preferences are formed and influenced by social variables and economic institutions. Similarly, our institutional framework, enabling and guiding economic activity, cannot be taken as a "given"; it interacts with individual preferences in a constant mutual interplay. Humanistic economics seeks to study that interaction from a critical perspective, not only to understand it but to guide it as well. And it is worth repeating that the values we employ in the process are not arbitrarily chosen and imposed, but are dictated by the human organism striving for wholeness, as observed by humanistic psychology.

The human enrichment of economics involves the recognition that we have a dual self. The self that we feel we are is at the same time perceived as divided. Its lower aspect–self-interest in its unambiguous interpretation–seeks one's own advantage regardless of the interests or well-being of others. This is the self that finds it rational to free ride. In contrast, the higher self is that which identifies with a common humanity and finds its rationality in objectivity, fairness, and the truth. The recognition of the existence of the higher self as well as the lower is necessary for an economics that is responsive to human needs and not merely human fancy driven by dollars. This is an economics that promotes the well-being of all, rather than just a commercialization of human activity which by itself eats away at the moral, social, and ecological fiber of society.

Derived from this economics is the concept that the governmental sphere should be as separate as possible from the market sphere so that the democratic principle of one-person, one-vote should not be compromised by the market principle of one-dollar, one-vote. The public funding of political campaigns is a practical example of a step in that direction.

But the market is crucial to a humanistic economy, and the prime example of a humanistic economic entity, the employee- or worker-owned business, can only function in a market economy where the business itself makes its own economic decisions and not the government on its behalf. This points to the recognition that it is not the existence of the market that is the human problem with capitalism, but the labor-hire contract of the conventional firm with its absentee ownership. The employee-owned firm eliminates these problems and presents a new economic form that resists being easily classified under the old economic rubrics.

Humanistic economics also recognizes that the market is not perfectly self-regulating, either in principle or in practice, and left to itself will lead to social inequality and not adequately meet human needs. Therefore, the market must always be adequately maintained, monitored, and nurtured by a democratic government in order to insure that competition continues to operate, that employment opportunities be adequately and fully available, that the basic needs of everyone be met, and that the environment is protected. The market is seen to be a certain kind of "game"–the economic game–and the government is necessary as the referee to insure that the rules be upheld and that the

"losers" are not unduly harmed, and in fact are helped to become winners.

Furthermore, in an increasingly interdependent world these same
principles have application on the international level and point to the
necessity of international economic bodies to play a similar role on that
level that government plays on the national level. The problem of international inequality and the unmet needs of literally a billion people on
this planet demand our attention. In this context, the implications of a
runaway international arms race are clear and compelling.

The social critic and anti-materialist G. K. Chesterton took as his
starting point for economic analysis the biblical injunction to be in the
world but not of it. Chesterton wrote: "Nowadays it is exactly those who
realize that we have here no abiding city who alone can build anything
like a city that will abide. It is exactly those who know that man on earth
is man in exile who can alone turn the earth into anything like a home."[3]

Chesterton concluded that the best way for this to be fulfilled is for
every individual to own a piece of the world, so as to be secure in it. We
find humanistic economics in general accord with this analysis. Being
in the world is the role and function of the lower self. But not being *of*
the world reflects the creative and spiritual aspirations of the higher self.
To attain the economic conditions that allow this to happen is the goal
of humanistic economics.

It is time to wrap things up, but not before entering a final plea to
the reader. If you are among the many who have approached economics
with many hopes, *do not give up!* Economics can be something more
than glorified market mechanics. Everywhere around the country there
are literally hundreds of economists busily involved in building a more
human science. Since the Second World War, two new professional associations have already sprung up and are challenging the long-estab-
lished American Economic Association. They are the Association for
Social Economics and the Association for Evolutionary Economics.
There is also a new organization called the Human Economy Center,
which specifically addresses itself to the basic issues discussed in this
book.[4] It is through these associations that humanistic economic
thought gets a sympathetic hearing and through which humanistic
economics can gather strength and inspiration.

Now that the organizational foundations have been laid, let us not
waste the opportunity to engage actively in the challenging task of en-
larging our economic house. Stand up and be counted among those who
are willing to work for what the Great Seal of the United States refers
to as NOVUS ORDO SECULORUM, a new world order!

References

1. Fred Hirsch, *Social Limits to Growth*. Cambridge, Massachusetts: Harvard University Press, 1976, p. 141.
2. John Stuart Mill, *Principles of Political Economy*. Vol II. New York: Colonial Press, 1857, pp. 320-326.
3. Quoted in Gerald Alonzo Smith's "Distribution and Conventional Economic Theory," *The Chesterton Review* (1979), p. 249.
4. Human Economy Center, Box 14, Department of Economics, Mankato State University, Mankato, Minnesota 56001.

Appendix I

WANTS, NEEDS, AND INDIFFERENCE*

Earlier in Chapter 2, we saw that social thinkers ever since Aristotle readily recognized that human beings have hierarchically structured and qualitatively different needs or wants. Economists from Adam Smith onwards were no exception, and they honored this basic conception, at least until 100 years ago.

Before that, to be more specific, human motivation and action in consumption had come to be understood by three different principles. First, it was T.C. Banfield who recognized and introduced the *principle of the subordination of wants:* "the satisfaction of every lower want in scale creates a desire of a higher character," obviously anticipating Maslow by more than a century. Next, there was H.H. Gossen's *principle of satiable wants*, meaning that the intensity of a want declines with its progressive satisfaction, eventually to zero. Finally, there was K. Menger's *principle of growth of wants* that tells us that as we satisfy a particular want, a new one will always pop up, herewith precluding us ever reaching a state of bliss or an absolute saturation of wants.

As already discussed earlier, economists in the second half of the nineteenth century no longer talked much about the structure of wants or needs. Neither did they recognize the principle of growth of wants. That was accomplished by collapsing everything into one single kind

---

* Most of the substance and essence of this chapter derives from a landmark article by Nicholas Georgescu-Roegen: "Choice, Expectations and Measurability," in the *Quarterly Journal of Economics* (1954), pp. 503-539.

of want: the want for utility. In essence, they proceeded with only one of the three principles: the principle of satiable wants, which was renamed the principle of diminishing marginal utility. This principle holds that the more we have of every commodity, the less an additional (or marginal) unit is worth to us. Every freshman student in economics will be familiar with its graphical representation.

Figure A.1

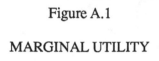

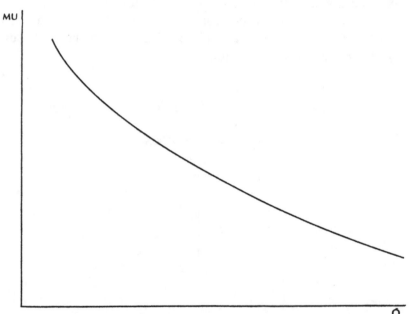

Grounding consumer behavior in the principle of diminishing marginal utility establishes what we alluded to earlier: the reduction of all qualitatively different kinds of needs to only one: utility. Such utility is contained in all useful goods, and because of this common property all goods are seen not only as comparable but also as commensurable or even substitutable. Appendix II seeks to dwell more on the questionable psychology that all this implies.

This marked a most radical step in reducing multiple needs into one single need: a mono-need for utility that can be obtained from consuming any good. But at the same time, according to Georgescu-Roegen, it implicitly attributes to man "faculties which he actually does not possess," unless we could drink paper, eat leisure, and wear steam engines.

Now, around the turn of the century, the principle of diminishing marginal utility was further developed to explain consumer choice by the great English economist Alfred Marshall. He called it the "equimarginal principle" and illustrated it by means of a housewife who has to allocate yarn between making socks and vests for her family. How is this problem solved? Simply by comparing the marginal utility of yarn in socks and in vests. If she has done the job most efficiently (i.e., without any waste of yarn), the utility of the last sock has to be equal to the utility generated by the last vest. Otherwise, "she will think she has failed if, when it is done, she has reason to regret that she did apply more to the making of, say socks, and less to vests."[1] Let us picture her choice problem by means of a graph showing the marginal utility curves and the equimarginal principle.

Figure A.2

VESTS VS. SOCKS

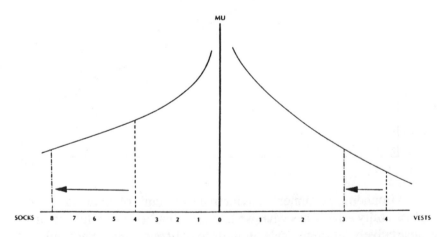

We have here two marginal utility curves. One is of wool for vests, and the other one (on the left) is the marginal utility of wool in socks. And assume the axis pictures eight socks and four vests, which seems reasonable since a sock generally uses less wool than a vest. Figure A.2 shows two different marginal utility curves that are both graphed together, rotated around the same axis measuring marginal utility. So what our housewife was complaining about was that after she was all done, she had four vests and something like four socks.

We can see now where the wool should have gone in order to maximize the utility of the household. The graph shows that the marginal utility of the fourth vest (the vertical distance under the right-hand curve) is much less than the marginal utility of the fourth sock made (the vertical distance under the left-hand curve). Accordingly, what she should do is equalize those two marginal utilities by cutting back vest production so that its marginal utility rises, and instead expand sock production until she gets to the same marginal utility in both uses. Now, one could show that this maximizes the total utility squeezed out of the wool by maximizing the area under the two utility curves, or the total utility drawn from the available yarn. Comparing the loss in total utility due to one less vest with the gain in total utility due to four more socks, you will observe that there has been a net gain in total utility by switching. In other words, what you gain by adding four socks is always greater than what you lose by reducing the vest output. It is important to understand that the rule is to allocate the wool so that the marginal utility is the same in all its uses, honoring Marshall's *equimarginal principle*.

Nicholas Georgescu-Roegen demonstrated that the equimarginal rule, assumed by all economists since Marshall to be applicable in the choice of all goods, is really only a special case valid within a certain need category, such as clothing. As soon as we want to apply it to basic goods representing different needs, it breaks down. For the sake of demonstrating this he uses an example pertaining to the allocation of water. Water can be used to drink or else to water plants (an aesthetic need). In order to demonstrate his example we now employ the same type graph used for socks and vests. On the left is the use of water in watering flower pots, lawns, and the like; on the right is the use of water (in gallons, quarts, etc.) for purposes of drinking.

Now, imagine a typical American household with running drinking water easily accessible in the kitchen and the bathroom. At any point in time we can assume that they will, as long as they are at home, not be thirsty. The easy access to water will keep their thirst close to zero. As a result, for all practical purposes, we can assume that the marginal utility of water for drinking is not significantly different from zero. In our diagram they would most likely be found around point D where the MU of an extra unit of water to drink is zero.

Figure A.3

DRINKING VS. WATERING

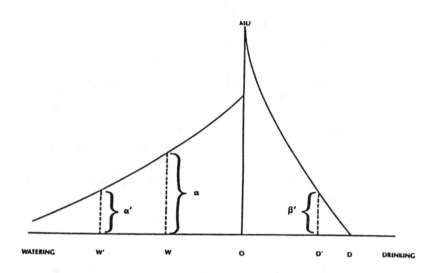

What about their spider plants decorating the kitchen? Usually, they are watered every two or three days. This implies that if we suddenly were to drop in on the family and check the plants, we would normally find that they could use a little water—unless, of course, they just happened to have been watered. The fact that most of the time they could need some extra water implies that the marginal utility of water to be used to water them is greater than zero, let us say α. At least this is what common sense thinking would have us assume. However, is this state of affairs now maximizing the well-being or utility of the household according to our economists and their equimarginal principle? Clearly not, as long as the MU of water for watering (α) is bigger than the MU of water for drinking, we can do better by drinking less (move from D to D') and watering a little more (move from W to W') until the marginal utility is the same in both (i.e., $\alpha' = \beta'$). Now, Georgesu-Roegen claims, and here the reader is welcome to disagree, that "no household would go thirsty in order to water a flowerpot." If you do not agree you are probably from another planet, one inhabited by Economic Man, and humanistic economics will sound strange and unnecessary to you. But, if you are not of that type, if you do not sacrifice yourself for your plants day after day, then you are one of us, a flesh-and-blood human being, biologically determined to honor what Georgescu-Roegen calls the *principle of irreducibility of wants* (or needs). All kinds of different commodities or actions fulfilling different needs cannot be pictured and measured along the same utility axis. In contrast, the reducibility of wants assumption underlying the equimarginal principle is, to repeat, an "improper concept constructed by attributing to Man faculties which he does not possess."

Since we are creatures with qualitatively different needs for, let us say, necessities, comforts, and luxuries, how do we go about choice? The answer is by a priority principle. Given a certain income, we first take care of the most important necessities–the food, the rent. What is left over we spend on new clothing, a newspaper, gasoline, savings for a rainy day, VCR rentals, perhaps even a ballgame. It is a budgeting process. If some money is still left over, we may start being interested in some real luxuries, like a bottle of thirty-year-old wine or a Lamborgini.

More generally, according to this budgeting principle, we start allocating our resources to the most urgent needs and then allow less and less important ones to be satisfied in turn.

It is basically in this manner that we choose among things we want, for example, two houses. First, they both have to be affordable. If so, we may then wonder whether each is big enough. Assuming this is so, we may have strong feelings about location. If one is in the right neighborhood and the other not, we go for it. But, assuming they both enjoy an acceptable location, we worry about the immediate neighbors. Usually, one will win out on that score, but what if not? Are we now really indifferent between the two alternatives? No, the principle of growth of wants tells us that other, even less important, considerations will now impose themselves. Ultimately, we may find, according to Georgescu-Roegen, that somebody chooses a particular house because "it offers a nice location for a bird house."

What is important here is that there is always a criterion to prefer one alternative over another. It may be, as in the house example, a trivial one, but it is enough to make up one's mind. With this kind of choice procedure there can never be any indifference; there is always something that manages to tilt one's preference one way or another. Choice between two combinations is always decided by the lowest relevant want that can be reflected in any of the two combinations.

Now, here comes the kicker: if choice precludes indifference, then it also precludes the modern economist's most precious tool–indifference curves. We can, of course, go ahead and assume that these curves exist anyway, but such may be at times a misleading procedure, especially when we compare commodities fulfilling different needs. That this is so can be gleaned from research pertaining to rats. Indifference curve analysis does explain their behavior when the choice is between ginger ale and Tom Collins. But explanation breaks down and rats become "irrational" when the choice is between water and food pellets.[2]

The economist with a vested interest in indifference curve analysis will probably defend their existence in two basic ways. One using logic, the other observation and experiments. Let us look at each briefly.

As a logical answer to Georgescu-Roegen's denial of the psychological necessity of indifference, we may interject that in going from positive preference to a negative preference (rejection), we are logically bound to pass through an in-between state called indifference. How can we have continuity without an intermediary class? Continuity certainly applies to numbers; we cannot get from a positive one to a negative one without going through zero. But why should this also be the case for the two mental states of preference and rejection? Take the example of life and death, both of which do indeed exist in continuous time. Is there an in-between here? And, if not, by what kind of logical necessity is there one between acceptance and rejection? Moreover, if continuity would after all require an intermediary state, what would we expect to find between indifference and preference? As such examples suggest, logic clearly does not compel the existence of indifference. If it exists, such existence will have to be proven in another way. And this brings us to the second defense.

Can we not test empirically for indifference? It is certainly not easy because indifference is in our minds and so not readily observable. Of course, we can observe somebody's behavior in choosing among two objects. If one-half of the time one is chosen, and the other half of the time the other, we may conclude that they are equally valuable to the choosing agent: that he or she is indifferent between the two. But we can never know how many times we have to repeat the experiment to know for sure. True, the longer we wait and the more we experiment, the more certain we can be. At the same time, the longer the duration of the experiment, the greater the likelihood that the subject might change his or her mind while still experimenting. If so, we could never prove wrong the idea that indifference exists, and the test would become meaningless.

However, what about revealed preference? Is that not a procedure that allows us to construct the perhaps controversial but certainly elusive indifference curves by merely observing people shopping? Soon after their introductory classes, are not students taught that ever since Paul Samuelson's insights decades ago, we do indeed have available such a procedure? And if this is correct, would not all fancy speculation about the existence of indifference curves be nothing more than an exercise of troublemakers wasting everybody's time?

Even though there are still many economists associated with reputable institutions that would want to cast the whole issue aside in this kind of manner, such a position is an indefensible one. The problem hinges on one of the very few assumptions underlying the Samuelson-type revelation of indifference curves, his celebrated *consistency postulate:* If an individual selects a particular bundle A of goods instead of another, bundle B, he does not also select the other bundle B over the first A. Yet how do we know that individuals do, in fact, act according to this type consistency? To find out, we need a criterion of choice which, if violated, would imply an inconsistency. It turns out that such a criterion to which the consistency postulate appeals is that the first bundle A cannot be both on a higher and a lower indifference curve than the second bundle B. (In technical jargon, this asserts the "asymmetry of preferences," and violation of this condition is shown in Figure A.4 below.)

Figure A.4

NON-ASYMMETRICAL PREFERENCES

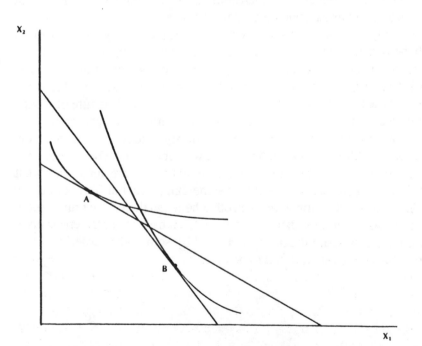

Whatever the ultimate merit of Samuelson's breakthrough, for our purposes the reader can surely already see a problem: in order to "reveal" preferences and indifference curves–and so prove their existence–we have to resort to a method and tool that already *presumes* their existence. Needless to say, such a type of revelation is not very revealing.

We may ask then, if such things as indifference, preference, indifference curves, or preference functions *cannot* be demonstrated to exist, logically or otherwise, does this imply chaotic choice behavior being totally unpredictable and random-like? Is nothing at all intelligibly comparable with anything else? Such a finding would appear in conflict with common sense and introspection, both of which suggest that comparisons are indeed made and that choice is, in fact, more often than not quite orderly.

Once again, it is Georgescu-Roegen who provides us with an answer. Yes, we do and can compare alternative actions, but we do so qualitatively, not quantitatively. Yes, we often choose according to a certain procedure, but we use this procedure to rank order our actions consistently, and in so doing we operate on many levels simultaneously. Instead of one single choice criterion–utility–we have many, and they are ordered according to some structure of priority that reflects need deprivation or higher aspirations. Being hungry, we go about choosing, let us say, with some sort of calorie-utility in mind. Yet once our hunger is adequately satisfied, a taste criterion may take on a number-one priority, and after that social factors may come to predominate. At any one point in time we deal with a whole bunch of different sets of utility functions and "indifference curves," one set of which will dominate the others. In this way, however, this vast structure of "indifference curves" is no longer one of true indifference because of what we said earlier: a tie-breaking lower priority criterion will resolve any initial semblance of indifference, one way or another. The indifference curves become "quasi-indifference curves"; they are really not what they appear to be, and they can do some things real indifference curves cannot do, such as touching each other here and there. The graph below shows such a quasi-indifference curve. Unlike a real indifference curve, all points on it are themselves ordered by some other criterion. Here point α would be preferred to point β.

Figure A.5

A QUASI-INDIFFERENCE CURVE

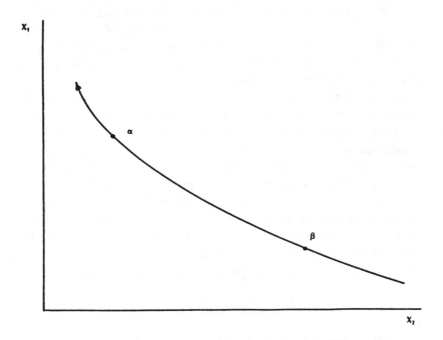

Such curves would vastly complicate ordinary analysis, but they may very well be more suitable for a reconstruction of economics that is no longer in conflict with human nature.

Meanwhile, let us conclude that the recognition of human needs has definite, perhaps even far-reaching, consequences for economic theory; it is likely that for this very reason economists refuse to deal with it. And if economic theory is meant to represent only consumer actions, where people no longer have to struggle with necessities and where shopping is more for pleasure and among roughly commensurable objects, it no doubt enjoys some applicability and a relevance of sorts. Yet, granting that much also means that the traditional theory is not a universal science and is dangerously irrelevant in dealing with allocation and choice, involving poor families or the Third World. For instance, with this type of need-based, so-called "lexicographic" choice theory, consumption patterns are primarily based on income and not on relative prices. This was recognized as early as 1943 by the French economist René Le Roy, according to whom "the variations in price concerning luxury goods have no influence on the demand of goods of the first necessity or on those products which afford a degree of comfort not quite approaching luxury."[3] Le Roy illustrates this with a typically French example: "Price variations of champagne have no influence on the consumption of table wine; but inversely a variation of the price of table wine must be expected to affect the demand for champagne."

More generally, take the policy of subsidizing the price of bread. According to all-is-mono-utility orthodox theory, lowering of the price of bread will induce an inefficient and excessive consumption of bread at the expense of, let us say, bicycles. It is a matter of changed relative prices effecting a *substitution* causing a change in relative outputs. However, in a structure-of-needs-based humanistic economics, subsidizing bread for the Third World city dweller will tend to boost the demand for bicycles more—not because of changing relative prices, but because of the *income effect.* The poor (as well as the rich) need to spend less on necessities, leaving more for comforts.

Of course, it is exactly in dealing with poverty and destitution where we need to solve the economic problem first and foremost, where we need a relevant and applicable body of theory: an economics that respects life, that addresses the problem of human privation and can help us find ways to resolve it. In short, an economics we can live with.

References

1. Alfred Marshall, *Principles of Economics.* 8th edition. London: Macmillan, 1920, p. 98.
2. J. Kagel, et al., "Experimental Studies of Consumer Demand Behavior Using Laboratory Animals," *Economic Inquiry,* 13 (1975), pp. 22-38.
3. René Le Roy, "La hierarchie des besoins et la notion des groupes dans l'économie de choix," *Econometrica,* 11 (1943), pp. 13-24.

People do not do calculus of rel. costs of @ item when budgeting — they prioritize!

Appendix II

THE FALLACY OF ALLOCATION BY MARGINAL COMPARISONS

John Hobson gives an example of the economist's typical account of how people allocate—what is sometimes known as the equimarginal principle. For example, I have $10 in my pocket and decide to spend $7.50 at the evening concert and the remaining $2.50 for African famine relief. Now, one can ask, why did I choose that particular expenditure pattern; why not give all the money to the charity and miss the concert? Alternatively, why not forget about the hunger problem and use the money to buy a better seat at the concert? In view of the fact that there is nothing sacrosanct about allocating the $10 in the way I did or any other way, there must be some reason why I did it in that particular manner. What is this reason?

Hobson explains the economist's way of accounting for this allocation as follows:

> I must have performed a very delicate spiritual operation of reducing my humanitarian feeling to common terms with love of music, and to have struck a balance which can only mean that I consider the additional satisfaction I would have gotten from giving another $2.50 to the Famine Fund to be a little less than the satisfaction I would get from the concert.[1]

We can now better appreciate how the process is supposed to work. In Appendix I we already discussed the idea of an equimarginal principle rooted in diminishing marginal utility. According to this principle, we apportion our money to different things by making sure that the last penny spent on a good—whether charity, music, beer, or shoes—yields the same amount of utility or satisfaction. Otherwise, we have to shuffle things around until it does. Only by following this procedure are we truly getting the biggest overall "bang for the buck." Whether such understanding is or is not supported by common sense, it is simply forced upon us by the merciless logic of the "marginalist" economist.

Now let us use another example to see how a change in prices is seen to effect changes in this equimarginal allocation. Consider the case of a mother accustomed to the weekly grocery shopping in accordance with some established routine and plan. One week, however, one of the kids is sick and needs some expensive prescription drugs, an additional expenditure that does not quite fit into the regular budget. There has to be some adjustment. The money has to come from somewhere, necessitating cutbacks elsewhere. What shall it be: less butter, less meat, a cheaper brand of coffee, or simply no more flowers? Again, the logic of the economist tells us that we compare the different potential sacrifices, and by such comparative calculus arrive at the least disagreeable way to cut back. In doing so he or she will have to focus on the prices and expected utility of every item. In other words, we are said to adjust our shopping by focusing on and comparing the individual *parts,* by calculating their prospective utility in order to rearrange their purchases in some optimal way. In the final analysis it is by the changing of the parts that we end up changing the "whole."

Hobson took issue with the above "adjustment process." He wrote regarding the shopper:

> I think it is a psychological error to represent her as doing this. The error consists in reading a psychological act which does not take place into an objective act that does. Undoubtedly she thinks, "How much does the new emergency require me to knock off this item, and how much off that, in order to provide for an estimated new expense?" But she doesn't perform the impossible task of comparing marginal values of two different kinds of satisfactions. The emergency has put into her mind a new standard of living with changed valuations for the old items, regarded *en bloc*. These changes of valuation *carry with them* reductions of purchases of different sizes and properties.[2]

What Hobson is pointing out is that the economist's analysis of the process that the economic actor goes through in allocating expenditures results from what is known as the "post hoc, ergo propter hoc" ("after the fact, therefore before the fact") fallacy. Just because it is possible to analyze expenditure decisions, as if the value of each additional change was determined by weighing and calculating each change against one another, by no means does this also imply that this is the actual process that we as economic actors go through.

Instead, Hobson proposes, the economic actor changes each of the items in a relation to the *whole,* rather than in relation to each other. As Hobson puts it, the changes happen at "the center" rather than at the margin. In the example of the mother the center or whole is the well-being and health of her family. When sickness occurs, demanding a new expensive drug, this item out of necessity goes to the top of a hierarchy of needs. The adjustment then will be made at the bottom of the hierarchy in terms of the least necessary item or items.

Yet another example will illustrate this fundamental difference in the explanation of the allocation process. Even in Hobson's day, as in ours, the forces of analytic "economics imperialism" were afoot, and there was the attempt to explain such things as why an artist painting a picture selects the various colors he or she uses. The economist would explain that the artist uses red, say, until the marginal value of red decreases to the point where he or she would get more artistic utility out of switching to brown. *Mirabile dictu!* How the theory of marginal utility can explain all manner of human behavior! But this is not how a real artist selects colors to use in a picture. Again, following Hobson's discussion, let us imagine the following. A painter decides to paint a portrait of a friend who characteristically wears a red hat. She has a picture in her mind of exactly what she wants to do in order to catch the right mood and represent the image. But as she is about to buy the necessary materials, she discovers that the price of red paint has just tripled, frustrating her intentions. Now what about the adjustments in her case? Is she going to paint the hat half red and half brown, as the economic way of thinking might recommend, or is she to simply paint a smaller hat? If she is an "Economic Man," she will focus on the first possibility of painting the hat in two colors—in other words, on the *parts*. But most artists would respond otherwise, adopting a new vision of the *whole.* This latter approach may simply imply reducing the size of the entire painting, or even choosing another object altogether. In so changing the whole all the parts will change "en bloc," as Hobson put it. And if this is the creative adjustment of an artist, then is it not also the way we make choices in the art of everyday living?

Another important implication emerges. If choice is holistic, rather than fragmented and part-oriented, relative price changes of one part versus another will have a relatively weak substitution effect. If price changes do induce adjustments, it is not so much by substitution of one part for another as it is due to the effect a price change will have on the overall budget. If it is large enough, the entire budget will have to be adjusted instead of just replacing the relatively more expensive item. It follows that rationing a shortage by price operates primarily by eliminating whole groups of people who can no longer afford the product, and not so much by a gradual and more easy process of substitution. As a result, demand curves tend to be quite insensitive to price changes, at least over a certain domain. Nothing has demonstrated this truth more than the stubbornness with which Americans have been clinging to foreign imports in spite of the drastically falling dollar.

In conclusion, if we are to build a more serious and meaningful economics, it will certainly be more holistic than marginalist in its underlying psychology. And this type of change in perspective alone points to an economic science where the focus is not so much on relative prices as it is on income and wealth.

References

1. John A. Hobson, *Work and Wealth* [1914]. New York: Augustus M. Kelley, 1968, pp. 326-327.
2. John A. Hobson, *Free Thought in the Social Sciences*. London: George Allen & Unwin, 1926, p. 128.

READER'S GUIDE TO ADDITIONAL LITERATURE

We have already tried to demonstrate in our earlier *Challenge of Humanistic Economics,* Menlo Park, 1979, that humanistic economics is not at all a new discipline created out of the blue. The present work continues in this almost 200-year-old tradition. Above all, it attempts to introduce readers–both those interested in a better world and those concerned with the current state of economic science inhibiting this goal–to some specific ideas that have long occupied social reformers, social philosophers, and social economists. In order for the reader to better appreciate the depth behind many of the issues discussed in this book, we believe it might be helpful for us to direct his/her attention to some of the basic material related to the present book. To simplify matters, we will proceed by arranging the readings by topics in accordance with the chapters in the book.

1. The Emergence of Humanistic Economics

The concept of "humanism" is unfortunately rather ambiguous and hard to pin down. Even worse, to many Anglo-Saxons it has come to be more or less synonymous with "atheism." To broaden such an overly narrow understanding we could recommend the late Martin Buber's *A Believing Humanism,* New York, 1969, or some other works categorized under the rubric of "Humanistic Theism," including "Christian Humanism" and "Hebrew Humanism."

The present book bypasses the theism/atheism debate and interprets the term "humanistic" more as in "humanistic psychology," which was created *against* the prevailing background of a *naturalistic* and behaviorist psychology grounded in animal laboratory experiments. Abraham Maslow's *Motivation and Personality,* first published in 1954 and republished in 1970, is generally considered to be the pioneering articulation of such recentering from human animal to the person. He followed up with a second book: *Toward a Psychology of Being* [1962], reprinted in 1982. An excellent account discussing the emergence of humanistic thinking in science and psychology can be found in Floyd Matson's *The Broken Image,* New York, 1964.

For a review of the history of humanistic economics, we refer to our earlier *Challenge of Humanistic Economics,* Menlo Park, CA, 1979, chapter 2.

2. The Place of Human Needs in Economics

Modern mainstream economics has been centered around human wants and preferences, not human needs. As a result, there is very little dealing explicitly with need satisfaction, at least in the economic literature. E.F. Schumacher's *Small is Beautiful,* New York, 1973, was an immensely popular attempt to refocus economics in that respect. There is also interesting and relevant work done by Bernhard Strumpel, ed., *Economic Means for Human Needs,* Ann Arbor, 1976, and by Walter Weisskopf, *Alienation and Economics,* New York, 1971.

Regarding economic theory, the recognition of needs does imply an entry of qualitative considerations that cannot be reduced to quantitative differences. One of the first who critically examined this general problem was the great John Hobson in "Social Science and Social Art," the last chapter of his *Work and Wealth* [1914], reprinted in New York by Augustus M. Kelley, 1968. For the effect of needs on the economist's concept of utility maximization, see Nicholas Georgescu-Roegen, "Utility and Value in Economic Thought," *Dictionary of the History of Ideas,* Vol. 4, 1973. There are many more advanced and technical writings on the subject, but we will refrain from listing them here and instead mention some of them at the end of this Guide under the section related to Appendix I.

3. Self-Interest and Economic Man: A History

Probably by far the best introduction to the history of self-interest can be found in Albert Hirschman's great little book, *The Passions and the Interests,* Princeton, 1977, as well as in a newer work by Milton Meyers, *The Soul of Modern Economic Man,* Chicago, 1983. The rise and early history of modern political economy is surveyed by Louis Dumont, *From Mandeville to Marx,* Chicago, 1977.

The subject of self-interested choice constituting the very foundation of modern economics is a central one in Lionel Robbins' classic *The Nature and Significance of Economic Science* [1932], London,

1984. Unfortunately, just about all serious humanistic reconstructions in economics will sooner or later have to struggle with this challenging masterpiece of real devil's advocacy.

For the reader interested in the history of economic thought, there are two excellent and pertinent books: one by Ray Canterbery, *The Making of Economics,* 3rd edition, Belmont, CA, 1987, and the other by an economist of the Austrian school, Israel Kirzner, *The Economic Point of View,* Kansas City, 1976.

4. The Problem of Self-Interest, and the Humanistic Response

Count Sismondi, the father of the humanistic tradition, spent most of his life in Geneva, Switzerland, and Italy. He wrote in French, perhaps an unfortunate circumstance that has helped to largely isolate him from the development of political economy in Great Britain. Today most of his writings, particularly his *New Principles of Political Economy* book, have still not been translated into English, although there do exist German and Russian versions of it. Americans interested in reading Sismondi will have to make do with two books: his slender *Political Economy* [1815], reprinted by Augustus M. Kelley, New York, 1966, and a compendium titled *Political Economy and the Philosophy of Government* [1847], also reprinted by Augustus M. Kelley, New York, 1972. Sismondi's underconsumption theory is critically but well discussed by M.F. Bleaney in *Underconsumption: A History and Critical Analysis,* New York, 1976.

John Ruskin, another towering figure in nineteenth century humanistic thought, wrote profusely, with insightful thoughts and bitter attacks on economics strewn everywhere. At the same time, he devoted two books exclusively to economic thought, his *Unto This Last* [1864] and his *Munera Pulveris* [1872]. Today there are two outstanding and scholarly books dealing with his economics, one by John T. Fain, *Ruskin and the Economists,* Nashville, 1956, and the other by John C. Sherbourne, *John Ruskin or the Ambiguity of Affluence,* Cambridge, MA, 1972.

For a brand new and generally excellent treatment of the influence of nineteenth century economists on social policy, we recommend Rajani K. Kanth's *Political Economy and Laissez-Faire,* Totowa, NJ, 1986.

5. Self-Interest and Contemporary Economics

The concept of economic rationality is critically discussed in Max Horkheimer's classic *Critique of Instrumental Reason,* New York, 1974, as well as in Martin Hollis and Edward Nell, *Rational Economic*

Man, New York, 1975. Slightly more relevant but perhaps also more difficult are the books by philosopher David Gauthier, *Morality and Rational Self-Interest,* Englewood Cliffs, NJ, 1970, and economist Stanley Wong, *The Foundations of Paul Samuelson's Revealed Preference Theory,* Boston, 1978.

The most enlightening and powerful critique, at least from a humanistic perspective, continues to be Amartya Sen's "Rational Fools: A Critique of the Behavioral Foundations of Economic Theory" [1976], reprinted in Frank Hahn and Martin Hollis, eds., *Philosophy and Economic Theory,* New York, 1979, pp. 87-109. Also relevant and inspiring is the recent book by Barry Schwartz, *The Battle for Human Nature,* New York, 1986.

In contrast, probably one of the best defenses of contemporary Economic Man can be found in Fritz Machlup's piece titled "The Universal Bogey" in Maurice Peston and Bernard Corry, eds., *Essays in Honor of Lord Robbins,* London, 1974, pp. 99-117.

6. Beyond Rational Man: The Reasonable Person

The work of the philosopher Kant is not easy reading, but we recommend two books: Immanuel Kant, *Ethical Philosophy* [1785, 1797], translated by James Ellington and published in Indianapolis, 1983. That book also contains as introduction a rather brilliant exposition of Kantian ethics by Warner Wick. Also very readable are Kant's lecture notes recorded by several of his own students: Immanuel Kant, *Lectures on Ethics,* translated by Louis Infield and published in Indianapolis, 1963. Finally, an interpretation of Kant's moral philosophy resembling the one used in our present book can be found in Robert Tucker, *Philosophy and Myth in Karl Marx,* Cambridge, 1972, chapter 1.

Among the leading books on the economics of altruism, we should point to David Collard's *Altruism and Economy,* New York, 1978, and Edmund S. Phelps, ed., *Altruism, Morality and Economic Theory,* New York, 1975. As background reading, Thomas Nagel's *The Possibility of Altruism,* Princeton, 1970, is unusually helpful.

As far as a constructive critique of utility theory is concerned, we suggest, in addition to the article by Sen mentioned in relation to the previous chapter, a book edited by Amartya Sen and Bernhard Williams, *Utilitarianism and Beyond,* New York, 1982. Similarly, there is also a highly relevant new book by Amitai Etzioni, *The Moral Dimension: Toward a New Economics,* New York (Free Press), 1988, especially part I.

For a mainstream treatment of different order preferences, see Thomas Schelling, *Choice and Consequence,* Cambridge, MA, 1984, and Howard Margolis, *Selfishness, Altruism, and Rationality,* New York, 1982.

Finally, there are two books centered around the type of human personality embraced in this chapter. They are Amelie Rorty, ed., *The Identities of Persons,* Berkeley, 1976, and R.S. Downie and Elisabeth Telfer, *Respect for Persons,* London, 1969.

7. Welfare Economics: Beyond the Old and the New

The reader seeking a clear and only moderately technical introduction to the evolution of welfare economics, both "new" and "old" alike, as well as the relation of such welfare economics to the more ethical kind advanced in this chapter, should start with Hly Myint's classic *Theories of Welfare Economics* [1948], reprinted by Augustus M. Kelley, New York, 1965.

For all practical purposes, however, the real beginning of a systematic humanistic welfare economics dates back to 1914 when John Hobson published his *Work and Wealth,* reprinted by Augustus M. Kelley, New York, 1968. Fifteen years later, the same author managed to present an even more carefully argued picture in his text, *Economics and Ethics,* London, 1929. To see how Hobson's welfare economics fits into his overall work, see John Allett, *New Liberalism (The Political Economy of J.A. Hobson),* Toronto, 1981.

We do have some mainstream attempts to relate economics to human welfare; see, for example, Sidney Hook, ed., *Human Values and Economic Policy,* New York, 1967, and the often technical and expensive but otherwise excellent book edited by Michael Boskin, *Economics and Human Welfare,* New York, 1979.

The heart of a humanistic critique of contemporary welfare economics relates to the issue of the alleged "solution" to the interpersonal comparison debate. The reader seeking to get to the bottom of things may greatly profit by a direct inspection of three landmark papers: N. Kaldor, "Welfare Propositions of Economics and Interpersonal Comparisons of Utility," *Economic Journal,* Vol. 43, December 1938, pp. 635-641; J.R. Hicks, "The Foundation of Welfare Economics," *Economic Journal,* Vol. 49, December 1939, pp. 696-700 and 711-712; and W.J. Baumol, "Community Indifference," *Review of Economic Studies,* 14:1, 1946-7, pp. 44-48. Then there is the great survey of these core issues by Robert Cooter and Peter Rappaport, "Were the Ordinalists Wrong about Welfare Economics?" *Journal of Economic Literature,* Vol. 22, June 1984, pp. 507-530.

Cost-benefit analysis has recently been critically and skillfully analyzed by James T. Campen, *Benefit, Cost and Beyond,* Cambridge, MA, 1986, as well as by James Kornai, "Appraisal of Project Appraisal" in the book mentioned above, and M. Boskin, ed., *Economics and Human Welfare,* New York, 1979, pp. 75-99.

8. Restructuring Work: Community in Enterprise

The struggle against the wage system was an early attribute of the emerging socialist movement long before Karl Marx tried to make it the centerpiece of his scientific socialism. The questions on how to deal with the wage system and the place of worker-owned cooperatives have also been long unresolved issues between the different strands of socialism. For a pertinent historical survey, see Martin Buber, *Paths in Utopia* [1945], reprinted by Beacon Press, Boston, 1958.

Unfortunately, a comprehensive volume representing the pioneering work by David Ellerman is only slowly in the making and not yet available, but a summary version of some of his key arguments can be found in his recent article, "The Corporation as a Democratic Social Institution" in Mark A. Lutz, ed., *Social Economics: Retrospect and Prospect,* Norwell, MA, 1989. Nevertheless, the new view on cooperatives is partially reflected in such books as Robert Jackall and Henry Levin, eds., *Worker Cooperatives in America,* Berkeley, 1984, and Frank Adams and Gary Hansen, *Putting Democracy to Work,* Eugene, OR, 1987.

More generally, for a brand new book relating the humanistic view of the person to questions of industrial psychology, see John Tomer, *Organizational Capital,* New York, 1988.

9. Economics Imperialism and the Need for Its Containment

This area of thinking is still too new to contain much literature. At this stage the reader should be aware of two basic books that go to the very heart of the issue. To hear a clear case for imperialism, see Richard Posner, *The Economics of Justice,* Cambridge, MA, 1981, and for a volume containing both pro and con, see Mark Kuperberg and Charles Bertz, eds., *Law, Economics and Philosophy,* Totowa, NJ, 1983. For a more comprehensive introduction to the field of law and economics, we recommend A. Mitchell Polinsky, *An Introduction to Law and Economics,* Boston, 1983, and Werner Hirsch, *Law and Economics: An Introductory Analysis,* New York, 1979.

Perhaps the most powerfully argued anti-imperialism piece is by Frank Michelman, "Norms and Normativity in the Economic Theory of Law," *Minnesota Law Review,* Vol. 62, 1978, pp. 1015-1048. But we obviously need something more comprehensive than that–and hopefully soon. Meanwhile, the reader may take a look at what appears to be one of the longest articles ever written, Peter Junger, "A Recipe for Bad Water: Welfare Economics and Nuisance Law Mixed Well," *Case Western Law Review,* Vol. 27, Fall 1976, pp. 3-335.

10. Government and the Market: The Vital Link

That it is incumbent on government to assume a strong guiding role in subordinating the economic sphere to social control has been a dominant theme for humanistic economists from Sismondi to Hobson. It has always been criticized by laissez-faire-oriented economists, particularly of the Austrian school, for whom active government policy is a sure instrument to drive society down the road towards a new serfdom. An eloquent and deeply humanistic response to such concerns was by John Maurice Clark, *Alternative to Serfdom,* New York, 1948.

For a more recent plea against laissez-faire and the self-defeating free reign of individualism, we recommend the excellent book by Fred Hirsch, *Social Limits to Growth,* Cambridge, MA, 1976.

A more mainstream economic conception of the general economic philosophy of government can be found in Robert A. Solo, *The Political Authority and the Market System,* Cincinnati, 1974.

A key issue in the market-government link concerns the desirability of economic regulation. Many books have been written on this subject. More importantly, perhaps, we are in the midst of a large-scale social experiment allowing us to taste the slowly maturing fruits of deregulation. One recent attempt to do just that is Larry N. Geston, et al., *The Deregulated Society,* Pacific Grove, CA, 1988.

The public choice view of government was formally introduced by James Buchanan and Gordon Tullock in *The Calculus of Consent,* Ann Arbor, MI, 1962. For a brief exposition of the contractarian view, see James Buchanan, "Political Economy and Social Philosophy" in Peter Koslowski, ed., *Economics and Philosophy,* Tuebingen, Germany, 1985, pp. 19-38. That book also contains a brief but relevant note by John Skorupski, "Utilitarianism and Contractualism," pp. 275-277.

11. Beyond the Welfare State: Full Employment

A good historical account of the evolution of the modern welfare state can be found in Walter Trattner, *From Poor Law to Welfare State: A History of Social Welfare in America,* 3rd edition, New York, 1984.

With respect to full employment policy, a very good historical and comparative account is provided by Helen Ginsberg, *Full Employment and Public Policy: The United States and Sweden,* Lexington, MA, 1983.

Martin Weitzman's new idea of profit sharing as an instrument for full employment is in his *The Share Economy,* Cambridge, MA, 1984, and sympathetically discussed in a much more technical book by James Meade, *Alternative Systems of Business Organization and Work Remuneration,* London, 1986.

12. Humanistic Enterprise: The Case of Mondragon

For the English-speaking hemisphere, the Mondragon cooperative movement is a relatively recent phenomenon first discovered only about fifteen years ago. One of the first books was by Alastair Campbell, *Mondragon 1980,* Leeds, Great Britain, 1980. Somewhat more recently, we have K. Bradley's and A. Gelb's *Cooperation at Work: The Mondragon Experience,* London, 1983. The best book currently available is by William Foote Whyte and Kathleen King Whyte, *Making Mondragon,* Ithaca, 1988. For the professional economist we recommend the article by Benedetto Gui, "Basque vs. Illyrian Labor-Managed Firms: The Problem of Property Rights" in *Journal of Comparative Economics,* Vol. 8, 1984, pp. 168-181.

The way to convert ESOPs into Mondragon-type equivalents is discussed in Peter Pitegoff, *The Democratic ESOP,* Somerville, MA, 1986, and worker ownership more generally in Corey Rosen, et al., *Employee Ownership in America: The Equity Solution,* Boston, 1986.

13. Towards a New World Economy

The field of international economic relations is as wide as it is complex. Fortunately, there exists an excellent little book shedding much light on how we got to where we are. It is W. Arthur Lewis, *The Evolution of the International Economic Order,* Princeton, NJ, 1977. Another introductory work, but more voluminous, comprehensive, and difficult, is A. G. Kenwood and A. L. Lougheed, *The Growth of the International Economy 1820-1980,* Boston, 1983.

One of the few books directly discussing the problem of building international economic instutitions to govern world trade is Todd Sandler, ed., *The Theory and Structure of International Political Economy,* Boulder, CO, 1980.

The conventional theory of comparative advantage underlying neoclassical trade theory can be found in every introductory economics textbook. Unfortunately, there appears to be little accessible material for a critical study of the doctrine. The exception to this rule is Culbertson's *International Trade and the Future of the West,* Madison, WI, 1984. We might add that this book had to be published at the author's own expense with the help of the local 21st Century Press. Otherwise, Professor Culbertson's writings are spread over various newspaper columns and union pamphlets.

The subject of world debt is a topic where we have to deal with rapid and accelerating changes that outdate serious publications the moment they appear in print. Nevertheless, we highly recommend a more popular but penetrating study resulting from a project of the Canadian churches titled *Debt Bondage or Self-Reliance,* published by GATT-Fly, Toronto, 1985. For a critical analysis of the International Monetary Fund, see M. Honeywell, et al., eds., *The Poverty Brokers: The IMF and Latin America,* London, 1983. More positively, a humanistic, basic alternative is explained in the recent UNICEF study by Giovanni A. Cornia, ed., *Adjustment with a Human Face,* New York, 1987.

With respect to modern development theory, one book stands out for its clarity and penetrating insight: Magnus Blomstrom and Hettne Bjorn, *Development Theory in Transition,* London, 1984. As a case study involving many of the problems discussed, you may want to take a look at Andres Coulson's *Tanzania: A Political Economy,* Oxford, 1982. Another brand new book is worth mentioning: E. Kisanga and O. Nudler, eds., *Alternative Development Experiences (Promise, Reality, Prospects),* London, 1988. It contains interesting case studies of Tanzania, Nicaragua, Iran, China, and Yugoslavia.

The Gandhian development strategy is masterfully presented in the slender volume by Amritananda Das, *Foundations of Gandhian Economics,* New York, 1979. There are two other books on Gandhian economics that provide additional insight: Romesh Diwan and Mark Lutz, eds., *Essays in Gandhian Economics,* New Delhi, 1985, and the small book by David Ross and Mahendra Kanthi, *Gandhian Economics,* Bangalore, 1983.

14. A Final Word

To repeat, human economy is primarily a relatively recent rediscovery and continuation of a school of thought that dates back to the early nineteenth century. The kick-off for the new wave of rearticulations was the publication of E. F. Schumacher's *Small is Beautiful,* New York, 1973. There have been a whole array of good books, many of which are designed to appeal more to laymen and practitioners than to professional academics. Among the more influential we have to point to Francis Moore Lappe and Joseph Collins, *Food First: Beyond the*

Myth of Scarcity, New York, 1979, and the recently published work edited by Paul Ekins, *The Living Economy,* New York, 1986. This latter book provides a representative collection of the serious and challenging way of thinking by many of today's leading "alternative economists." A similar perspective is coherently presented in David Ross and Peter Usher, *From the Roots Up: Economic Development as if Community Mattered,* 1985. Both these books are available through the Council on International and Public Affairs, P.O. Box 337, Croton-on-Hudson, NY 10520.

Appendix I. Wants, Needs, and Indifference

The material dealing with this theoretically important topic is rather technical and not recommended for the non-economist. We restrict ourselves here to one book by D. S. Ironmonger, *New Commodities and Consumer Behavior,* Cambridge, 1972, and three key articles: Nicholas Georgescu-Roegen, "Utility" in David Sills, ed., *International Encyclopedia of the Social Sciences,* Vol. 16, New York, 1968, and the same author's famous "Choice, Expectations, and Measurability" in *Quarterly Journal of Economics,* 68:4, November 1954, pp. 503-534. The reader who is comfortable with mathematical set theory may want to read the brief piece by J. Encarnacion, "A Note on Lexicographical Preferences," *Econometrica,* 1:2, 1964, pp. 215-217.

It is worth repeating that the list of readings selected here in this Guide is by no means exhaustive. However, it does provide valuable background material to better understand the approach taken in this book: an economics designed to tame Mammon. Everyone committed to this challenging but rather distant goal can take solace in Kenneth Boulding's eloquent wisdom in observing that "We still have a long way to go before we establish securely in the organization of society that Hidden Hand which transmutes the dross of Self-Interest into the gold of General Welfare." But, he adds, "the taming is under way and Mammon-taming is a fine career."[*]

---

[*] *Beyond Economics,* Ann Arbor, MI, 1968, p. 42.

INDEX

ness, 56, 96-99; as way of life, 40
Self-reliance: and foreign trade, 307-8; in Third World development, 300, 309
Seligman, Peter, 301
Sen, Amartya, 98, 114
Senior, Nassau, 39, 61, 70-74, 77
Seventh Circuit Court of Appeals in Chicago, 187
Seymour Specialty Wire Co., 275, 277
Share economy: and dignity, 242; as industrial sharecropping, 241; as tool for full employment, 240-42; and vacuum cleaner effect, 241
Sherman Anti-Trust Act, 204
Sidwick, Henry, 130-31
Sismondi, Jean Charles Leonard Simonde de, 64-68, 75, 289, 313
Skinner, B.F., 5, 7-8
Slavery, 149, 154, 158, 165-67
Sleeman, J.F., 225, 232
Smith, Adam, 13, 33, 35-39, 43-44, 46-48, 56-57, 61, 64-66, 70, 78, 86, 98, 108, 129, 202, 205-7, 210, 313-14
Smith, Gerald A., 321
Social Conservation Service, 142
Social justice: as justice maximization, 192; as wealth maximization, 192; as welfare maximization, 192
Social Security, 205, 219, 225
Social Security Act, 224
Socialism, 149, 154-55, 163, 168, 171; and democracy, 163; scientific, 154
Socioeconomic power, 27, 109
Socrates, 7
Solow, Robert, 70
Stalin, 168
Steady state economy, 317
Stigler, George, 105, 179, 187
Suarez, Francis, 166
Summum bonum, 317
Swift, 34
Tanzania, Republic of, 293, 296, 298-99
Tawney, Richard, 76
Ten Hour Act of 1847, 204
Tennessee Valley Authority, 142
Third World debt: African, 292-96; causes of, 294-96; environmental exploitation, 301; situation today, 292-94; in socialist countries, 302-4; solutions, 300-10
Thompson, William, 154
Thurow, Lester, 283
Titmus, Richard, 143
Torrens, 72
Toynbee, Arnold, 76
Trust, as common lubricant, 84-86
Tucker, A.W., 79
Tullock, Gordon, 199
Unemployment: and discouraged workers,

236; natural, 239; part-time, 236; rate-adjusted, 236-37; rational, 240; rising trend of, 233; statistical measurement of, 233-37
United Nations Declaration of Human Rights, 167
United States Job Service, 244
Utilitarianism, 8, 40-41, 52; beginnings of, 5; and the economic analysis of law, 191; and the pleasure principle, 7, 52
Utility: commensurability of, 30-31, 49; diminishing marginal, 22, 132, 322-24; interpersonal comparisons of, 133-35; marginal, 48, 54; mono-dimensional theory of, 27-30-31, 207; moral, 114; and moral commitment, 113; as ophelimity (subjective) 137; overarching, 113-16, 218; want for, 323. See also Maximization behavior
Value: as ability to pay, 143, 188, 190; dictated by organic need for wholeness, 319; of dignity, 149; as efficiency, 118; human, 209; and "human standard" of, 149; implicit judgment of, 188; market, 190; neutral, 146; non-market, 143
Veblen, Thorstein, 57
Voltaire, 4, 34
Wage fund theory, 72
Wage system, 154-55; case against, 157-58; and cooperatives, 259-63; as implicit contract, 166; as self-rental, 158, 161, 166
Walras, Leon, 51, 136-37
Watson, John B., 4
Wealth maximization: See Economic efficiency as wealth maximization
Weitzman, Martin, 240-42
Welfare: economic, 146; international diffusion of, 232; legislative history, 223-24; and work force, 231
Welfare economics, 86, 99, 129; classical, 129-30; and externalities, 131; humanistic, 146-50; neoclassical, 130-33; "new," 138-146, 147; Pareto criterion, 313
Welfare state: and minimum wage, 238-39; and safety net, 232-33. See also Welfare
Wesley, John, 34
Wicksteed, Philip Henry, 54-58, 60-61, 97, 108, 179, 208
Wieser, 55, 61
Winter, Ralph, 187
Wordsworth, 41
Work: humanistic approach to, 155-57; important topic in humanistic economics, 153; as meaningless or meaningful, 149-50, 156; quality of, 153, 156
Work force, 77, 231, 233
Works Project Administration (WPA), 224
World Bank, 290
Yugoslavia, 170-71, 302